Augsburger Rechtsstudien

Herausgegeben im Auftrag der
Juristischen Fakultät der Universität Augsburg von

Professor Dr. Arnd Koch
Professor Dr. Thomas M.J. Möllers
Professor Dr. Matthias Rossi

Band 88

Charl Hugo/Thomas M.J. Möllers (eds.)

Legality and Limitation of Powers

Values, Principles and Regulations in Civil Law, Criminal Law, and Public Law

Nomos

JUTA

The Deutsche Nationalbibliothek lists this publication in the Deutsche Nationalbibliografie; detailed bibliographic data are available on the Internet at http://dnb.d-nb.de

ISBN: HB (Nomos) 978-3-8487-4951-5
ePDF (Nomos) 978-3-8452-9163-5

British Library Cataloguing-in-Publication Data
A catalogue record for this book is available from the British Library.

ISBN: HB (Juta) 978-1-4851-2826-7

Library of Congress Cataloging-in-Publication Data
Hugo, Charl / Möllers, Thomas M.J.
Legality and Limitation of Powers
Values, Principles and Regulations in Civil Law, Criminal Law, and Public Law
Charl Hugo / Thomas M.J. Möllers (eds.)
347 p.
Includes bibliographic references and index.

ISBN 978-1-4851-2826-7 (hardcover Juta)

1st Edition 2019

Preface

The University of Augsburg School of Law is able to look back on a long lasting partnership and lively scientific exchange with the University of Johannesburg (South Africa), which in 2016, with the conference and the corresponding conference book under the title Transnational Impacts on Law: Perspectives from South Africa and Germany, found its most notable event to date.

One year later, the 2017 conference was already the second symposium between both faculties and the "return visit" of Augsburg scientists to Johannesburg, after the conference in 2016 had taken place on German soil. The event was titled Legality and Limitation of Powers: Values, Principles and Regulations in Civil Law, Criminal Law, and Public Law. Inspired by current political and societal developments in both hemispheres, participants explored the implications of legality maxims and the regulation of power in various areas of law from a South African and German perspective.

Topics of high current interest from various branches of law (international private law, European law, constitutional law, legal methods, company law, antitrust law, and employment law) are addressed by German scholars and responded to by their South African counterparts, which leads to a deeper understanding of open legal questions in both legal systems.

Together with the combination of paper and comment, we kept up the innovative concept of promoting young talent. As in 2016, we were pleased to have had both junior and experienced researchers on both sides sharing their elucidating research.

This volume is the result of our collaborative research and of great interest for legal scientists internationally. Fittingly, publishers in both countries – Nomos in Germany and Juta in South Africa – again reflect this German-South-African collaboration.

As indicated in 2016, it is the intention of both faculties to continue the fruitful and enriching cooperation between the law schools on both continents. In this context, we are proud to announce another symposium, which is planned for 2019, focusing mainly on different impacts of fundamental rights in legal systems.

The conference and the respective book was again supported by the Augsburg Center for Global Economic Law and Regulation (ACELR). In this respect, we owe much thanks to the staff of the ACELR, in particular Michael Biesinger, for his organizational support as well as supervising the conference transcript. We would also sincerely like to thank the University of Augsburg for its generous financial support of junior researchers' travel expenses.

The editors

Prof. Dr. Thomas M.J. Möllers (Augsburg)
Prof. Dr. Charl Hugo (Johannesburg)

January 2019

Contents

Introduction

I.

> "To prevent the weaker members of the community from being preyed upon by innumerable vultures, it was needful that there should be an animal of prey stronger than the rest, commissioned to keep them down. But the king of the vultures would be no less bent upon preying on the flock than any of the minor harpies [...]."

This passage from John Stuart Mill's *On Liberty* (1859) vividly allegorizes what happens when the powerful remain unchecked. In his text, the British philosopher calls for a constitution to defend the "flock" from their "beak and claws". In a world where autocratic tendencies are becoming increasingly popular and constitutional values seem jeopardized in several countries around the globe this topic appears to be as important today as it was back in the year 1859.

It was already Mill who claimed "limits to the power which the ruler should be suffered to exercise over the community". Following this idea, the first part of the title, "Legality and Limitations of Powers" emphasizes the maxim of legality as an essential and constitutionally prescribed aspect of power limitation. However, as reflected by the second part of the title, "Values, Principles, and Regulations in Civil Law, Criminal Law, and Public Law", this volume does not focus on solely constitutional aspects but allows authors to deal with different manifestations of that idea and the implications of the legality maxim in their areas of law. Here, the "law" is understood to be the overall designation for the respective legal area on the German and South African side. Both nations unite the need for power limitations to a socially sound and legally envisaged level. At the same time, parallel structures can be revealed. Nevertheless, due to the different legal traditions, different approaches are available, each of which is critically examined.

The concept of the symposium between the law schools from Augsburg and Johannesburg, however, again demonstrates immense will and interest in learning from the respective other legal system. Interesting parallels have been uncovered, not least through the Augsburg-Johannesburg conference.

This publication constitutes a further step towards a deeper cooperation between both nations in the legal field.

II.

This volume starts with the contribution of *Rensmann* on normative values in modern constitutionalism. He hereby relates to the 60th anniversary of the *Lüth* decision, the leading case for "value-oriented" constitutionalism in Germany, although it is not a German invention. His remarks revisit the *Lüth* judgement with a view to developing the contention that the "value-oriented" jurisprudence of the German Federal Constitutional Court is not as idiosyncratically German as many German constitutional lawyers would like us to believe. The conceptual development leading up to the famous *Lüth* dictum of the constitution as an "objective value system", is instead closely linked to the emergence of international human rights law – and hence from its very beginnings the result of an intense transnational and inter-cultural discourse. He points out that although we live in different hemispheres and although our legal systems are embedded in different cultural, social and political contexts, Germans and South Africans are united by a distinctive "value-oriented" vision of the constitution. As the Constitutional Court of South Africa famously stated in Carmichele v. Minister of Safety and Security, the South African Constitution "is not merely a formal document regulating public power. It also embodies, like the German Constitution, an objective, normative value system". Whereas human dignity, proportionality, and all other attributes of modern "value-oriented" constitutionalism are inextricably woven into the fabric of the South African Constitution, the text of the German Constitution ("Basic Law") is much more ambiguous in this regard. *Rensmann* concludes that *Lüth* constituted a milestone in the evolution of "value-oriented" and human rights-based constitutionalism to which both the German and the South African constitutions subscribe.

Venter comments on the paper, stating that values and principles play a central role in the South African Constitution because they created a new democratic system and transformed society, even though there is criticism that it has not lived up to its goals. However, transformation takes time and is hard to measure. In the end, there is no ultimate transformation that can be reached. In this process, however, she calls for constitutional values to be our guide so that every application of these values leaves society and the legal system more transformed than it was before.

Starting with a statement of J.H.H. Weiler that the enhancing importance of constitutional identity replaces the former discussion about the much-contested concept of state sovereignty, *Hölzlwimmer* analyses the potentials of the legal concept of constitutional identity in (quasi-)federal systems of government to find a balance of powers between federal and sub-federal bodies in general, but concurrently raises cautions against an extended use of this notion leading to judicial activism contradicting the principle of separation of powers. She first focuses on the concept of constitutional identity from a Member State's view and in particular its interpretation and application in the case law of the German Constitutional Court as national constitutional court with one of the longest traditions and hence most powerful voices within the European Union. Thereafter, the sides are switched and the meaning of constitutional identity is examined in detail from the European Union's point of view. In the following comparative part, it is questioned whether there is a common concept of constitutional identity within the European legal system. Evaluating the pros and cons of a legal concept of constitutional identity applied by the judiciary and predicting the future development of identity claims, in particular within the European Union but also regarding its transferability to other (quasi-) federal systems of government, she calls for a restrictive interpretation of national constitutional identity with respect to the principle of general openness towards European Union law and the principle of sincere cooperation between national and Union bodies. To protect the (quasi-) federal structure of the European project "unified in diversity", *Hölzlwimmer* suggests a more precise definition not solely on a case-by-case basis but also as a clear dogmatic structure and classification to support the efficacy of this legal remedy within the European Union.

In this context *Barrie* reclaims the fundamental ideas and historical roots of the European Union. Since it is an association of sovereign states without a European Federal Constitution or federal people, the EU is not an incipient federal state but a quasi-federation. The aim of the Maastricht Treaty was to integrate the member states to a tighter economic and political union. He points out the importance of the principle of subsidiarity to guarantee the autonomy of the member states. *Barrie* also refers to Australia, where there is a debate on subsidiarity because the legislative powers were influenced by the Commonwealth. Similar to the EU there is the problem of losing constitutional identity. His solution is a stricter application of the principle of subsidiarity.

Rossi's contribution initially gives an overview of the basic principles of democracy and the constitution. The paper then points out that democratic legislation and the binding nature of a constitution can´t be viewed as antipodes and sets out the multidimensional relations between them which enable societies to develop a self-determined life. Liberating stability and flexibility must be brought into balance, otherwise they threaten to damage the constitution and democracy. The article focusses on liberating stability through concepts such as liability, stability evolving from historical experience, stability through resilience and unchangeable core guarantees. The next chapter is devoted to the democratic principles where *Rossi* states that democracy stands less for stability than for flexibility. *Rossi* then points out the reasons for this flexibility and why flexibility is necessary in the political process.

In her response to Rossi's paper, *Roux* views the model of constitutional democracy as described in Rossi's paper in light of the historical background of the South African Constitution. Applying it to the South African Constitution she tests whether it holds true for the South African modern constitutional democracy. The paper starts with the concept of a constitution as an "anchor of stability" as described by Rossi, which is reflected in a constitution as an "historical experience", as a regulatory framework, and lastly in its "changeability" that is the "guarantee" to its "self-preservation". The paper also focuses on Rossi's concepts of "democratic flexibility", as reflected in "governance for a limited period of time", in "legislative amendment as the standard type of law", and finally in "political self-restriction". Especially in ever and fast moving times, in the ever-changing context, the South African Constitution cannot ignore the circumstances in which it finds application. Therefore, the Constitution has to transform again by coming into its own by realising its purpose. At the same time, Roux concludes, as being transformative, and as it were, flexible, it will have to provide much-needed stability in a South African society that is finding it a challenge to continue believing in the high aspirations of the constitutional project.

In light of the before mentioned centuries of segregation and discrimination, holocaust and apartheid *Benecke* and *Henrico* refer to revolutionary efforts in both hemispheres to overcome discrimination. *Benecke* focuses on the European way to end discrimination. Since the EU passed the main directives regarding employment and social law around the year 2000, the Member States have been experimenting with various implementations. *Benecke* compares the German approach, the implementation of the *General Equal Treatment Act (Allgemeines Gleichbehandlungsgesetz/AGG)*, to the legislation of other Member States and sheds light on the effectiveness of the various procedural and material approaches. On one side, questions arise whether an act of discrimination should lead to criminal or civil consequences, whether the injured person, a law enforcement agency or a NGO should be able to bring an action and, if so, against whom the action should be brought. On the other side, the paper covers questions whether the prohibited grounds should be exhaustive and how the directives' demands for damages can be adequately met without enabling fraud and abuse of the legislation. On his part, *Henrico* puts these legal problems into a South African context. The unique historical, social and legal circumstances of South Africa call for a special handling of discrimination. Consequently, *Henrico* explains how Sec. 9 of the South African Constitution protects the equality among all people. He describes how the legal framework in South Africa provides relief in the form of civil liability, how the legal protection covers a much wider area than just the workplace and how designated institutions investigate and institute class actions against perpetrators.

Our conference title, of course, also indicates the inclusion of a paper, with methodological questions addressing the heart of jurisprudence. The contribution of *Möllers* and *Brosig* presents a fundamental analysis on how to work with principles in Capital Markets Law. The paper starts with an overview of the meaning and the creation of legal principles. The authors outline the characteristics of legal principles and illustrate why it is important to distinguish between codified principles and unwritten legal principles when analysing the derivation of principles. They examine several different approaches to derivation in the literature and expose their flaws. Furthermore, they shine a light on the limits of the development of legal principles, i.e. how the arbitrariness of dogmatic justification is an issue. Eventually, the writers look at aspects of deduction and the formation of principles at a European level. In their outlook they conclude by stressing the importance of establishing legal principles at a European level and present implication for further research.

Ius est ars boni et aequi (law is the art of the good and the just): this statement by the ancient Roman jurist Celsius shows how law essentially is a dialectical, argumentative exercise of discourse and persuasion. *Van der Merwe* uses this quote to illustrate the great importance of principle in closing the inevitable gaps that every normative superstructure leaves. In his response to the paper by *Möllers* and *Brosig* he commends the authors on their work and shows how South African jurists deal with the application of principles as there is no South African "Methodenlehre". His response pictures how South African jurists harvest the fruits of Ancient Roman civil- and English case law. His comparison of the situation in South Africa and the situation in Europe shows how different approaches reach similar results.

Drawing our attention to law enforcement under US Antitrust Law and EU Competition Law, *Kort* brings up another aspect of legality. Analysing leniency programmes under US antitrust law and EU competition law, *Kort* calls for a worldwide cooperation and coordination concerning leniency programmes, as leniency programmes are a key tool for competition authorities to uncover illegal cartels which often operate across borders. Companies thinking about coming clean need to know that they will benefit from leniency in the same way – whichever competition authority deals with the case. In his contribution, *Kort* compares leniency programmes in South Africa, the US and EU and finds much similarity between the different jurisdictions. As in the US and in Europe, leniency programmes in South Africa are only applicable to horizontal agreements (i.e. cartels) as such agreements are the most difficult to uncover. All three jurisdictions have in common that there is one central antitrust authority. Furthermore, in every focal region immunity only protects against fines imposed by the authorities but not from civil liability. This has made confidentiality a very important aspect in every country. As leniency programmes in the US were introduced much earlier than in other parts of the world its regulations served as a blueprint for other countries.

In turn, *Alberts* provide a closer look at the situation in South Africa and some thoughts on current questions in South African Competition Law. He briefly illustrates the role of the competition commission, the central competition authority in South Africa, and famous leniency cases, involving South African companies. The most important concern is that the effectiveness of leniency programmes might suffer from criminal prosecution of cartel conduct by the National Prosecution Authority (NPA) from which the Competition Commission cannot grant immunity. In order to ensure that leniency programmes remain an effective tool to combat such conduct a close cooperation between the two authorities is required. It remains to be seen whether this concept that has previously worked in other industrial countries will work in developing countries.

The principle of legality is the legal idea that requires all law to be clear, ascertainable and non-retrospective. In this context, *Biesinger* asks whether this also affects liability issues in company law: 20 years after the famous ARAG/Garmenbeck case, he addresses the question whether the court was right in defining corporate reputation as a possible justification to refrain from the enforcement of existing damage claims against members of the management board of a corporation. For purposes of legal consideration, he first calls for a definitional common denominator of the multi-disciplinary but legally understudied concept of corporate reputation. Pointing out today's importance of corporate reputation and the difficulties of measuring it, *Biesinger* advocates for qualifying the enforcement decision of the supervisory board as an entrepreneurial decision. However, non-enforcement merely with reference to corporate reputation runs the risk of developing a silver bullet and abolishing legal justifications for turning away from a legal basic concept. According to his social and economic findings, the general suitability of corporate reputation as a consideration should generally be critically scrutinized.

Van der Linde gives a South African perspective on this question. She highlights structural differences and similarities of corporate governance between both legal systems. Due to the unitary board structure of South African companies, either the board itself or someone else on behalf of the company can bring proceedings against a director. *Van der Linde* states that in both instances the company's best interests is the main factor determining the decision whether proceedings should be brought. While the business judgement rule may offer some guidance for the difficult assessment there has not been any judicial guidance so far.

Turning to private international law, the paper of *Wurmnest* and *Kübler-Wachendorff* states that over the last few decades, German courts have more and more relied on provisions of the Grundgesetz to discard the application of foreign law. The article discusses the implications of this development and gives an overview of important cases in which the public policy exception has been successfully applied. They then discuss whether the European reservation clauses are to be interpreted according to autonomous European standards. Furthermore, the authors review how the most important national values can be protected and why the importance of public policy will diminish in the future.

Neels and *Fredericks* consider that the device of public policy may also be used in South African private international law to exclude the application of so-called "unwelcome" foreign law. They then pose the question whether the Bill of Rights is necessarily applicable to foreign law because the issue has not pertinently been considered by the South African courts. The authors discuss why, unlike in Germany, no reservations have been expressed in South African case law or in doctrine about the increasing influence of the Constitution in South African private international law.

The paper of *Lorenzmeier* and *Strydom* analyses basic external trade actions, Association Agreements (AA) and Economic Partnership Agreements (EPA). *Lorenzmeier* initially gives an overview of the EU's strategies and intentions of the EU's trade agreements. The first chapter is devoted to the structure of the European Union's external (trade) actions and and the corpus of legislation of the TFEU that gives the EU the power to conclude these agreements. The paper then outlines how the aims of the Union have been achieved in the course of the negotiations of the Association Agreement with Ukraine and the Economic Partnership Agreement with the SADC countries. Furthermore the paper demonstrates the differences between these types of agreements but also focusses on its political issues. *Lorenzmeier* finally tries to gage the prospective success of these two approaches. From an African perspective, *Strydom* presents the main objectives and principles of the African Continental Free Trade Area (ACFTA) Agreeement, which was signed by 44 state parties in March 2018. The contribution also discusses problems that might occur between state parties regarding the interpretation of the agreement.

III.

As mentioned in our preface above, this publication is a product of the second Augsburg-Johannesburg conference and is the result of our collaborative research. The relatively new concept of combining papers authored by senior and junior researchers was introduced by the South African partners and has willingly been adopted by the University of Augsburg. The generous financial support by both Universities is indicative of how important both universities consider developing capacity in research. To keep the successful joint research going and to intensify our good relationship, further publications with more interesting and up-to-date topics are planned. The Augsburg-Johannesburg cooperation thereby again demonstrates groundbreaking international cooperation on a scientific level.

The editors

Prof. Dr. Thomas M.J. Möllers (Augsburg)
Prof. Dr. Charl Hugo (Johannesburg)

January 2019

Normative Values in Modern Constitutionalism Reflections on the Constitution as an "Objective Value System" 60 years after *Lüth*

*Thilo Rensmann**

Abstract: *Germany and South Africa are united by a distinctive value-oriented vision of the constitution. As the Constitutional Court of South Africa famously stated in Carmichele v. Minister of Safety and Security, the South African Constitution "... is not merely a formal document regulating public power. It also embodies, like the German Constitution, an objective, normative value system."*
Whereas human dignity, proportionality, and all other attributes of value-oriented constitutionalism are inextricably woven into the fabric of the South African Constitution, the text of the German Constitution is much more ambiguous. Although the solemn commitment to human dignity is conspicuously placed in its very first article, the subsequent provisions, and in particular the Bill of Rights, are much more reminiscent of traditional liberal constitutionalism.
It was not until 1958 that the Federal Constitutional Court in its seminal Lüth judgement laid the foundations for the value-oriented approach which is today closely associated with German constitutionalism. On the occasion of the 60th anniversary of Lüth, the following article reflects on the significance of this case for modern constitutionalism from both a German and a comparative perspective.

---

* Thilo Rensmann, *Dr. iur.*; Professor, University of Augsburg, Faculty of Law. Chair of Public Law, International Law and European Law.

I. Introduction: Modern constitutionalism on a desert island

In his fascinating book "The Strange Alchemy of Life and Law" Albie Sachs applies the popular "desert island" hypothetical to constitutional principles. Justice Sachs writes that if he "were to be stranded on a desert island and allowed to take only two constitutional elements with [him], [he] would take human dignity and proportionality."[1]

Most German constitutional lawyers would probably be quite happy with his choice, because both elements – human dignity and proportionality – lie at the heart of a "value-oriented" understanding of the constitution, which has become a hallmark of German constitutionalism.[2] Indeed, it should not really come as a surprise that German and South African castaways would choose essentially the same constitutional principles as the foundation of their "desert island republic". Although we live in different hemispheres and although our legal systems are embedded in different cultural, social and political contexts, Germans and South Africans are united by a distinctive "value-oriented" vision of the constitution. As the Constitutional Court of South Africa famously stated in *Carmichele v. Minister of Safety and Security*, the South African Constitution

1 Albie Sachs, *The Strange Alchemy of Life and Law* (2009), 203.

2 See Michaela Hailbronner, *Traditions and Transformations – The Rise of German Constitutionalism* (2015), 97–123; Thilo Rensmann, 'The Constitution as a Normative Order of Values', in: Pierre-Marie Dupuy, Bardo Fassbender, Malcom N. Shaw and Karl-Peter Sommermann (eds), *Common Values in International Law – Essays in Honour of Christian Tomuschat* (2006), 259–278; Thilo Rensmann, *Wertordnung und Verfassung* (2007).

> "… is not merely a formal document regulating public power. It also embodies, like the German Constitution, an objective, normative value system."[3]

Had Justice Sachs, in our desert island-hypothetical, been allowed to choose only one constitution to take along, he would undoubtedly have opted for the South African Constitution – both as a matter of passion and reason. For a German constitutional lawyer intent on securing a "value-oriented" constitutional order on his or her desert island this would be a much more vexing question.

Whereas human dignity, proportionality, and all other attributes of modern "value-oriented" constitutionalism[4] are inextricably woven into the fabric of the South African Constitution, the text of the German Constitution ("Basic Law"[5]) is much more ambiguous. Although the solemn commitment to human dignity is conspicuously placed in its very first article[6], the subsequent provisions of the Basic Law, and in particular the Bill of Rights, are much more reminiscent of traditional liberal constitutionalism. To quite a few post-war constitutional scholars in Germany the entrenchment of human dignity in article 1 paragraph 1 of the Basic Law therefore appeared to be strangely at odds with the overall liberal thrust of the constitution.[7] Indeed, in the early 1950s, some scholars even went so far as to brand the human dignity-clause a "drafting error" and thus devoid of any true normative force.[8] It was only about 10 years after the promulgation of the Basic

3 Constitutional Court of South Africa, Case CCT 48/00, 16.8.2001, *Carmichele v Minister of Safety and Security*, 2001 (4) SA 938 (CC).

4 On the idiosyncratic features of the ideal-type of "value-oriented" constitutionalism, see Thilo Rensmann, *Wertordnung und Verfassung* (2007), 266–301.

5 Basic Law for the Federal Republic of Germany, 23 May 1949, Bundesgesetzblatt (Federal Law Gazette) 1949, 1; English translation available at: https://www.gesetze-im-internet.de/englisch_gg/ (18-06-2018).

6 Article 1 para. 1 Basic Law reads: "Human dignity shall be inviolable. To respect and protect it shall be the duty of all state authority".

7 See, e.g., Friedrich Klein, 106 (1950) *Zeitschrift für die gesamte Staatswissenschaft (ZgS)*, 390 (404).

8 Franz W. Jerusalem, 5 (1950) *Süddeutsche Juristen-Zeitung (SJZ)*, 1; see also, Ernst Forsthoff, 'Die Umbildung des Verfassungsgesetzes', in: id. and Klaus Frey (eds), *Rechtsstaat im Wandel: Verfassungsrechtliche Abhandlungen 1950–1973* (2nd Edition, 1976), 130 (146).

Law that the German Federal Constitutional Court in its seminal *Lüth* decision[9] laid the foundations for the "value-oriented" approach which is today closely associated with German constitutionalism[10].

Accordingly, if a German constitutional lawyer were presented with the choice between the German and South African constitutions, he or she would be well advised to opt for South Africa's 1996 Constitution, which in clear and unambiguous language entrenches all essential features of modern "value-oriented" and human rights-based constitutionalism[11].

However, were one permitted to take along a copy of one court judgment in addition, then it would certainly be a close call. In the end, a German constitutional lawyer would probably go for the "bundle" of the German Basic Law and *Lüth*, not least because the complex and multifaceted nature of this judgment – as well as its remarkable career as one of the leading cases of global constitutionalism – provide for fascinating research and hence a welcome pastime during banishment to the island.

2018 marks the 60th anniversary of the Federal Constitutional Court handing down its *Lüth* judgment. It is thus a particularly timely moment to reflect on the significance of *Lüth* for modern constitutionalism – from both a German and a comparative perspective.

The following remarks revisit the *Lüth* judgement with a view to developing the contention that the "value-oriented" jurisprudence of the German Federal Constitutional Court is not as idiosyncratically German as many German constitutional lawyers would like us to believe. It is argued that the conceptual development leading up to the famous *Lüth* dictum of the constitution as an "objective value system", is instead closely linked to the emergence of international human rights law – and hence from its very beginnings the result of an intense transnational and inter-cultural discourse.

9 BVerfG 15.1.1958 – 1 BvR 400/51 – BVerfGE 7, 198. For English translations see Jürgen Bröhmer, Clauspeter Hill and Marc Spitzkatz, *60 Years German Basic Law: The German Constitution and Its Court: Landmark Decisions of the Federal Constitutional Court of Germany in the Area of Fundamental Rights* (2nd Edition, 2012), 352–357; Donald P. Kommers and Russel A. Miller, *The Constitutional Jurisprudence of the Federal Republic of Germany* (3rd Edition, 2012), 442–448.

10 See references in note 2.

11 See Thilo Rensmann, *Wertordnung und Verfassung* (2007), 269–301 with further references.

II. Lüth as a global precedent for "value-oriented" constitutionalism

The German Federal Constitutional Court, however, can legitimately be credited with the distinction of having been amongst the first to give clear expression to this novel approach to constitutionalism. In the 1958 *Lüth* decision the Court held with regard to the Basic Law:

> "Without doubt, the primary purpose of fundamental rights is to safeguard the individual sphere of liberty against interference by public authority. They are defensive rights of the citizen against the state. … It is equally true, however, that the Basic Law … has, in its section on fundamental rights, also set up an objective order of values. … This value system, which centres around human dignity and the human personality freely developing within the social community, must be regarded as a fundamental constitutional decision for all areas of law; it provides guidelines and impulses to the legislature, the executive and the judiciary."[12]

Today this dictum is not only echoed in South Africa[13] and other African states[14], but by many constitutions and courts around the globe. Pertinent examples are provided by the Spanish and Portuguese constitutions of the late 1970s[15], which in turn strongly influenced many modern constitutions in Latin America[16]. After the collapse of the Soviet Empire, practically all post-communist states in Central and Eastern Europe adopted this new type of "value-oriented" constitutionalism.[17]

It would, however, undoubtedly overstate the significance of German constitutionalism, were one to draw a direct genealogical line between the

---

12 BVerfG 15.1.1958 – 1 BvR 400/51 – BVerfGE 7, 198, 205. Translation based on Donald P. Kommers and Russel A. Miller, *The Constitutional Jurisprudence of the Federal Republic of Germany* (3rd Edition, 2012), 443 et seq.

13 See Constitutional Court of South Africa, Case CCT 48/00, 16.8.2001, *Carmichele v Minister of Safety and Security*, 2001 (4) SA 938 (CC).

14 For a more recent example, see High Court of Kenya, Miscellaneous Civil Application 391 of 2017, 17 January 2018, *Republic v National Assembly, Speaker of National Assembly & 6 others Ex parte George Wang'ang'a*, [2018] eKLR, para. 78 (with a direct reference to the *Lüth* decision).

15 See Thilo Rensmann, *Wertordnung und Verfassung* (2007), 267 et seq.

16 See Armin von Bogdandy et al., 'Ius Constitutionale Commune en América Latina: A Regional Approach to Transformative Constitutionalism', in: Armin von Bogdandy et al. (eds), *Transformative Constitutionalism in Latin America* (2017), 3 (15–20).

17 See Wojciech Sadurski, *Rights Before Courts – A Study of Constitutional Courts in Postcommunist States of Central and Eastern Europe* (2nd Edition, 2014); Herman Schwartz, *The Struggle for Constitutional Justice in Post-Communist Europe* (2000).

Lüth decision and the increasing number of "value-oriented" constitutions around the world. The surprising and enduring international appeal of *Lüth* is rather based on the fact that the Federal Constitutional Court in 1958 led the way in wholeheartedly embracing the emerging "value system" of international human rights and resolutely merging it with the strict normativity and supremacy of constitutional law.

III. The constitutional commitment to the "value system" of the Universal Declaration of Human Rights

In stark contrast to the Weimar Constitution of 1919[18] and to many modern constitutional texts such as the South African Constitution, the German Basic Law – as it still stands today – restricts itself almost exclusively to setting forth classical liberal rights and is therefore practically devoid of social rights and other guarantees establishing positive State obligations.[19]

This observation seems difficult to reconcile with the fact that the Basic Law, in the first two paragraphs of its article 1, proclaims human dignity as the highest constitutional value and makes a solemn commitment to "inviolable and inalienable human rights [as] … the basis of every community, of peace and of justice in the world." It has gone largely unnoticed in Germany, that these two paragraphs are borrowed – practically *in haec verba* – from the Universal Declaration of Human Rights (UDHR)[20] and thereby give expression to the unequivocal aspiration of the mothers and fathers of the Basic Law to base the new constitutional order on the emerging "value system" of international human rights.

---

18 Constitution of the German Empire, 11 August 1919, Reichsgesetzblatt (Law Gazette of the German Empire) 1919 No. 152, 1383; English translation available at: http://germanhistorydocs.ghi-dc.org/pdf/eng/ghi_wr_weimarconstitution_Eng.pdf (18-06-2018).

19 The observations in sections III and IV draw on Thilo Rensmann, 'Domestic Courts as International Human Rights Courts – A German Perspective', in: Stefan Kadelbach, Thilo Rensmann and Eva Rieter (eds), *Judging International Human Rights – Courts of General Jurisdiction as Human Rights Courts* (forthcoming 2019).

20 Cf. preamble, para. 1 UDHR, according to which the "recognition of the inherent dignity and of the equal and inalienable rights of all members of the human family is the foundation of freedom, justice and peace in the world".

The UDHR – which had been adopted six months before the entry into force of the German Basic Law – marked a paradigm shift in the evolution of both human rights and modern constitutionalism. It is built on a "value system"[21] in which human dignity as the highest value[22] overarches the trinity of freedom, equality and brotherhood[23] (or "solidarity" in modern parlance[24]).

The ultimate goal of human rights is thus no longer limited to ensuring "liberty" in the sense of the individual's "right to be let alone"[25] by the State. The drafters of the UDHR had lost the liberal optimism that the free interplay of societal forces would be sufficient to guarantee "freedom from fear" and "freedom from want".[26] In the UDHR the reach of human rights is therefore extended to the societal conditions which are indispensable for the "full and free development of the human personality"[27].

This communitarian vision of "freedom" changes the substantive reach and structure of human rights in two essential ways:

Firstly, in addition to the classical negative rights of the enlightenment period, the UDHR also guarantees "economic, social and cultural rights"[28]. All human rights – liberal and social rights – are considered equally fundamental, they are "indivisible ... interdependent and interrelated"[29].

Secondly, by tearing down the "wall of separation" which the liberal human rights conception establishes between the governmental and the societal spheres[30], the UDHR endows human rights with an additional dimension. This new dimension of human rights finds its clearest expression in

---

21 As to the conceptualisation of the UDHR as a "value system" see René Cassin, 79 (1951–II) *Recueil des cours de l'académie de droit international*, 237 (277–279); Thilo Rensmann, *Wertordnung und Verfassung* (2007), 18–21.

22 Article 1 sentence 1; preamble, para. 1 UDHR.

23 Article 1 sentences 1 and 2 UDHR.

24 Thus, e.g. the terminology of the Charter of Fundamental Rights of the European Union which in its preamble (para. 2) reaffirms "the universal values of human dignity, freedom, equality and solidarity" and in Titles I–IV spells out the fundamental rights corresponding to each of these values.

25 As to this notion see Samuel Warren and Louis Brandeis, 4 (1890) *Harvard Law Review (Harv L Rev)*, 193.

26 See preamble, para. 2 UDHR (quoting Roosevelt's "Four Freedoms").

27 Article 22 UDHR.

28 Article 22 UDHR. See also 23–27 UDHR.

29 Thus the formulation in Vienna Declaration and Programme of Action, 25 June 1993, (1993) 32 ILM 1661, chapter I, para. 5.

30 Carl Schmitt describes this as the "fundamental distributive principle" (*fundamentales Verteilungsprinzip*) of the liberal human rights conception, see Carl Schmitt,

article 28 of the UDHR according to which "everyone is entitled to a social and international order in which the rights and freedoms set forth in this Declaration can be fully realised."

Human rights are thus not only understood as individual rights but also as normative "values" or "principles"[31] which structure the social order at national and international level; they provide – in the words of the *Lüth* judgment – "guidelines and impulses" to all branches of government[32], or – as it is often put today – human rights assume a "transformative" dimension[33].

The essence of "value-oriented" constitutionalism had hence already been fully developed by the international community in the UDHR, a full decade before it found its much-quoted expression in the *Lüth* decision of the German Federal Constitutional Court.

IV. Endowing international human rights with the teeth of Marbury v. Madison

The mothers and fathers of the German Constitution were determined not to repeat the mistakes, which had led to the downfall of the Weimar Republic.[34] The Weimar Republic had proved defenceless against the rise of the Nazi movement, which had availed itself of the democratic process as a Trojan horse. The Achilles' heel of the Weimar Constitution was considered to have been its procedural, relativistic approach to democracy and, in particular the weak normative power of its bill of rights.

Verfassungslehre (1928), 164; English translation: Carl Schmitt, *Constitutional Theory* (trans. Jeffrey Seitzer, 2008), 203.

31 On the interrelationship between "values" and "principles", see Robert Alexy, *A Theory of Constitutional Rights* (trans. Julian Rivers, 2010), 86–93.

32 BVerfG 15.1.1958 – 1 BvR 400/51 – BVerfGE 7, 198, 205. Translation based on Donald P. Kommers and Russel A. Miller, *The Constitutional Jurisprudence of the Federal Republic of Germany* (3rd Edition, 2012), 443 et seq.

33 Karl E. Klare, 14 (1998) *South African Journal on Human Rights*, 146–188. See also Michaela Hailbronner, 65 (2017) *American Journal of Comparative Law*, 527–565; Armin von Bogdandy et al., 'Ius Constitutionale Commune en América Latina: A Regional Approach to Transformative Constitutionalism', in: Armin von Bogdandy et al. (eds), *Transformative Constitutionalism in Latin America* (2017), 3 (15–20).

34 See Thilo Rensmann, *Wertordnung und Verfassung* (2007), 33–36.

As a response, article 1 paragraph 3 of the Basic Law, which immediately follows the "quotation" from the UDHR, declares the bill of rights binding on all three branches of government as "directly applicable law".

In the eyes of the drafters of the Basic Law the intention of transforming human rights into "directly applicable law" – while at the same time shaping their normative ambit and content in accordance with the UDHR – created a virtually irreconcilable conflict. Faithfully following the model of the UDHR would have required the inclusion of social rights and other positive human rights dimensions.[35] On the other hand, the goal of endowing human rights with strict normativity seemed to militate against the inclusion of social rights, which under the Weimar Constitution had been widely considered mere "programmatic" provisions devoid of any normative clout.[36]

The fathers and mothers of the Basic Law did not succeed in resolving this conflict. The baton was thus handed over to the Federal Constitutional Court.

The breakthrough came in 1958 with the *Lüth* decision. At the heart of this case lay a crime against humanity and the impunity of its perpetrator.[37] Adolf Hitler's propaganda minister Josef Goebbels had commissioned Veit Harlan to direct the blatantly anti-Semitic film "Jud Süss". After the war, Harlan was charged before German courts with aiding and abetting a crime against humanity for his involvement with the Nazi's propaganda war against the Jews. He was eventually acquitted on spurious grounds and subsequently resumed his career as a film director.

Erich Lüth – at the time the press officer for the city-state of Hamburg but acting, however, in his private capacity – made a public appeal for the boycott of Harlan's films. Harlan's film production company sought an injunction against Lüth, enjoining him from making any further boycott calls. The Hamburg Regional Court granted the injunction on the basis that calling for a boycott was contrary to public policy.[38] Lüth took the case to the

---

35 See articles 22–28 UDHR.

36 Thilo Rensmann, *Wertordnung und Verfassung* (2007), 53–62 with further references.

37 For a summary of the facts see BVerfG 15.1.1958 – 1 BvR 400/51 – BVerfGE 7, 198, 199–203.

38 LG Hamburg 22.11.1951 – 15 O 87/51. The injunction was based on Section 826 of the German Civil Code which reads: "A person who, in a manner contrary to public policy, intentionally inflicts damage on another person is liable to the other person to make compensation for the damage." English translation taken from: https://www.gesetze-im-internet.de/englisch_bgb/index.html (15-06-2018).

Federal Constitutional Court claiming that the injunction violated his right to freedom of speech under article 5 paragraph 1 of the Basic Law.

In terms of legal doctrine, the *Lüth* case raised the question of the horizontal application of fundamental rights to what was essentially a private law dispute between Lüth and Harlan's film production company. Many scholars at the time categorically denied any third party-effect (*Drittwirkung*) of fundamental rights since in their view the German bill of rights only provided for classical liberal rights against State interference.[39] Others tried to reconstruct the horizontal application of fundamental rights within the paradigm of negative liberties by arguing that it was the court injunction, which represented the relevant act infringing Lüth's freedom of speech.[40]

The Federal Constitutional Court relied instead on a novel approach based on a positive duty to protect the "values" embodied in the bill of rights, which ingeniously brought together the "value system" of the UDHR and the strict normativity of the German Constitution.

The constitutional "order of values" referred to by the Federal Constitutional Court in its famous and much quoted *Lüth* dictum[41] in fact replicates and hence internalises the "value system" of the UDHR[42]. Both "value systems" centre "around human dignity and the human personality freely developing within the social community."[43] By virtue of this communitarian notion of freedom, the fundamental rights of the Basic Law – in the same way as international human rights – assume additional, positive dimensions.

---

39 See references in Franz Laufke, 'Vertragsfreiheit und Grundgesetz', in: Hans Carl Nipperdey (ed), *Das deutsche Privatrecht in der Mitte des Jahrhunderts – Festschrift für Heinrich Lehmann*, Volume 1 (1956), 145–188.

40 See e.g. Hans Carl Nipperdey, 'Die Würde des Menschen', in: Franz L. Neumann, Hans Carl Nipperdey and Ulrich Scheuner (eds), *Die Grundrechte – Handbuch der Theorie und Praxis der Grundrechte*, Volume 2 (1954), 1 (21). On the links between Nipperdey's approach, the US Supreme Court's "state action-doctrine" and international human rights law see Thilo Rensmann, 'The Constitution as a Normative Order of Values: The Influence of International Human Rights Law on the Evolution of Modern Constitutionalism', in: Pierre-Marie Dupuy, Bardo Fassbender, Malcom N. Shaw, Karl-Peter Sommermann (eds) *Common Values in International Law – Essays in Honour of Christian Tomuschat* (2006), 259 (274–275).

41 BVerfG 15.1.1958 – 1 BvR 400/51 – BVerfGE 7, 198, 205. Translation based on Donald P. Kommers and Russel A. Miller, *The Constitutional Jurisprudence of the Federal Republic of Germany* (3rd Edition, 2012), 443 et seq.

42 As to the "value system" of the UDHR see supra section III.

43 See the quotation from *Lüth* in note 12.

Freedom in dignity guarantees not only negative "liberty against interference by public authority"[44] but also "freedom from want" and "freedom from fear"[45], which each require positive State action.

Indeed, article 1 paragraph 1 sentence 2 of the Basic Law explicitly sets forth the duty of all state authority to "respect *and protect*" human dignity. By transforming the bill of rights into a "value system" based on human dignity, the Federal Constitutional Court projected the dual obligation "to respect and protect" onto all fundamental rights. As an integral part of each fundamental right, the duty to protect corresponds with an individual right to be protected[46] and binds all three branches of government "as directly applicable law"[47].

The approach based on the duty to protect allowed the Federal Constitutional Court to view the horizontal effect of fundamental rights through the prism of the separation of powers. Whereas the negative duty to respect equally applies to all three branches of government, the Court considered the responsibility for discharging the duty to protect to lie primarily with the legislature.[48] The protective duties of the judiciary and the executive are thus in principle limited to taking account of the "guidelines and impulses" "radiating" from the bill of rights when interpreting and applying legislation.[49]

Building on these doctrinal foundations, the Federal Constitutional Court eventually held that the Hamburg Regional Court had failed in its duty to accord proper weight to Lüth's freedom of speech when finding that his boycott call was contrary to public policy.[50] Under the new human rights-based German Constitution, no one was to be denied the right to speak out against a crime against humanity.

The Federal Constitutional Court had thereby not only vindicated those citizens who had publicly stood up for the cause of human rights in the early formative years of the Federal Republic of Germany. By resolutely merging

---

44 BVerfG 15.1.1958 – 1 BvR 400/51 – BVerfGE 7, 198, 205. Translation based on Donald P. Kommers and Russel A. Miller, *The Constitutional Jurisprudence of the Federal Republic of Germany* (3rd Edition, 2012), 443 et seq.

45 See preamble, para. 2 UDHR.

46 BVerfG 15.1.1958 – 1 BvR 400/51 – BVerfGE 7, 198, 207.

47 Article 1 para. 3 Basic Law.

48 BVerfG 15.1.1958 – 1 BvR 400/51 – BVerfGE 7, 198, 205.

49 BVerfG 15.1.1958 – 1 BvR 400/51 – BVerfGE 7, 198, 205–207.

50 BVerfG 15.1.1958 – 1 BvR 400/51 – BVerfGE 7, 198, 213–230.

the "value system" of the UDHR with the supremacy of the constitution effectuated by the power of judicial review, the FCC had also added an important element to the evolution of modern constitutionalism: *Lüth* had endowed international human rights with the teeth of *Marbury v. Madison*[51].

V. Conclusion: The legacy of Lüth

Against this backdrop, it seems fair to conclude that *Lüth* constituted a milestone in the evolution of "value-oriented" and human rights-based constitutionalism to which both the German and the South African constitutions subscribe.

At the core of this new ideal-type of constitutionalism lies the premise that the legitimacy of governmental power is not exclusively based on the will of "we the people" but also on the universal values of human dignity and human rights. The judicial branch is empowered to ensure that the democratic process pays due respect to these foundational values. Accordingly, judicial review does not pose a "counter-majoritarian difficulty"[52] but is rather the natural consequence of reining in the democratic process by constitutionally entrenched values.

Since this new generation of "value-oriented" constitutions share the commitment to the universal values of human dignity and human rights, the interpretation of domestic fundamental rights becomes part of a common endeavour to shed light on the exact meaning of the lodestar of the UDHR.[53] The comparative analysis of other "value-oriented" and human rights-based constitutions hence becomes an integral part of the hermeneutic process of constitutional interpretation.[54]

---

51 United States Supreme Court, 24.2.1803, *Marbury v. Madison*, 5 U.S. (1 Cranch) 137 (1803).

52 Alexander M. Bickel, *The Least Dangerous Branch* (1962), 16.

53 The obligation to interpret domestic fundamental rights in the light of international human rights finds a clear expression in section 39 (1) (a) and (b) South African Constitution. For Germany see, BVerfG 14.10.2004 – 2 BvR 1481/04 – BVerfGE 111, 307, 317; BVerfG 8.2.2011 – 2 BvR 2365/09 – BVerfGE 128, 326, 367–368; BVerfG 12.6.2018 – 2 BvR 1738/12 – http://www.bverfg.de/e/rs20180612_2bvr173812.html (15-06-2018).

54 See section 39 (1) (c) South African Constitution: "When interpreting the Bill of Rights, a court, tribunal or forum … may consider foreign law." For Germany, see, with further references, Karl Peter Sommermann, 'Funktionen und Methoden

Whilst in South Africa, and other democracies subscribing to human rights-based constitutionalism, much attention is given to German constitutional thought, the German constitutional discourse since *Lüth* has been comparatively introspective. The 60th anniversary of *Lüth* should serve as a reminder to German constitutional lawyers that the advent of "value-oriented" constitutionalism in Germany was itself the result of an intense international discourse.

Today the center of this discourse has shifted to the emerging democracies in Latin America, Africa and Asia. Under designations such as "neo-constitucionalismo"[55] and "transformative constitutionalism"[56] a rich and creative debate on "value-oriented" and human rights-based constitutionalism has unfolded in the Global South.

The new surge of nationalist populism in Europe demonstrates that 60 years along the road human rights-based constitutionalism is not as firmly entrenched in our societies and legal systems as many of us thought. Populist movements strike at two basic pillars of "value-oriented" constitutionalism: Human rights are discredited as libertarian principles which undermine traditional national values, and judicial review is perceived as the rule of a technocratic elite disregarding the true will of "we the people".

Currently the examples of Poland and Hungary highlight the precarious state of human rights-based constitutionalism in Europe. The past elections in Austria, the Netherlands, France, Germany and Italy demonstrate that the more entrenched European democracies are also under enormous populist pressure.

Constitutional thought in Europe needs to adapt to these new challenges, which in many ways resemble the problems faced by the fledgling democracies in the Global South. The *ius constitutionale commune* emerging amongst "value-oriented" democracies around the globe, provides a rich source of inspiration for devising adequate strategies for faithfully transforming the promise of human dignity and human rights into constitutional reality.[57] It is therefore high time that German constitutional lawyers more

---

der Grundrechtsvergleichung', in: Detlef Merten and Hans-Jürgen Papier (eds), *Handbuch der Grundrechte*, Volume 1 (2004), 631–678.

55 Miguel Carbonell, *Teoría del neoconstitucionalismo: ensayos escogidos* (2007).

56 See references in note 33.

57 As to the global relevance of Latin American constitutionalism, see Armin von Bogdandy et al., 'Ius Constitutionale Commune en América Latina: A Regional Approach to Transformative Constitutionalism', in: Armin von Bogdandy et al.

actively rejoined this global discourse. This is what we owe to the legacy of *Lüth*.

Bibliography

Robert Alexy, *A Theory of Constitutional Rights* (trans. Julian Rivers, Oxford University Press, Oxford 2010).

Alexander M. Bickel, *The Least Dangerous Branch* (Bobbs-Merrill, Indianapolis 1962).

Jürgen Bröhmer, Clauspeter Hill and Marc Spitzkatz, *60 Years German Basic Law: The German Constitution and Its Court: Landmark Decisions of the Federal Constitutional Court of Germany in the Area of Fundamental Rights* (2nd Edition, The Malaysian Current Law Journal, Ampang 2012).

Miguel Carbonell, *Teoría del neoconstitucionalismo: ensayos escogidos* (Instituto de Investigaciones Jurídicas, UNAM, Madrid 2007).

René Cassin, 'La déclaration universelle et la mise en œuvre des droits de l'homme' 79 (1951–II) *Recueil des cours de l'académie de droit international*, 237.

Ernst Forsthoff, 'Die Umbildung des Verfassungsgesetzes', in: id., Klaus Frey (eds), *Rechtsstaat im Wandel: Verfassungsrechtliche Abhandlungen 1950–1973* (2nd Edition, C.H. Beck, München 1976), 130.

James Fowkes, 'Transformative Constitutionalism and the Global South: The View From South Africa', in: Armin von Bogdandy et al. (eds), *Transformative Constitutionalism in Latin America* (Oxford University Press, Oxford 2017), 97.

Michaela Hailbronner, *Traditions and Transformations – The Rise of German Constitutionalism* (Oxford University Press, Oxford 2015).

Michaela Hailbronner, 'Transformative Constitutionalism: Not Only in the Global South' 65 (2017) *American Journal of Comparative Law (Am J Comp L)*, 527.

Franz W. Jerusalem, 'Die Grundrechte des Bonner Grundgesetzes und ihre Durchsetzung in der Rechtsprechung' 5 (1950) *Süddeutsche Juristen-Zeitung (SJZ)*, 1.

Karl E. Klare, 'Legal Culture and Transformative Constitutionalism' 14 (1998) *South African Journal on Human Rights*, 146.

Friedrich Klein, 'Bonner Grundgesetz und Rechtsstaat' 106 (1950) *Zeitschrift für die gesamte Staatswissenschaft (ZgS)*, 390.

Donald P. Kommers and Russel A. Miller, *The Constitutional Jurisprudence of the Federal Republic of Germany* (3rd Edition, Duke University Press, Durham 2012).

(eds), *Transformative Constitutionalism in Latin America* (2017), 3 (8–9); on a South African perspective, see James Fowkes, 'Transformative Constitutionalism and the Global South: The View From South Africa', in: Armin von Bogdandy et al. (eds), *Transformative Constitutionalism in Latin America* (2017), 97–121.

Franz Laufke, 'Vertragsfreiheit und Grundgesetz', in: Hans Carl Nipperdey (ed), *Das deutsche Privatrecht in der Mitte des Jahrhunderts – Festschrift für Heinrich Lehmann*, Volume 1 (De Gruyter, Berlin 1956), 145.

Hans Carl Nipperdey, 'Die Würde des Menschen', in: Franz L. Neumann, Hans Carl Nipperdey and Ulrich Scheuner (eds), *Die Grundrechte – Handbuch der Theorie und Praxis der Grundrechte*, Volume 2 (Duncker & Humblot, Berlin 1954), 1.

Thilo Rensmann, 'Domestic Courts as International Human Rights Courts – A German Perspective', in: Stefan Kadelbach, Thilo Rensmann and Eva Rieter (eds), *Judging International Human Rights – Courts of General Jurisdiction as Human Rights Courts* (Springer, Heidelberg forthcoming 2019).

Thilo Rensmann, 'The Constitution as a Normative Order of Values', in: Pierre-Marie Dupuy, Bardo Fassbender, Malcom N. Shaw and Karl-Peter Sommermann (eds), *Common Values in International Law – Essays in Honour of Christian Tomuschat* (N.P. Engel, Kehl 2006), 259.

Thilo Rensmann, *Wertordnung und Verfassung* (Mohr Siebeck, Tübingen 2007).

Albie Sachs, *The Strange Alchemy of Life and Law* (Oxford University Press, Oxford 2009).

Wojciech Sadurski, *Rights Before Courts – A Study of Constitutional Courts in Post-communist States of Central and Eastern Europe* (2nd Edition, Springer, Dordrecht 2014).

Carl Schmitt, *Constitutional Theory* (trans. Jeffrey Seitzer, Duke University Press, Durham, 2008).

Carl Schmitt, *Verfassungslehre* (Duncker & Humblot, Munich, Leipzig 1928).

Herman Schwartz, *The Struggle for Constitutional Justice in Post-Communist Europe* (University of Chicago Press, Chicago, London 2000).

Karl Peter Sommermann, 'Funktionen und Methoden der Grundrechtsvergleichung', in: Detlef Merten and Hans-Jürgen Papier (eds), *Handbuch der Grundrechte*, Volume 1 (C.F. Müller, Heidelberg 2004), 631.

Armin von Bogdandy, Eduardo Ferrer Mac-Gregor, Mariela Morales Antoniazzi, Flávia Piovesan and Ximena Soley, 'Ius Constitutionale Commune en América Latina: A Regional Approach to Transformative Constitutionalism', in: Armin von Bogdandy et al. (eds), *Transformative Constitutionalism in Latin America* (Oxford University Press, Oxford 2017), 3.

Samuel Warren and Louis Brandeis, 'The Right to Privacy' 4 (1890) *Harvard Law Review (Harv L Rev)*, 193.

Register of Cases

Germany

BVerfG 15.1.1958 – 1 BvR 400/51 – BVerfGE 7, 198.

BVerfG 14.10.2004 – 2 BvR 1481/04 – BVerfGE 111, 307.

BVerfG 8.2.2011 – 2 BvR 2365/09 – BVerfGE 128, 326.

BVerfG 12.6.2018 – 2 BvR 1738/12.

LG Hamburg 22.11.1951 – 15 O 87/51.

Kenya

High Court of Kenya, Miscellaneous Civil Application 391 of 2017, 17 January 2018, *Republic v National Assembly, Speaker of National Assembly & 6 others Ex parte George Wang'ang'a*, [2018] eKLR.

South Africa

Constitutional Court of South Africa, Case CCT 48/00, 16.8.2001, *Carmichele v Minister of Safety and Security*, 2001 (4) SA 938 (CC).

United States

United States Supreme Court, 24.2.1803, *Marbury v. Madison*, 5 U.S. (1 Cranch) 137 (1803).

Comment: Constitutional Values and Transformative Constitutionalism

*Roxan Venter**

I. The transformative nature of normative constitutional values

It is virtually impossible to deny the importance of the role of values in the South African constitutional order. From the advent of our new constitutional democracy values played, and continue to play, a central role in the South African constitutional system. Ever since the inclusion of the constitutional principles in the Constitution of the Republic of South Africa 200 of 1993 (hereafter the Interim Constitution), which the Constitutional Court later used to certify the current Constitution of the Republic of South Africa of 1996 (hereafter the Constitution), values and principles have taken centre stage in South African constitutional law. It is also important to appreciate what these values had to achieve – not only did these values have the function of creating a new democratic system, but they also needed to continue to transform society long after the adoption of the new Constitution. These values were therefore never meant merely to be used to form the foundation of our new democracy and then conveniently to disappear into the annals of history – like a faint recollection or a fond memory which can nostalgically be remembered once in a while, only to disappear into obscurity once more.

These two functions of the South African Constitution and its values, namely forming the basis of a new democratic order and transforming the

* Roxan Venter, *B.Com. (Law), LL.B., LL.M., LL.D.*, Senior Lecturer in Constitutional Law and Human Rights Law, Faculty of Law, University of Johannesburg.

South African society, are clearly illustrated by the following passage from the postamble of the Interim Constitution:

> 'This Constitution provides *a historic bridge between the past of a deeply divided society* characterised by strife, conflict, untold suffering and injustice, *and a future founded on the recognition of human rights, democracy and peaceful co-existence and development opportunities for all South Africans, irrespective of colour, race, class, belief or sex.* The pursuit of national unity, the well-being of all South African citizens and peace require reconciliation between the people of South Africa and the reconstruction of society.'[1] [own emphasis]

This is the ongoing project of the South African Constitution and its values: transformative constitutionalism. In the words of Mureinik the South African Constitution is the "bridge" from a 'culture of authority' to a 'culture of justification'.[2] The Constitution can, however, not merely remain a bridge – a bridge is static and only connects one place with another. The Constitution needs to allow society to move forward, change and transform. Therefore, where the Constitution has established a new kind of society, the values need to be used to make that society move forward and transform in order to correct the injustices and inequalities of the past, as well as to address new challenges as they emerge.

Among the values of human dignity, freedom and equality enshrined in section 1 of the Constitution, the indigenous value of *ubuntu* is also central to the new constitutional order and its transformative goal. In *Dikoko v Mokhatla* the court referred to *ubuntu* as 'intrinsic to and constitutive of our constitutional culture'.[3] The court in the *Dikoko* judgment further emphasised the double function of the Constitution and its underlying values:

> 'Historically it [*ubuntu*] was *foundational to the spirit of reconciliation and bridge-building* that enabled our deeply traumatised society to overcome and transcend the divisions of the past. In present day terms it has *an enduring and creative character*, representing the element of human solidarity that binds together liberty and equality to create an affirmative and mutually supportive triad of central constitutional values.' [4] [own emphasis]

1 The postamble of the Interim Constitution under the heading 'National Unity and Reconciliation'.

2 Etienne Mureinik, *South African Journal on Human Rights (SAJHR)*, 1994, 31 (32).

3 *Dikoko v Mokhatla* 2006 (6) SA 235 (CC) par 113.

4 *Dikoko v Mokhatla* 2006 (6) SA 235 (CC) par 113.

Constitutional values, including the value of ubuntu, have also been emphasised in many judgments, for example *S v Makwanyane,*[5] *Minister of Health v New Clicks South Africa (Pty) Ltd,*[6] *Director of Public Prosecutions, Transvaal v Minister for Justice and Constitutional Development,*[7] *Doctors for Life International v Speaker of the National Assembly,*[8] and in many other cases and in various different contexts. Furthermore, various provisions of the Constitution enforce and underlie the transformative nature of the Constitution and its values. Section 1 of the Constitution, which enshrines the values on which our constitutional order is founded, are entrenched with a special higher majority, which means that the national assembly would need a 75% majority and the support of six of the nine provinces in the national council of provinces in order to amend this provision – which further illustrates the importance of these values in the South African constitutional system. Section 39(1) of the Constitution, for example, expressly prescribes that its underlying values must be promoted when interpreting the Bill of Rights, while section 39(2) provides that when any legislation is interpreted, or when the common or customary law is developed, the 'spirit, purport and objects of the Bill of Rights' must be promoted. Some of the most important examples of provisions that contribute to the Constitution's transformative goals are the affirmative action provision contained in the equality clause,[9] the land reform provision contained in the property clause[10] and the various socio-economic rights[11] enshrined in the Constitution.

This normative constitutional value system that was created by the Interim Constitution and the current South African Constitution was driven firstly by the negotiation processes and compromises reached between the various parties responsible for the drafting of the new constitutional documents, in the spirit of reconciliation and transformation. Secondly, the South African constitutional value system was developed in recognition of international values that were aimed at setting international norms and standards for the international community, for instance in the Universal Declaration of Human Rights and Fundamental Freedoms as well as other international instruments, that have gone mostly unacknowledged in South

5 1995 3 SA 391 (CC).
6 2006 2 SA 311 (CC).
7 2009 4 SA 222 (CC).
8 2006 6 SA 416 (CC).
9 Sec. 9(2) of the Constitution.
10 Sec. 25 of the Constitution.
11 For instance housing (sec. 26) and health care (sec. 27).

Africa's constitutional history since their recognition by the international community nearly five decades earlier. Section 39(1)(*b*) of the South African Constitution also expressly provides that when the Bill of Rights is interpreted the international law must be considered.

The German system, similar to that of South Africa, had to embark on a transformation process of its own following World War II. It is also easy to compare this process with the one that South Africa had to follow after the end of the Apartheid era. It is undeniable that the German Constitutional Court's value-based approach in the *Lüth* judgment[12] to the interpretation and application of the German Constitution, in line with the values set out in the Universal Declaration of Human Rights, has had a profound effect on this transformation process in the German system and will continue to do so.

II. The future of constitutional values in transformation

Although the transformative goals of the South African Constitution have made great progress in transforming society in the years following its adoption, there is much more that could be done. It is no wonder that constitutional values and their contribution to transformation are increasingly criticised and threatened by proponents of populist theories. *Rensmann* rightly points out that these populist movements strike at the heart of the transformative constitutional value system and would rather have such a system replaced with a system which recognises the 'true will of the people' – one that is not enforced by 'libertarian principles' and judicial review by a 'technocratic elite'. These arguments are also rife in South Africa and many feel that the Constitution has not lived up to its transformative goals – and never will. Populist movements however lose sight of the fact that, not only is the 'will of the people' as changeable as the weather and difficult to ascertain, but also cannot provide an objective system to evaluate legislation, government and private action or provide a defined system of higher level goals to strive towards.

Transforming a society does not happen overnight; it is also not a road with a clear destination. It may even be asked whether it is at all possible to reach a stage when one could sit back and say that our society has been completely transformed. It would seem that this is an unattainable goal. We should, however, not be disheartened by this realisation. Transformation is

12 BVerfG 15.01.1958 – 1 BvR 400/51 – BVerfGE 7, 198 – Lüth.

an ongoing process that needs to be implemented every day, applied to every situation, every law, and every government and private action. In this process constitutional values should be our guide so that every application of these values leaves society and the legal system more transformed than it was before, always coming closer but never reaching ultimate transformation. It seems that transformation, like life, is about the journey and not a destination. It is therefore important, as *Rensmann* rightly points out, that constitutional lawyers in Germany, and also in South Africa, not disregard the threat of populist theories to value-oriented constitutionalism, but that they emphasise the importance of these values in addressing the injustices of the past which, in many ways, were in fact caused by the application of populist theories. It is only when we compare our society with higher ideals and values that we can aspire to truly begin to transform society.

Bibliography

Mureinik, Etienne, 'A bridge to where? Introducing the Interim Bill of Rights', 1994, *South African Journal on Human Rights (SAJHR)*, 31.

Register of cases

South Africa

Dikoko v Mokhatla 2006 6 SA 235 (CC).

Director of Public Prosecutions, Transvaal v Minister for Justice and Constitutional Development 2009 4 SA 222 (CC).

S v Makwanyane 1995 3 SA 391 (CC).

Doctors for Life International v Speaker of the National Assembly 2006 6 SA 416 (CC).

Minister of Health v New Clicks South Africa (Pty) Ltd 2006 2 SA 311 (CC).

Germany

BVerfG 15.01.1958 – 1 BvR 400/51 – BVerfGE 7, 198 – Lüth.

The Concept of Constitutional Identity in (Quasi-) Federal Systems of Government – From Limitation of Powers to Judicial Policy Making

*Jennifer Hölzlwimmer**

Abstract: *The concept of constitutional identity has evolved to a well-known and controversial legal instrument in the case law of the German Constitutional Court as well as of other constitutional or higher courts all over Europe. Also at the EU level one is familiar with the concept of national constitutional identity as proven e.g. by Art. 4(2) TEU and the preamble of the EU Charter of Fundamental Rights. But looking into detail, there is no common concept of constitutional or national identity. Rather both concepts support and complement each other, i.e. the concept of constitutional identity at the national level is mirrored in the concept of national identity at the European (quasi-federal) level but with both of them having diverse approaches, addressees and final interpreters. In combination it provides a legal instrument of interest for every federal system trying to set limits on federal powers, and hence finding a balance between federal and sub-federal competences and interests.*

* Jennifer Hölzlwimmer, senior research and teaching position, PhD candidate, University of Augsburg, Faculty of Law. Chair for Public Law, Public Regulatory Law and European Law.

I. Introduction

At least since the judgment on the Lisbon treaty in 2009,[1] the concept of constitutional identity originating in Article 79(3) the Basic Law (*Grundgesetz* – GG) has evolved to a well-known and controversial legal instrument in the case law of the German Constitutional Court (*Bundesverfassungsgericht* – BVerfG).

At the European level, *J.H.H. Weiler* already articulated the enhanced importance of constitutional identity in 2002, replacing the former discussion about the much-contested concept of state sovereignty[2]:

> 'Mobilizing in the name of sovereignty is passé; mobilizing to protect identity by insisting on constitutional specificity is à la mode.'[3]

Nowadays, national constitutional or higher courts all over Europe have joined the 'rally round the concept of constitutional identity'[4].[5] It can surely

1 BVerfG 30.06.2009 – 2 BvE 2/08 a. o. – BVerfGE 123, 267 (344, 353 et seq.) – Lissabon. For further cases with reference to constitutional identity, see only BVerfG 18.07.2005 – 2 BvR 2236/04 – BVerfGE 113, 273 (295 et seqq.) – Europäischer Haftbefehl; BVerfG 06.07.2010 – 2 BvR 2661/06 – BVerfGE 126, 286 (302 et seq.) – Ultra-vires-Kontrolle; BVerfG 19.07.2011 – 1 BvR 1916/06 – BVerfGE 129, 78 (100) – Anwendungserweiterung; BVerfG 14.01.2014 – 2 BvR 2728/13 a. o. – BVerfGE 134, 366 (384 et seq.) – OMT-Urteil (Vorlagebeschluss).

2 See, for example, the various contributions in Neil Walker (ed), *Sovereignty in Transition* (2003).

3 Joseph H.H. Weiler, 40 (2002) *Journal of Common Market Studies (JCMS)*, 563 (569).

4 Monica Claes, 'National identity: Trump card or up for negotiation?, in: Alejandro Saiz Arnaiz and Carina Alcoberro LLivina (eds), *National Constitutional Identity and European Integration* (2013), 109 (109).

5 Starting with the Conseil Constitutionnel (French Constitutional Court) 27.07.2006 – Decision No. 2006-540 DC – para. 19 and followed by Conseil Constitutionnel 30.11.2006 – Decision No. 2006-543 DC – para. 6; Trybunal Konstytucyjny (Polish Constitutional Court) 24.11.2010 – K 32/09 – paras. III.1.1.2, III.2.1–III.2.2, III.3.3 and III.3.8; similar Corte Costituzionale (Italian Constitutional Court) 27.12.1973 – Decision No. 183/1973 – EuR 1974, 255 – Frontini; Corte Costituzionale 08.06.1984 – Decision No. 170/1984 – EuGRZ 1985, 98 – Granital ('controlimiti'); Tribunal Constitucional (Spanish Constitutional Court) 13.12.2004 – Declaration DTC 1/2004 – EuR 2005, 339 (the 'basic values and principles' of the constitution); Ústavní soud (Czech Constitutional Court) 08.03.2006 and 03.05.2006 – Pl ÚS 50/04 and Pl ÚS 66/04 (the 'essential attributes of a democratic state governed by the rule of law'); Ústavní soud

be concluded that the concept of constitutional identity suddenly takes the leading part not only in the play 'Who`s afraid of the Charter?'[6] but generally in 'Who's afraid of the European Union?' with the national constitutional courts as its 'fighting soldiers and never capitulating guardians'.

This article aims to analyse the potential of the legal concept of constitutional identity in (quasi-)federal systems of government in order to find a balance of powers between federal and sub-federal bodies in general. At the same time, it also raises cautions against an extended use of this notion leading to judicial activism contradicting the principle of separation of powers. Therefore, the paper first focuses on the concept of constitutional identity from a Member State's view, and in particular its interpretation and application in the case law of the German Constitutional Court as national constitutional court with one of the longest traditions and most powerful voices within the European Union (part II). Afterwards, the sides are switched and the meaning of constitutional identity is examined in detail from the European Union's point of view (part III). In the following comparative part, it is questioned if there is a common concept of constitutional identity within the European legal system (part IV). The paper ends with an evaluation of the pros and cons of a legal concept of protection of constitutional identity applied by the judiciary as such, and some thoughts on the future development of identity claims – in particular within the European Union, but also regarding its transferability to other (quasi-)federal systems of government (part V).

II. Constitutional identity from a Member State's perspective

The European Union's Member States' constitutional or higher courts' legal argument to protect constitutional identity must first be analysed against its broader background. As used in nowadays jurisdiction, the Member States' claim for constitutional identity is usually regarded as belonging to the group of 'counter-limits' (*controlimiti*) to the general precedence of European Union law. The idea of the counter-limits doctrine goes back to a

---

26.11.2008 and 03.11.2009 – Pl ÚS 19/08 and Pl ÚS 29/09 (the 'material' or 'substantive' or 'essential core' of the constitution).

6 Taking up the title and introduction of Daniel Sarmiento's article, 50 (2013) *Common Market Law Review (CMLRev.)*, 1267 (1267).

decision of the *Corte Costituzionale* (= Italian Constitutional Court) in 1973 in the *Frontini*-case, stating that an EC Regulation would only be applied in Italy if it is not in conflict with the unbreakable principles of the Italian constitutional order.[7] The ratio of this doctrine is that because the precedence of European Union law is based on the national constitutions, it necessarily finds its limits within these constitutions. In the words of the Federal Constitutional Court of Germany (BVerfG):

> '[T]he precedence (of application) of European Union law does not apply unrestrictedly, but [...] is restricted by national (constitutional) law.'[8]

This is at least true as long as the European Union constitutes a supranational body *sui generis* with the Member States as the 'Masters of the Treaties', and not a federal state such as the Republic of Germany with its sub-federal bodies, the German *Länder*.

In German constitutional law, three variations of counter-limits have been introduced by the case law of the Federal Constitutional Court within

---

7 Corte Costituzionale (Italian Constitutional Court) 27.12.1973 – Decision No. 183/1973 – EuR 1974, 255 – Frontini; cf. further Oreste Pollicino, 'The Italian Constitutional Court and the European Court of Justice: A progressive overlapping between the supranational and the domestic dimensions', in: Monica Claes, Maartje De Visser, Patricia Popelier and Catherine Van De Heyning (eds), *Constitutional Conversations in Europe: Actors, Topics and Procedures* (2012), 101 (105).

8 Translated from the original German. BVerfG 15.12.2015 – 2 BvR 2735/14 – BVerfGE 140, 317 (339 et seqq.) – Identitätskontrolle, with reference to several case law of other constitutional or supreme courts within the European Union, e.g. for the French Republic: Conseil Constitutionnel 27.07.2006 – Decision No. 2006-540 DC – 19th recital; Conseil Constitutionnel 09.06.2011 – Decision No. 2011-631 DC – 45th recital; for the Italian Republic: Corte Costituzionale 22.06.1966 – Decision No. 98/1965 – EuR 1966, 146 – Acciaierie San Michele; Corte Costituzionale 27.12.1973 – Decision No. 183/1973 – EuR 1974, 255 – Frontini; Corte Costituzionale 08.06.1984 – Decision No. 170/1984 – EuGRZ 1985, 98 – Granital; Corte Costituzionale 21.04.1989 – Decision No. 232/1989 – Fragd; Corte Costituzionale 08.04.1991 – Decision No. 168/1991 – S.p.a Industria dolciaria Giampaoli; Corte Costituzionale 23.03.1994 – Decision No. 117/1994 – Zerini; for the Republic of Poland: Trybunal Konstytucyjny 11.05.2005 – K 18/04 – paras. 4.1., 10.2.; Trybunal Konstytucyjny 24.11.2010 – K 32/09 – paras. 2.1. et seq.; Trybunal Konstytucyjny 16.11.2011 – SK 45/09 – paras. 2.4., 2.5.; for the Kingdom of Spain: Tribunal Constitucional 13.12.2004 – Declaration DTC 1/2004 – EuR 2005, 339 (343) – Ground 2 and Tribunal Constitucional 13.02.2014 – Decision STC 26/2014 – HRLJ 2014, 475 (477 and 478) – No. 3 of the recitals.

the last decades. First, in its famous *Solange II*-decision the Federal Constitutional Court acknowledged the precedence of European Union law also over the fundamental rights catalogue of the German Constitution (set out in the Basic Law, GG), but only

> '(a)s long as the European Communities, in particular European Court case law, generally ensure effective protection of fundamental rights as against the sovereign powers of the Communities which is to be regarded as substantially similar to the protection of fundamental rights required unconditionally by the Constitution, and in so far as they generally safeguard the essential content of fundamental rights'.[9]

This principle has been elaborated and contoured in further decisions, but with no essential change in meaning.[10] Secondly, the Federal Constitutional Court multiply confirmed that there is a limit to the precedence (in application) of European Union law over national law in case the European Union is acting *ultra vires*, i.e. without any competence transferred to the European level by its Member States.[11] And thirdly, as already mentioned above (part I), the Federal Constitutional Court in its Lisbon decision in 2009 clearly stated that the protection of constitutional identity sets a limit to the precedence of European Union law, and that the Court itself will be the guarantor of this identity. This sets limits to the national government transferring national sovereignty to the European level or activating its own right to judicial review of EU secondary law when the latter touches aspects of the constitutional identity of the Federal Republic of Germany.[12]

---

9 Translated from the original German. BVerfG 22.10.1986 – 2 BvR 197/83 – BVerfGE 73, 339 (387) – Solange II. Prior to this, BVerfG 29.05.1974 – 2 BvL 52/71 – BVerfGE 37, 271 (285) – Solange I.

10 BVerfG 12.10.1993 – 2 BvR 2159/92 a. o. – BVerfGE 89, 155 (175) – Maastricht; BVerfG 07.06.2000 – 2 BvL 1/97 – BVerfGE 102, 147 (164) – Bananenmarktordnung; BVerfG 13.03.2007 – 1 BvF 1/05 – BVerfGE 118, 79 (79, 95 et seqq.) – Emissionshandel; BVerfGE 30.06.2009 – 2 BvE 2/08 a. o. – BVerfGE 123, 267 (335) – Lissabon. For a detailed history of the Solange jurisprudence, see Bill Davies, 21 (2015) *European Law Journal*, 434.

11 BVerfGE 08.04.1987 – 2 BvR 687/85 – BVerfGE 75, 223 (242) – Kloppenburg; BVerfG 12.10.1993 – 2 BvR 2134, 2159/92 – BVerfGE 89, 155 (188) – Maastricht; BVerfGE 30.06.2009 – 2 BvE 2/08 a. o. – BVerfGE 123, 267 (353 et seq.) – Lissabon; BVerfG 06.07.2010 – 2 BvR 2661/906 – BVerfGE 126, 286 (302 et seqq.) – Ultra Vires-Kontrolle.

12 BVerfG 30.06.2009 – 2 BvE 2/08 a. o. – BVerfGE 123, 267 (343 et seq., 353 et seq.) – Lissabon. Regarding the further development of the identity control by the German Constitutional Court, cf. Sara Dietz, 142 (2017) *Archiv des öffentlichen Rechts (AöR)*, 78 (83 et seqq.).

The relationship between these three counter-limits still is highly disputed in academic literature. In particular since the Federal Constitutional Court's decision of 15 December 2015 regarding the European arrest warrant,[13] some comments speak of a '*Solange III'* decision'[14] or 'Solange two and a half'[15], implicating a replacement of the former *Solange II* principles by the 'newly developed' identity review. However, this view ignores the concrete limits of identity control, i.e. its terminated scope of application covers only a mandatory minimum stock of fundamental rights and those matters touching human dignity next to the general structure of a federal, social and constitutional democracy. The *Solange II* decision or Article 23(1) sentence 1 of the Basic Law repeating these principles encompasses a much broader scope of fundamental rights with a higher level of protection.[16] Hence, the identity review must be acknowledged and dogmatically classified as a further remedy next to the fundamental rights review according to the *Solange II* case.

In view of the relationship between the identity review and the *ultra vires* review, the opinion of the *ultra vires* review as special case of an identity review seems to prevail in the academic literature.[17] However, in 2016 the Federal Constitutional Court stated:

> 'Both the identity review and the ultra vires review are derived from Art. 79 sec. 3 GG [Basic Law] but constitute independent types of review using different standards'.[18]

---

13 BVerfG 15.12.2015 – 2 BvR 2735/14 – BVerfGE 140, 317 (333 et seq., 336 et seqq.) – Identitätskontrolle.

14 Mathias Hong, 'Human Dignity and Constitutional Identity: The Solange-III-Decision of the German Constitutional Court', Verfassungsblog, https://verfassungsblog.de/ (18-02-2016); Frank Schorkopf, 'Karlsruhe will Kommunikation, nicht Konfrontation', Legal Tribune Online (LTO), https://www.lto.de/ (29-01-2016).

15 Christoph Goos, 'Solange Zweieinhalb', Junge Wissenschaft im öffentlichen Recht-Blog (JuWiss-Blog), https://www.juwiss.de/, (10 and 11-01-2016).

16 Also Sara Dietz, 142 (2017) *Archiv des öffentlichen Rechts (AöR)*, 78 (119).

17 See, for example, Sara Dietz, 142 (2017) *Archiv des öffentlichen Rechts (AöR)*, 78 (123 et seqq., 127).

18 Translated from the original German. BVerfG 21.06.2016 – 2 BvR 2728/13 – BVerfGE 142, 123 (188) – OMT-Urteil.

It is at least questionable whether this statement is in line with the interpretation of the *ultra vires* review as special case of identity review.[19] Convincingly, *Thiele* classifies all three types of reviews as tools based on Article 23(1) of the Basic Law and as falling under the term *Integrationsidentität* (integration identity) without ignoring the individual autonomy of each kind of review regarding scope of application and purpose.[20]

However, the dogmatic and structural classification of the identity review of the Federal Constitutional Court insofar remains fraught with uncertainties. Nevertheless, it can be confirmed that the concept of constitutional identity has primarily been used within the last years by the Federal Constitutional Court in connection with European integration, i.e. in order to set limits on the national government transferring competences to the European level or on the precedence of EU law itself,[21] and in contrast to its original historical intent[22]. This is also true for all other national (constitutional) courts of EU Member States applying the concept of constitutional identity in their jurisdiction. In conclusion, the protection of constitutional identity in the interpretation of the national (constitutional) courts generally aims to set a limit to (quasi-)federal power and to safeguard relevant power at the state level. It is therefore applied to balance the distribution of powers in the European (nowadays at least quasi-federal) project of economic and political integration, and to protect the unique diversity between the European Member States. Admittedly, it is of a 'strongly casuistic character'[23] and hence induces legal uncertainty[24] due to a lack of a self-contained content list and (theoretically) 28 possible interpreters each claiming different subjects as component of their individual constitutional identity.

---

19 Pleading for confirmity, Sara Dietz, 142 (2017) *Archiv des öffentlichen Rechts (AöR)*, 78 (128 et seqq.) with reference to BVerfG 21.06.2016 – 2 BvR 2728/13 – BVerfGE 142, 123 (203) – OMT-Urteil.

20 Alexander Thiele, *Europarecht (EuR)* 2017, 367 (367).

21 See Monika Polzin, 14 (2016) *International Journal of Constitutional Law (I•CON)*, 411 (412 et seq.) with further references to the 'vigorous' debate in Fn. 6.

22 In detail to the historical origin of the concept of constitutional identity in German constitutional law, Monika Polzin, 14 (2016) *International Journal of Constitutional Law (I•CON)*, 411 (414 et seqq.).

23 Alexander Thiele, *Europarecht (EuR)* 2017, 367 (368).

24 Alexander Thiele, *Europarecht (EuR)* 2017, 367 (368).

III. Constitutional identity from the European Union's perspective

Next to the discussion about constitutional identity at the Member States level, the question on identity issues also arises at the European level.

Early in the history of the European Union, the European Court of Justice (ECJ) at least implicitly expressed its point of view regarding the need for uniform application of European Union law and its supremacy over 'domestic legal provisions, however framed'[25].[26] According to the ECJ, it is further 'impossible for the States, as corollary, to accord precedence to a unilateral and subsequent [national] measure over a legal system accepted by them on a basis of reciprocity'.[27] Hence in contrast to the counter-limits doctrine explained above, but convincingly from a European – quasi-federal – point of view, European Union law also takes precedence over national constitutional law leaving no room for unilateral national exemptions even if based on constitutional arguments. In the wording of the ECJ:

> '[T]he validity of a [Union] measure or its effect within a Member State cannot be affected by allegations that it runs counter to either fundamental rights as formulated by the Constitution of that state or the principles of a national constitutional structure'.[28]

If explained in EU law textbooks, national deviations from the general concept of supremacy of EU law are usually conceived as 'pathological instances' but not as proof of there still being an existing dependence of EU law upon national (constitutional) law.[29] So first, there is the impression that there is no room for the protection of constitutional identity in the meaning

25 European Court of Justice, Case C-6/64, 15.07.1964, *Costa/E.N.E.L.*, ECR 585 (594). Similar European Court of Justice, Case C-11/70, 17.12.1970, *Internationale Handelsgesellschaft*, ECR 1125, para. 3.

26 See Ferdinand Wollenschläger, in: Horst Dreier (ed), *Grundgesetz-Kommentar, Band 2* (3rd Edition, 2015), Art. 23 para. 14.

27 European Court of Justice, Case C-6/64, 15.07.1964, *Costa/E.N.E.L.*, ECR 585 (593 et seq.).

28 European Court of Justice, Case C-11/70, 17.12.1970, *Internationale Handelsgesellschaft*, ECR 1125, para. 3. Even clearer e.g. the French wording saying the validity of EU law cannot be questioned by national norms 'quellesqu'ellessoient'. Also European Court of Justice, Case C-409/06, 08.09.2010, *Winner Wetten*, ECR I-8015, paras. 60 et seq.

29 Miguel Poiares Maduro, 'Contrapunctual Law: Europe's Constitutional Pluralism in Action', in: Neil Walker (ed), *Sovereignty in Transition* (2003), 501 (503).

of protection of national constitutional basic values as described above. A view into the original European Treaties confirms this impression, with the word 'identity' completely absent from the legal wording as well as from the legal discourse in the early days of European integration. The reason surely lies in the fact that the European project focused on economic integration in these days was not considered as challenge to national or constitutional identities able to affect constitutional matters, or even basic constitutional values of the Member States.

Yet, the European Union of 2017 is familiar with the concept of national constitutional identity at least on a textual basis. For, nowadays Article 4(2) TEU reads:

> 'The Union shall respect the equality of Member States before the Treaties as well as their national identities, inherent in their fundamental structures, political and constitutional, inclusive of regional and local self-government. It shall respect their essential State functions, including ensuring the territorial integrity of the State, maintaining law and order and safeguarding national security. In particular, national security remains the sole responsibility of each Member State.'[30]

Additionally, respect for national identity is stipulated in the preamble to the EU Charter of Fundamental Rights. It states:

> 'The Union contributes to the preservation and to the development of these common values while respecting the diversity of the cultures and traditions of the peoples of Europe as well as the national identities of the Member States and the organisation of their public authorities at national, regional and local levels'.[31]

Article 4(2) TEU was introduced with the Lisbon Treaty in 2009 and replaced former Article 6(3) TEU which already stipulated respect for national identity of the Member States since the Treaty of Maastricht in 1992. The wording now goes back to the first draft on the Constitutional Treaty of the European Union and its Article I-5 and has been kept identical after the negative referendums and the following failure of the Constitutional Treaty. However, the systematic connection with the envisaged brand-new primacy clause in Article I-6 is now missing due to the general dismissal of

30 Italics not included in the original but set by the author herself for analytical reasons.

31 Recital 3 of the preamble to the EU Charter of Fundamental Rights.

an implementation of the precedence of European Union law within the Articles of the Lisbon Treaty.[32] Article 4(2) TEU now supplements the former Article 6(3) TEU with at least an 'idea' of a possible content of national identity. According to the wording of Article 4(2) TEU, national identity consists of 'fundamental structures, political and constitutional, inclusive of regional and local self-government'. Still, this definition includes a broad scope for interpretation. In view of a uniform application of EU law, an autonomous interpretation by EU law is appreciated,[33] but it is self-evident that fundamental political and constitutional structures differ from one Member State to the other. Hence, some argue that the term 'national identity' within the meaning of Article 4(2) TEU must be further concretised by national courts in conformity with the principle of sincere cooperation, Art. 4(3) TEU.[34] This suits the opinion of the Federal Constitutional Court of Germany as formulated in its Lisbon decision, which claims the final say in identity matters.[35] But still, Article 4(2) TEU is part of EU primary law and as such object of interpretation solely by the ECJ.[36] Material aspects cannot justify a deviation from this principle.

---

32 In more detail to the history of Article 4(2) TEU cf. CONV 375/02, 10 et seqq. Of its declaration as 'Christophersen-clause' see CONV 251/02, 3. Further Monica Claes, 'National identity: Trump card or up for negotiation?', in: Alejandro Saiz Arnaiz and Carina Alcoberro LLivina (eds), *National Constitutional Identity and European Integration* (2013), 109 (118 et seqq.).

33 Walter Obwexer, in: Hans von der Groeben, Jürgen Schwarze and Armin Hatje (eds), *Europäisches Unionsrecht* (7th Edition, 2015), Art. 4 EUV para. 27; Rudolf Streinz, in: idem (ed), *EUV/AEUV* (2nd Edition, 2012), Art. 4 EUV para. 14.

34 Rudolf Streinz, in: idem (ed), *EUV/AEUV* (2nd Edition, 2012), Art. 4 EUV para. 20; Armin Hatje, in: Jürgen Schwarze, Ulrich Becker, Armin Hatje and Johann Schoo (eds), *EU-Kommentar* (3rd Edition, 2012), Art. 4 EUV para. 12.

35 BVerfG 30.06.2009 – 2 BvE 2/08 a. o. – BVerfGE 123, 267 (353 et seqq.) – Lissabon.

36 Walter Obwexer, in: Hans von der Groeben, Jürgen Schwarze, Armin Hatje (eds), *Europäisches Unionsrecht* (7th Edition, 2015), Art. 4 EUV para. 27; Monica Claes, 'National identity: Trump card or up for negotiation?', in: Alejandro Saiz Arnaiz and Carina Alcoberro LLivina (eds), *National Constitutional Identity and European Integration* (2013), 109 (111 et seq., 123). See also GA Miguel Poiares Maduro, Case C-53/04, 07.09.2006, *Marrosu and Sardino*, ECR I-7213, para. 40: '(T)he national authorities, in particular the constitutional courts, (…) are best placed to define the constitutional identity of the Member States which the European Union has undertaken to respect. The fact remains, however, that it is the duty of the Court of Justice to ensure that that assessment is

Unfortunately, the ECJ has so far not sufficiently answered the question of interpretation of Article 4(2) TEU. Analysing the few decisions on national identity according to Article 4(2) TEU, the lack of a general definition becomes obvious – in particular regarding concrete aims and purposes. In view of content, at least 'the protection of the official language',[37] the 'republican state structure',[38] the 'constitutional order of a Member State – whether it is centralist or federal'[39] and, as corollary, 'the division of competences within a Member State'[40] – and 'regional sovereignty'[41] have already explicitly been acknowledged as part of national identity by the Court, but the list is (naturally) left open for amendments.

Due to a lack of a general definition of national identity within the meaning of Article 4(2) TEU by the ECJ, it is also interpreted differently by legal scholars. Some simply describe the content of national identity as the 'untouchable' objects of a state.[42] Others are going into more detail, claiming the 'federal construction of a State and the public institutions which are characteristic for the variety of its cultural life, like e.g. in Germany the role of public service broadcasting as well as [...] decisions concerning the school and education system, family law, language, certain areas of media regulation, and the status of churches and religious and non-denominational

---

made in accordance with the fundamental rights and objectives with which it must ensure compliance within the Community context.'

37 European Court of Justice, Case C-473/93, 02.07.1996, *Commission/Luxembourg*, ECR I-3207, para. 35; European Court of Justice, Case C-391/09, 12.05.2011, *Runevič-Vardyn and Wardyn*, ECR I-3818, para. 86; European Court of Justice, Case C-51/08, 24.05.2011, *Commission/Luxembourg*, ECR I-4235, para. 124; European Court of Justice, Case C-202/11, 16.04.2013, *Las*, ECLI:EU:C:2013:239, para. 26. See also Carl Otto Lenz, in: idem and Klaus-Dieter Borchardt (eds), *EU-Verträge* (6th Edition, 2012), Art. 4 EUV para. 4.

38 European Court of Justice, Case C-208/09, 22.12.2010, *Sayn-Wittgenstein*, ECR I-13693, para. 92.

39 GA Juliane Kokott, Cases C-428/06 and C-434/06, 11.09.2008, *Unión General de Trabajadores de la Rioja*, ECR I-6747, para. 54.

40 GA Juliane Kokott, Case C-428/06 and C-434/06, 11.09.2008, *Unión General de Trabajadores de la Rioja*, ECR I-6747, para. 54.

41 European Court of Justice, Case C-156/13, 12.06.2014, *Digibet*, ECLI:EU:C:2014:1756; European Court of Justice, Case C-51/15, 21.12.2016, *Remondis*, ECLI:EU:C:2016:985.

42 Thomas Oppermann, *Deutsches Verwaltungsblatt (DVBl.)* 2003, 1165 (1170).

communities'[43] or 'statehood and sovereignty of Member States, basic organizational structures (federalism, centralism), democracy, rule of law, individual freedoms and human rights'[44] as elements embraced by Article 4(2) TEU.

In conclusion, it seems to be at least widely acknowledged that the basic principles of state organization and basic values of the relevant Member State (with 'basic' meaning 'constitutive for the relevant political system') do fall under the term national identity within the meaning of Article 4(2) TEU.[45] Questions and disputes arise that touch on cultural specificities and their possible relevance for identity claims under Article 4(2) TEU.[46] Insofar, it is still unclear what pertains to national identity according to Article 4(2) TEU, and it is a matter of fact that national actors are in a better position to judge these issues than the ECJ itself. Yet, the final say on national identity goes to the latter, with the national courts only able to claim for protection and insofar start the negotiation of possible components of national identity.

This has to be remembered when analysing the specific approach of Article 4(2) TEU. In addition to the discussion about the diverse subjects covered by the term national identity, the interpretations of the purpose of this Article deviate greatly from each other. For example, *von Bogdandy* and *Schill* understand Article 4(2) TEU 'as permitting domestic constitutional courts to invoke, under certain limited circumstances, constitutional limits to the primacy of EU law' and insofar as confirmation of the counter-limits doctrine. *Claes* clearly contradicts this opinion, expressively claiming that

---

43 Rudolf Geiger, in: idem, Daniel-Erasmus Khan and Markus Kotzur (eds), *European Union Treaties* (2014), Art. 4 TEU para. 3.

44 Armin Hatje, in: Jürgen Schwarze, Ulrich Becker, Armin Hatje and Johann Schoo (eds), *EU-Kommentar* (3rd Edition, 2012), Art. 4 EUV para. 11. Similar with reference to Article 20 Basic Law Christoph Vedder, in: idem and Wolff Heintschel von Heinegg (eds), *Europäisches Unionsrecht* (2nd Edition, 2018), Art. 4 EUV para. 6.

45 Also Rudolf Streinz, in: idem (ed), *EUV/AEUV* (2nd Edition, 2012), Art. 4 EUV para. 14.

46 In favour of an inclusion of cultural matters Rudolf Streinz, in: idem (ed), *EUV/AEUV* (2nd Edition, 2012), Art. 4 EUV para. 15; Rudolf Geiger, in: idem, Daniel-Erasmus Khan and Markus Kotzur (eds), *European Union Treaties* (2014), Art. 4 TEU para. 3. Expressively against Monica Claes, 'National identity: Trump card or up for negotiation?', in: Alejandro Saiz Arnaiz and Carina Alcoberro LLivina (eds), *National Constitutional Identity and European Integration* (2013), 109 (118 et seq.).

this Article 'was not designed as a shield or a sword in the hands of the Member States, which their national (constitutional) courts can raise in order to fence off or challenge European law'[47]. The latter opinion at least fits into the favoured picture of distribution of competences regarding the interpretation of Article 4(2) TEU between the ECJ and the national (constitutional) courts. Article 4(2) TEU solely obliges the European Union itself to exceptionally provide for a possibility to derogate from the uniform application of EU law, and the ECJ to engage with national claims concerning identity matters.[48] It can therefore be interpreted as a 'general obligation for the EU to respect the constitutional identities of Member States'[49], but not as confirmation of the counter-limits doctrine[50] with the national courts as its final interpreter and the aim to approve or even justify national unilateralism in contradiction to the general precedence in application of European Union law.

In conclusion, the concept of constitutional identity is also visible at the European level, but is attached with legal uncertainty and unanswered questions due to a lack of a general definition of content and purpose, and guidance for application. Therefore, the functionality and reasonability of Article 4(2) TEU, with its stipulation for respect for national identity, is uncertain but still open for further contouring and enhancement.

IV. A common concept of constitutional identity?

The analyses have proven that while the notion of constitutional identity or national identity is known at both the European and the Member States level, the content and purpose of these concepts are still unclear and cause

---

47 Monica Claes, 'National identity: Trump card or up for negotiation?', in: Alejandro Saiz Arnaiz and Carina Alcoberro LLivina (eds), *National Constitutional Identity and European Integration* (2013), 109 (111).

48 Monica Claes, 'National identity: Trump card or up for negotiation?', in: Alejandro Saiz Arnaiz and Carina Alcoberro LLivina (eds), *National Constitutional Identity and European Integration* (2013), 109 (112).

49 Allan Rosas, 'Five Years of Charter Case Law: Some Observations', in: Sybe de Vries, Ulf Bernitz and Stephen Weatherill (eds), *The EU Charter of Fundamental Rights as a Binding Instrument* (2015), 11 (20).

50 Monica Claes, 'National identity: Trump card or up for negotiation?', in: Alejandro Saiz Arnaiz and Carina Alcoberro LLivina (eds), *National Constitutional Identity and European Integration* (2013), 109 (111 et seq.).

legal uncertainty due to the lack of guidance from the judiciary. In consequence, there are controversial discussions among legal experts as to whether there is a common concept of constitutional identity, i.e. a common content of both notions – constitutional and national identity – or whether they relate to each other at all.

Some treat them as synonyms with the same content[51] and primarily refer to the historical background of these concepts.[52] According to *Besselink* and *Faraguna*, for example, Article 4(2) TEU in its new 2009 version developed the former notion of national identity into the concept of constitutional identity as interpreted by the national courts of the Member States.[53] *Von Bogdandy* and *Schill* understand Article 4(2) TEU as confirmation of the counter-limits doctrine of the national courts (see above, part III).[54] The Federal Constitutional Court of Germany also clearly referred to Article 4(2) TEU to justify the application of its constitutional identity review in its Lisbon decision.[55] Others clearly reject any power of Article 4(2) TEU to limit the supremacy of European Union law.[56] Often the concepts of national and

---

51 Christian Calliess, Wolfgang Kahl and Adelheid Puttler, in: Christian Calliess and Matthias Ruffert (eds), *EUV/AEUV* (5th Edition, 2016), Art. 4 EUV para. 17. Same content to a large extent: Armin Hatje, in: Jürgen Schwarze, Ulrich Becker, Armin Hatje and Johann Schoo (eds), *EU-Kommentar* (3rd Edition, 2012), Art. 4 EUV para. 13. Cf. also GA Miguel Poiares Maduro, Case C-213/07, 16.12.2008, *Michaniki*, ECR I-9999, para. 31.

52 Christian Calliess, Wolfgang Kahl and Adelheid Puttler, in: Christian Calliess and Matthias Ruffert (eds), *EUV/AEUV* (5th Edition, 2016), Art. 4 EUV para. 15.

53 Leonard F.M. Besselink, 6 (2010) *Utrecht Law Review*, 36 (42 et seqq.); Pietro Faraguna, 41 (2016) *Brooklyn Journal of International Law (Brook. J. Int'l L.)*, 492 (497 et seq.).

54 Armin von Bogdandy and Stephan Schill, 48 (2011) *Common Market Law Review (CMLRev.)*, 1417 (1417).

55 BVerfG 30.06.2009 – 2 BvE 2/08 a. o. – BVerfGE 123, 267 (350, 354) – Lissabon.

56 Monica Claes, 'National identity: Trump card or up for negotiation?', in: Alejandro Saiz Arnaiz and Carina Alcoberro LLivina (eds), *National Constitutional Identity and European Integration* (2013), 109 (111 et seq.). Interpreting the case law of the European Court of Justice in this way Walter Obwexer, in: Hans von der Groeben, Jürgen Schwarze and Armin Hatje, *Europäisches Unionsrecht* (7th Edition, 2015), Art. 4 EUV para. 37. Disagreeing Thomas Oppermann, *Deutsches Verwaltungsblatt (DVBl.)* 2003, 1165 (1170) in regard to Article I-5 Verfassungsvertrag.

constitutional identity are described as diverse, but related[57] or 'intermingled'[58] principles.

In view of the analyses above, it must be concluded that both concepts definitely cover similar and – at least in parts – identical subjects. However, the purposes or approaches clearly differ:

At the Member States level, the concept of constitutional identity is used as both 'a Shield and (...) a Sword'[59] against an 'ever closer Union',[60] with enhanced legislative activity also in sensitive areas, such as budgetary discipline. From a German perspective, this is in line with Article 23(1) of the Basic Law (GG)[61] reading:

> 'With a view to establishing a united Europe, the Federal Republic of Germany shall participate in the development of the European Union that is committed to democratic, social and federal principles, to the rule of law, and to the principle of subsidiarity, and that guarantees a level of protection of basic rights essentially comparable to that afforded by this Basic Law. To this end the Federation may transfer sovereign powers by a law with the consent of the Bundesrat. The establishment of the European Union, as well as changes in its treaty foundations and comparable regulations that amend or supplement this Basic Law, or make such amendments or supplements possible, shall be subject to paragraphs (2) and (3) of Article 79.'

The concept of national identity originating in Article 4(2) TEU however stipulates respect for national identity on part of the European Union, and hence contains a duty for cooperation and negotiation. Therefore, it can be classified as an expression of constitutional pluralism[62] and an indispensable tool for the European Union to remain 'united in diversity'[63].

---

57 Elke Cloots, *National Identity in EU Law* (2015), 3.

58 Krystyna Kowalik-Bańczyk, 33 (2013) *Polish Yearbook of International Law (PYIL)*, 171 (185).

59 Cf. Theodore Konstadinides, 13 (2011) *The Cambridge Yearbook of European Legal Studies*, 195 (195).

60 Term adopted from European Council's Solemn Declaration on European Union (Stuttgart, 19.06.1983), Bull. EC 6-1983, point 1.1, 24 (25).

61 Christoph Vedder, in: idem and Wolff Heintschel von Heinegg (eds), *Europäisches Unionsrecht* (2nd Edition, 2018), Art. 4 EUV para. 12.

62 Armin von Bogdandy and Stephan Schill, 70 (2010) *Zeitschrift für ausländisches öffentliches Recht und Völkerrecht (ZaöRV)*, 701 (705, 710).

63 Cf. Gabriel N. Toggenburg, 'Unity in Diversity: Searching for the Regional Dimension in the Context of a Someway Foggy Constitutional Credo', in: Roberto Toniatti, Marco Dani and Francesco Palermo (eds), *An Ever More Complex Union* (2004), 27. Also explaining the concept of constitutional identity by its origin in this motto Monica Claes, 'National identity: Trump card or up for negotiation?', in: Alejandro Saiz Arnaiz and Carina Alcoberro LLivina (eds), *National Constitutional Identity and European Integration* (2013), 109 (112 et seq.).

In other words, the concept of constitutional identity at the national level is mirrored in the concept of national identity at the European (quasi-federal) level. Looking at the possible content of these concepts, they vary if viewed from a different angle, with both of them having diverse approaches, addressees and final interpreters. While there is no common concept of constitutional or national identity, both concepts support and complement each other.

It seems reasonable to conclude that the national concept of constitutional identity in combination with the (quasi-)federal concept of national identity is a legal instrument of interest for every federal system trying to set limits on federal powers, and hence finding a balance between federal and sub-federal competences and interests.

V. Pros and cons of the use of the concept of constitutional identity by the judiciary and its future development

In support of this last finding, possible advantages of the implementation of the combined concepts of constitutional identity and national identity will be highlighted in this last chapter.

First, as the analyses of the European examples have proven, these concepts are able to activate and guide negotiations on sovereignty matters and guarantee a dialogue between affected authorities. It is even almost indispensable in a (quasi-)federal system such as the European Union in order to protect the unique diversity between the Member States. It gives people room for identification and shows respect for traditions and history. Furthermore, it shifts the discussions about sovereignty to questions about identity issues – possibly strengthening the idea of a Union that respects diversity, instead of challenging the general sovereignty of the national states. Lastly, the combined concepts are a useful tool to find a vertical balance of powers in all federal structures.

On the other hand, disputes about identity issues might possibly affirm negative attitudes towards federal activity as such. Specifically within the European Union, the concept of identity has already been used in order to support nationalists' or anti-European opinions. The former British Prime Minister, David Cameron, for example, linked speeches on multi-culturalism and the euro crisis to the term national identity.[64] Therefore, a restrictive

64 David Cameron, Speech at the Munich Security Conference 5 February 2011; idem, Speech at the Lord Mayor's Banquet 14 November 2011.

interpretation of national constitutional identity is needed with respect to the principle of general openness towards European Union law and the principle of sincere cooperation between national and Union bodies. Additionally, there is the danger that misleading judicial activism[65] will threaten the principle of the (horizontal) separation of powers. Therefore, one can only warn against an overhasty adoption of identity issues by the national (constitutional) courts contrary to a political decision of the majority of the parliament to transfer competences to the federal level.[66] This would not only contradict the principle of separation of powers but annul the advantages of the concept of constitutional identity in federal systems as such.

Anyway, the concept of constitutional identity will keep legal scholars as well as the ECJ and the national (constitutional) courts busy over the next couple of years due to a general and increasing trend for Euro-scepticism and a revival of nationalism within the Member States. To protect the (quasi-)federal structure of the European project 'unified in diversity', a more precise definition (not solely on a case-by-case basis) and a clear dogmatic structure and classification will be required to support the efficacy of this legal remedy within the European Union. At this point, it might be worth taking a look at other (federal) systems (such as South Africa), and the solutions they have found regarding the allocation of powers between the different levels and the protection of national or regional specificities and sovereignty.

Bibliography

Leonard F.M. Besselink, 'National and constitutional identity before and after Lisbon' 6 (2010) *Utrecht Law Review*, 36.

Armin von Bogdandy and Stephan Schill, 'Overcoming Absolute Primacy: Respect for National Identity under the Lisbon Treaty' 48 (2011) *Common Market Law Review (CMLRev.)*, 1417.

Armin von Bogdandy and Stephan Schill, 'Die Achtung der nationalen Identität unter dem reformierten Unionsvertrag – Zur unionsrechtlichen Rolle nationalen Verfassungsrecht und zur Überwindung des absoluten Vorrangs' 70 (2010) *Zeitschrift für ausländisches öffentliches Recht und Völkerrecht (ZaöRV)*, 701.

Christian Calliess and Matthias Ruffert (eds), *EUV/AEUV*, Commentary (5th Edition, C.H. Beck, Munich 2016).

---

65 See Thomas M.J. Möllers and Katharina Redcay, *Europarecht (EuR)* 2013, 409 (420 et seq., 429 et seq.).

66 Alexander Thiele, *Europarecht (EuR)* 2017, 367 (379).

David Cameron, Speech at the Munich Security Conference 05.02.2011, www.number10.gov.uk/news/pms-speech-at-munich-security-conference/ (27-04-2018).

David Cameron, Speech at the Lord Mayor's Banquet 14.11.2011, www.number10.gov.uk/news/lord-mayors-banquet/ (27-04-2018).

Monica Claes, 'National identity: Trump card or up for negotiation?', in: Alejandro Saiz Arnaiz and Carina Alcoberro LLivina (eds), *National Constitutional Identity and European Integration*, Law and Cosmopolitan Values, Volume 4 (Intersentia, Cambridge 2013), 109.

Elke Cloots, *National Identity in EU Law*, Studies in European Law (Oxford University Press, Oxford 2015).

Bill Davies, 'Resistance to European Law and Constitutional Identity in Germany: Herbert Kraus and *Solange* in its Intellectual Context' 21 (2015) *European Law Journal*, 434.

Sara Dietz, 'Die europarechtsfreundliche Verfassungsidentität in der Kontrolltrias des Bundesverfassungsgerichts' 142 (2017) *Archiv des öffentlichen Rechts (AöR)*, 78.

Horst Dreier (ed), *Grundgesetz-Kommentar, Volume 2* (3rd Edition, Mohr Siebeck, Tübingen, 2015).

Pietro Faraguna, 'Taking Constitutional Identities Away from the Courts' 41 (2016) *Brooklyn Journal of International Law (Brook. J. Int'l L.)*, 492.

Rudolf Geiger, Daniel-Erasmus Khan and Markus Kotzur (eds), *European Union Treaties* (C.H. Beck, München 2014).

Christoph Goos, 'Solange Zweieinhalb' *Junge Wissenschaft im öffentlichen Recht-Blog (JuWiss-Blog)* of 10- and 11-01-2016, https://www.juwiss.de/14-2016/ and https://www.juwiss.de/15-2016/ (27-04-2018).

Hans von der Groeben, Jürgen Schwarze and Armin Hatje (eds), *Europäisches Unionsrecht* (7th Edition, Nomos, Baden-Baden 2015).

Mathias Hong, 'Human Dignity and Constitutional Identity: The Solange-III-Decision of the German Constitutional Court' *Verfassungsblog* of 18-02-2016, http://verfassungsblog.de/human-dignity-and-constitutional-identity-the-solange-iii-decision-of-the-german-constitutional-court/ (27-04-2018).

Theodore Konstadinides, 'Constitutional Identity as a Shield and as a Sword: The European Legal Order within the Framework of National Constitutional Settlement' 13 (2011) *The Cambridge Yearbook of European Legal Studies*, 195.

Krystyna Kowalik-Bańczyk, 'À la recherche d'une coherence perdue – Possible Arguments for the Non-application of EU Law in Member States' 33 (2013) *Polish Yearbook of International Law (PYIL)*, 171.

Carl Otto Lenz and Klaus-Dieter Borchardt (eds), *EU-Verträge*, Commentary (6th Edition, Bundesanzeiger Verlag and Linde Verlag, Köln and Wien 2012).

Miguel Poiares Maduro, 'Contrapunctual Law: Europe's Constitutional Pluralism in Action', in: Neil Walker (ed), *Sovereignty in Transition* (Hart Publishing, Oxford 2003), 501.

Thomas M.J. Möllers and Katharina Redcay, 'Das Bundesverfassungsgericht als europäischer Gesetzgeber oder als Motor der Union?' *Europarecht (EuR)* 2013, 409.

Thomas Oppermann, 'Eine Verfassung für die Europäische Union' *Deutsches Verwaltungsblatt (DVBl.)* 2003, 1165.

Oreste Pollicino, 'The Italian Constitutional Court and the European Court of Justice: A progressive overlapping between the supranational and the domestic dimensions', in: Monica Claes, Maartje De Visser, Patricia Popelier and Catherine Van De Heyning (eds), *Constitutional Conversations in Europe: Actors, Topics and Procedures* (Intersentia, Cambridge 2012), 101.

Monika Polzin, 'Constitutional identity, unconstitutional amendments and the idea of constituent power: The development of the doctrine of constitutional identity in German constitutional law' 14 (2016) *International Journal on Constitutional Law (I•CON)*, 411.

Allan Rosas, 'Five Years of Charter Case Law: Some Observations', in: Sybe de Vries, Ulf Bernitz and Stephen Weatherill (eds), *The EU Charter of Fundamental Rights as a Binding Instrument*, Studies of the Oxford Institute of European and Comparative Law (Hart Publishing and Bloomsbury, Oxford 2015), 11.

Daniel Sarmiento, 'Who's afraid of the Charter? The Court of Justice, national courts and the new framework of fundamental rights protection in Europe' 50 (2013) *Common Market Law Review (CMLRev.)*, 1267.

Frank Schorkopf, 'Karlsruhe will Kommunikation, nicht Konfrontation' *Legal Tribune Online (LTO)* of 29-01-2016, http://www.lto.de/recht/hintergruende/h/bverfg-2bvr273514-eu-haftbefehl-auslieferung-verfassungsidentitaet-menschenwuerde-gg-eu-recht-emrk/_(27-04-2018).

Jürgen Schwarze, Ulrich Becker, Armin Hatje and Johann Schoo (eds), *EU-Kommentar* (3rd Edition, Nomos, Baden-Baden 2012).

Rudolf Streinz (ed), *EUV/AEUV*, Commentary (2nd Edition, C.H. Beck, Munich 2012).

Alexander Thiele, 'Integrationsidentität des Art. 23 Abs. 1 GG als (einzige) Grenze des Vorrangs des Europarechts' *Europarecht (EuR)* 2017, 367.

Gabriel N. Toggenburg, 'Unity in Diversity: Searching for the Regional Dimension in the Context of a Someway Foggy Constitutional Credo', in: Roberto Toniatti, Marco Dani and Francesco Palermo (eds), *An Ever More Complex Union* (Nomos, Baden-Baden 2004), 27.

Christoph Vedder and Wolff Heintschel von Heinegg (eds), *Europäisches Unionsrecht*, Commentary (2nd Edition, Nomos, Baden-Baden 2018).

Neil Walker (ed), *Sovereignty in Transition* (Hart Publishing, Oxford 2003).

Joseph H.H. Weiler, 'A Constitution for Europe? Some Hard Choices' 40 (2002) *Journal of Common Market Studies (JCMS)*, 563.

Register of Cases

Germany

BVerfG 29.05.1974 – 2 BvL 52/71 – BVerfGE 37, 271 – Solange I.

BVerfG 22.10.1986 – 2 BvR 197/83 – BVerfGE 73, 339 – Solange II.
BVerfGE 08.04.1987 – 2 BvR 687/85 – BVerfGE 75, 223 – Kloppenburg.
BVerfG 12.10.1993 – 2 BvR 2159/92 a. o. – BVerfGE 89, 155 – Maastricht.
BVerfG 07.06.2000 – 2 BvL 1/97 – BVerfGE 102, 147 – Bananenmarktordnung.
BVerfG 18.07.2005 – 2 BvR 2236/04 – BVerfGE 113, 273 – Europäischer Haftbefehl.
BVerfG 13.03.2007 – 1 BvF 1/05 – BVerfGE 118, 79 – Emissionshandel.
BVerfG 30.06.2009 – 2 BvE 2/08 a. o. – BVerfGE 123, 267 – Lissabon.
BVerfG 06.07.2010 – 2 BvR 2661/06 – BVerfGE 126, 286 – Ultra-vires-Kontrolle.
BVerfG 19.07.2011 – 1 BvR 1916/06 – BVerfGE 129, 78 – Anwendungserweiterung.
BVerfG 14.01.2014 – 2 BvR 2728/13 a. o. – BVerfGE 134, 366 – OMT-Urteil (Vorlagebeschluss).
BVerfG 15.12.2015 – 2 BvR 2735/14 – BVerfGE 140, 317 – Identitätskontrolle.
BVerfG 21.06.2016 – 2 BvR 2728/13 a. o. – BVerfGE 142, 123 – OMT-Urteil.

France

Conseil Constitutionnel 27.07.2006 – Decision No. 2006–540 DC.
Conseil Constitutionnel 30.11.2006 – Decision No. 2006–543 DC.
Conseil Constitutionnel 09.06.2011 – Decision No. 2011-631 DC.

Poland

Trybunal Konstytucyjny 11.05.2005 – K 18/04.
Trybunal Konstytucyjny 24.11.2010 – K 32/09.
Trybunal Konstytucyjny 16.11.2011 – SK 45/09.

Italy

Corte Costituzionale 22.06.1966 – Decision No. 98/1965 – EuR 1966, 146 – Acciaierie San Michele.
Corte Costituzionale 27.12.1973 – Decision No. 183/1973 – EuR 1974, 255 – Frontini.
Corte Costituzionale 08.06.1984 – Decision No. 170/1984 – EuGRZ 1985, 98 – Granital.
Corte Costituzionale 21.04.1989 – Decision No. 232/1989 – Fragd.
Corte Costituzionale 08.04.1991 – Decision No. 168/1991 – S.p.a Industria dolciaria Giampaoli.
Corte Costituzionale 23.03.1994 – Decision No. 117/1994 – Zerini.

Spain

Tribunal Constitucional 13.12.2004 – Declaration DTC 1/2004 – EuR 2005, 339.

Tribunal Constitucional 13.02.2014 – Decision STC 26/2014 – HRLJ 2014, 475.

Czech Republic

Ústavní soud 08.03.2006 – Pl ÚS 50/04.

Ústavní soud 03.05.2006 – Pl ÚS 66/04.

Ústavní soud 26.11.2008 – Pl ÚS 19/08.

Ústavní soud 03.11.2009 – Pl ÚS 29/09.

European Court of Justice

European Court of Justice, Case C-6/64, 15.07.1964, *Costa/E.N.E.L.*, ECR 585.

European Court of Justice, Case C-11/70, 17.12.1970, *Internationale Handelsgesellschaft*, ECR 1125.

European Court of Justice, Case C-473/93, 02.07.1996, *Commission/Luxembourg*, ECR I-3207.

GA Miguel Poiares Maduro, Case C-53/04, 07.09.2006, *Marrosu and Sardino*, ECR I-7213.

GA Juliane Kokott, Case C-428/06 – C-434/06, 11.09.2008, *Unión General de Trabajadores de la Rioja*, ECR I-6747.

GA Miguel Poiares Maduro, Case C-213/07, 16.12.2008, *Michaniki*, ECR I-9999.

European Court of Justice, Case C-409/06, 08.09.2010, *Winner Wetten*, ECR I-8015.

European Court of Justice, Case C-208/09, 22.12.2010, *Sayn-Wittgenstein*, ECR I-13693.

European Court of Justice, Case C-391/09, 12.05.2011, *Runevič-Vardyn and Wardyn*, ECR I-3818.

European Court of Justice, Case C-51/08, 24.05.2011, *Commission/Luxembourg*, ECR I-4235.

European Court of Justice, Case C-202/11, 16.04.2013, *Las*, ECLI:EU:C:2013:239.

European Court of Justice, Case C-156/13, 12.06.2014, *Digibet*, ECLI:EU:C:2014:1756.

European Court of Justice, Case C-51/15, 21.12.2016, *Remondis*, ECLI:EU:C:2016:985.

Comment: "The Concept of Constitutional Identity in (Quasi-) Federal Systems of Government – From Limitation of Powers to Judicial Policy Making"

*George Barrie**

In 1946 at a post-World War II conference in Zurich, Winston Churchill proposed a United States of Europe based on a partnership between France and Germany. Five years later in 1951 with the Treaty of Paris a common market in coal and steel products came into existence (Belgium, Netherlands, Luxembourg, France, Germany and Italy). Six years later in 1957 these six countries created a European Common Market with the Treaty of Rome ending *inter alia* all restrictions on movements of persons, service and capital and harmonising competition between them.

This Treaty of Rome was seen to be a bargain of *mutual sacrifice* – with the emphasis on the term 'sacrifice'. The Treaty of Rome has developed into 28 European states (*separate and independent)* becoming part of the European Union (EU) with the Treaty of the European Union (TEU) signed at Maastricht which came into force on 1 November 1993. The EU was seen by some to be the resurrection of the Holy Roman Empire. The EU can for our purposes be referred to as a *quasi-federation* – the term used in the paper by Jennifer Hölzlwimmer. In the *Lisbon Treaty Case*[1] the German Federal Constitutional Court (Bundesverfassungsgericht) saw the European Union as an association of sovereign states (Staatenverbund) and not an incipient federal state (Bundesstaat or Staatsverband).[2] The court held that the Treaty of Lisbon decided against the concept of a European Federal Constitution and a *new* federal people. The court could not see the Lisbon Treaty aiming at founding a *state*. The court insisted that the sovereign power of the European Union had *outer limits* and that the civil society, or *demos*, essential

---

* George N. Barrie, *B.A. (Law), LL.B., LL.D.*, Emeritus Professor, Faculty of Law, University of Johannesburg.

1 BVerfG 30.06.2009 – 2 BvR 1010/08 – BVerfGE 123, 267.

2 See Paul Kirchhof, 'The Legal Structure of the European Union as a Union of States', in: Armin von Bogdandy and Jürgen Bast (eds), Principles of European Constitutional Law (2nd Edition, 2011), 765 (778). This view is disputed by Christoph Schönberger, 129 (2004) Archiv des öffentlichen Rechts (AöR), 81.

to democracy is still centered on the nation state, framed by a common language, culture and history. The term *quasi-federation* to refer to the EU would thus seem to be an apt reference.

A federation enables separate entities or communities to make decisions *for themselves* in some matters while joining together the make decisions *about matters of interest to all of them.* People who live in a federation will thus always be subject to *two sets* of governments or two centres of power. An obvious question then arises: What remains of the *constitutional identity* of the separate entities or states of a federation or quasi-federation? This question has been pertinently raised by Ms Hölzlwimmer in her paper. The answer to this question, in the case of the EU, will differ depending whether the emphasis is placed on the competencies of the governing bodies of the EU or the competencies of the separate states which constitute the EU.

The stated aim of the TEU (Maastricht Treaty) was to assist in the European evolution from being a 'community' into a 'closer union among the peoples of Europe'. The aim was that member states weld themselves into a tighter economic and political union. It was hoped that a single European currency supervised by a European Central Bank would culminate in deeper integration. It was hoped that a greater political union would be achieved by an European Parliament, European Commission and European Council.

The TEU (Maastricht Treaty) further called for a significant *transfer* of member states' governing powers and extensive cooperation between governments which involved a wide range of topics which traditionally belonged to the *sovereign power* of states. The question invariably arose *who* holds the balance of powers? This question is also pertinently raised in Ms Hölzlwimmer's paper.

In the EU we have bodies such as the European Parliament, the European Court of Human Rights and the European Court of Justice *which* in practice conclusively determine the demarcation of powers between the separate member states of the EU and the EU governing bodies? Must those EU bodies only play a *supporting* role in governing the EU and *only act* if the constituent states are incapable or unwilling?

Pope Pius XI believed that in governing the vast Catholic Church the principle of *subsidiarity* must prevail. He saw the principle of *subsidiarity* meaning that the individual congregations must be empowered with decision–making as close to the individual congregations as possible – at grassroots level as it were. That the Catholic Church as such must not intervene if the congregation is capable of resolving the issue itself. Transposed to a quasi–federation (as we are describing the EU) subsidiarity *discourages centralisation* unless there is a justification of central involvement in affairs that *cannot* be handled adequately at state level. *Subsidiarity* seen in this manner, is a *characteristic* of federalism or quasi-federalism.

This principle of *subsidiarity* is a *key principle* of EU law and is *incorporated* in article 5(3) of the TEU because several of the Member States of the EU were initially concerned about compromising their *national autonomy* should they join the EU. Thus article 5(3) of the TEU provides that if a matter does *not* fall within the exclusive competence of the European Community and can be resolved *better* by the individual member state the central authority of the EU should *not* intervene.

In the EU, however, it is a moot point whether the principle of *subsidiarity* has been *effective* as a safeguard in *guarding* against *centralisation*? At a judicial level it would appear that the principle of subsidiarity has been *disregarded* by the European Court of Justice as is evidenced by the fact that *no* directives or regulations emanating from the EU governing bodies have been annulled on the basis of *subsidiarity*. This is because the European Court of Justice regards the principles of *subsidiarity* as a *political judgment* best left to the European Parliament and Council of Ministers.

The paper of Ms Hölzlwimmer refers to the *Solange II Case*[3] of the German Federal Constitutional Court where *precedence* of EU law *over* the fundamental rights-catalogue of the German Constitution was *acknowledged*. In *Solange II* the German Federal Constitutional Court found that improvements in the *democratic character* of the European Community's policy making and in the Community's protection of fundamental rights justified that Court's *retreat* from constantly patrolling the border between Europe's supranational authority and Germany's *constitutional identity*. While the German Federal Constitutional Court did not surrender its right to monitor the Basic Law's (Grundgesetz) principles against the EU's supranational power – jurisdiction it secured for itself in the *Solange I Case*[4] – it was satisfied that it would *not* have to exercise its review powers so long as the European Community's enhanced *democracy* and protection of rights remained in force.[5] *Solange I* and *Solange II* continue to be much debated as set out by DP Kommers and RA Miller.[6]

In the *Maastricht Treaty Case*[7] the German Federal Constitutional Court, in keeping with its *Solange II* decision, *refused* to accept jurisdiction over

3 BVerfG 22.10.1986 – 2 BvR 197/83 – BVerfGE 73, 339.

4 BVerfG 29.05.1974 – 2 BvL 52/71 – BverfGE 37, 271.

5 Carl Lebeck, 7 (2006) German Law Journal, 907.

6 Donald P. Kommrs and Russell A. Miller, The Constitutional Jurisprudence of the Federal Republic of Germany (3rd Edition, 2012), 327–331.

7 BVerfG 12.10.1993 – 2 BvR 2134/92 – BVerfGE 89, 155.

fundamental rights complaints because it remained satisfied that the European Court of Justice adequately ensured the protection of fundamental rights. In the *Maastricht Treaty Case* the German Federal Constitutional court addressed critical issues related to the meaning of democracy, separation of powers, federalism and national sovereignty. The court described the absolute limits of further European integration and announced its intent to ensure that Europe exercised *only* those sovereign powers democratically and constitutionally assigned to it by member states. The conclusions arrived at by the court advanced the sovereigntist view that the EU is a *Staatenverbund* and not a *Staatsverband* or *Bundessstaat.*

The paper of Ms Hölzlwimmer rightly concludes that the debate as to what is meant by *constitutional identity* in the EU will continue especially with the rise of Europe-skepticism and the revival of nationalism. It is also clear that the social and political consensus over full German integration into a united European Union has, over the last generations, begun to weaken. The German Federal Constitutional Court's hesitance towards an enthusiastic acceptance of the European Union has also, looked at objectively, been a matter of tone and not of action. As far as European integration is concerned, the German Federal Constitutional court seems to have given priority to the Basic Law's preamble that Germany is an equal partner in a united Europe.

The paper of Ms Hölzlwimmer states that a view into other federal systems and *their* allocation of powers between the different levels of sovereignty might be helpful in the debate as to Germany's '*constitutional identity'*. I would suggest taking a closer look at Australia where there is a lively debate on *subsidiarity* and measures which must be taken to *counter* the incremental taking over of the financial and legislative powers by the federal government (the Commonwealth) from the states. This Australian debate mirrors to a large extent the issues relating the '*constitutional identity*' in the EU raised by Ms Hölzlwimmer in her paper. Despite the federal intentions of the framers of the Australian Constitution the Australian federal landscape has become increasingly centralised. This has happened because, put simply, the principle of *subsidiarity* has been largely overlooked in the Australian federal system. The turning point towards centralisation was the decision of the Australian High Court in *Amalgamated Society of Engineers v. Adelaide Steamship Co Ltd*[8] which irrepably altered the balance of powers between the Commonwealth and the separate states. The *Engineers* de-

8 (1920) 28 CLR 129.

cision resulted in the legislative powers of the states being increasingly encroached upon by the Commonwealth. In this way, similarly to the EU, the federal states of Australia are slowly but surely losing their '*constitutional identity*'. A stricter application of the principle of subsidiarity, however, would restore a proper balance between the federal states.[9] This would restore the authenticity of Australian federalism and safeguard against future centralisation.[10] The same holds for the quasi-federal nature of the EU. Only a strict application of the principle of subsidiarity will restore the rightful '*constitutional identity*' of the separate states of the EU.[11]

The German Basic Law makes a fundamental commitment to national sovereignty. Section 24(1) of the Basic Law also provides that the "Federation may by law transfer sovereign powers to international organizations." The question remains that when transferring sovereign powers to a supranational entity like the EU, what remains of German '*constitutional identity*'? Does the German Federal Constitutional Court not have to exercise *greater vigilance* to preserve the sovereignty secured by the Basic Law? Are there not *constitutional limits* to the transfer of German sovereign powers to the EU? Must the German Federal Constitutional Court not be more active in seeking to safeguard German state sovereignty, German '*constitutional identity*', as an essential framework for Germany's participation in the European Union?

Animated by a desire to overcome the pariah status Germany had earned with its repeated acts of hostility in the twentieth century, the Basic Law's framers decided to pursue a programme of international integration.[12] The Basic Law's preamble envisions Germany as an equal partner in a *united* Europe. To achieve this a constitutional mechanism was set in place with the aim of achieving a deeper European unity (section 24(1) of the Basic Law). This culminated in the transfer of sovereign powers to a supranational organisation like the EU. It could never have been the intention of the Basic Law's framers to sacrifice Germany's '*constitutional identity*' in this pro-

---

9 Michelle Evans, 'Subsidiarity and Federalism: A Case Study of the Australian Constitution and its Interpretation', in: Michelle Evans and Augusto Zimmerman (eds), Global Perspectives on Subsidiarity (2014), 185 (186).

10 Anne Twomey and Glen Withers, Federalist Paper 1 Australia's Federal Future (2007), 46.

11 Gary W. Vause, 27 (1995) Case Western Reserve Journal of International Law, 61.

12 Donald P. Kommers and Russell A. Miller, The Constitutional Jurisprudence of the Federal Republic of Germany (3rd Edition, 2012), 325.

cess. It is for the German Federal Constitutional Court to confront the tensions raised between supranational and domestic authority brought about by Germany's deeper integration into European governance, and to emphasise that there are constitutional limits to that European governance.

Bibliography

Michelle Evans, 'Subsidiarity and Federalism: A Case Study of the Australian Constitution and its Interpretation', in: Michelle Evans and Augusto Zimmerman (eds), *Global Perspectives on Subsidiarity* (Springer, Dordrecht 2014), 186.

Paul Kirchhof, 'The Legal Structure of the European as a Union of States', in: Armin von Bogdandy and Jürgen Bast (eds), *Principles of European Constitutional Law* (2nd Edition, Hart/C.H.Beck/Nomos, Oxford 2011) 765.

Donald P. Kommers and Russell A. Miller, *The Constitutional Jurisprudence of the Federal Republic of Germany* (3rd Edition, Duke University Press, Durham 2012).

Carl Lebeck, 'National Constitutionalism, Openness to International Law and the Pragmatic Limits of European Integration. European Law in the German Constitutional Court from EEC to the PJCC' 7 (2006) *German Law Journal,* 907.

Anne Twomey and Glen Withers, *Federalist Paper 1. Australia's Federal Future* (April 2007), https://www.caf.gov.au/documents/australiasfederalfuture.pdf (6 March 2018).

Gary W. Vause, 'The Subsidiarity Principle in European Union Law – American Federalism Compared' 27 (1995) *Case Western Reserve Journal of International Law*, 61.

Register of cases

Australia

Amalgamated Society of Engineers v. Adelaide Steamship Co Ltd (1920) 28 CLR 129.

Germany

BVerfG 30.06.2009 – 2 BvR 1010/08 – BVerfGE 123, 267 – Lisbon Treaty.

BVerfG 12.10.1993 – 2 BvR 2134/92 - BVerfGE 89, 155 – Maastricht Treaty.

BVerfG 29.05.1974 – 2 BvL 52/71 – BverfGE 37, 271 – Solange I.

BVerfG 22.10.1986 – 2 BvR 197/83 – BVerfGE 73, 339 – Solange II.

Democratic Flexibility and Constitutional Stability

*Matthias Rossi**

Abstract: *Constitutional democracies are characterised by the tension between political freedom of scope and the constitutional order. Democracy means change – or at least changeability – while constitutions, firm as a rock, guarantee reliability with stability. These poles, however, are not in rigid contrast to each other. Constitutions have not only limiting but also enabling functions. And for reasons of self-preservation they must themselves be changeable and convertible. On the other hand, democratic legislation is rigid not only for constitutional reasons. Against this background, this paper sets out the multi-dimensional relations between democratic legislation and the binding nature of a constitution.*

* Matthias Rossi, *Dr. iur.*; Professor, University of Augsburg, Faculty of Law. Chair for Constitutional Law, Administrative Law, European Union Law and Theory of Legislation.
I would like to thank my colleague, Aqilah Sandhu, and Gill Mertens for their assistance in translating this paper.

I. Introduction

The model of constitutional democracy has prevailed in many countries across the world. Especially from the perspective of the 'western world' – if this rather undefined, yet comprehensive, concept may be used – it is considered to be the only political system that fully respects the principle of liberal self-determination.

Nevertheless, the fundamental tension between democracy as governance by the people and the legally binding force of the constitutional order frequently suffers ruptures.

Young democracies in Central and Eastern Europe often find it difficult to exercise their right to self-determination within the boundaries set by their constitution and by the legal order of the European Union. Even old democracies like Switzerland find it difficult to accept that referendums on banning the construction of minarets are incompatible with fundamental rights and human rights provisions.

In Germany, it also took the young Weimar Republic a long time to accept that the fundamental rights as guaranteed in the constitution have a binding force upon Parliament as an expression of institutionalised democracy. This only became a matter of fact after the experience of National Socialism.

Despite this fundamental tension, it would be wrong to consider democracy and the binding force of the constitution to be antipodes. The interplay between constitutional stability and democratic flexibility enables societies to develop a self-determined life, while at the same time sticking to their historical origins and preserving, and further enhancing their cultural identity.

In this respect, constitutions have the dual task of simultaneously ensuring stability and acting as an open proposal for change in the future.[1] This dual function of constitutions – ensuring stability on the one hand, facilitating development on the other – has been described often.[2] In the following, we will therefore focus solely on liberating stability and flexibility from their supposed antagonism, making it clear that both must be brought into balance and can be brought into balance.

II. Constitutional stability

1. Stability by liability

Constitutions serve as "anchors of stability". From a legal point of view, this is – or should be – nothing new.

Without doubt, all state authority is bound by the constitution. The differentiation between the '*pouvoir constituant*' that creates this basic order (not in the sense of *Kelsen*) or these 'rules of play' and the '*pouvoir constitué*' – which is created (and at the same time limited) by this constituent power – is compatible with the idea of democracy. However, this is only the case if an assembly representing the people has exercised the constituent power, or if it was at least adopted or even later accepted by the majority of the people. Even Germany suffers from a birth defect in this respect, because such a popular vote on the Basic Law for the Federal Republic of Germany (GG) – which was initially conceived merely as a provisional arrangement – has never taken place. Instead, the parliaments of the German *Länder* (Federal states), which have only indirect democratic legitimacy, ratified the Basic Law. In political reality, there are no doubts as to the democratic foundation of the Basic Law.

---

1 See *Gunnar Folke Schuppert*, 120 (1995) *Archiv für öffentliches Recht (AöR)*, 32 (35).

2 See *Gunnar Folke Schuppert*, 120 (1995) *Archiv für öffentliches Recht (AöR)*, 32 et seqq., with much further evidence.

2. Stability by historical experiences

The Basic law probably derives its stability from its content, as constitutions are the product of a specific historical experience.The power of constitutions to give a sense of identity and legitimacy to the people derives largely from central and shared moral values resulting from injustice suffered. We will give just a few examples. The struggle for religious freedom is the reason why the fundamental right to freedom of religion is of particular significance. The inviolability of human dignity is a reaction to its complete denial in history. The lack of the right to self-dissolution of the *Bundestag* under the Basic Law is explained by the instability of the Parliament under the Weimar Constitution. The list of examples could be continued – especially in countries such as South Africa.

The fact that to a certain extent constitutions relate to the past does not confer a backwards character upon them. Rather, constitutions refer to collective experiences and thereby form the basis of what we today call a narrative. Insofar, they are a point of focus (or of reference, at least) which the development of statehood takes as its starting point and on which it may fall back once again – especially in times of crisis.

3. Stability by sticking to a framework regime

Aside from this rather cultural relevance, constitutions have a primarily legal significance. The constitution is the founding, organising and limiting source for the exercise of state power. Its limiting function is certainly the focus of every legal analysis. However, in most cases, the question of whether or not certain acts are constitutional, does not only prevent an impartial and objective debate. It also obscures the perspective of the many opportunities that are available within that framework. At the same time, the question paves the way for a constructive approach – by defining the space, actors and instruments. The constitution insofar creates the institutional infrastructure, without which the peaceful resolution of disputes would be as much impossible as the problem analysis itself.

4. Stability through resilience

In the sense of such an institutional infrastructure, the main purpose of a constitution is certainly “to be at its core a fundamental, systematic, consequently permanent, independent order of state life, which is therefore emphasised and shaped in a law”.[3]

The comparison with an ‘infrastructure’ shows that constitutions regularly provide only instruments, but do not specify how these are supposed to be used. Such a rather formalised role of a constitution is perfect to guarantee its function of ensuring stability and also enables the necessary balance with the flexibility that is primarily founded in democracy. Paradoxically, however, an overly formal understanding can also jeopardise the very stability intended by a constitution. The problems that can result from an overly narrow understanding of bindingness and from a rigidity of constitutions are indeed history in Germany. But they are still present – the seizure of power by the National Socialists was formally compatible with the *Weimar Reichsverfassung* (WRV). A historian analyses aptly: “In order to preserve the rule of law, its defenders would have had to violate the letter of a constitution that was neutral against their own validity during the final crisis in Weimar. But this was opposed by an attitude that Ernst Fraenkel denounced at the end of 1932 as ‘constitutional patriotism’. The relinquishment of governmental power to Hitler was not brought about by this failure, but was made possible by it.”[4]

The elimination of democracy through the abuse of democracy was the beginning of the end of the most liberal German constitution, the Weimar Reichsverfassung, and ended in the demise of the Third Reich. Knowing full well that every monocausal attempt to explain these events allows only a partial and necessarily incomplete analysis, there is undoubtedly an essential (contributory) cause for this in the limitless liberality and value neutrality of the WRV: It was liberal to the point of self-abasement, because it contained no effective safeguards against its opponents.[5]

---

3 Translated from the original German. Hasso Hofmann, *Recht – Politik – Verfassung. Studien zur Geschichte der politischen Philosophie* (1986), 261 et seqq.

4 Translated from the original German. Heinrich August Winkler, *Weimar 1918–1933. Die Geschichte der ersten deutschen Demokratie*, (1993), 594.

5 Günter Dürig, in: Theodor Maunz and Günter Dürig (eds), *Grundgesetzkommentar* (83rd Edition, 2018), Art. 18 mn. 7.

The WRV did not have the manifold safeguards against internal erosion as provided for today in the GG. It could therefore be effectively repealed without violating the Constitution. To prevent this from happening again, the GG has devoted special attention to the protection of the Constitution[6] and for good reason opted for a 'fortified, 'resilient or 'defensive' democracy – the terminology varies. From the pluralism of goals and values, certain absolute values are excluded and resolutely defended against all attacks.[7]

5. Stability by changeability

Beyond the special instruments of resilience, which intend "to guarantee that enemies of the Constitution cannot invoke the freedoms guaranteed by the Basic Law and their protection to endanger, undermine or destroy the constitutional order or the existence of the state",[8] the task of the constitution to "bring the state into form" and to preserve it requires a degree of flexibility and adaptability of constitutional law.[9]

The framework itself, however, is not rigid and unchangeable. It is in many ways flexible and amendable. Depending on their respective content, constitutional provisions are subject to transformation, capable of interpretation and some depend on statutory definition even from the very outset. The constitutional jurisdiction, which is responsible for the interpretation of the Constitution, turns out to be remarkably future-oriented and progressive in many cases (at least in Germany), and it is quite obvious that its perspective is not merely to be the keeper of the Grail. Above all, the Constitution itself may be amended. The Amendment is subject to special procedures and formal requirements, because it is the *pouvoir constituent constitué* that is acting. After all, the Constitution itself provides for an amendment procedure that respects the principle of democracy, and also secures its own preservation. A constitution that is not amendable will – once it is incapable of solving the problems of its time convincingly – first lose its acceptance and then lose its validity, before it is replaced by a new one. It is the specific

6 Konrad Hesse, *Grundzüge des Verfassungsrechts der Bundesrepublik Deutschland* (20th Edition, 1999), mn. 695.

7 BVerfG, 17.08.1956 – 1 BvB 2/51 – BVerfGE 5, 85, para. 138 et seq.

8 BVerfG 17.01.2017 – 2 BvB 1/13 – BVerfGE 144, 20, para. 418 (prohibition of the NPD).

9 Gunnar Folke Schuppert, 120 (1995) *Archiv für öffentliches Recht (AöR),* 32 (37).

claim of its binding force that makes the changeability of a constitution necessary. Therefore, for the sake of their self-preservation, constitutions are intelligently designed if they provide for flexibility clauses and the possibility of amendment. (Considering its binding nature, it is rather questionable when a constitution provides for its own abrogation if the constituent power decides to adopt a new constitution. Such a provision, as is included in Article 146 of the Basic Law, may be explained by the provisional character of the Basic Law of 1949 and the lack of foresight in 1990).

From a political or social science perspective, two types of constitutional change can be distinguished: Those that react only to a changed reality (and can therefore be described as changes of adaptation), and conversely those that want to control reality itself (and can thus be described as changes of behaviour).[10] This distinction is of course irrelevant under constitutional law – the formal constitution does not question the reasons for or motives behind constitutional amendments, but treats them all equally. In particular, they must satisfy the requirements of Article 79 of the Basic Law.

In Germany, the primacy of the constitution is initially secured by the requirement to amend the text as stated in Article 79(1) sentence 1 of the Basic Law: Any amendment or extension of the legal provisions contained in the Constitutional Charter require a law expressly amending or supplementing the wording of the Basic Law. Article 79(1) sentence 1 of the Basic Law thus serves the "authenticity and visibility of every constitutional amendment",[11] the primary purpose of which is to prevent (formal) breaches of the constitution. Thus Article 79(1) sentence 1 of the Basic Law deprives the parliamentary legislator of the possibility of 'hiding' norms that amend or supplement the constitution in simple (federal) laws. In this way, the Basic Law guarantees that all (formal) constitutional law is written in the Basic Law and nowhere else, and that every constitutional amendment is reflected in the Basic Law. This excludes a legal situation such as under the WRV, according to which laws amending the Constitution were valid if they had been adopted by the majorities required for constitutional amendments. Article 79(1) sentence 1 of the Basic Law is thus primarily directed against "constitutional violations from above", i.e. against attacks

10 See Peter Häberle, 'Zeit und Verfassungskultur', in: Anton Peisl, Armin Mohler (eds), *Die Zeit* (1983), 289 et seqq.

11 BVerfG, 16.06.1959 – 2 BvL 10/59 – BVerfGE 9, 334, para. 336.

by state organs themselves against the constitution, as they appear historically in *coups d'état*.[12] However, rules that remove the constitutional obligation for certain future exercise of sovereignty (as was possible by recourse to Art. 48 WRV at the time of the Weimar Republic) by recourse to the constitution itself are also prohibited.

Otherwise, constitutions can only be amended if certain specific procedural requirements are met – in Germany laid down in Article 79(2) of the Basic Law according to which constitutional amendments must be carried by an absolute majority of two thirds of the Members of each house, the *Bundestag* and the *Bundesrat*. These majorities, which can be quite difficult to achieve depending on the party-political composition of the individual houses, primarily provide protection against over-hasty change and deliberately contain elements to slow down the process. It is all the more astonishing and alarming, of course, if in times of a Grand Coalition, in which both the *Bundestag* and the *Bundesrat* are dominated by the same party-political majority, constitutional articles are amended almost arbitrarily. Apart from such special party-political constellations, the requirement of an absolute majority prevents constitutional provisions from being subjected to the usual political horse trading in the day-to-day parliamentary business. In this respect, these majority requirements have a stabilising effect.

6. Stability through unchangeable core guarantees

Lastly, the strongest protection of the constitution is found in the eternity clause of Article 79(3) of the Basic Law, abolishing any amendment to the Basic Law that affects the division of the Federation into *Länder*, their participation in principle in the legislative process, or the principles laid down in Articles 1 and 20 of the Basic Law – even if the majorities in the *Bundestag* and *Bundesrat* as required under Article 79(2) of the Basic Law are met. Thus the Basic Law establishes an absolute guarantee of the existence of a constitution with certain unchangeable core principles, subject only to the adoption of a new constitution as provided for in Article 146 of the Basic Law.

As the Federal Constitutional Court (BVerfG) rightly pointed out, the principles of Article 1 of the Basic Law do not only include the principle of human dignity enshrined in paragraph 1. “The commitment to inviolable

---

12 Klaus Stern, *Das Staatsrecht der Bundesrepublik Deutschland I*, (2nd Edition, 1984), 184.

and inalienable human rights as the basis of the human community, peace and justice contained in Article 1(2) of the Basic Law also gains significance; together with the reference to the following fundamental rights in Article 1(3) of the Basic Law, their guarantees are in principle not subject to restriction insofar as they are indispensable for the maintenance of an order corresponding to Article 1(1) and 1(2) of the Basic Law."[13] Therefore, the legislature amending the constitution and the original legislature must not disregard fundamental postulates of justice, such as the principle of equality of rights and the prohibition of arbitrariness.[14] However, "Article 79(3) of the Basic Law only requires that the principles mentioned are not affected.It does not prevent the legislature amending the constitution from modifying the positive legal expression of these principles for appropriate reasons."[15]

This provision results from a distrust in the parliamentary legislature, which abused its legislative power at the beginning of the National Socialist era. The Constitution therefore protects itself not only against executive powers, but also against the constituent power by prohibiting its representatives from making certain constitutional amendments. This is new, and undoubtedly a constitutional risk as it restricts even the sovereignty of the people with regard to the core provisions of the constitution (Article 20(2) sentence 1 of the Basic Law). It thus increases the – at least theoretical – danger that, due to the normative stipulations of future generations, any pressure will not be discharged by way of a legal constitutional amendment, but via other (revolutionary) valves.[16]

Nevertheless, Article 79(3) of the Basic Law deserves unconditional approval. Certainly revolutionary upheavals with the consequence of creating new constitutional law cannot be ruled out by a single provision, and it is undisputed that every constitution lives only as long as it enjoys the appropriate standing among the people and possesses normative power.[17] However, Article 79(3) of the Basic Law prevents the core principles from being

13 Translated from the original German. BVerfG, 23.04.1991 – 1 BvR 1170/90 – BVerfGE 84, 90, para. 121.

14 Translated from the original German. BVerfG, 23.04.1991 – 1 BvR 1170/90 – BVerfGE 84, 90, para. 121.

15 Translated from the original German. BVerfG, 23.04.1991 – 1 BvR 1170/90 – BVerfGE 84, 90, para. 121, with reference to BVerfG, 15.12.1970 – 2 BvF 1/69 – BVerfGE 30, 1, para. 24.

16 Ludwig Thoma, in: Hans Carl Nipperdey, *Die Grundrechte und Grundpflichten der Reichsverfassung* I (1929), 25.

17 On this aspect Konrad Hesse, *Grundzüge des Verfassungsrechts der Bundesrepublik Deutschland*, (20th Edition 1995), mn. 701.

overturned by means of a seemingly legal procedure – as in 1933 – by abusing existing constitutional provisions. Anyone who wants to eliminate the fundamental principles of the Constitution mentioned in Article 79(3) of the Basic Law – such as by abolishing elections or by entrusting the task of judicature to the executive bodies – will be forced into illegality as an opponent of the Constitution.

III. Democratic flexibility

However, the constitutional boundaries are not fixed once and for all. Constitution in the normative sense and constitutional reality have a mutual relationship. This is shaped, among other things, by state practice – which in turn is expressed in the political decisions of parliaments and governments. Such political decisions can lead to a modification of the content of constitutional provisions without explicitly changing their text. Through such a constitutional amendment, they enable the further development of constitutional law within the limits of Article 79(3) of the Basic Law, compliance with which is ensured by the Federal Constitutional Court.[18] The most recent example of this in Germany is 'marriage for all' (*Ehe für alle*): While 'marriage' implicitly meant to only include the heterosexual relationship between two people – not least because of its systematic position in connection with the protection of the family, traditionally consisting of husband, wife and children – the constitutional concept has now been changed by an amendment to an ordinary legal provision, not the Basic Law. Possibly, one must certainly add, because there is no binding decision of the Federal Constitutional Court and as such a decision is unlikely at the moment.[19]

Such a changed understanding of a central constitutional concept is by no means uncommon. It is a normal expression of democracy. Democracy

---

18 On constitutional change, see Ernst-Wolfgang Böckenförde, 'Anmerkungen zum Begriff Verfassungswandel', in: Peter Badura and Scholz, Ruppert (eds), *Wege und Verfahren des Verfassungslebens* (1998), 3 (3 et seq.); Konrad Hesse, 'Grenzen der Verfassungswandlung', in: Horst Ehmke, Joseph H. Kaiser, Wilhelm A. Kewenig, Karl Matthias Meessen and Wolfgang Rüfner (eds), *Festschrift für Ulrich Scheuner zum 70. Geburtstag* (1973), 123 et seqq. See also the numerous contributions in: Christoph Hönnige, Sascha Kneip, Astrid Lorenz (eds), *Verfassungswandel im Mehrebenensystem* (2011) passim.

19 In detail, see Ferdinand Wollenschläger and Dagmar Coester-Waltjen, *Ehe für alle* (2018) passim.

stands less for stability than for flexibility. The rule of the people means the will of the people, and this can change over the course of time.

1. Multi-faceted concept of democracy

Admittedly, caution is required with regard to the concept of democracy. Due to its historical-philosophical background, democracy is a complex concept that is increasingly used in an undifferentiated way. It is therefore all the more important to bear in mind that the concept of democracy under the Basic Law also encompasses four aspects:

- It is a manifestation of political domination – here there is most room for historical-philosophical references.
- It is a method of legitimising domination.
- It is a specific process of procuring justice – with numerous overlaps with the rule-of-law principle.
- It is a substantive principle aimed at participation, co-determination and equal opportunities.[20]

Against this background, it should be emphasised that the principle of democracy is not so much aimed at setting or limiting the content of policies. Rather, it aims to channel and discipline the political process, while at the same time enabling it in the first place. In this respect, the principle of democracy is also a term to describe the task of the democratic constitution to organise decision-making processes that are open to the future and to content.[21]

In this respect, constitutional law is not only capable of being concretised, but above all it is also in need of concretisation. The density of constitutional requirements must not be overestimated: Constitutional law is "not as concrete as settled law".[22] It is to be further concretised by the legislator, which has a creative leeway that it can exercise in accordance with

20 Gunnar Folke Schuppert, 120 (1995) *Archiv für öffentliches Recht (AöR)*, 32, 63.

21 Gunnar Folke Schuppert, 120 (1995) *Archiv für öffentliches Recht (AöR)*, 32, 82.

22 Peter Lerche, *deutsches Verwaltungsblatt (DVBl)* 1961, 690 (692 et seq.). See also Eberhard Schmidt-Aßmann, *Das allgemeine Verwaltungsrecht als Ordnungsidee* (2004), 11.

the majority decision taken in the political decision-making process. Legislation is precisely not an 'enforcement' of constitutional law, but rather the exercise of political power to shape policy. This creative power not only presupposes flexibility, but at the same time also requires it.

2. Flexibility through temporary rule

Aside from theoretical aspects – especially from philosophically charged questions – there is virtually no doubt that in a constitutional democracy the will of the people can only be expressed through special procedures, and only when certain formal requirements are met. In a representative democracy, the expression of the will of the people – not necessarily consensus-building – is exercised through specific bodies, and first and foremost through the legislative body. However, the conferral of powers is only for a limited period of time. This already shows the special flexibility, which is immanent to democracy. Democracy means governance for a specified period, a time that is defined in the constitution. Governance is characterised primarily by the power to enact laws.

These laws decouple themselves from their respective initiator, as the enactment is the shared responsibility of the Parliament as institution and not of the individual Member of Parliament. Therefore, laws in principle remain in force and effect even beyond the duration of a legislative period. Governance for a limited period of time insofar makes it possible to rule even beyond the prescribed limited period of time.

3. Flexiblity by legislative amendments

Laws can undoubtedly be changed, and even repealed, by enacting a new law as *actus contrarius*. This changeability is an expression of the special flexibility, which is a result of the principle of democracy.

With view to the high extent of statutory standardisation in the social welfare state of the 21st century, it is no surprise that the everyday business of the legislature primarily consists of amending existing laws, and not enacting new laws. This is true irrespective of whether one takes into account only singular provisions or whole laws. The legislature deals with a series of laws that are meant either to replace, extend or repeal existing laws, and thereby is always concerned with 'settled' law. The discussion on temporary provisions insofar does not concern the question of the changeability (and repeal) of laws, but rather the question of whether the future legislature will have to actively repeal or change a law.

Nota bene: The disadvantage of temporary provisions is that there are only two options: the temporary provision either lapses completely, or remains in force as a whole. The option to improve the law or certain provisions (the amendment of laws) is widely ignored. However, this option is not only highly relevant from a theoretical point of view of a 'learning' legislature, but also from a practical view. But if the legislature is willing (or even forced) to amend the law anyway – for instance, because the limitation of a provision also affects other legal provisions that now have to be corrected for clarification purposes – the main argument in favor of temporary provisions (which is to unburden the legislature) no longer works.

4. Path dependency of laws

Despite the fundamental changeability of laws, many legal decisions turn out to be surprisingly stable. However, considering the wide variety of laws, democratic flexibility is not only and foremost limited by the constitution, but also by the existing legal statutes. When each provision leads to a variety of subsequent amendments in other statutes, which again may involve further players – for example in the federal multi-level system – the legislature will not be inclined to amend the law. The legislative process is path dependent, and these paths are at times much narrower than the broad path provided for by the constitution.

5. Political self-restriction

But even if the path seems to be sufficiently clear to go back the same way and take another route, a surprisingly large number of laws that had faced fierce opposition from political opponents when enacted during one legislative period are not repealed by the very same opponents after a change of government in the next legislative period. This is not only the case for laws that increase taxes and levies, but also for material laws (*Sachgesetz*).

This restraint is understandable when it comes to laws that are qualified as substantive constitutional law. These are provisions that contain fundamental rules of play and that set out the conditions that govern the exercise of power. The most prominent example for such a law that is meant to have a longer legal validity is the Federal Electoral Act (*Bundeswahlgesetz*), the

Political Parties Act (*Gesetz über die politischen Parteien*), the (*Abgeordnetengesetz*), and (not least) the Federal Constitutional Court Act (*Bundesverfassungsgerichtsgesetz*) with its provisions on the Court's jurisdiction – on the Court's power, so to speak.

But even beyond this material approach, there are legal provisions that are not changed in the following legislative period, even if they had been fiercely criticised at the time of their adoption in the previous period. The reason for this might well lie in political self-restraint, but more likely it is the need for legal certainty and reliance on the law. It may also be for the very pragmatic reason of saving resources. It is impossible to implement an unlimited agenda during one legislative period – be it four or five years. The short period forces the legislature to focus on certain priorities. Moreover, if the agenda is predetermined by exogenous events – a financial crisis here, a refugee crisis there, by foreign policy issues or even by natural disasters – the possibility of dealing with all topics diminishes over time. Futhermore, the participation of all relevant actors in the legislative process reduces the timeframe to such an extent that fundamental changes cannot be reached during one legislative procedure. Democratic flexibility thereby quickly falls victim to political expediency.

This also applies to the constitutional amendments that are possible within the framework of Article 79 of the Basic Law. Dieter Grimm put it aptly: "In modern societies, everything is changeable, but only a certain amount of simultaneous or abrupt change is bearable. Constitutions stabilise the relationship between continuity and change by institutionalising greater continuity at the level of principles and procedures than at the level of their implementation and concretisation. They do this less often by preventing change than by increasing consensus and justification requirements." And he continues that "constitutions introduce different time horizons into politics, which have two effects: They form a self-protection of society against haste and create a space for social learning. The constitution itself cannot be exempt from change, but must provide for its own adaptation or change."[23]

23 Translated from the original German. Dieter Grimm, *Staatswissenschaften und Staatspraxis* 1990, 23.

IV. Interrelation between democratic flexibility and constitutional stability

Strangely enough, it is sometimes the stability-oriented constitution that forces the legislature to act. Legislative duties not only derive from the supranational law of the European Union, but also from the Constitution, as concretised further and formulated by the Federal Constitutional Court. This shows that democratic flexibility and constitutional stability are certainly interrelated: constitutional law draws the limits for the democratic exercise of powers, but also urges it to take action, when it is necessary to ensure the stability of the basic order. Conversely, democracy requires a flexible constitution in order not to lose the reconnection with the will of its citizens, and thereby not to lose its validity.

What is crucial is that the stabilising and dynamic elements are balanced – once they lose their balance, they threaten to damage the constitution and democracy.

Bibliography

Ernst-Wolfgang Böckenförde, 'Anmerkungen zum Begriff Verfassungswandel', in: Peter Badura, Scholz, Ruppert (eds), *Wege und Verfahren des Verfassungslebens* (C.H. Beck, Munich 1998), 3.

Dieter Grimm, 'Die Zukunft der Verfassung' *Staatswissenschaften und Staatspraxis* (Suhrkamp, Berlin 1990), 23.

Peter Häberle,'Zeit und Verfassungskultur', in: Anton Peisl, Armin Mohler (eds), *Die Zeit* (Oldenbourg Wissenschaftsverlag, Oldenbourg 1983), 289.

Konrad Hesse, *Grundzüge des Verfassungsrechts der Bundesrepublik Deutschland* (20th Edition, C.F. Müller, Heidelberg 1999).

Konrad Hesse, 'Grenzen der Verfassungswandlung', in: Horst Ehmke, Joseph H. Kaiser, Wilhelm A. Kewenig, Karl Matthias Meessen and Wolfgang Rüfner (eds), *Festschrift für Ulrich Scheuner zum 70. Geburtstag* (Duncker & Humblot, Berlin 1973), 123.

Christoph Hönnige, Sascha Kneip and Astrid Lorenz (eds), *Verfassungswandel im Mehrebenensystem* (Springer, Wiesbaden 2011).

Hasso Hofmann, *Recht – Politik – Verfassung. Studien zur Geschichte der politischen Philosophie* (Metzner, Frankfurt am Main, 1986).

Peter Lerche, 'Stil, Methode, Ansicht' 76 (1961) *deutsches Verwaltungsblatt (DVBl)*, 690.

Theodor Maunz and Günter Dürig (eds) *Grundgesetz Kommentar, Band III* (loose-leaf 83rd Edition, C.H. Beck, Munich, April 2018).

Hans Carl Nipperdey (ed) *Die Grundrechte und Grundpflichten der Reichsverfassung, Band I* (Reimar Hobbing, Berlin 1929).

Eberhard Schmidt-Aßmann, *Das allgemeine Verwaltungsrecht als Ordnungsidee* (Springer, Wiesbaden 2004).

Gunnar Folke Schuppert, 'Rigidität und Flexibilität von Verfassungsrecht' 120 (1995) *Archiv für öffentliches Recht (AöR)*, 32.

Klaus Stern, Das Staatsrecht der Bundesrepublik Deutschland, Band I (2nd Edition, C.H. Beck, Munich 1984).

Heinrich August Winkler, *Weimar 1918-1933. Die Geschichte der ersten deutschen Demokratie* (C.H. Beck, Munich 1993).

Ferdinand Wollenschläger and Dagmar Coester-Waltjen, *Ehe für alle* (Mohr Siebeck, Tübingen 2018).

Register of Cases

BVerfG 17.08.1956 – 1 BvB 2/51 – BVerfGE 5, 85.

BVerfG 17.01.2017 – 2 BvB 1/13 – BVerfGE 144, 20.

BVerfG 16.06.1959 – 2 BvL 10/59 – BVerfGE 9, 334.

BVerfG 23.04.1991 – 1 BvR 1170/90 – BVerfGE 84, 90.

Comment: "Democratic Flexibility and Constitutional Stability"

*Mispa Roux**

I. Introduction

In Rossi's paper 'Democratic flexibility and constitutional stability', he describes the tension between democracy and a constitutional order based on the former's 'changeability', and the latter's guarantee to offer 'reliability by stability'. However, the tension does not mean that democracy and constitutionalism are opposites: as Rossi rightly states, this relationship 'enables societies to develop a self-determined life while at the same time sticking to their historical origins and thereby not only preserve, but also further enhance their cultural identity'.

* Mispa Roux, *LL.B., LL.M., LL.D.*, Senior Lecturer in Public Law and Deputy Director of the South African Institute for Advanced Constitutional, Public, Human Rights and International Law, a centre of the Faculty of Law, University of Johannesburg.

This certainly rings true for our South African constitutional democracy. The postamble of the interim Constitution provided for the Constitution as an

> 'historic bridge between the past of a deeply divided society characterised by strife, conflict, untold suffering and injustice, and a future founded on the recognition of human rights, democracy and peaceful co-existence and development opportunities for all South Africans, irrespective of colour, race, class, belief or sex. The pursuit of national unity, the well-being of all South African citizens and peace require reconciliation between the people of South Africa and the reconstruction of society. The adoption of this Constitution lays the secure foundation for the people of South Africa to transcend the divisions and strife of the past, which generated gross violations of human rights, the transgression of humanitarian principles in violent conflicts and a legacy of hatred, fear, guilt and revenge. These can now be addressed on the basis that there is a need for understanding but not for vengeance, a need for reparation but not for retaliation, a need for ubuntu but not for victimisation.'[1]

The South African Constitution can therefore certainly not be studied in the abstract, and a balance must be struck between the apartheid history, and our current reality, whether at a social, economic or political level that have a 'bearing on (the) interpretation and evaluation of the various provisions' of the Constitution.[2] Keeping in mind that a constitution provides much-needed 'stability' in a democratic state, it must also be remembered that it is not a 'static' document that is oblivious to the ever-changing context within which it finds application. South Africa today is vastly different from the South Africa that existed at the time of writing and adopting the Constitution: it has been said that our Constitution represents a 'snapshot of the hopes and dreams of (our) nation at the time of its writing or – more cynically – (as representing) a snapshot of the relative political power and influence of various political formations involved in the drafting of (our) Constitution'.[3] Rossi writes that a constitutional order frequently suffers ruptures, and in South Africa we have also experienced several such 'ruptures' between our democracy as governed by the people, and the legally binding force of our constitutional order. Twenty three years after the establishment of our constitutional democracy we are unfortunately nowhere near having achieved the hopes and dreams that influenced the constitutional drafters.

1 Constitution of the Republic of South Africa, Act 200 of 1993.

2 Pierre de Vos, Warren Freedman, Danie Brand and others *South African Constitutional Law in Context*, (2014), 3.

3 Pierre de Vos, Warren Freedman, Danie Brand and others *South African Constitutional Law in Context*, (2014), 4.

In the following response to Rossi, the model of constitutional democracy as decribed in his paper will be applied to the South African Constitution in an attempt to test whether it holds true for our constitutional democracy. This paper will start with the concept of a constitution as an 'anchor of stability' as described by Rossi, which is reflected in a constitution as an 'historical experience', as a regulatory framework, and lastly in its 'changeability' that is the 'guarantee' to its 'self-preservation'. Thereafter the paper will focus on Rossi's concepts of 'democratic flexibility', as reflected in 'governance for a limited period of time', in 'legislative amendment as the standard type of law', and finally in 'political self-restriction'.

II. The Constitution as an 'Anchor of Stability'

The South African Constitution certainly serves as an 'anchor of stability' in our democratic state. All state power derives from the Constitution: it authorises, limits and regulates the exercise of this power, and sets out the basic principles of our constitutional order. Basic principles in the Constitution include the concept of constitutionalism and the rule of law, which in turn manifests in constitutional supremacy and justiciability, especially with regards to the Bill of Rights. Other constitutional principles such as democracy, accountability and the separation of powers of different branches of government all 'directly govern the structure and functioning of state power'.[4]

Perhaps the most important 'anchor of stability' that our Constitution provides lies first and foremost therein that it was firstly an instrument in ensuring the smooth transition from an authoritarian, racially oppressive and divisive autocracy to a constitutional democracy based on human dignity, equality and freedom. The interim Constitution was 'transitional' in nature: it provided for the procedures for negotiating and drafting of a 'final' Constitution, and fell away once this was achieved.[5]

South Africa does not suffer from a 'birth defect' in the same way that Germany does in that 'an assembly representing the (majority of the) people' did not accept and adopt its Basic Law. The 1996 'final'

4 Iain Currie and Johan De Waal, *The Bill of Rights Handbook*, (6th Edition, 2005), 1.

5 Iain Currie and Johan De Waal, *The Bill of Rights Handbook*, (6th Edition, 2005), 5.

Constitution was drafted and adopted by an elected Constitutional Assembly, in essence consisting of the Parliament that was elected during the first democratic election in 1994: Chapter 5 of the interim Constitution made provision for the process of the adoption of the final Constitution, which had to be passed by 'a majority of at least two-thirds of all the members of the Constitutional Assembly'.[6] Public-participation was also encouraged, by holding public meetings and workshops in an effort to involve South Africans 'in the constitution-writing process'.[7] It must be pointed out that the certification of the final Constitution had to be done by an unelected Constitutional Court,[8] thereby granting it the power to declare on the validity of the endeavors of a democratically elected Constitutional Assembly. Nevertheless, the final Constitution came into effect after its certification by the Constitutional Court on 4 February 1997.

1. The Constitution as historical experience

As pointed out earlier, the South African Constitution initially served as a transititional document, a 'bridge' between an authoritarian, racially oppressive and divisive autocracy to a constitutional democracy.[9] In this regard, our Constitution is 'transformative':[10] South Africa was revolutionised in that the Constitution replaced the doctrine of parliamentary sovereignty with constitutional supremacy. Rigid centralised government power was replaced with the principle of separation of powers ensuring the division of power among the executive, legislative and judicial

---

6 Section 73(2) of the interim Constitution.

7 Iain Currie and Johan De Waal, *The Bill of Rights Handbook*, (6th Edition, 2005), 6, footnote 21.

8 See in this regard: *Ex parte Chairperson of the Constitutional Assembly: in re Certification of the Constitution of the Republic of South Africa 1996 (First Certification Judgment)* 1996 (4) SA 744 CC; *Certification of the Amended Text of the Constitution of the Republic of South Africa, 1996* (Second Certification Judgment) 1997 (2) SA 97 (CC).

9 Etienne Mureinik, 10 (1994) *South African Journal on Human Rights (SAJHR)*, 31.

10 Pierre de Vos, Warren Freedman, Danie Brand and others *South African Constitutional Law in Context*, (2014), 26 et seqq.; Etienne Mureinik, 10 (1994) *South African Journal on Human Rights (SAJHR)*, 31; Karl E. Klare, 14 (1998) *South African Journal on Human Rights (SAJHR)*, 146.

speheres at national, provincial and local levels. Human rights were guaranteed to all South Africans, thereby ending three hundred years of colonialism, segregation and apartheid. The preamble of the Constitution sets out the purpose of adopting the Constitution

> 'so as to [h]eal the divisions of the past and establish a society based on democratic values, social justice and fundamental human rights'; [l]ay the foundations for a democratic and open society in which government is based on the will of the people and every citizen is equally protected by law; [i]mprove the quality of life of all citizens and free the potential of each person'.[11]

The Bill of Rights is described as the 'cornerstone of democracy'[12] for South Africa, enshrining the rights of all people in our country and affirming the democratic values of human dignity, equality and freedom.'[13] Rossi points out that the power of a constitution lies therein that it gives 'a sense of identity and legitimacy to its people' which 'derives largely from central and shared moral values as a result of the injustice suffered'. The entire design of apartheid was the absolute denial of human dignity, equality and freedom of the majority South Africans. The reason for the particular significance of for example, the rights to equality,[14] human dignity,[15] life,[16] freedom and security of the person,[17] freedom of expression,[18] political rights,[19] freedom of movement and residence,[20] and property[21] in a South African context, results from their complete denial to all South African citizens for decades.

The 'transformativeness' of the South African Constitution goes further than its early nature as a transitional document: South Africa is is still a deeply unequal society with 'great disparaties in wealth', most notably between the different races, and 'as long as these conditions continue to

11 Preamble of the Constitution.
12 Ibid.
13 Section 7(1) of the Constitution.
14 Section 9 of the Constitution.
15 Section 10 of the Constitution.
16 Section 11 of the Constitution.
17 Section 12 of the Constitution.
18 Section 16 of the Constitution.
19 Section 19 of the Constitution.
20 Section 21 of the Constitution.
21 Section 25 of the Constitution.

exist (the transformative) aspiration (of the Constitution) will have a hollow ring.'[22]

2. The Constitution as regulatory framework

As Rossi points out, a constitution is not only of 'cultural relevance', but is 'primarily of legal significance' in that it serves as 'the founding, organising and limiting source for the exercise of state power'. In South Africa the Constitution has been used on a number of occasions to test the constitutionality of 'law and conduct',[23] and even our President's conduct relating to 'security upgrades' at his private residence in Nkandla, KwaZulu-Natal Province has been declared a failure to 'uphold, defend and respect the Constitution as the supreme law of the land'[24] by the Constitutional Court.

The 'regulatory framework' of the Constitution is further reflected in the constitutional principles of constitutional supremacy, separation of powers and 'checks and balances'.[25] The doctrine of separation of powers lies central to judicial independence and judicial review, which is a characteristic of a constitution as 'regulatory framework'.

3. Amendment of the Constitution as guarantee to self-preservation

An 'intelligently designed' constitution, according to Rossi, provides for 'flexibility clauses and the possibility of amendment', and a constitution 'that is not amendable will, once it is incapable of solving the problems of its time convincingly, first lose its acceptance and then lose its validity, before it is replaced by a new one.' The South African Constitution has been amended 17 times to date, and section 74 of the Constitution requires

---

22 *Soobramoney v Minister of Health (KwaZulu-Natal)* 1998 (1) SA 765 (CC) paras 8–9.

23 Section 172(1)(a) of the Constitution.

24 *The Economic Freedom Fighters and The Speaker of the National Assembly, Republic of South Africa, President Jacob Gedleyihlekisa Zuma, and the Public Protector* 2016 (3) SA 580 (CC) para 83.

25 Iain Currie and Johan De Waal, *The Bill of Rights Handbook*, (6th Edition, 2005), 18 et seqq.

special procedures and majorities that have to be adhered to in order to prevent the Constitution from being amended too easily.[26] It is therefore 'flexible' in that way, and definitely 'future-oriented and progressive'.

The next part of the paper will focus on Rossi's concept of 'democratic flexibility' which is reflected in, as he describes, 'governance for a limited period of time', in 'legislative amendment as the standard type of law', and finally in 'political self-restriction'.

III. Democratic flexibility

The South African Constitution provides in its preamble that our Constitution is to 'lay the foundations for a democratic and open society in which government is based on the will of the people and every citizen is equally protected by law'. Democracy is also a basic constitutional principle of our constitutional order, and is mentioned in several places in the Constitution. Democracy cannot be described as a static concept, as the will of the people is known to be changeable as time goes by.

1. Governance for a limited period of time

The South African Constitution recognises three types of democracy: representative democracy, participatory democracy, and direct democracy. It is, however, the first form of democracy, namely representative democracy, upon which our Constitution is founded, specifically by

---

26 Sections 1 and 74(1) of the Constitution may be amended by a bill passed by the National Assembly, with a supporting vote of at least 75 per cent of its members, and the National Council of Provinces, with a supporting vote of at least six provinces. The Bill of Rights may be amended by a bill passed by the National Assembly, with a supporting vote of at least two thirds of its members, and the National Council of Provinces, with a supporting vote of at least six provinces. Any other provision of the Constitution may be amended by a bill passed by the National Assembly, with a supporting vote of at least two thirds of its members, and also by the National Council of Provinces, with a supporting vote of at least six provinces, if the amendment relates to a matter that affects the Council, or alters provincial boundaries, powers, functions or institutions; or amends a provision that deals specifically with a provincial matter.

guaranteeing political rights in the Bill of Rights.[27] It is through representative democracy that the will of the people is expressed, that is in turn brought to fruition by the legislature. The legislature exercises the will of the people by enacting new laws, which is a central characteristic of governance. Several pieces of legislation have been enacted in recent years that reflect the founding values of human dignity, equality and freedom, or to ensure that effect is given to provisions in the Constitution. Examples of constitutional order-laws abound;[28] two notable examples include the Civil Union Act 17 of 2006, which provides for the legalisation of same-sex marriage, and the Promotion of Equality and Prevention of Unfair Discrimination Act 4 of 2000, which, inter alia, prohibits hate speech. However, the South African legislature very often runs into difficulty in passing new laws, as a balance has to be struck between enacting laws as part of governmental power, and ensuring that these laws reflect the will of the people in a multi-party democracy.

Rossi further points out that laws 'remain in force and effect even beyond the duration of a legislative period', which is true even for South Africa. For example, several pieces of legislation adopted before 1994 are still in operation, provided of course that they are consistent with the Constitution.

2. Legislative amendment as the standard type of law

Rossi's 'flexibility' of democracy is not only reflected in the ability of the legislature to enact new legislation, but also in the ability to amend and repeal laws. Racially-motivated apartheid-era legislation was automatically

27 Iain Currie and Johan De Waal, *The Bill of Rights Handbook*, (6th Edition, 2005), 14 et seq.

28 The Recognition of Customary Marriages Act 120 of 1998 gives effect to 'marriages concluded under any tradition, or a system of religious, personal or family law' in terms of section 15(3) of the Constitution; the Promotion of Access to Information Act 2 of 2000 gives effect to the right to access to information, the Promotion of Administrative Justice Act 3 of 2000 gives effect to the right to just administrative action, and various labour laws were adopted in terms of section 23 of the Constitution (for example the Labour Relations Act 66 of 1995, the Basic Conditions of Employment Act 75 of 1997, the Employment Equity Act 55 of 1998, to name a few).

invalidated as a result of its inconsistency with the Constitution,[29] whereas other pre-1994 laws were amended to ensure its constitutional validity.

However, as Rossi states, it is the 'everyday business of the legislator' rather to amend existing laws, and not to enact new laws. An example of a looming, highly divisive, legislative amendment involves the continued membership of South Africa to the International Criminal Court.[30] The precursor to this looming legislative amendment is the saga involving South Africa's decidedly embarrassing and controversial failure to arrest and surrender President Al-Bashir from the Sudan when he visited the country in 2015 to attend an African Union summit. The opportunity of South Africa to have arrested and surrendered Al-Bashir to the international criminal court was not only a failure to fulfil international legal obligations, but also a failure to act in conformity with our own Constitution[31] and existing legislation.[32] In reaction to the controversy caused by the failure to arrest and surrender Al-Bashir, the South African national executive delivered a notice of withdrawal from the Rome Statute of the ICC to the Secretary-General of the United Nations.[33] This shocking move by the executive was done without prior parliamentary approval, which gave rise to a North Gauteng High Court application by the Democratic Alliance to declare the decision by the executive to withdraw as member state from the International Criminal Court and its subsequent notice of withdrawal as unconstitutional and invalid.[34] Shortly after the withdrawal notice the Minister of Justice and Correctional Services also tabled a bill to repeal the South African Implementation of the Rome Statute Act.[35] The North Gauteng High Court declared the decision to withdraw from the Rome

29 Section 172(1)(a) of the Constitution.

30 Mispa Roux,(2018) *Tydskrif vir die Suid-Afrikaanse Reg (TSAR)* 2018,106 (114).

31 Sections 1, 2, 7(2), 8(1), 10-12, 39(2), 231(4), 232 and 233 of the Constitution.

32 Diplomatic Immunities and Privileges Act 37 of 2001; and Implementation of the Rome Statute of the International Criminal Court Act 27 of 2002.

33 Declaratory statement by the Republic of South Africa on the decision to withdraw from the Rome Statute of the International Criminal Court, United Nations Treaty Collection, reference: CN 786.2016.TREATIES-XVIII.10 (Depositary Notification), 19 Oct 2016.

34 *Democratic Alliance v Minister of International Relations and Cooperation* 2017 3 SA 212 (GP).

35 Implementation of the Rome Statute of the International Criminal Court Repeal Bill B 23—2016.

Statute and the notice of withdrawal without parliamentary approval unconstitutional and invalid, and ordered the Minister of International Relations and Cooperation, the Minister of Justice and Correctional Services, and the President of South Africa to revoke the notice of withdrawal.[36] Fortunately the government complied with the court order, and revoked the notice of withdrawal.[37] In December 2017, the International Crimes Bill was tabled in parliament.[38] It is envisaged that South Africa will in all probability withdraw from its ICC membership, undoubtedly as a result of growing push-back on the African continent against the ongoing relationship between African states with the ICC. African criticism against the International Criminal Court specifically surrounds the controversy regarding 'selective enforcement' of international criminal justice and claims of neo-colonialism.[39]

3. Political self-restriction

This example of a unilateral decision by the national executive being challenged by a political opposition party is a perfect example of Rossi's description of democratic flexibility reflected in political self-restriction. South Africans have come to expect opposition parties to bring court applications challenging the legislature's new laws, amendments, and repeals. These laws, amendments and repeals attract harsh criticism and heated debate, both in parliament and in civil society. Arguably the most controversial bills that have been tabled in parliament are the Prevention

36 *Democratic Alliance v Minister of International Relations and Cooperation* 2017 3 SA 212 (GP) para 84.

37 South Africa: Withdrawal of Notification of Withdrawal, United Nations Treaty Collection, reference: CN 121.2017.TREATIES-XVIII.10 (Depositary Notification), 7 March 2017.

38 International Crimes Bill [B 37 – 2017].

39 Steve Odero, 'Politics of international criminal justice, the ICC's arrest warrant for Al Bashir and the African Union's neo-colonial conspirator thesis', in: Chacha Murungu and Japhet Biegon (eds), *Prosecuting International Crimes in Africa* (2011), 145; James Nyawo, *Selective Enforcement and International Criminal Law: The International Criminal Court and* Africa (2017), 187 et seqq.; Paulo Gaeta, 7 (2009), *Journal of International Criminal Justice (JICJ)*, 315; Mia Swart and Karin Krisch, 1 (2014), *African Journal of International Criminal Justice (AJICJ)*, 38; Gus Waschefort, 98 (2016) *International Review of the Red Cross (IRRC)*, 593 (611–615).

and Combating of Hate Crimes and Hate Speech Bill,[40] the Expropriation Bill,[41] the Protection of State Information Bill,[42] and the International Crimes Bill.[43] However, these all serve as excellent examples characterising our constitutional democracy and the role of the Constitution in preventing centralising of government power.

IV. Conclusion

To conclude, a comparison between South Africa and Germany is to be welcomed, especially considering the fact that the constitutional democracies of both states followed a period of gross denial and violation of human rights. In the case of Germany, the holocaust; in South Africa, apartheid. In both states the meaning and context behind the constitutional democracy was much more charged than in states that did not go through periods of mass atrocity and human rights violations.

At the time when negotiations started for the drafting of the Constitution, the starkest inequality experienced in South Africa was along racial lines. Today South African society is still unequal, the starkest inequality being along social and economic circumstances. At first glance it seems to be non-racist, but the reality is that white South Africans are still socially and economically advantaged above the majority black South Africans. Populist rhetoric finds fertile soil in South Africa; perhaps one of the reasons Bell Pottinger's 'white monopoly capital'[44] was easily repeated and believed was because of an element of truth. The #feesmustfall movement often turned to the fact that the majority students studying at economically exclusive universities happen to be mostly English- and Afrikaans-speaking white South Africans.[45] The so-called 'born free generation' is disillusioned with the difference between the South Africa they were promised, and the South Africa they got.

It is in this context that the Constitution has to transform again by coming into its own by realising its purpose in healing the divisions of the past and

40 Prevention and Combating of Hate Crimes and Hate Speech Bill [B – 2016].

41 Expropriation Bill [B4 – 2015].

42 Protection of State Information Bill [B6D – 2010].

43 See fn. 38.

44 N.N., 'Report fingers Bell Pottinger in "white monopoly capital" campaign', in: Times LIVE (04-09-2017).

45 Nuran Davids and Yusef Waghid, '#FeesMustFall: History of South African student protests reflects inequality's grip', in: *Mail & Guardian* (10-10-2016).

improving the quality of life of all South African citizens. At the same time as being transformative, and as it were, flexible, it will have to provide much-needed stability in a South African society that is finding it a challenge to continue believing in the high aspirations of the constitutional project. Conceivably the biggest test for the 'transformative' South African Constitution is whether it can reinvent itself by shifting its focus in addressing the great disparities still experienced in social and economic circumstances. It is very apparent that the South African Constitution cannot ignore the ever-changing context within which it finds application. Our Constitution is amendable, therefore an 'intelligent' one as Rossi describes, but the risk of our Constitution being replaced by a new one lies not in its failure to be amendable, but in being found as 'incapable of solving the problems of its time convincingly', thereby first losing acceptance and credibility, and then finally, its validity.

Bibliography

Iain Currie and Johan De Waal, *The Bill of Rights Handbook* (6th Edition, Juta, Cape Town 2013).

Nuran David and Yusef Waghid, '#FeesMustFall: History of South African student protests reflects inequality's grip', in: *Mail & Guardian* (10-10-2016), https://mg.co.za/article/2016-10-10-feesmustfall-history-of-south-african-student-protests-reflects-inequalitys-grip (07-05-2018).

Pierre De Vos and Warren Freedman (eds), *South African Constitutional Law in Context,* (Oxford University Press Southern Africa, South Africa 2014).

Paulo Gaeta, 'Does President Al Bashir enjoy immunity from arrest?' 7 (2009) *Journal of International Criminal Justice (JICJ)*, 315.

Karl E. Klare, 'Legal culture and transformative constitutionalism' 14 (1998) *South African Journal on Human Rights (SAJHR)*, 146.

Etienne Mureinik, 'A bridge to where? Introducing the interim Bill of Rights' 10 (1994) *South African Journal on Human Rights (SAJHR)*, 31.

N.N., 'Report fingers Bell Pottinger in "white monopoly capital" campaign', in *Times LIVE* (04-09-2017), https://www.timeslive.co.za/news/south-africa/2017-09-04-report-fingers-bell-pottinger-in-white-monopoly-capital-campaign/ (07-05-2018).

James Nyawo, *Selective Enforcement and International Criminal Law: The International Criminal Court and Africa* (Intersentsia, Cambridge 2017).

Steve Odero, 'Politics of international criminal justice, the ICC's arrest warrant for Al Bashir and the African Union's neo-colonial conspirator thesis', in: Chacha Murungu and Japhet Biegon (eds), *Prosecuting International Crimes in Africa* (Pretoria University Law Press, Cape Town 2011), 145.

Mispa Roux, 'Obstacles to the prevention of gross human rights violations' *Tydskrif vir die Suid-Afrikaanse Reg (TSAR)* 2018, 106.

Mia Swart and Karin Krisch, 'Irreconcilable differences? An analysis of the standoff between the African Union and the International Criminal Court' 1 (2014) *African Journal of International Criminal Justice (AJICJ)*, 38.

Gus Waschefort, 'Africa and international humanitarian law: The more things change, the more they stay the same' 98 (2016) *International Review of the Red Cross (IPRC)*, 593.

Register of cases

Democratic Alliance v Minister of International Relations and Cooperation 2017 3 SA 212 (GP).

Economic Freedom Fighters and The Speaker of the National Assembly, Republic of South Africa, President Jacob Gedleyihlekisa Zuma, and the Public Protector 2016 3 SA 580 (CC).

Ex parte Chairperson of the Constitutional Assembly: in re Certification of the Constitution of the Republic of South Africa 1996 (First Certification Judgment) 1996 4 SA 744 CC; Certification of the Amended Text of the Constitution of the Republic of South Africa, 1996 (Second Certification Judgment) 1997 2 SA 97 (CC).

Soobramoney v Minister of Health (KwaZulu-Natal) 1998 1 SA 765 (CC).

Discrimination in Working Life and Anti-Discrimination Law – Experiments and Experiences in Germany and Europe

*Martina Benecke**

Abstract: *Ten years ago, the European directives against discrimination were implemented into national law. The directives ended a long period of a passionate and emotional discussion about discrimination in working life, and were accompanied by hopes on one side and fears on the other. Ten years later, the issues are quite different from the original hopes and fears. This paper will summarise the experiences and the focus in practice and legislation.*

* Martina Benecke, *Dr. iur.*; Professor, University of Augsburg, Faculty of Law. Chair for Civil Law, Commercial Law, Labor Law and Economic Law.

I. Introduction: An era of experiments and experiences in legislation against discrimination

In the 1990s, legislation against discrimination had come into the focus of the EU.[1] As a result, the EU passed four new or revised directives around the year 2000:

- Council Directive 2000/43/EC of 29 June 2000 implementing the principle of equal treatment between persons irrespective of racial or ethnic origin,
- Council Directive 2000/78/EC of 27 November 2000 establishing a general framework for equal treatment in employment and occupation,
- Directive 2002/73/EC of the European Parliament and of the Council of 23 September 2002 amending Council Directive 76/207/EEC on the implementation of the principle of equal treatment for men and women as regards access to employment, vocational training and promotion, and working conditions, and
- Council Directive 2004/113/EC of 13 December 2004 implementing the principle of equal treatment between men and women in the access to and supply of goods and services.

With a small delay, Germany implemented these directives into national law by adopting the General Equal Treatment Act (*Allgemeines Gleichbehandlungsgesetz*, AGG).[2] Note that the term 'discrimination' does not appear in the name of the Act. This name is the result of a long discussion,

1 Comparison of European equality law in 2003: Mark Bell and Lisa Waddington, 28 (2003) *European Law Review (E.L.R.)*, 349.

2 Official citation manner: Allgemeines Gleichbehandlungsgesetz vom 14. August 2006 (BGBl. I S. 1897), last amended by Article 8 of the law dated 3 April

which is typical for this era. For Germany and most of the other Member States of the EU, anti-discrimination legislation was a new, special and quite sensitive subject. Of course, there had been legislation against gender discrimination and disabilities acts, but hardly anyone had cared about age discrimination. Ten years ago, in the European Year of Equal Opportunities for All (2007)[3], most Member States implemented the directives into their domestic law.

So whilst some advocated as much protection against discrimination as possible, others worried about fraud and feared innumerable claims.[4] More than ten years later, most experiences show that neither approach was entirely reasonable. There had been some legal proceedings, but not an extraordinary number of them, and some instances of fraud, but the main problems were unexpected ones.

Nearly all legal proceedings focus on the fields of employment law and social law. This correlates with the subject matter of the directives, especially Directive 2000/78/EC and Directive 2002/73/EC. Apart from that, discrimination is more likely to be found in the processes of working life than in the process of buying an apple. Furthermore, most legal proceedings were filed in Germany, for the obvious reason is that Germany is the most populous country of the EU. Apart from that, Germans have a reputation for knowing their rights and being willing to go to court, and perhaps for being particularly sensitive to discrimination.[5]

In the following paper, I will discuss the main legislation in Germany and the other Member States – the implementation of which into domestic law has resulted in some intriguing experiments. Because of this, courts faced new challenges. Over the last ten years, several legal proceedings and

2013 (BGBl. I S. 610). For an English version, see http://www.antidiskriminierungsstelle.de/SharedDocs/Downloads/DE/publikationen/AGG/agg_in_englischer_Sprache.html

3 Decision No 771/2006/EC of the European Parliament and of the Council of 17 May 2006 establishing the European Year of Equal Opportunities for All (2007) – towards a just society, OJ L 146 of 31.5.2006. See also Communication from the Commission to the Council, the European Parliament, the European Economic and Social Committee and the Committee of the Regions - Implementation, results and overall assessment of the 2007 European Year of Equal Opportunities for All {SEC(2009)781} /COM/2009/0269 final).

4 Summary of the discussion: Tobias Lock, 38 (2013), *European Law Review (E.L.R.),* 655 (659).

5 In Eastern Europe, the society seems to be more reluctant concerning anti-discrimination law, see Barbara Havelková, 17 (2016) *German Law Journal (GLJ)*, 2016, 627.

important judgments have led to some interesting experiences. Based on these experiences, my aim is to evaluate some European, and especially German, anti-discrimination legislation.

II. Prosecution of discrimination and available sanctions

The first matter, comprising three independent issues, concerns the legal consequences of a discriminating act, its sanctioning and the method of prosecution. First, the legislature has to decide whether an act of discrimination is to be considered as a crime, an offence or a civil wrong. This correlates with the question of the persons authorised to prosecute such discrimination. It may be the law enforcement agency of the Member State, some kind of NGO, or the discriminated person as the injured party. The third inter-dependent matter concerns the sanctions for the discrimination which, due to its importance, merits a section of its own.

Some Member States of the EU opted for a solution in the field of criminal law or in the law of offences. Others – including Germany – opted for solutions in the field of civil law. Some chose a combination of both solutions – for example, racial discrimination is treated as a crime[6], but age discrimination leads only to a civil claim. The most common solution is a solution in civil law, but this leads to a second option: Is there a possibility of collective action, or must the discriminated person assert his or her rights and claims individually?

During the legislative process, I voted for a solution in offence law[7] and I am still not convinced that the current law is the best solution. If a certain act is a legal criminal offence, this legal implementation clarifies the immediate concerns of the state that the law is designed to address. Furthermore, prosecution of discrimination is not the responsibility of the discriminated person but the responsibility of the state. Therefore, there is less danger of fraud. On the other hand, the discriminated person may be too shy or intimidated to take legal action against the discrimination.

On the other hand, the responsibility of the discriminated person has several benefits. It ensures a prosecution even if the discrimination may seem

6 On the subjects of racial justice in Germany and the current law see Wolfram Bechtel, 'The State of Racial Justice in Germany', in: María Elósegui and Cristina Hermida (eds), *Policies and Courts' Legal Reasoning in Europe*, (60, 2017), 157.

7 Martina Benecke and Gisela Kern, 16 (2005) *Europäische Zeitschrift für Wirtschaftsrecht (EuZW)*, 360.

rather trivial. In particular, the sanction of prosecution immediately benefits the discriminated person und may restore his or her dignity. Over the last ten years, there have been several instances of civil proceedings against discrimination, and very few criminal proceedings. It may be that experience has shown that the civil compensation for victims by means of civil action against the offender is the more effective path. However, one must add that there are some cases of fraud and abuse of rights – and they will be addressed below. Also discussed below will be the issue of collective action, because of its connection with the question of institutions extending the protection against discrimination.

III. Persons protected and persons responsible in cases of discrimination

When considering the question of possible claimants and defendants under anti-discrimination laws, one must differentiate between employment law legislation and discrimination under civil law, Sections 19–21 of the General Equal Treatment Act (AGG). The latter pools certain listed legal relations under civil law – especially bulk business, private insurance and housing rental (see Section 19 AGG). Of course, both the claimant and opponent may be subject to private law. This part of the AGG has turned to be of little practical importance, with the exception of very few cases concerning private insurance.[8]

In practice, the AGG is a part of the employment laws, and most of its rules deal with employment law – especially the protection of employees against discrimination (Sections 6–18 AGG). Pursuant to the anti-discrimination directives,[9] Section 6 AGG lists the persons covered. The term 'employee' as a possible claimant refers not only to persons in dependent employment and persons employed for the purposes of their vocational training, but also to persons of similar status on account of their dependent economic status. Section 6(3) points out that insofar as the conditions for access to gainful employment and promotion are affected, the provisions apply, mutatis mutandis, to the self-employed and to members of an organ of an enterprise, in particular directors and board members. In most cases, the defendant is the employer who, of course, may be a natural or a legal person or an unincorporated firm with the legal capacity to employ persons.

8 Cases in Germany summed up by Michael Heese, (65) 2012 *Neue Juristische Wochenschrift (NJW)*, 572.

9 See above p. 104.

Pursuant to Section 18 AGG, the provisions set out in Part 2 concerning employment law apply, mutatis mutandis, to membership of or involvement in a party to a collective bargaining agreement and similar organisations. This regulation may give an entitlement when the rejection of a membership in the listed organisation turns out to be discriminatory. Fortunately, this is hardly ever the case.[10]

IV. Prohibited grounds of discrimination

1. Legal situation in Germany

The name of the German Anti-discrimination act – *Allgemeines Gleichbehandlungsgesetz* (General Equal Treatment Act) – is misleading. It suggests that the purpose of the law is to ensure equal treatment of all the possible claimants addressed above. On the contrary – not every discrimination, unequal treatment or harassment will lead to legal consequences and sanctions. It is characteristic for each anti-discrimination legislation – directives as well as their national implementations – to refer to certain prohibited grounds of discrimination.

In the German act, these are set out in Section 1 AGG.[11] The translated wording is the following: "The purpose of this Act is to prevent or to stop discrimination on the grounds of race or ethnic origin, gender, religion or belief, disability, age or sexual orientation." The discrimination grounds have not only been established to protect minorities. As a result, 'sexual orientation' not only protects homosexual people, but in the same way heterosexual and religion covers not only the religions or minorities but also the mainstream one or ones. Age means old, young and middle-aged and gender means each gender.[12] On the other hand, only disabled persons are

---

10 Monika Schlachter, in: Rudi Müller-Glöge, Ulrich Preis and Ingrid Schmidt (eds), *Erfurter Kommentar zum Arbeitsrecht* (17th Edition, 2017), AGG § 18 para 2.

11 Wording of the paragraph: *§ 1 Ziel des Gesetzes: - Ziel des Gesetzes ist, Benachteiligungen aus Gründen der Rasse oder wegen der ethnischen Herkunft, des Geschlechts, der Religion oder Weltanschauung, einer Behinderung, des Alters oder der sexuellen Identität zu verhindern oder zu beseitigen.*

12 Monika Schlachter, in: Rudi Müller-Glöge, Ulrich Preis and Ingrid Schmidt (eds), *Erfurter Kommentar zum Arbeitsrecht* (17th Edition, 2017), AGG § 1 para. 12 et seqq.

protected against discrimination – a discrimination as a result of not being disabled is hardly imaginable – and 'race' does not suggest the existence of human races but takes a stand against racism and racial discrimination.[13]

Pursuant to Section 3 AGG, the protection against discrimination includes the following acts: direct discrimination,[14] indirect discrimination,[15] harassment, sexual harassment and instructions to discriminate against a person. As mentioned above, these acts have to be motivated by one of grounds referred to under Section 1 AGG. Furthermore, the law provides some possible reasons of justification, so a different treatment on the prohibited grounds does not necessarily always have to be discriminatory. For example, pursuant to Section 8 AGG, differences of treatment may be permissible on grounds of occupational requirements.

2. Legal comparison in Europe: More or less prohibited grounds?

The prohibited grounds are the main item of each anti-discrimination act. Comparison of the different laws shows that several Member States have installed further prohibited grounds into their acts – such as marital or family status, financial status or membership in a party or trade union. Some Member States even regard their list of the prohibited ground as a non-exhaustive list.[16]

It must be asked whether this is a better concept. At first glance, because the struggle against discrimination is a most important issue, it may appear that the scope of an anti-discrimination act cannot be wide enough. In Germany, there is a slogan – *viel hilft viel* – which may be translated as "much helps much". Quoting it leads to some reservations, because in legislation much is not the same as best or optimal. This already emerges from the fact that the wider the scope of a law is, the greater also the risk of legal uncertainty.

13 Siobhan McInerney, 56 (2008) *International and Comparative Law*, 211.

14 A case of direct discrimination is to be assumed where one person has been treated less favourably than another has been or would be treated in a comparable situation on any of the grounds referred to under Section 1.

15 Indirect discrimination occurs where an apparently neutral provision, criterion or practice would put persons at a particular disadvantage compared with other persons on any of the grounds referred to under Section 1, unless that provision, criterion or practice is objectively justified by a legitimate aim and the means of achieving that aim are appropriate and necessary.

16 See Martina Benecke, *Rechtsvergleich der europäischen Systeme zum Antidiskriminierungsrecht*, 2010, p. 19 et seqq., para. 68 et seqq.

Legislation against discrimination has two aims: the prohibition and sanctioning of certain discriminatory acts, and also the political aim of increasing sensitivity and awareness against discrimination on both sides. So, the European directives and the current German law point out the precise concerns of the legislature and, moreover, of society. In contrast, a non-exhaustive list is necessarily vague and difficult to apply. It relativises the concern of the legislature, and the act gives the impression of an obscure and unrealistic entity.

A very long and extensive list of prohibited ground raises similar concerns. For example, the anti-discrimination act of Hungary lists 19 prohibited grounds. I cannot fault a critic who says this is a foolish law. Experience has shown that the anti-discrimination acts with an exhaustive list of prohibited grounds going no further than the areas of discrimination set out in directives have demonstrated the greatest practical importance. If there are legal gaps, there are usually also ways to close them. For example, there has been a discussion, about whether discrimination on grounds of an individual's weight should be incorporated into anti-discrimination law.[17] In 2014, the CJEU ruled that obesity of a worker constitutes a 'disability' within the meaning of Directive 2000/78/EC of 27 November 2000.[18]

3. Practical significance of the listed grounds

The question of the practical significance of the particular prohibited grounds leads to some surprising answers. The situation at the turn of the century was the following: There were two prohibited grounds, which were familiar and generally accepted – gender and the protection of disabled persons. In most countries, including Germany, laws concerning these matters had existed for more than twenty years. The other prohibited grounds were less familiar as subjects of civil law. Some hypothesized that the prohibition

17 International comparison between U.S. and France: Michael Huggins, 38 (2015) *Fordham International Law Journal (Fordham Int'l L. J.)*, 889.

18 This is the case where it entails a limitation resulting in particular from long-term physical, mental or psychological impairments which in interaction with various barriers may hinder the full and effective participation of the person concerned in professional life on an equal basis with other workers; Judgment of the European Court of Justice, Case 354/13 18.12.2014, *Fag og Arbejde*, ECLI:EU:C:2014:2463.

of racial discrimination might become the most important item. Hardly anyone considered the importance of protection against discrimination because of age – especially of young age. For example, most collective agreements provided more vacation days for older workers than for younger workers, and payment in public services was essentially age-dependent.

Ten years later, most legal proceedings under the anti-discrimination law seem to concern age discrimination.[19] Apart from that, gender discrimination and claims of disabled people have not become less important than ten years ago. Claims on the grounds of racial discrimination mostly concern religion and dress codes, especially the Islamic headscarf. The attitude of employers and customers towards Islamic women wearing headscarves seems to be one of the most controversial issues at the moment,[20] although overall more legal proceedings relate to age discrimination.

V. Legal consequences of discrimination, and sanctions against discrimination

1. Challenges for the legislature

One of the challenges of anti-discrimination acts for legislatures is defining the sanctions that the law provides in cases of discrimination. The directives

---

19 See only European Court of Justice European Court of Justice 22/11/2005, Case 144/04, *Mangold*, ECLI:EU:C:2005:709; European Court of Justice, Case 411/05, 16.10.2007 *Palacios*, ECLI:EU:C:2007:604; European Court of Justice, Case 388/07, 5.3.2009, *Age Concern England*, ECLI:EU:C:2009:128; European Court of Justice, Case 555/07, 19.1.2010, *Kücükdeveci*, ECLI:EU:C:2010:21; European Court of Justice, Case 45/09, 12.10.2010, *Rosenbladt*, ECLI:EU:C:2010:601; European Court of Justice, Case 499/08, 20.10.2010, *Ingeniørforeningen i Danmark/Andersen*, ECLI:EU:C:2010:600; European Court of Justice, Case 297/10, 08.09.2011, *Hennings*, ECLI:EU:C:2011:560; European Court of Justice, Case 501/12, 19.06.2014, *Specht*, ECLI:EU:C:2014:2005; International comparison see Joanna N. Lahey, 32 (2010) *Res Aging*, 679. On the issue of demographic chance as a possible reason Melanie Regine Hack, 3 (2010) *Europäische Zeitschrift für Arbeitsrecht (EuZA)*, 347.

20 See from a comparative legal perspective concerning German and UK law Tobias Lock, 38 (2013) *European Law Review (E.L.R.)*, 655; relating to Germany Joyce Marie Mushaben, 14 (2013) *German Law Journal (GLJ)*, 1757. The German problem is even discussed in Canada. See Tina Mirzazadeh 28 (2015) *Pacific McGeorge Global Business & Development Law Journal*, 411.

require that Member States to lay down sanctions rules applicable to infringements of the national provisions adopted pursuant to each directive, and to take all measures necessary to ensure that they are applied. The sanctions – which may comprise the payment of compensation to the victim – must be effective, proportionate and dissuasive.[21]

With this wording, the directives point towards the possibility of a solution in the form of civil claims – in particular, the payment of compensation to the victim. As mentioned above, most Member States (including Germany) voted for this option. The result is a quite exceptional legal regulation. Because of the provisions of the directives, the law has to take into account both the prevention of discrimination and compensation for damages.

This leads to three peculiarities of damages in German anti-discrimination law.[22] Firstly, the directives demand liability without fault, although traditional German indemnity law and tort law are based on the principle of fault. Secondly, the required sanctioning and dissuasive effect may be inconsistent with the proportionality of the damages. Thirdly, the directives demand a sanction even in cases without an actual victim.[23]

2. Current German law

Current German law – especially Section 15 AGG – is a complex compromise between these demands. It distinguishes between material and non-material damages, damages and compensation. Pursuant to Section 15(1)

---

21 Council Directive (EC) No 2000/43/EU of 29 June 2000, art. 15; Council Directive (EC) No 2000/78 of 27 November 2000, art. 17; Council Directive (EC) No 2006/54 of 5 July 2006, art. 25.

22 See Martina Benecke, in: Beate Gsell, Wolfgang Krüger, Stephan Lorenz and Jörg Mayer (eds), *beck-online.GROSSKOMMENTAR BeckOGK* (Edition 1.4.2017) AGG § 15 para. 1.

23 Such a case is the origin of the *Feryn* judgment – Judgment of the European Court of Justice, Case 54/07, 10.7.2008, *Feryn*, ECLI:EU:C:2008:397. The director of the company Feryn had given a public statement that his undertaking was looking to recruit fitters but that it could not employ "immigrants" because its customers were reluctant to give them access to their private residences. There is little doubt about the racial discrimination, but because of the public statement, one cannot identify a certain violated person.

AGG, the employer is under an obligation to compensate the damage arising from a violation of the prohibition of discrimination. It is important that this does not apply where the employer is not responsible for the breach of duty.

By contrast, no responsibility is necessary if the damage arising does not constitute economic loss. In this case, the employee may demand appropriate monetary compensation. This compensation is limited: In the event of non-recruitment, it may not exceed three monthly salaries if the employee would not have been recruited if the selection had been made without unequal treatment. Apart from that, pursuant to Section 15(6) AGG, any violation of the prohibition of discrimination on the part of the employer will not justify a claim to the establishment of an employment relationship, a vocational training relationship or to promotion, unless such a relationship or promotion results from another legal ground. So in employment law there is generally no obligation to contract.[24]

3. Experiences and evaluation

Since the General Equal Treatment Act (AGG) entered into force, critics have raised doubts that the current legislation meets the demands of the directives – which, as has already been stated, require 'effective, proportionate and dissuasive' sanctions. Apart from that, the claim for damages is fault-based, whereas the directives demand otherwise. Only the claim for non-material damages fulfils this requirement: Section 15 AGG has to be seen in conjunction with Section 22 AGG. This legal regulation lessens the burden of proof of the claimant, and it may even shift when the person claiming to be the victim of discrimination can establish a presumption of discrimination. In this circumstances, it is for the respondent to prove that there has been no discrimination.[25]

Evaluating the law, one has to consider the most frequent application in practice – the application procedure. Most cases concern job advertisement

---

24 Concerning the obligation to contract in general civil law, see Franz Christian Ebert and Tobias Pinkel, 10 (2009) *German Law Journal (GLJ)*, 1417; Joachim Wiemann, 11 (2010) *German Law Journal (GLJ)*, 1131.

25 Communication from the Commission, the European Parliament, the European Economic and Social Committee and the Committee of the Regions about the application of Council Directive (EC) No. 2000/78 of 27 November 2000 establishing a general framework for equal treatment in employment and occupation, COM(2008) 225 final/2, p. 8.

with discriminatory wording – such as 'young applicants wanted'. Many other mistakes occur in the staffing procedure concerning disabled applicants. In these cases, it should be considered that it is almost impossible to prove that there has been no discrimination. It may be that the prevention of legal abuse is an argument in favour of the current law. There have been several cases of fraud that will be discussed below. An overview of the anti-discrimination law shows a great variety of legal consequences, but also quite similar monetary amounts. The amount of financial sanctions – penalty or damages – lies between a few hundred euros or even €10,000–30,000. Nobody in Europe has become rich (or impoverished!) as a result of a discrimination claim.

VI. Institutions against discrimination

The greatest differences between the national implementations of the directives may concern legal institutions against discrimination. Of course, there are courts applying the law – in some countries civil law, in others criminal law. Apart from that, Article 13 of the Racial Equality Council Directive 2000/43/EC demands that the Member States designate a body or bodies for the promotion of equal treatment of all persons without discrimination on the grounds of racial or ethnic origin. In accordance with the Directive, these bodies may form part of agencies charged at the national level with the defence of human rights or the safeguarding of individuals' rights.

Some Member States designated an existing body to be the Article 13 body, while others set up a new body. In several Member States, including Germany, the competences of their independent, specialised body include not only racial discrimination but also the other discrimination grounds. Furthermore, there is a wide variety of the competences allocated to such bodies.

Apart from that, all implementations of the anti-discrimination directives share the commonality that the prosecution of discrimination is never the sole responsibility of the independent body. In some Member States, the specialised body has been given the authority to impose fines and/or to support discriminated claimants during legal proceedings. All specialised bodies offer consulting services concerning legal and other options to fight against discrimination.

Another fundamental legislative decision was the question of popular actions. Some Member States - except Germany – provide for collective actions against discriminatory acts. The complaining party may be the specialised body, a public institution and/or a NGO. Usually, the collective action depends on the consent of the discriminated person, but some Member States provide for the possibility of collective action even without consent. One can debate for hours the question of whether legal proceedings against discrimination without the consent of the victim are sensible. Of course, the dissuasive effect is greater, because attempts to intimidate the victim are useless. Nevertheless, it is a questionable matter to start legal proceedings without the consent of the most affected person. Germany does not provide for the possibility of collective actions in such a case.

In Germany, Sections 25–30 AGG regulate the formation, legal status and competences of the specialised body. It is called the Federal Anti-Discrimination Agency.[26] The agency is attached to the Federal Ministry for Family Affairs, Senior Citizens, Women and Youth (BMFFSJ), but is independent in its decisions and is not subject to instructions or directives of the minister. The agency works under the control of its head, whose legal status is regulated in Section 26 AGG.

Section 27 AGG sets out the tasks of the Anti-Discrimination Agency, and Section 28 AGG its competences. Concerning the tasks, it differentiates between tasks to the benefit of individuals and tasks concerning society as a whole. Accordingly, any person who believes he or she has been discriminated against on any of the prohibited grounds may take their case to the Federal Anti-Discrimination Agency, which will give independent assistance. Pursuant to Section 27(3)–(5), the general tasks of the Agency concerning society are publicity work, measures to prevent discrimination, and academic studies into such discrimination. Compared with other specialised bodies in Europe, its position is relatively weak.[27] The competences of the Agency comprise requests to the involved parties to make submissions, requests to supply necessary information, and co-operation with NGOs.

The Federal Anti-Discrimination Agency is not in an ideal position, and suffers from two chronic problems. Although its financial resources seem to be considerable, it is understaffed,[28] and its employees have little legal expertise. But the main problem of the Federal Anti-Discrimination Agency

---

26 In German, *Antidiskriminierungsstelle des Bundes*, http://www.antidiskriminierungsstelle.de.

27 Melanie Regine Hack, 3 (2010) *Europäische Zeitschrift für Arbeitsrecht (EuZA)*, 347 (352 et seqq.).

28 Wolfram Bechtel, 'The State of Racial Justice in Germany', in: María Elósegui and Cristina Hermida (eds), *Policies and Courts' Legal Reasoning in Europe*, (60, 2017), 157 (162).

is its natural ideological orientation. Of course, its direction is as much a fight against discrimination as possible whereas I think a sensible fight against discrimination is the better solution.

VII. The problem of abuse of the law and fraud: major problem or a trivial matter?

1. Problems in law and society

One of the main problems of any legislation against discrimination is the possibility of abuse and fraud. The main problem itself is to blame for it. In principle, there is a broad consensus in society that discrimination is to blame, to proceed against and to fight. This leads to two other consensuses: first, that the victim of a discrimination is in need of legal help, and secondly that there have to be noticeable sanctions against the perpetrator.

If someone abuses anti-discrimination law or misuses it to commit fraud, this consensus is perverted and so is the legal system against discrimination. The abuser pretends to be a victim, though a sense of justice raises reluctance to allow this person to benefit and to penalize the act of the perpetrator. This leads to the main legal problem: The greater the benefits for the (apparent) victim, the stronger the incentive for abuse. In addition, legal help for real victims – such as a statutory easing of the burden of proof – facilitates abuse. On the other hand, sanctions for discrimination are the wrong legal consequence and the (apparent) perpetrator is the real victim.

Apart from the legal dilemma, the misuse of anti-discrimination law is a problem of society. Firstly, it jeopardises the consensus against discrimination. Secondly, it jeopardises the legal help for real victims of discrimination. As pointed out, naivety endangers discrimination and the real aim is a sensible fight against discrimination – but this is cheap criticism.

The real legal problems can be summed up in two questions. The first is the definition of abuse or fraud: Which conduct will lead to application of the legal rules, and which has to be excluded for reasons of abuse? One questions whether intent is essential and where the borderline between over-sensitive persons and real victims is located. Linked to this is the second question: do claims of over-sensitive individuals have to be accepted in order not to endanger the claims of the true victims of a mischievous discrimination?

2. Experiences in practice

Before the AGG was adopted, and in the first few years after its adoption, critics had feared an 'industry of claimants' and what they called (in a typical mixture of English and German) 'AGG-hopping'.[29] Ten years later, there is no evidence of an industry. Nevertheless, there are a considerable number of cases that lead to a discussion about the abuse of anti-discrimination law. They have in common claimants who brought a noticeable number of court proceedings, and nearly all of them relate to the processes concerning job applications. Some of these cases deal with disabled claimants. German law provides quite a complex procedure to ensure the protection of disabled applicants, and some applicants seem to apply for a lot of advertised positions, look for mistakes and consequently claim for compensation.[30]

The most discussed anti-discrimination claimant in Germany, and maybe even in Europe, is a Munich lawyer called Nils Kratzer.[31] He is middle-aged and passed his exams with an average grade. Usually his claims concern a job advertisement saying that the potential employer is looking for young applicants, e.g. 'young professionals', 'you will fit into our young and dynamic team', 'we are looking for job starters'. His applications may be described as made without love, and in many cases he is not qualified for the position.

The German Federal Labour Court (*Bundesarbeitsgericht*) is rather reluctant to assume a case of abuse of the law. In a 2016 judgment,[32] the Court stressed that the term *Bewerber für ein Beschäftigungsverhältnis* (applicant for an employment relationship) is a formal one, so the seriousness of the application is no necessary condition for the protection through the Act. Furthermore, the qualification for the position is not necessary, so it did not matter whether the potential employer was looking for applicants who passed their exams with outstanding marks. Neither is the quality of the application or the number of them of any relevance.

---

29 Christian Rolfs, 33 (2016) *Neue Zeitschrift für Arbeitsrecht (NZA)*, 586; Steffen Krieger, 27 (2016) *Europäische Zeitschrift für Wirtschaftsrecht (EuZW)*, 696 with English summary.

30 Martin Diller, 24 (2007) *Neue Zeitschrift für Arbeitsrecht (NZA)*, 1321.

31 See for example: http://www.spiegel.de/karriere/diskriminierung-bei-der-bewerbung-anwalt-aus-muenchen-gilt-als-agg-hopper-a-1062076.html.

32 BAG 19.5.2016 – 8 AZR 470/14, BAGE 155, 149.

In contrast, in another case the CJEU refused Mr. Kratzer the protection of the Anti-discrimination Directives.[33] The First Chamber has ruled that a situation in which a person who in making an application for a post does not seek to obtain that post, but only seeks the formal status as an applicant with the sole purpose of seeking compensation, does not fall within the definition of 'access to employment, to self-employment or to occupation', within the meaning of those provisions. If the requisite conditions under EU law are met, this may be considered to be an abuse of rights. To summarise the judgments, the CJEU is less reluctant than the Federal Labour Court of Germany.

In conclusion: these cases may be annoying, though they are entertaining. Although the abuse of the law is not the greatest problem of anti-discrimination law in Europe. As pointed out above, damages, compensation and penalties are moderate. If there are few opportunities to become rich, but many to become unpopular, working as an Anti-discrimination Act claimant is not the most attractive proposition.

VIII. Conclusion

Over ten years ago, the General Equal Treatment Act (AGG) was an experiment. Although Germany has considerable experience and tradition in fundamental rights review, there was no anti-discrimination act in civil law, and the few legal regulations concerning gender discrimination and protection of disabled persons were fragmentary. Even then, their main application field was employment law and working life. The same can be said of the AGG, which does not have any practical relevance in other fields of law.[34] I recall a 2006 conversation with a judge at the Federal Labour Court, who told me: "We – the judges – have had a first look at the AGG, and have no idea at all how to deal with this piece of law!"

Ten years, and some experiences later, the AGG has ceased to be an experiment and has – surprisingly – become quite a normal and ordinary act. Courts in Europe and its Member States had second and third looks at the acts, developing reasonable ideas about how to deal with anti-discrimination law. There is considerable legal certainty about the interpretation of the

33 European Court of Justice, Case 423/15, 28.7.2016, *Nils-Johannes Kratzer*, ECLI:EU:C:2016:604.

34 Very few cases concern private insurance law, e.g. age or sex discrimination in insurance conditions.

prohibited grounds, the illegal acts of discrimination and their legal consequences. The problem of abuse of the law is annoying, but the AGG has this problem in common with other protective legislation, such as consumer protection legislation. At least the law had some consequences, and it may have changed social attitudes in some way. Nevertheless, it cannot be said that private autonomy and freedom in business decision-making have been seriously jeopardised. In summary, I would like to appeal for a collective cool-down.

Bibliography

Wolfram Bechtel, 'The State of Racial Justice in Germany', in: María Elósegui and Cristina Hermida (eds), *Policies and Courts' Legal Reasoning in Europe,* Ius Gentium: Comparative Perspectives on Law and Justice (60, Springer International Publishing AG, Cham 2017, 157).

Mark Bell and Lisa Waddington, 'Reflecting on equalities in European equality law', 28 (2013) *European Law Review (E.L.R.)*, 349.

Martina Benecke and Gisela Kern, 'Sanktionen im Antidiskriminierungsrecht - Möglichkeiten und Grenzen der Umsetzung der europäischen Richtlinien im deutschen Recht', 16 (2005) *Europäische Zeitschrift für Wirtschaftsrecht (EuZW)*, 360.

Martina Benecke, *Rechtsvergleich der europäischen Systeme zum Antidiskriminierungsrecht*, Expertise im Auftrag der Antidiskriminierungsstelle des Bundes, 2010, http://www.antidiskriminierungsstelle.de/SharedDocs/Downloads/DE/publikationen/Expertisen/Expertise_Rechtsvergleich_europ_Systeme_zum_Antidiskr-Recht.pdf?__blob=publicationFile (27-02-2018).

Martin Diller, 'AGG-Hopping durch Schwerbehinderte', 24 (2007) *Neue Zeitschrift für Arbeitsrecht (NZA)*, 1321.

Franz Christian Ebert and Tobias Pinkel, 'Restricting freedom of contract through non-discrimination provisions: a comparison of the Draft Common Frame of Reference (DCFR) and the German «General Equality Law»', 10 (2009) *German Law Journal (GLJ)*, 1417.

beck-online.GROSSKOMMENTAR BeckOGK, Beate Gsell, Wolfgang Krüger, Stephan Lorenz and Jörg Mayer (eds) (Edition 1.4.2017, C.H.Beck, Munich, 2017).

Melanie Regine Hack, 'Impact or potential of anti-discrimination legislation in light of the demographic change – Comparisons between Norway and Germany', 3 (2010) *Europäische Zeitschrift für Arbeitsrecht (EuZA)*, 347.

Barbara Havelková, 'Resistance to anti-discrimination law in Central and Eastern Europe: a post-communist legacy?', 17 (2016) *German Law Journal (GLJ)*, 627.

Michael Heese, 'Offene Preisdiskriminierung und zivilrechtliches Benachteiligungsverbot', 65 (2012) *Neue Juristische Wochenschrift (NJW)*, 572.

Michael Huggins, 'Not «fit» for hire: the United States and France on weight discrimination in employment', 38 (2015) *Fordham International Law Journal (Fordham Int'l L. J.)*, 889.

Steffen Krieger, 'Rechtsmissbrauch durch «AGG-Hopping»', 27 (2016) *Europäische Zeitschrift für Wirtschaftsrecht (EuZW)*, 696.

Joanna N. Lahey, 'International Comparison of Age Discrimination Laws', 32 (2010) *Res Aging*, 679.

Tobias Lock, 'Religious freedom and belief discrimination in Germany and the United Kingdom: towards a common European standard?', 38 (2013) *European Law Review (E.L.R.)*, 655.

Siobhan McInerney, 'The Development of Legal Instruments to Combat Racism in a Diverse Europe', 56 (2007) *International & Comparative Law*, 211.

Tina Mirzazadeh, 'Discrimination in the name of secularism: a ban of religious symbols in Québec', 28 (2015) *Pacific McGeorge Global Business & Development Law Journal*, 411.

Erfurter Kommentar zum Arbeitsrecht, Rudi Müller-Glöge, Ulrich Preis and Ingrid Schmidt (eds) (17th Edition, C.H.Beck, Munich, 2017).

Joyce Marie Mushaben, 'Women between a rock and a hard place: state neutrality vs. EU antidiscrimination mandates in the German headscarf debate', 14 (2013) *German Law Journal (GLJ)*, 1757.

Christian Rolfs, 'AGG-Hopping', 33 (2016) *Neue Zeitschrift für Arbeitsrecht (NZA)*, 586.

Joachim Wiemann, 'Obligation to contract and the German general act of equal treatment (Allgemeines Gleichbehandlungsgesetz)', 11 (2010) *German Law Journal (GLJ)*, 1131.

Register of cases

Germany

BAG 19.5.2016 – 8 AZR 470/14, BAGE 155, 149.

European Court of Justice

European Court of Justice, Case 144/04, 22/11/2005, Mangold, ECLI:EU:C:2005:709.

European Court of Justice, Case 411/05, 16.10.2007, Palacios, ECLI:EU:C:2007:604.

European Court of Justice, Case 54/07, 10.7.2008, Feryn, ECLI:EU:C:2008:397.

European Court of Justice, Case 388/07, 5.3.2009, Age Concern England, ECLI:EU:C:2009:128.

European Court of Justice, Case 555/07, 19.1.2010, Kücükdeveci, ECLI:EU:C:2010:21.

European Court of Justice, Case 45/09, 12.10.2010, Rosenbladt, ECLI:EU:C:2010:601.

European Court of Justice, Case 499/08, 20.10.2010, Ingeniørforeningen i Danmark/Andersen, ECLI:EU:C:2010:600.

European Court of Justice, Case 297/10, 08.09.2011, Hennings, ECLI:EU:C:2011:560.

European Court of Justice, Case 501/12, 19.06.2014, Specht, ECLI:EU:C:2014:2005.

European Court of Justice, Case 354/13 18.12.2014, Fag og Arbejde, ECLI:EU:C:2014:2463.

European Court of Justice, Case 423/15, 28.7.2016, Nils-Johannes Kratzer, ECLI:EU:C:2016:604.

Beyond Mere Rules and Regulatory Frameworks: A Reply to M. Benecke, “Discrimination in Working Life and Anti-Discrimination Law – Experiments and Experiences in Germany and Europe”

*Radley Henrico**

I. Introduction

A vignette is given by Benecke of the manner in which certain European directives were noteworthy for informing the adoption of the General Equal Treatment Act (AGG)[1] in Germany. Initial reservations were expressed on

---

* Radley Henrico, *B.Proc., LL.B., LL.M., LL.D.*, Senior Lecturer in the Department of Procedural and Public Law, Faculty of Law, University of Johannesburg.

1 Allgemeines Gleichbehandlungsgesetz vom 14. August 2006 (BGBI. I S. 1897).

the part of scholars and judges alike as to the extent to which such an anti-discrimination law would be effective in the workplace and beyond. Since its adoption in 2006, greater factual and legal certainty now exists that the AGG has a definitive role to play in combatting discrimination in the workplace. But it would appear that uncertainty continues to overshadow the AGG, particularly regarding its practical relevance in areas of law beyond the workplace.

The purpose of this reply is to address some of the concerns raised by Benecke.[2] This is done with reference to unfair discrimination in the South African context. It is argued that unfair discrimination is regulated in terms of a legislative framework – informed by constitutional imperatives. It is further argued that, whilst disputes are capable of resolution in terms of the aforesaid framework, something more than a mere regulatory regime is required. This *something else* is insistence upon a celebratory culture of diversity in our society.

II. The Phenomenon of Unfair Discrimination in Society

Equality jurisprudence arises as a consequence of a necessity to address unfair discrimination in society. Benecke contends that unfair discrimination is more likely to arise in the workplace than 'in the process of buying an apple',[3] in other words, greater (civil) society. This is not unique to Germany. Whilst certainly not all, at least many reported instances of unfair discrimination in South Africa can be traced to the workplace.[4] A feasible

2 Aspects of this reply draw on the author's unpublished doctoral thesis, Radley Henrico, *Religious Discrimination in the South African Workplace* (Unpublished LLD Thesis, NWU 2016).

3 Martina Benecke p. 101.

4 See, for example, *Hoffman v. South African Airways,* 2000 1 SA 1 (CC) paras. 34–38; *Zabala v. Gold Reef City Casino,* 2009 1 BLLR 94 (LC) para. 21; *Motaung v. Department of Education,* 2013 34 ILJ 1199 (LC) para. 12; *FAWU v. Rainbow Chicken Farms,* 2000 1 BLLR 70 (LC) paras. 30–34; *Dlamini v. Green Four Security,* 2006 11 BLLR 1074 (LC) paras. 14–18; *Lewis v. Media24 Ltd,* 2010 31 ILJ 2416 LC paras. 32–45; *Kievits Kroon Country Estate (Pty) Ltd v. Mmoledi,* 2014 35 ILJ 209 (SCA) paras. 23–32; *SACTWU v. Berg River Textiles, a division of Seardel Group Trading (Pty) Ltd,* 2012 33 ILJ 972 (LC) paras. 38–48; *Department of Correctional Services v. POPCRU,* 2013 JOL 30347 (SCA) paras. 10–25. For non-workplace unfair discrimination cases, see *Christian Education South Africa v. Minister of Education,* 2000 4 SA 757 (CC) paras.

explanation is what I would call the 'proximity phenomenon', namely that the workplace, which is a micro-image of our macrocosmic society, is ripe terrain for potential conflict of rights by the respective parties to the employment relationship.[5]

Sensitivity to the notion of unfair discrimination on the part of Germans is shared by South Africans. A history steeped in inequality and arbitrary, capricious treatment of persons on the basis of race officially recognised through the apartheid regime is a sombre reminder of just how pertinent and sensitive unfair discrimination was and continues to be in our equality jurisprudence.[6] Ongoing debate concerning radical economic transformation and white-owned monopoly alongside spectres of inequality, poverty and corruption threaten to divide and polarise our growing democratic system along racial lines.[7]

The right to equality as expressed in terms of section 9 of the Constitution of the Republic of South Africa, 1996 (Constitution), is made all the more emphatic by references in subsections 3 and 4 to the fact that neither the state nor any other person may unfairly discriminate, directly or indirectly,

---

19–27; *De Lange v. Presiding Bishop of the Methodist Church,* 2016 1 SA 1 (CC) paras. 38–43; *Prinsloo v. Van der Linde,* 1997 6 BCLR 759 (CC) paras. 15–22; *President of the RSA v. Hugo* 1997 4 SA 1 (CC), paras. 39–43; *Harksen v. Lane* 1998 1 SA 300 (CC) paras. 40–53; *S v. Lawrence, S v. Negal, S v. Solberg,* 1997 4 SA 1176 (CC) paras. 100–107; *Prince v. President of the Law Society of the Cape of Good Hope,* 2002 2 SA 792 (CC) paras. 33–50; *MEC for Education: Kwazulu-Natal v. Pillay,* 2008 1 SA 474 (CC) paras. 36–52; and *Strydom v. NG Gemeente Moreleta Park,* 2009 30 *ILJ* 868 (EqC) paras. 25–47.

5 Given R. Moloto, Lizelle Brink and Alewyn J. Nel, 12 (2014) *SA Journal of Human Resource Management (SAJHRM)*, 1 (12) and Edwin Cameron, 'Dignity and Disgrace – Moral Citizenship and Constitutional Protection', in: Christopher McCrudden (ed), *Understanding Human Dignity* (2013), 128 (132).

6 Henk J. Kloppers and Gerrit J. Pienaar, 17 (2014) *Potchefstroom Electronic Law Journal (PELJ)*, 677 (680–687); Becky L. Jacobs, 18 (2006) *Pace International Law Review (PILR)*, 407 (414–423); John Dugard, *Human Rights and the South African Legal Order* (1978), 261; Anthony S. Mathews, *Freedom, State, Security and the Rule of Law* (1986), 15-16; Edwin Cameron, *Justice: A Personal Account* (2014), 36–44 and 58–61; and Ian Currie and Johan De Waal, *The Bill of Rights Handbook* (5th Edition, 2005), 2–3.

7 See Colleen Scribner, (2017) *Journal of International Service (JIS)*, 57 (60) and Haroon Bhorat *et al*, *Betrayal of the Promise: How South Africa is Being Stolen* (May 2017) (http://www.pari.org.za/wp-content/uploads/2017/05/Betrayal-of-the-Promise-25052017.pdf).

against anyone on the basis of religion.[8] Mere differentiation does not constitute discrimination in the legal sense of the word. It is important to conceive of the distinction between 'discrimination' in the pejorative (hurtful) and non-pejorative (non-hurtful) sense of 'differentiation' (mere distinction). Differentiation in the pejorative sense translates into the notion of 'unfair discrimination'.[9] The need to address unfair discrimination can be seen as the need to address the imperative of equality guaranteed in terms of section 9 of the Constitution. But it is important that effect is given to a substantive, as opposed to a formal, notion of equality. This is captured in the *dictum* by Goldstone J in *President of the RSA v. Hugo*[10] where the following is stated:

> "We need, therefore, to develop a concept of unfair discrimination which recognises that although a society which affords each human being equal treatment on the basis of equal worth and freedom is our goal, we cannot achieve that goal by insisting upon identical treatment in all circumstances before that goal is achieved."[11]

A discrimination case where dignity was highlighted by the Constitutional Court as a significant aspect of the impact unfair discrimination had upon the individual is *Hoffman v. South African Airways*.[12] In dealing with whether or not the airline's policy had discriminated against the applicant on the basis of his HIV-positive status, Ncgobo J observed as follows:

> "At the heart of the prohibition of unfair discrimination is the recognition that under our Constitution all human beings, regardless of their position in society, must be accorded equal dignity. That dignity is impaired when a person is unfairly discriminated against. The determining factor regarding the unfairness of the discrimination is its impact on the person discriminated against. Relevant considerations in this regard include … the human dignity of the victim."[13]

---

8 Other grounds as listed under s. 9(3) include race, gender, sex, pregnancy, marital status, ethnic or social origin, colour, sexual orientation, age, disability, conscience, belief, culture, language and birth.

9 See Patrick Lenta, 126 (2009) *South African Law Journal (SALJ)*, 827 (835); Johan D. Van der Vyver, 14 (2011) *Potchefstroom Electronic Law Journal (PELJ)*, 1 (14); Radley Henrico, 36 (2015) *Obiter*, 275 (288); Clive Thompson and Paul S. Benjamin, *South African Labour Law* (loose-leaf Vol I, Service 43, 2002), 1-27 and the authorities cited at fn. 169.

10 1997 4 SA 1 (CC).

11 Para. 41.

12 2000 1 SA 1 (CC).

13 Para. 27.

Consequently, substantive equality and human dignity are essential to determining whether or not unfair discrimination has taken place. They are the *raison d'être* informing the end purpose of the determination.

The right to freedom of religion is enshrined in section 15(1) of the Constitution. In the context of the workplace, this must be considered together with the constitutional guarantee that everyone has the right to fair labour practices.[14] By implication, an employer would have the right to insist on compliance with an inherent requirement of the job (IROJ). Whether the nature of the IROJ necessitates a reasonable and justifiable limitation, or even an exclusion, of the expression of a religious freedom is not always dispositive of a simple answer – nor is it an easy exercise. Hence, the determination of whether discrimination is fair can be fraught with difficulties.

Addressing conflicting fundamental rights in the workplace can be achieved through reasonable accommodation. In the interest of fair labour practices, it is often necessary to require mutual accommodation of conflicting rights.[15]

III. Addressing the Consequences of Unfair Discrimination

The concern raised by Benecke – and validly so – is the manner in which it is incumbent on government to address unfair discrimination. Put differently, should any instance of unfair discrimination be dealt with as a criminal offence or as a civil wrong, or, alternatively, a combination thereof? In circumstances where unfair discrimination is dealt with as a civil wrong, the question arises whether the possibility of collective action on behalf of the victims is mooted, or whether the victims themselves must assert such claim.

Germany has elected, in instances of racial discrimination, to address this as a crime,[16] whilst choosing to address other instances of unfair discrimination, such as age or religion, as civil matters. Claimants in such

14 S. 23(1) of the Constitution.

15 Radley Henrico, 33 (2012) *Obiter*, 503.

16 Martina Benecke and Gisela Kern, (2005) *Europäische Zeitschrift für Wirtschaftsrecht (EuZW)*, 360 (360).

cases must prosecute claims themselves, given that collective actions are not possible.[17]

The benefits said to arise from the criminal prosecutions of unfair discrimination claims[18] are in and of themselves insufficient to fully justify and warrant such criminal prosecutions. This is so for the following reasons. Making any unfair discrimination claim a criminal offence (as opposed to a civil enforceable right against the offender) does not make the status of the prevailing law any more certain. The current legislative framework in South Africa[19] makes clear the basis upon which unfair discrimination is regulated in the workplace and civil society. Concerns of timidity or fear of intimidation on the part of victims is at the end of the analysis a factor which should not detract from the nature of legal process regulating unfair discrimination. A more pressing concern is that the overall issue of the prosecution of criminal offences in South Africa is not without grave concerns ranging from inadequately and incompetently investigated offences to their (in)effective prosecution, all of which impact adversely upon an accused's right to a fair trial and in respect of which our criminal justice system does not actually have capacity.[20]

The above considerations all conspire to indicate that a civil legislative framework is the most adequate and suitable means available for addressing and prosecuting – in the loose sense of the word – instances of unfair discrimination. Underscoring this assertion is Benecke's finding that in the last ten years there have been several civil proceedings on the basis of unfair discrimination and very few criminal proceedings.[21]

---

17 Martina Benecke p. 110.

18 Such as, for example, clarifying the law in terms of making the act in question a criminal offence, making it the responsibility of the state to prosecute (as opposed to the victim), and thereby in effect addressing situations in which the victim is either too shy or fears intimidation (see Martina Benecke, p. 102).

19 As discussed below.

20 See in this regard, for example, Judge Deon Van Zyl, *Annual Report for period 1 April 2009 to 31 March 2010* (2010) (https://acjr.org.za/resource-centre/jics-annual-report-2009-2010.pdf) (11–14) which found that in Gauteng alone, over 1 000 awaiting trial persons were held in detention on remand for periods of between two to six years, in prison conditions described as 'shockingly inhumane'. See also A. Gopaul, *The Impact and Constitutionality of Delayed Trials on the Rights of a Suspect or Accused Person During Criminal Proceedings* (Unpublished LLM Thesis, UNISA 2015), 86 at footnote 623.

21 Martina Benecke p. 103.

IV. Notional Victims and Respondents in Unfair Discrimination Cases

The application of the General Equal Treatment Act in Germany[22] is more pertinent to the realm of the workplace and labour law.[23] This coverage aligns itself – as pointed out by Benecke – with the EU Council Directive aimed at establishing a framework for equal treatment in employment and occupation.[24]

Achieving a more egalitarian society is imperative to the foundation and sustenance of a democratic order.[25] In seeking to establish such an order, the Constitution provides that everyone is equal before the law and has the right to equal protection and benefit of the law.[26] The right to equality is reinforced by the following provision:

> "Equality includes the full and equal enjoyment of all rights and freedoms. To promote the achievement of equality, legislative and other measures designed to protect or advance persons, or categories of persons, disadvantaged by unfair discrimination may be taken."[27]

Protection against the violation of equality is demonstrated with reference to the prohibition against unfair discrimination by the state.[28] Unfair discrimination is also prohibited in the case of non-state entities.[29]

The non-formal approach to equality which our law recognises – as do both legal systems – is consonant with a substantive approach to equality, as previously stated.[30] Allowance may be made for differentiation between

---

22 To areas such as big business, private insurance and housing rental, see Martina Benecke p. 103.

23 In terms of § 6–8 of the AGG. See also Martina Benecke p. 103.

24 Council Directive 2000/78/EC of 27 November 2000.

25 *AZAPO v. President of the Republic of South Africa,* 1996 4 SA 671 (CC) para. 1; *Brink v. Kitshoff,* 1996 4 SA (CC) para. 40; *President of the Republic of South Africa v. Hugo,* 1997 4 SA 1 (CC) para. 41; *Bato Star Fishing v. Minister of Environmental Affairs,* 2004 4 SA 490 (CC) para. 36; and *Minister of Finance v. Van Heerden,* 2004 6 SA 121 (CC) para. 26.

26 S. 9(1) of the Constitution.

27 S. 9(2) of the Constitution.

28 S. 9(3) of the Constitution.

29 S. 9(4) of the Constitution.

30 See *Minister of Finance v. Van Heerden,* 2004 6 SA 121 (CC) para. 26; *Minister of Home Affairs v. Fourie,* 2006 1 SA 524 (CC) para. 60; Cathi Albertyn, 'Constitutional Equality in South Africa', in: Ockert C. Dupper and Christoph Garbers (eds), *Equality in the Workplace: Reflections from South Africa and Beyond*

persons on various grounds embracing a host of factors. A substantive approach to equality demands that we take account of and celebrate the diversity of the individuals our society presents.[31] A caveat in the workplace may be where the accommodation of such diversity would be out of kilter with the IROJ, or accommodation of the diversity would result in undue hardship.[32]

V. Prohibited Grounds of Unfair Discrimination

1. Relevance of Listed Grounds

Listing grounds upon which certain acts will constitute unfair discrimination translates into certainty in law. There can no doubt as to the ground(s) upon which conduct will be a violation of rights to fundamental equality, freedom and human dignity. It comes as little surprise that article 3(3) of the Basic Law for the Federal Republic of Germany[33] lists ten grounds upon which no person shall be favoured or disfavoured for fear of contravening article 3(1) and (2).[34] Similarly, in South Africa, the Constitution lists seventeen grounds[35] upon which neither the state nor any person may unfairly discriminate against another person.

(2010), 77; and Andre Van Niekerk *et al*, *Law@work* (3rd Edition, 2015), 121–122.

31 See C. Albertyn, 'Constitutional Equality in South Africa', in: Ockert C. Dupper and Christoph Garbers (eds), *Equality in the Workplace: Reflections from South Africa and Beyond* (2010), 77 and the authorities cited at footnote 16; *Minister of Finance v Van Heerden* 2004 6 SA 121 (CC), para. 26; *Minister of Home Affairs v. Fourie,* 2006 1 SA 524 (CC) para. 60; and *National Coalition for Gay & Lesbian Equality v. Minister of Justice,* 1999 1 SA 6 (CC) para. 62. Also see Cathi Albertyn, 23 (2007) *South African Journal on Human Rights (SAJHR)*, 253 (257–258) and Sandra Fredman, 21 (2005) *South African Journal on Human Rights (SAJHR)*, 163 (168–169). *Cf* Murray Wesson, X11 (2007) *Juridica International (JurInt)*, 74 (76).

32 *NEHAWU v. University of Pretoria,* 2006 5 BLLR 437 (LAC) para. 55; *Kotze v. Rebel Discount Liquor Group (Pty) Ltd,* 2000 21 ILJ 129 (LC) paras. 132–133; *Johnson & Johnson (Pty) Ltd v. CWIU,* 2006 27 ILJ 269 (LAC); and *Dlamini v. Green Four Security*, 2006 11 BLLR 1074 (LC) para. 67.

33 Grundgesetz für die Bundesrepublik Deutschland in der im Bundesgesetzblatt Teil III, Gliederungsnummer 100-1 .

34 The right to equality before the law and of persons respectively.

35 Under s. 9(3) of the Constitution.

The relevance of such grounds, in terms of whether they give rise to claims of direct or indirect unfair discrimination, is considered below.

2. Legislative Framework and Direct or Indirect Unfair Discrimination

The purpose of legislation, namely to prohibit and sanction unfair discrimination,[36] cannot be gainsaid. However, the overarching effect thereof is to give effect to the principle of subsidiarity.[37] The number of prohibited (listed) grounds of unfair discrimination can only properly be accounted for when regard is had to both the constitutional and legislative provisions. Whether a particular country will ever achieve so-called 'optimum inclusivity' of grounds sufficient to cover all grounds of unfair discrimination is moot. The inclusion of obesity as a basis of unfair discrimination, is novel,[38] but with the ever-increasing phenomenon of obesity worldwide,[39] it would appear that this is a ground that will gain traction in equality jurisprudence.

A practical concern arises from unidentifiable grounds, such as the notion of 'arbitrary' appearing under section 11(2) of the Employment Equity Act[40] (EEA). Although listed, this ground would impose upon a complainant the additional onus of proving that the conduct is irrational, amounts to discrimination and is unfair.[41]

Is the lesson to be drawn from this that the further the net of potential liability is cast, the heavier the onus upon the applicant? By doing so the

---

36 Martina Benecke p. 106.

37 *S v. Mlungu,* 1995 3 SA 867 (CC) para. 95; *Mazibuko v. City of Johannesburg,* 2010 4 SA 1 (CC) para. 73; *Sidumo v. Rustenburg Platinum Mines Ltd,* 2008 2 SA 24 (CC) para. 248; *SANDU v. Minister of Defence,* 2007 5 SA 400 (CC) para. 51; *Minister of Health v. New Clicks SA (Pty) Ltd,* 2006 2 SA 311 (CC) paras. 94–96 and 437; *My Vote Counts MPC v. Speaker of the National Assembly,* [2015] ZACC 31 para. 50 and the authorities therein cited; and *De Lange v. Presiding Bishop of the Methodist of Southern Africa for the time being and Another*, 2016 2 SA 1 (CC) paras. 53–59.

38 Martina Benecke p. 106.

39 See Edward W. Gregg and Jonathan E. Shaw, 1 (2017) *The New England Journal of Medicine (N Engl J Med)*, 80 (80); Martin J. Friedrich, 7 (2017) *Journal of the American Medical Association (JAMA),* 603 (605); and Danielle Dellorto, 'Global Report: Obesity Bigger Health Crisis than Hunger', (14 December 2012), *CNN.*

40 55 of 1998.

41 S. 11(2)(a)–(c) of the EEA.

legislature evidently seeks to address this situation by means of a balance of convenience regarding the respective parties.

VI. Legal Consequences and Sanctions Arising from Unfair Discrimination

For almost three decades the primary legislation regulating unfair discrimination in the South African workplace has been the EEA and the Labour Relations Act[42] (LRA). Functioning outside the workplace is the Promotion of Equality and Prevention of Unfair Discrimination Act (PEPUDA).[43] The scope for determining whether discrimination is unfair under PEPUDA is notionally and conceptually much broader than what is provided for under either the EEA or LRA. This is so not only on account of it being non-workplace related, but also due to the nature of factors to be taken into account in determining whether an act of discrimination can be regarded as being unfair.[44]

All three legislative instruments provide relief in the form of civil liability. Whereas the EEA and LRA both provide, *inter alia*, for awards of compensation,[45] alternatively damages, PEPUDA, due to its non-workplace application, offers relief to applicants in the form of an order for damages, which can be granted in addition to any other remedy the court may order.[46]

There can be no doubt that unfair discrimination disputes are heavily regulated in terms of the above legislative regime. To the extent that it resolves disputes it must be accepted, even welcomed. However, the reality is that this formal framework is not dispositive of all potential disputes arising from our multicultural and diverse society. Something else is required. People themselves must learn to break through the barriers of mere toleration of individual differences and embrace a culture of celebration of the differences that are characteristic of our heterogeneous society.[47]

---

42 66 of 1995.

43 4 of 2000, which entered into force on 16 June 2003.

44 As set out under s. 14(3)(a)–(i).

45 Which award is limited with reference to a ceiling of 24 months and the claimant's salary.

46 Under s. 21(2)(a)–(p) of PEPUDA.

47 For further reading, see R. Henrico, 38 (2017) *Obiter*, 229 (230); *City of Tshwane Metropolitan Municipality v. Afriforum & Another*, 2016 9 BCLR

VII. Institutions against Unfair Discrimination

Under the unfair discrimination legislative framework, a claimant pursues relief in the *fora* established pursuant to such legislation. In workplace-related unfair discrimination matters, disputes have their origin in the statutory forum of the Commission for Conciliation, Mediation and Arbitration (CCMA),[48] alternatively the bargaining council having jurisdiction,[49] and they culminate in the Labour Court.[50] In non-workplace related disputes, a claimant pursues relief in the equality court.[51]

Article 13 of the Racial Equality Council Directive[52] prescribes that member states designate bodies that will promote equal treatment of persons aimed at non-discrimination on certain grounds.[53] An equally relevant measure in South Africa would be the Chapter 9 State Institutions Supporting Constitutional Democracy.[54] In particular, in this regard, we have three specific bodies, namely the South African Human Rights Commission;[55] the Commission for the Promotion and Protection of the Rights of Cultural, Religious and Linguistic Communities;[56] and the Commission for Gender Equality.[57]

Benecke raises concerns regarding the effectiveness of such institutions. Noting that in certain member states they are vested with the authority to impose fines for infractions of legislation, in others, with the exception of

---

1133 (CC) paras. 123 and 130–134; and Chief Justice Mogoeng Mogoeng's sentiments in his OR Tambo memorial lecture to the effect that 'all South Africans can make a contribution to improve the situation in our country' (see Nomahlubi Jordaan, "Please Stop the Insatiable Hunger for Money", says Chief Justice Mogoeng', (28 October 2016), *Business Live*).

48 A juristic person established under s. 112, as read with s. 191(1)(a)(ii) of the LRA. The Labour Court is considered a High Court, see s. 157(1) and (2) of the LRA, as read with ss. 165, 166, 169 and 170 of the Constitution.

49 S. 191(1)(a)(i) of the LRA.

50 S. 191(5)(b)(i), as read with s. 187(1)(f) of the LRA. See also s. 46(1), as read with s. 49 of the EEA.

51 In terms of s. 16(1)(a) of PEPUDA, every High court is an equality court for the area of its jurisdiction.

52 Council Directive 2000/43/EC of 29 June 2000.

53 Martina Benecke, p. 110.

54 Established pursuant to s. 181 of the Constitution.

55 Established under s. 181 (b), as read with s. 184 of the Constitution.

56 Established under s. 181 (c), as read with ss. 185–186 of the Constitution.

57 Established under s. 181(d), as read with s. 187 of the Constitution.

Germany, they do not have *locus standi* to institute so-called popular or class actions in instances of unfair discrimination.

In South Africa, the aforesaid three institutions are established in terms of the Constitution as commissions that possess the necessary powers to investigate instances of, *inter alia*, unfair discrimination or an abuse of human rights. Their powers do not include the imposition of fines. As opposed to the position in Germany, these institutions can also factually and legally institute class actions against perpetrators.[58]

The actual impact these institutions have upon quality jurisprudence should be more in terms of the public awareness they are capable of generating[59] than in the class actions they are capable of instituting, which rarely occurs.

VIII. Considerations Regarding Abuse of the Legislative Framework

Benecke raises the valid concern regarding the extent to which, if any, unfair discrimination mechanisms may be employed to advance *mala fide* motives. This would clearly be contrary to the intention of the legislature.

The South African legislative framework must be understood in the context of enabling provisions, which would dissuade potential claimants proceeding on a basis that is anything less than *bona fide*. Whilst not suggesting

58 Acting in terms of s. 34, as read with s. 38 of the Constitution.

59 See, for example, the incident regarding the assault of a South African citizen by former Zimbabwean President Robert Mugabe's wife, Grace Mubabe, upon her recent visit to South Africa. Ironically, the remonstrations by the Commission for Gender Equality that Mrs Grace Mugabe be prosecuted were not shared by the South African Minister of Police who officially declared that Mrs Grace Mugabe was apparently protected by diplomatic immunity. Apart from making recommendations and investigating issues, its ability to enforce effectively issues pertaining to gender discrimination is limited by, for example, not being able to issue subpoenas. See Phumzile Bhengu, *Commission for Gender Equality Quarter 1 Performance* (5 September 2017) (https://www.pmg.org.za/committee-meeting/24965/). Also see Commission for the Promotion and Protection of the Rights of Cultural, Religious and Linguistic Communities, *Preliminary Report of the Hearings on the Commercialisation of Religion and Abuse of People's Belief Systems* (2017) (http://www.crlcommission.org.za/docs/Report%20On%20Commecialization%20of%20Religion%20and%20Abuse%20of%20People's%20Believe%20Systems%20final.pdf).

for one moment that such conduct cannot occur, the reality is that the material deterrence arises from an appropriate cost order which the tribunal or court is capable of handing down against a vexatious claimant.[60] In exceptional cases, where the respondent has reason to believe the claimant may be pursuing a spurious claim or be acting maliciously, nothing precludes the respondent from seeking an interim security of costs order against the claimant. These are, it is contended, the most appropriate means of addressing concerns of systemic abuse and fraud.

IX. Conclusion

Although it may have commenced as a perceived socio-legal experiment in Germany, the AGG has shown itself to be an inexorable part of Germany's unfair discrimination landscape.[61] To its credit, the AGG has injected legal certainty regarding the prohibited (listed) grounds of unfair discrimination and the consequences that will result from an infraction of the law. The potential of abuse of the AGG by claimants remains a social phenomenon in Germany. By comparison, in South Africa, a rather unique and different concern is raised. It is the concern of uniting a diversity of cultures in a manner, which transcends the norm of mere tolerance. There is a clamant call for a celebration of differences. The more people of different cultures celebrate their differences, and are thereby united, the less the need to rely on the regulated legislative framework to enforce unfair discrimination claims and resort to formal dispute mechanisms to resolve conflicts.[62]

Bibliography

Cathi Albertyn, 'Constitutional Equality in South Africa', in: Ockert C. Dupper and Christoph Garbers (eds), *Equality in the Workplace: Reflections from South Africa and Beyond* (Juta, Cape Town 2010), 77.

60 See, for example, the costs award a CCMA arbitrator may make in terms of Rules 142 and 143 of the CCMA Guidelines on Misconduct Arbitration (published under GN R224, in *Government Gazette* 38573 of March 2015); the powers of the Labour Court in respect of costs under s. 158(1)(a)(vii) of the LRA or s. 50(2) of the EEE; and the High Court's power to make any appropriate order of costs against any party under s. 21(2)(o) of PEPUDA.

61 Martina Benecke p. 114.

62 For further reading see Radley Henrico (fn. 47), 236–239.

Cathi Albertyn, 'Substantive Equality and Transformation in South Africa' 23 (2007) *South African Journal on Human Rights (SAJHR)*, 253.

Martina Benecke and Gisela Kern, 'Sanktionen im Antidiskriminierungsrecht: Möglichkeiten und Grenzen der Umsetzung der Europäischen Richtlinien im deutschen Recht' (2005) *Europäische Zeitschrift für Wirtschaftsrecht (EuZW)*, 360.

Phumzile Bhengu, *Commission for Gender Equality Quarter 1 Performance* (5 September 2017), https://pmg.org.za/committee-meeting/24965/ (01-10-2017).

Haroon Bhorat et al., *Betrayal of the Promise: How South Africa is Being Stolen* (May 2017), http://pari.org.za/wp-content/uploads/2017/05/Betrayal-of-the-Promise-25052017.pdf (02-10-2017).

Edwin Cameron, 'Dignity and Disgrace – Moral Citizenship and Constitutional Protection', in: Christopher McCrudden (ed), *Understanding Human Dignity* (Oxford University Press, Oxford 2013), 132.

Edwin Cameron, *Justice: A Personal Account* (Tafelberg, Cape Town 2014).

Commission for the Promotion and Protection of the Rights of Cultural, Religious and Linguistic Communities, *Preliminary Report of the Hearings on the Commercialisation of Religion and Abuse of People's Belief Systems* (2017), http://www.crlcommission.org.za/docs/Report%20On%20Commecialization%20of%20Religion%20and%20Abuse%20of%20People's%20Believe%20Systems%20final.pdf (01-10-2017).

Ian Currie and Johan De Waal, *The Bill of Rights Handbook* (5th Edition, Juta, Cape Town 2005).

Danielle Dellorto, 'Global Report: Obesity Bigger Health Crisis than Hunger', (14 December 2012), *CNN*, http://edition.cnn.com/2012/12/13/health/global-burden-report/index.html (30-09-2017).

John Dugard, *Human Rights and the South African Legal Order* (Princeton University Press, Princeton 1978).

Ockert C. Dupper and Christoph Garbers, *Equality in the Workplace: Reflections from South Africa and Beyond* (Juta, Cape Town 2010).

Sandra Fredman, 'Providing Equality: Substantive Equality and the Positive Duty to Provide' 21 (2005) *South African Journal on Human Rights (SAJHR)*, 163.

Martin J. Friedrich, 'Global Obesity Epidemic Worsening' 7 (2017) *Journal of the American Medical Association (JAMA)*, 603.

Arusha Gopaul, *The Impact and Constitutionality of Delayed Trials on the Rights of a Suspect or Accused Person During Criminal Proceedings* (Unpublished LLM Thesis, UNISA 2015).

Edward W. Gregg and Jonathan E. Shaw, 'Global Health Effects of Overweight and Obesity' 1 (2017) *The New England Journal of Medicine (N Engl J Med)*, 80.

Radley Henrico, 'Mutual Accommodation of Religious Differences in the Workplace – A Jostling of Rights' 33 (2012) *Obiter*, 503.

Radley Henrico, 'Revisiting a Culture of Tolerance Relating to Religious Unfair Discrimination in South Africa (Part 1)' 38 (2017) *Obiter*, 229.

Radley Henrico, 'South African Constitutional and Legislative Framework on Equality: How Effective is it in Addressing Religious Discrimination in the Workplace?' 36 (2015) *Obiter*, 275.

Radley Henrico, *Religious Discrimination in the South African Workplace* (Unpublished LLD Thesis, NWU 2016).

Becky L. Jacobs, 'The Post-Apartheid City in the New South Africa: A Constitutional "Triomf"' 18 (2006) *Pace International Law Review (PILR)*, 407.

Nomahlubi Jordaan, '"Please Stop the Insatiable Hunger for Money", says Chief Justice Mogoeng', (28 October 2016), *Business Live*, http://www.timeslive.co.za.local/2016/20/28%E2%80%98Please-stop-the-insatiable-hunger-for-money%E2%80%99---Chief-Justice-Mogoeng (03-10-2017).

Henk J. Kloppers and Gerrit J. Pienaar, 'The Historical Context of Land Reform in South Africa and Early Policies' 17 (2014) *Potchefstroom Electronic Law Journal (PELJ)*, 677.

Patrick Lenta, 'Taking Diversity Seriously: Religious Associations and Work-related Discrimination' 126 (2009) *South African Law Journal (SALJ)*, 827.

Anthony S. Mathews, *Freedom, State, Security and the Rule of Law* (University of California Press, Berkeley 1986).

Given R. Moloto, Lizelle Brink and Alewyn J. Nel, 'An Exploration of Stereotyping Perceptions amongst Support Staff within a South African Higher Education Institution' 12 (2014) *SA Journal of Human Resource Management (SAJHRM)*, 1.

Colleen Scribner, 'Multiculturalism in South Africa: Forces at Play in the "Rainbow Nation"' 2017 *Journal of International Service (JIS)*, https://jis-online.org/2017/07/24/multiculturalism-in-south-africa/ (03-10-2017).

Thompson, Clive and Benjamin, Paul S., *South African Labour Law* (loose-leaf Vol I, Service 43, Juta, Cape Town 2002).

Johan D. van der Vyver, 'The Right to Self-determination of Cultural, Religious and Linguistic Communities' 14 (2011) *Potchefstroom Electronic Law Journal (PELJ)*, 350.

Andre van Niekerk et al., *Law@work* (3rd Edition, LexisNexis, Durban 2015).

Deon H. van Zyl, *Annual Report for period 1 April 2009 to 31 March 2010* (2010).

Murray Wesson, 'Discrimination Law and Social Rights: Intersections and Possibilities' 2007 *Juridica International (JurInt)*, 74.

Register of cases

AZAPO v. President of the Republic of South Africa 1996 4 SA 671 (CC).

Bato Star Fishing v. Minister of Environmental Affairs 2004 4 SA 490 (CC).

Brink v. Kitshoff 1996 4 SA (CC).

Christian Education South Africa v. Minister of Education 2000 4 SA 757 (CC).

City of Tshwane Metropolitan Municipality v. Afriforum & Another 2016 9 BCLR 1133 (CC).
De Lange v. Presiding Bishop of the Methodist Church 2016 2 SA 1 (CC).
Department of Correctional Services v. POPCRU 2013 JOL 30347 (SCA).
Dlamini v Green Four Security 2006 11 BLLR 1074 (LC).
FAWU v Rainbow Chicken Farms 2000 1 BLLR 70 (LC).
Harksen v. Lane 1998 1 SA 300 (CC).
Hoffman v. South African Airways 2000 1 SA 1 (CC).
Johnson & Johnson (Pty) Ltd v. CWIU 2006 27 ILJ 269 (LAC).
Kievits Kroon Country Estate (Pty) Ltd v. Mmoledi 2014 35 ILJ 209 (SCA).
Kotze v. Rebel Discount Liquor Group (Pty) Ltd 2000 21 ILJ 129 (LC).
Lewis v. Media24 Ltd 2010 31 ILJ 2416 LC.
Mazibuko v. City of Johannesburg 2010 4 SA 1 (CC).
MEC for Education: Kwazulu Natal v. Pillay 2008 1 SA 474 (CC).
Minister of Finance v. Van Heerden 2004 6 SA 121 (CC).
Minister of Health v. New Clicks SA (Pty) Ltd 2006 2 SA 311 (CC).
Minister of Home Affairs v. Fourie 2006 1 SA 524 (CC).
Motaung v. Department of Education 2013 34 ILJ 1199 (LC).
My Vote Counts MPC v. Speaker of the National Assembly [2015] ZACC 31.
National Coalition for Gay & Lesbian Equality v. Minister of Justice 1999 1 SA 6 (CC).
NEHAWU v. University of Pretoria 2006 5 BLLR 437 (LAC).
President of the Republic of South Africa v. Hugo 1997 4 SA 1 (CC).
President of the RSA v. Hugo 1997 4 SA 1 (CC).
Prince v. President of the Law Society of the Cape of Good Hope 2002 2 SA 792 (CC).
Prinsloo v. Van der Linde 1997 6 BCLR 759 (CC).
S v. Lawrence, S v. Negal, S v. Solberg 1997 4 SA 1176 (CC).
S v. Mlungu 1995 3 SA 867 (CC).
SACTWU v. Berg River Textiles, a Division of Seardel Group Trading (Pty) Ltd 2012 33 ILJ 972 (LC).
SANDU v. Minister of Defence 2007 5 SA 400 (CC).
Sidumo v. Rustenburg Platinum Mines Ltd 2008 2 SA 24 (CC).
Strydom v. NG Gemeente Moreleta Park 2009 30 ILJ 868 (EqC).
Zabala v. Gold Reef City Casino 2009 1 BLLR 94 (LC).

Law-Enforcement in Turbulent Times – How to Work with Principles in Capital Markets Law

Thomas M.J. Möllers[*]
Isabella Brosig[**]

Abstract: *The search for, establishment, and application of new legal principles is among the most challenging of legal methods for academics, lawyers, and judges. One precondition for formulating new principles is a consistent internal and external legal system of terms, conditions and values – a system that was fostered by several Pandectists (German legal scholars) in the early 19th century. Once established, principles may fill gaps in the law, may be used as one argument among many to find a balanced solution, and may even establish the supremacy of one solution over the other. They may thus provide the necessary flexibility to find solutions and enforce rules and regulations – especially in the fast-paced and ever-changing capital markets.*

* Thomas M.J. Möllers, *Dr. iur.*; Professor, University of Augsburg Faculty of Law. Managing Director of the Center for European Legal Studies. Chair for Civil Law, Economic Law, European Law, Private International Law and Comparative Law.

** Isabella Brosig, Academic Assistant at the Chair of Thomas M.J. Möllers.

I. Introduction and structure of the paper

In our society, being principled is usually seen as a positive character trait for an individual to have. People who stand by their principles are considered to be strong-willed, sincere, and straightforward. In this respect, politicians and elected representatives are far too often assumed to put honest convictions aside during elections in order to secure power and influence, or of acting opportunistically in the interests of the strongest lobby, and against the interests of the sovereign people. 'Politics without principles' is one of Gandhi's famous seven deadly sins of modern society.[1] It is therefore hardly a new insight that both Germany's Basic Law (GG) and the ordinary law are permeated with numerous principles which are meant to ensure that the law is as straightforward as possible.

However, it is all the more astonishing that only a few of these legal principles are set out in positive law. So, for example, there is as little explicitly recorded on the principle in the law of obligations of freedom of contract[2] in the German Civil Code (BGB) as there is on the principle of contractual fidelity (*pacta sunt servanda*).[3] However, no one seriously disputes the existence and applicability of these principles. On the contrary, other states have codified numerous principles.[4] It is generally assumed that the BGB presupposes that these principles are obviously valid.[5]

---

1 Mahatma Gandhi, 'Seven Social Sins', *Young India* No. 43 (October 22, 1925), 361: "politics without principles".

2 The term is even referred to in the *Motive zu dem Entwurfe eines Bürgerlichen Gesetzbuches für das Deutsche Reich* (Statements on the Draft of a Civil Code for the German Reich), Volume 2 (1896), p. 2: "By virtue of the principle of freedom of contract, which governs the law of contractual obligations, the parties can determine their legal relationships and associations between themselves at their discretion with binding effect, insofar as there are no conflicting general or specific individual absolute legal provisions."

3 In contrast, the principle was even found in the original Article 77 of the *Entwürfe eines Bürgerlichen Gesetzbuches für das Deutsche Reich* (Draft of a Civil Code for the German Reich) (1888): "In order to conclude a contract, it is necessary for the contracting parties to declare their corresponding intentions to each other"; This Article 77 was then deleted by the second commission, see Commission's Report, p. 156, in: Mugdan, *Die gesamten Materialien des Bürgerlichen Gesetzbuchs für das Deutsche Reich*, Volume I (1899), p. 688.

4 For *pacta sunt servanda*, see fn. 64, for instance; for the violation of moral principles, see fn.70.

5 Thus Werner Flume, 'Rechtsgeschäft und Privatautonomie', in: Ernst von Caemmerer, Ernst Friesenhahn and Richard Lange (eds), *Festschrift zum hundertjährigen Bestehen des Deutschen Juristentages 1860-1960* (1960), 135 (136 et seq).; Werner Flume, *Allgemeiner Teil des Bürgerlichen Rechts, Das Rechtsgeschäft*, Volume 2 (1965), Section 1.1, 1; agreeing Claus-Wilhelm Canaris, 200

However, there are also explicitly stated legal principles. The Basic Law (GG) already contains the best known: fundamental rights are principles *par excellence*. At the European level, it is particularly important to mention the fundamental freedoms set out in the Treaty on the Functioning of the European Union (TFEU) and the Charter of Fundamental Rights of the European Union (CFR). The mere fact that legal principles dominate our highest-ranking codifications shows their enormous importance in reaching legally sound decisions, and forces legal scholars to discuss them.

This paper discusses the issue of whether and how legal principles can be called upon to resolve questions of law in German and European company, capital markets and antitrust law. The purpose of legal methodology is to clarify how legal principles affect the resolution of a case, and how they can be usefully harnessed for this purpose. The main area of application of methodological work with legal principles is to instances where the law does not provide a resolution – or at least does not contain a clear resolution – to a legal problem. If there is a gap in the law, such cases need to be resolved by a court. This is because the judge is obligated to make a decision.[6] Moreover, the judge cannot simply decide, but rather needs to be able to justify the decision rationally with good arguments.[7] For this purpose, the judge can make use of the appraisals of existing law as part of an extensive methodological arsenal, and develop a solution from these. In particular, in addition to the option to interpret existing laws, the judge also has

(2000) *Archiv für die civilistische Praxis (AcP)*, 273 (277); Reinhard Bork, *Allgemeiner Teil des Bürgerlichen Gesetzbuchs* (4th Edition, 2016), para. 99.

6 Ludwig Enneccerus and Hans Carl Nipperdey, *Lehrbuch des Bürgerlichen Rechts* (15th Edition, 1957), 336; Arthur Meier-Hayoz, 36 (1981) *JuristenZeitung (JZ)*, 417 (417), Bernd Rüthers, Christian Fischer and Axel Birk, *Rechtstheorie* (8th Edition, 2015), para. 314; see also Karl Larenz, *Methodenlehre der Rechtswissenschaft* (6th Edition, 1991), 368 (402); Historically on the so-called prohibition on denying justice see Ekkehard Schumann, 81 (1968) *Zeitschrift für Zivilprozeß (ZZP)*, 79 (83 et seq.); Marie Theres Fögen, 'Schrittmacher des Rechts – Anmerkungen zum Justiz- und Rechtsverweigerungsverbot', in: Heinrich Honsell (ed), *Privatrecht und Methode: Festschrift für Ernst August Kramer* (2004), 3 (3 et seq).

7 On the obligation to give reasons, German Federal Constitutional Court (BVerfG) 19.05.1992 – 1 BvR 986/91 – BVerfGE 86, 133 (144 et seq.); see from the ordinary law, Sec. 30 (1) German Federal Constitutional Court Act (BVerfGG); Sec. 313 (1) No. 6 (3) Code of Civil Procedure (ZPO); Sec.s 267 (1), 275 Code of Criminal Procedure (StPO) or Sec. 117 (2) No. 5 Rules of the Administrative Courts (VwGO); Sec.s 60 (2), 4, 96 (2) Labour Courts Act (ArbGG).

the power to develop the law.[8] The judge must therefore inevitably pose the question as to how to resolve a legal problem in the spirit of the existing law when it is not regulated. The judge has to explore existing appraisals of the law, and harness them to solve the specific legal problem.

A line of argument based on principles gains its power of persuasion from this alone. Principles provide for stability in law, legal certainty, and transparency. Principles can also only be rebutted with difficulty; they have a superordinate character compared with individual selective legal provisions. Objections can only be raised against them with difficulty – unless one can claim that the circumstances are sufficient for an exception to the principle. However, for this one then bears the burden of argumentation.

Despite the advantages of reasoning with legal principles, there is also a risk that the mere reference to a principle replaces the deeper analysis of the specific case and its circumstances, and thus the justice of the individual case might get left behind. Decisive aspects of the individual case that could force a departure from the principle are in danger of being overlooked. Furthermore, the fact that legal principles are often uncodified can lead to a temptation to 'invent' new legal principles without sufficient connection to the existing law. Moreover, the lack of precise determination of their scope – particularly for unregulated legal problems – opens the floodgates to decisions being made without transparent justification and, ultimately, to arbitrariness.

It is therefore necessary to identify legal principles from a methodological point of view, and clarify the question as to whether and how they can be called upon to resolve the specific case without constitutional objections. For this purpose, the first requirement is a conceptual and characterising delimitation and narrowing down (section B). Following this, the prerequisites for the development and formation of legal principles must be clarified (section C) and the limits in their evolution must be demonstrated (section D). The focus then turns to the application of legal principles as a methodological construction in the specific individual case (section E). Eventually, a methodological consideration of legal principles at the European level is required (section F).

---

8 Explicitly BVerfG 14.02.1973 – 1 BvR 112/65 – BVerfGE 34, 269, 286 et seq. – Soraya; BVerfG 08.04.1987 – 2 BvR 687/85 – BVerfGE 75, 223, 243 et seq. – Kloppenburg.

II. What characterises a legal principle

A definition of a 'general legal principle' must include various components. In the same way that legal doctrine is more than the law,[9] so legal principles are more than the legal norms of the laws. Legal principles develop from the totality of the written and unwritten legal norms. Principles build structures that underlie the law.[10] They create meaning by means of their interaction and allow for a certain degree of generalisation.[11] Like the concept of good faith in Section 242 of the Civil Code (BGB), they are only codified by way of exception[12] – which is why they are often obtained from development of the law.[13] Consequently, there are numerous codifications that refer to the general legal principles as part of permissible development of the law.[14] Instead of deriving principles simply from 'justice' or 'legal concord', they must be obtained from the legal system. Many principles claim normative validity and give rise to presumptions.[15] Legal rules are labelled as legal principles although they are often "undeserving of that term".[16] Before principles can be subsumed, they need to be further substantiated. Working with legal principles methodically requires two steps (see below).

---

9 Here Andreas Voßkuhle, 'Neue Verwaltungswissenschaft', in: Wolfgang Hoffmann-Riem, Eberhard Schmidt-Aßmann and Andreas Voßkuhle (eds), *Grundlagen des Verwaltungsrechts*, Volume 1 (2nd Edition, 2012), § 1 para. 6; see the various conceptualisations for Christian Waldhoff, in: Gregor Kirchhof, Stefan Magen and Karsten Schneider (eds), *Was weiß Dogmatik?* (2012), 17, 22 et seq.; Christoph Möllers, 'Methoden', in: Wolfgang Hoffmann-Riem, Eberhard Schmidt-Aßmann and Andreas Voßkuhle (eds), *Grundlagen des Verwaltungsrechts*, Volume 1 (2nd Edition, 2012), § 3 para. 35 et seq.

10 Klaus Friedrich Röhl and Hans Christian Röhl, *Allgemeine Rechtslehre* (3rd Edition, 2008), § 33.I., 283.

11 Jürgen Basedow, 200 (2000) *Archiv für die civilistische Praxis (AcP)*, 445 (453). In detail also Claus Wilhelm Canaris, *Die Feststellung von Lücken im Gesetz* (2nd Edition, 1983), 47 et seqq.

12 Also Ernst August Kramer, 'Funktionen allgemeiner Rechtsgrundsätze – Versuch einer Strukturierung' in: Helmut Koziol, Peter Rummel (eds), *Im Dienste der Gerechtigkeit: Festschrift für Franz Bydlinski* (2002), 197 (203).

13 Karl Larenz (Fn. 6), 421 as 'legal discovery'.

14 Thus Sec. 46 Introduction. Preuß. ALR: "If there is no law… the judge must decide based on the general legal principles adopted by the statute;" explicitly also Sec. 7 ABGB: "make a decision according to the natural principles of law".

15 Klaus Friedrich Röhl and Hans Christian Röhl (Fn. 10), § 33 I, 284.

16 Explicitly on the following Klaus Friedrich Röhl and Hans Christian Röhl (Fn. 10), § 33 I, 283.

Building on *Dworkin* and *Esser,*[17] *Alexy* developed a theory of basic rights.[18] According to his strict hypothesis of differentiation, principles are in direct contrast to rules,[19] although distinct limits do not exist. Rules – namely, norms that can be subsumed – are either satisfied or not satisfied. The decision is made on the basis of factual elements or similar factual conditions. But principles do not necessarily lead to a decision, because they need to be balanced with other principles.[20] Thus, principles establish requirements for optimisation.[21] They allow for rational decisions, for instance, by defending a minor violation of a legally protected right with serious reasons for violation.[22] Viewing principles as requirements for optimisation is considered commonplace.[23] The hypothesis of differentiation is able to consistently describe the basic rights' mode of action when applying the principle of proportionality.[24]

A large part of academic literature, however, adopts a critical attitude towards the claim of Alexy's theory to absoluteness.[25] The differentiation between principles and rules cannot be derived from the Constitution.[26]

---

17 Josef Esser, *Grundsatz und Norm in der richterlichen Fortbildung des Privatrechts* (4th Edition, 1990), 39 et seqq., 87 et seqq.

18 Whereas Ronald Dworkin, *Taking Rights Seriously* (1977), 278 et seqq. adopted the 'one right answer'-Theory; Robert Alexy, 25 (1985) *Archiv für Rechts- und Sozialphilosophie – Beihefte (ARSP-B)*, 13 (28) rejects such.

19 Robert Alexy (Fn. 18), 13, 15 et seqq.

20 Ronald Dworkin, *Taking Rights Seriously* (2nd Edition, 1978), 26.

21 Robert Alexy (Fn. 18), 13 (19); ibid., *Theorie der Grundrechte* (1986), 75 et seqq.; ibid., 18 (1987) *Rechtstheorie*, 405 (407); concurring Karl Larenz (Fn. 6), 475; Nils Jansen, *Die Struktur der Gerechtigkeit* (1998), 106 et seqq.; Anne Röthel, *Normkonkretisierung im Privatrecht* (2004), 146 et seqq., 225 et seqq.

22 Robert Alexy, 61 (2002) *Veröffentlichungen der Vereinigung der Deutschen Staatsrechtslehrer (VVDStRL)*, 7, 18 et seqq.; before ibid. (Fn. 21), 143 et seqq.

23 Matthias Jestaedt, *Grundrechtsentfaltung im Gesetz* (1999), 213: "widely met with approval."

24 Matthias Jestaedt, 'Die Abwägungslehre – ihre Stärken und ihre Schwächen', in: Otto Depenheuer, Markus Heintzen and Peter Axer (eds), *Staat im Wort: Festschrift Josef Isensee* (2007), 253 (258 et seq.); Jan Henrik Klement, 63 (2008) *JuristenZeitung (JZ)*, 756 (761).

25 Josef Franz Lindner, *Theorie der Grundrechtsdogmatik* (2005), 54; Jan Henrik Klement (Fn. 24), 756 et seqq.; ibid., 64 (2009) *JuristenZeitung (JZ)*, 560 et seqq.

26 Josef Franz Lindner (Fn. 25), 54.

Thus, it is not clear when a norm is a principle or when it is a rule.[27] This is also why critics oppose the hypothesis of differentiation, thus giving a clear differentiation between principles and rules. After all, there is a danger that the courts might obtain new competences as a result of the requirements of optimisation that do not arise out of the Constitution.[28] *Sieckmann* further developed the theory of principles, and more carefully considers principles only as "rudiments of argumentation".[29]

III. The derivation of legal principles

1. Codified principles

If a principle is codified, the question of its derivation is unnecessary. Here, the only issue is whether a law 'elevated' into a legal principle – and thus having a ripple effect on other provisions – can be taken into consideration for their interpretation, or can serve as the basis for further development of the law in the area of law concerned. First, there is the possibility that the law itself ascribes the status of a legal principle to a legal rule. Article 5(1) sentence 1 (3) TEU, for example, explicitly speaks of the principle of conferral and of the principle of subsidiarity. But one rarely finds such clear statements in German law.[30]

If such a clear legislative emphasis is missing, the distinction between procedural and substantive practicability developed by *Jhering* may help in clarifying whether a codified law is a principle or a rule. According to the

27 Michael Sachs, 'Die Grundrechte als objektives Recht u. als subjektives Recht', in: Klaus Stern (ed), *Das Staatsrecht der Bundesrepublik Deutschland*, Volume III/1 (1988), § 65, 502; Matthias Jestaedt (Fn. 23), 214; ibid. (Fn. 24), 253 (261); Jan Henrik Klement (Fn. 24), 760.

28 Martin Gellermann, *Grundrechte im einfachgesetzlichen Gewand* (2000), 71; Josef Franz Lindner (Fn. 25), 55; Jan Henrik Klement (Fn. 24), 560 et seq.; warning Bernd Rüthers, Christian Fischer and Axel Birk, *Rechtstheorie* (8th Edition, 2015), para. 757a.

29 Jan Sieckmann, *Recht als normatives System* (2009), 41 et seqq.

30 For example, critical of the "General Principles" set out in Sec. 3 German Securities Acquisition and Takeover Act (WpÜG), Peter Versteegen, in: Heribert Hirte and Christoph von Bülow (eds), *Kölner Kommentar zum WpÜG* (2nd Edition, 2010), § 3 para. 2: Declared aims, use of which is questionable; Ulrich Noack and Timo Holzborn, in: Eberhard Schwark and Daniel Zimmer (eds), *Kapitalmarktrechts-Kommentar* (4th Edition, 2010), § 3 para. 1.

opposing view by *Alexy* discussed above, the distinction between principles and rules has only a gradual nature.[31] Legal norms are formally practicable depending on the ease and safety with which they can be applied to the specific case. Consequently, a schematical age limit regulating the legal age is significantly more practical than determining the "necessary comprehension and strength of character"[32]. Legal norms are substantively practical if, as principles, they allow for single-case justice because the relevant valuation is clearly discernible[33] – as, for instance, under the general right to protection of personality or the standard of negligence according to Section 276(2) of the Civil Code (BGB).[34] Thus formal and substantive practicability are complementary.[35] According to this distinction, rules are formally practicable, but principles are substantively practicable legal provisions.

Based on their breadth and vagueness, the 'general rules of conduct' under Section 63(1) (formerly Section 31(1)) of the German Securities Trading Act (WpHG) need to be fleshed out and further specified, and may therefore be considered as substantively practicable principles instead of rules.

2. The derivation of unwritten legal principles

It is more difficult to derive legal principles that are not explicitly stated. In large parts of the ordinary law, this is actually the norm. For this purpose, there are several different approaches.

---

31 For example Marietta Auer, *Materialisierung, Flexibilisierung, Richterfreiheit* (2005), 48, 135.

32 Rudolf von Jhering, *Geist des römischen Rechts*, Volume 1 (4th Edition, 1878), 51, 53.

33 Duncan Kennedy, 89 (1976) *Harvard Law Review (Harv.L.Rev.),* 1685 (1688) mentions "good faith, due care, reasonableness"; Jack M. Balkin, 39 (1986) *Rutgers Law Review (Rutgers L. Rev.),* 1 (44).

34 Marietta Auer (Fn. 31), 48, 54 et seqq.

35 Josef Esser, 'Realität und Ideologie der Rechtssicherheit in positiven Systemen', in: Siegfried Hohenleitner, Ludwig Linder and Friedrich Nowakowski (eds), *Festschrift für Theodor Rittler* (1957), 13 (14): "Plurality of style and content" („Pluralität von Form und Inhalt"); Jack M. Balkin (Fn. 33), 43 et seqq.

a) Previous attempts justifying the derivation of general legal principles

Dworkin describes principles as standards that, without being rules, may be suitable as arguments for individual rights.[36] They need to be specified by balancing, and constitute requirements for optimisation.[37] In specifying principles, however, such a formal description is only partially suitable. In particular, in this way legal principles are still not derived on the basis of the law.

Some would like to explain legal principles from a historical perspective.[38] It is certainly the case that numerous legal principles come from centuries of tradition – in some cases even millennia.[39] Legal constructions such as the prohibition in *laesio enormis* or *clausula rebus sic stantibus* can only provide initial approaches to justifying the current principles of law or legal rules. On closer inspection, however, one will find that many legal principles have developed over the centuries. Because conditions change, the comparison with the historical examples is not always convincing.[40] Ultimately, the necessary flexibility would not be achieved by forming new principles if these were derived exclusively from the past.[41] Legal doctrine,

---

36 Ronald Dworkin (Fn. 18), 90.

37 On Civil Law, thus Manfred Wolf and Jörg Neuner, *Allgemeiner Teil des Bürgerlichen Rechts* (10th Edition, 2012,), para. 4 para. 49.

38 See the examples in Josef Esser, *Grundsatz und Norm in der richterlichen Fortbildung des Privatrechts* (4th Edition, 1990), 317 et seq.; Joachim Rückert, 'Das BGB und seine Prinzipien', in: Mathias Schmoeckel, Joachim Rückert and Reinhard Zimmermann (eds), *Historisch-kritischer Kommentar zum BGB* (2003), § 1 para. 80 et seq.; and Reinhard Zimmermann, *Law of Obligations* (1992); ibid., 47 (1992) *Juristenzeitung (JZ)*, 8 et seq.; ibid., 193 (1993) *Archiv für die civilistische Praxis (AcP)*, 121 et seq., who calls for a European ius commune.

39 See, for example Aristotle, *Nicomachean Ethics*, 5th Book, 4–9 (Justice and Fairness); Art. 104 et seq. Constitutio Criminalis Carolina (CCC) of 27/07/1532 (Principle of Legality); Christian Wolff, *Grundsätze des Natur- und Völkerrechts* (1754), § 438: "When two or more jointly agree on one or more promises, it is a contract (pactum or pactio)." (pacta sunt servanda); Ulp.D. 1.1.10.1. "Juris praecepta sunt haec: honeste vivere, alterum non laedere, suum cuique tribuere" (alterum non laedere).

40 See only the various groups of cases of frustration of contract which have developed in the course of time in the case law. For example, the overview in Christian Grüneberg, in: Otto Palandt (ed), *BGB* (77th Edition, 2018), § 313 para. 25 et seq.

41 Critical against Reinhard Zimmermann (Fn. 38) for example, Dieter Simon, 11 (1992) *Rechtshistorisches Journal*, 574 (577 et seq.); Wolfgang Wiegand, 12

correctly understood, does not remain in the jurisprudence of concepts, but instead changes with the requirements of the legislature and case law.[42]

Some describe principles as legal and as having a hybrid status between law and morals because they comprise elements of both.[43] *Larenz* described principles as guiding criteria of legal standardisation that are able to justify decisions on the basis of their own persuasiveness.[44]

Legal principles have already been traced back to early legal ideas such as justice, practicality and legal certainty.[45] Certain forms of justice by *Aristoteles* have been referred to as natural law. Ultimately, such legal ideas claim higher standards than legal principles. Such values,[46] however, are too general for the resolution of a case. They need to be further substantiated.[47]

Deriving principles directly from the valuations of legal rules and regulations, therefore, seems more persuasive. Consequently, deriving legal principles legal literature favours induction – which means making an inference from the specific to the general.[48] According to *Canaris*, deriving

---

(1993) *Rechtshistorisches Journal*, 277 et seq.; Friedrich Kübler, 12 (1993) *Rechtshistorisches Journal*, 307 (310 et seq).

42 Thus Rudolf von Jhering, *Geist des römischen Rechts*, Volume 1 (4th Edition, 1878), 14: "Through Roman law, but beyond it"; here Wolfgang Fikentscher, *Methoden des Rechts in vergleichender Darstellung*, Volume II (1976), 165. On the necessary flexibility, see Winfried Brohm, 30 (1972) *Veröffentlichungen der Vereinigung der Deutschen Staatsrechtslehrer (VVDStRL)*, 245 (249); Uwe Volkmann, 60 (2005) *Juristenzeitung (JZ)*, 261 (262 et seq).

43 Franz Bydlinski, *Fundamentale Rechtsgrundsätze* (1988), 128.

44 Karl Larenz, *Methodenlehre der Rechtswissenschaft* (6th Edition, 1991), 421.

45 Before Gustav Radbruch, *Grundzüge der Rechtsphilosophie* (8th Edition, 1973), § 9, 164 et seqq.; Karl Larenz, *Richtiges Recht* (1979), 31 et seqq.; Arthur Kaufmann, *Rechtsphilosophie* (2nd Edition, 1997), 191 et seqq.

46 Wolfgang Fikentscher, *Methoden des Rechts*, Volume IV (1977), 394 et seqq.

47 Franz Bydlinski, *Juristische Methodenlehre und Rechtsbegriff* (2nd Edition, 1991), 133; Axel Metzger, *Extra legem, intra ius: Allgemeine Rechtsgrundsätze im Europäischen Privatrecht* (2009), 22.

48 Explicitly Aristotle, *Aristoteles' Erste Analytiken oder: Lehre vom Schluss* (Issue Kirchmann, 1877), 23. ch., 142; Francis Bacon, *Novum Organum*, Book I (1620, Issue Joseph Devey (ed), 1902), Aphorismus CIV, 82.

an idea is based on several legal provisions.[49] Some claim that principles result from an isolated analogy[50] or from a cumulative analogy.[51]

This description is too narrow, because legal principles cannot only be derived from several legal provisions. The isolated analogy frequently makes an inference from the specific to the specific; it frequently fulfils a missing factual element by comparing the missing element with the existing element. The general legal principle, however, is derived by making an inference from the specific to the general.[52] The legal principle is, thus, usually broader than the provision(s) it is derived from. Moreover, *ratio legis* is only a means to an end of the methodical process construing an analogy. But carving out a general legal idea already constitutes the end.[53] The comparison to the cumulative analogy must be rejected as well, because the purpose is to close a gap. It requires the underlying case to show a large degree of congruence and comparability. The general legal principle, on the contrary, requires validity also for an indefinite number of cases that cannot yet be identified conclusively.[54] Eventually, the general legal principles can be based on other criteria of validity as well, whereas the cumulative analogy is derived exclusively from the general principle of legal equality.[55]

b) Induction: a systematic and valuing comparison for the derivation of new general legal principles

The systematic derivation of a general legal principle can be achieved through positive provisions. For example, the principle of promissory estoppel is based on Sections 171, 172 and 405 of the Civil Code (BGB). This

---

49 For example, Claus-Wilhelm Canaris (Fn. 11), 97 et seq. "One common legal concept is obtained by several statutory regulations and it is characterized as a general legal principle"; Neil MacCormick, *Legal Reasoning and Legal Theory* (1978), 153 et seq., 232 et seq.

50 For Section 254 BGB Christian Grüneberg, in: Otto Palandt (ed), *BGB* (77th Edition 2018), § 254 para. 3.

51 Ernst August Kramer (Fn. 12), 208; Axel Metzger (Fn. 47), 20, 161 et seqq.

52 Explicitly Claus-Wilhelm Canaris (Fn. 11), 98.

53 Claus-Wilhelm Canaris (Fn. 11), 98.

54 Claus-Wilhelm Canaris (Fn. 11), 98.

55 Claus-Wilhelm Canaris (Fn. 11), 98 et seqq.

principle, consequently, is valid for authority by estoppel[56] or apparent authority,[57] but also in commercial and corporate law.[58] It is also possible to derive a principle from a single provision.[59] It is generally accepted that the provision in Section 254 of the Civil Code on contributory negligence in the law of damages is considered to be a legal principle, and the concept of contributory negligence is to be understood in non-technical terms. Those who disregard the necessary duty of care when one of their legal interests is harmed breach an obligation, along with the actual injuring party. They are then to be accused of 'culpability to themselves', so that it would be unconscionable to claim full compensation.[60] The provision also applies outside of the law on damages to provisions that do not require any fault at all, such as strict liability,[61] or the claim for compensation under neighbourhood law in Section 906(2) sentence 2 of the Civil Code[62] or for the claim for disposal in Section 1004 of the Civil Code.[63] The principle also applies in public law.[64] Thus one can find principles that are only indirectly inferred from the law. This derivation is among the most difficult circumstances in which to determine the legal position. Therefore, principles such as freedom of contract and individual limits are to be substantiated further, which will be an issue further below.

---

56 BGH 15.10.1987 – III ZR 235/86 – BGHZ 102, 60, 64; without dogmatic derivation then: BGH 11.05.2011 – VIII ZR 289/09 – BGHZ 189, 346 para. 15 – Usage of another member's eBay account.

57 BGH 20.01.1983 – VII ZR 32/82 – BGHZ 86, 273, 274 et seqq. – Authority by estoppel.

58 Claus-Wilhelm Canaris, *Die Vertrauenshaftung im deutschen Privatrecht* (1971), 150 et seqq.

59 For example Arthur Meier-Hayoz, in: Arthur Meier-Hayoz (ed), *Berner Kommentar on Swiss Private Law, Introduction to Art. 1-10 ZGB* (1962), Art. 1 para. 406: "A legal rule of a broader scope is often designated as a general legal principle."

60 BGH 18.04.1997 – V ZR 28/96 – BGHZ 135, 235, 240 – roots in the tennis court.

61 BGH 23.06.1952 – III 297/51 – BGHZ 6, 319, 320 – Duty to compensate among drivers; BGH 13.04.1956 – VI 347/54 – BGHZ 20, 259, 263 et seqq. – Operational Risk.

62 BGH 18.09.1987 – V ZR 219/85 – NJW-RR 1988, 136, 138.

63 BGH 18.04.1997 – V ZR 28/96 – BGHZ 135, 235, 239 et seq. – roots in the tennis court.

64 BGH 29.03.1971 – III ZR 98/69 – BGHZ 56, 57, 63: "the legal rationale contained in Section 254 BGB."

IV. *Limits to the development of legal principles and the rules and legal doctrines derived hereby*

1. Rejecting the arbitrariness of a legal dogmatic justification

The obligation to contract and contracts with protective effect for the benefit of third parties are legal doctrines that form part of the basis of legal training and have been recognised for decades. It is therefore surprising that the legal dogmatic justifications underlying them are so disputed and seem to be arbitrary.[65] As the danger of illegal development of law *contra legem* is thus increased, this seems to be astounding. Neglecting the justification for the development of law means concluding based on previous understanding[66] and thus violates the obligation to justify the development of law.

2. Rejection of empty phrases (interpretation of contracts, nature of the matter)

Using empty phrases is also not sufficient. Establishing the legal doctrine of contracts with protective effect for the benefit of third parties by the supplementary interpretation of contracts is not enough, because the reference to the intents of a party then becomes a mere fiction as the party ordinarily does not want to be held liable. The contract is interpreted on the basis of objective criteria instead of the parties' contractual intent.[67] Sometimes legal principles are derived from the "nature of the matter", which was first

---

65 On contracts with protective effect to the benefit of third parties, see for example BGH 11.01.1977 – VI ZR 261/75 – NJW 1977, 2073, 2074: "indifferent"; Christian Grüneberg, in: Otto Palandt (ed), *BGB* (77th Edition 2018), § 328 para. 14: "As a practical result both views are broadly consistent."

66 Here Hans-Georg Gadamer, *Wahrheit und Methode* (6th Edition, 1990), 281 et seqq., 296 et seqq.; Josef Esser, *Vorverständnis und Methodenwahl in der Rechtsfindung* (1970), 139 et seqq., 149 et seqq.

67 Wolfgang Fikentscher and Andreas Heinemann, *Schuldrecht* (10th Edition, 2006), para. 305, 158.

established by *Dernburg*[68] and adopted in academic literature[69] and jurisdiction.[70] This must be rejected as well, because 'nature of the matter' does not establish anything in its own right.[71] Legal ethical principles, such as justice and fairness, must also be further specified to allow for transparent persuasive trains of thought and reasoning.

3. Justification derived from the valuations and limits of the law

Therefore, the derivation and development of a legal principle are among the most difficult parts of working with legal principles. Consequently, it may take decades to establish new legal principles and legal doctrines. It is easier to derive the legal principles from *one or more legal rules*. As shown above, this is rarely the case – which is why the development of new legal principles must be established strictly on the basis of the law and the valuations of the law.

V. Deduction: Specification and scope of principles

Deduction means the inference of the specific from the general. In the underlying context, deduction describes how a general principle works its way into the resolution of a specific legal problem, which is the way from the principle to the rule. Just as the deduction of a general legal principle by inference constitutes judicial development of the law, the legal principles and doctrines derived by means of deduction constitute development of the law. Principles, therefore, serve the development of the law on the basis of pre-existing valuations. Figuratively speaking, legal principles serve as a bridge connecting the existing law and the new law.

---

68 Heinrich Dernburg, *Pandekten*, Volume 1 (4th Edition 1894), 87; ibid., *System des römischen Rechts*, Volume 1 (8th Edition, 1911), 64; Andreas von Thur, *Allgemeiner Teil des Bürgerlichen Rechts*, Volume 1 (1910), 42.

69 In detail Karl Larenz (Fn. 6), 417 et seqq. with further references; Claus-Wilhelm Canaris (Fn. 11), 100.

70 BVerfG 20.02.1952 – 1 BvF 2/51 – BVerfGE 1, 117, 131.

71 Critical Ralf Dreier, *Zum Begriff der „Natur der Sache“* (1965), 127 et seq.; Klaus Friedrich Röhl and Hans Christian Röhl (Fn. 10), § 7.V., 74: "It appears that the concept of the essence as well as of the nature of the matter do not provide for a new argument anywhere"; Peter Raisch, *Juristische Methoden: vom antiken Rom bis zur Gegenwart* (1995), 178; Bernd Rüthers, Christian Fischer and Axel Birk (Fn. 28), para. 929.

1. The specification of a legal principle in general

a) Priority of a legal principle

The case is relatively easy if different principles conflict with each other, but the conflict can be solved by the priority of one principle with respect to the other. According to the *lex specialis* rule, for instance, one principle is superseded by another principle. While here only the conflict between two legal rules needs to be solved, the conflict of legal principles entails more – because a legal principle can be inherent in several legal rules, or even be valid with no legal justification whatsoever. The German Federal Court of Justice (BGH)[72] and the Austrian Supreme Court (OGH),[73] for example, considered an investor's claim for damages as ranking above to the principle of capital preservation.

b) Development of categories, sub-categories, and similar factual conditions

Further specification is possible by creating categories, subcategories, and similar factual conditions. The same procedure applies to general stipulation. The general stipulation too is specified by means of sub-principles, categories, and similar factual conditions. Case law is primarily subject to specification without such legal justification.

c) From legal principle to legal rule

Eventually, there is one last step to obtain a new legal norm, such as a new basis for a claim, from a legal principle by way of development of law. This

72 BGH 09.05.2005 – II ZR 287/02 – NJW 2005, 2450 – EM.TV; BGH 28.11.2005 – II ZR 80/04 – ZIP 2007, 681 para. 3 – Comroad I.

73 OGH 30.03.2011 – Ob 77/10i – GesRZ 2011, 251 No. II.1.1; OGH 15.03/2012 – 6 Ob 28/12d – ÖBA 2012, 548/1828, No. 2.2.et seqq., 9.3.et seq. with comparative references.

is often attached with great uncertainty about the legal dogmatic justification. The classic example is the obligation to contract,[74] the frustration of contract,[75] and contracts with protective effect for the benefit of third parties.[76] The new legal rules were specified by jurisdiction, applying categories and similar factual conditions. As inherent in judicial development, the approaches are made cautiously and the practical application can sometimes only be developed through a *trial-and-error* process.

d) Conflicting legal principles

Conflicting legal principles limit certain specifications of a legal principle. Moreover, one or more legal principles can oppose a legal resolution. This is an issue examining basic rights. Even basic rights granted unconditionally, such as artistic freedom under Article 5(3) sentence 1 of the Basic Law (GG), are limited by the so-called inner-constitutional limitations.[77] These inner-constitutional limitations are conflicting basic rights of others or other constitutionally protected goods. The same applies to legal principles.

Conflicting principles need to be balanced with each other. They need to be weighed according to the schematic examination of proportionality in the stricter sense. First, the conflicting principles must be examined in relation to each other, according to the abstract value assigned to them by the constitution or the law. Then, the specific case must be examined. How much does one principle have to be restricted for the benefit of the other principle? Are the resulting consequences acceptable? Then again: which

---

74 Still arguing for Sec. 826 BGB: RG 07.11.1931 – V 106/31 – RGZ 133, 388, 392 – Theater; critic or for example BGH 02.12.1974 – II ZR 78/72 – BGHZ 63, 282, 285 – Compulsory admission of a monopoly organisation; see for the more recent view which derives an obligation to contract from an injunctive relief Karsten Schmidt, *Deutsche Richterzeitung (DRiZ)* 1977, 97 (98); Reinhardt Bork, in: Julius v. Staudinger (ed), *Bürgerliches Gesetzbuch* (edited 2015), Einl §§ 145 et seqq. para. 27; Jan Busche, in: Jürgen Säcker, Roland Rixecker, Hartmut Oetker and Bettina Limperg (eds), *Münchener Kommentar BGB* (6th Edition 2012), Vorbem § 145 para. 21; Christian Armbrüster, in: Erman, *Bürgerliches Gesetzbuch* (14th Edition 2014), Vorbem § 145 para. 29.

75 See for example BGH 25.02.1993 – VII 24/92 – BGHZ 121, 378 para. 48.

76 Thus RG 10.02.1930 – VI 270/29 – RGZ 127, 218, 221 – gas meter.

77 Settled case law, cf. BVerfG 26.05.1970 – 1 BvR 83/69, 244/69, 345/69 – BVerfGE 28, 243, 261 – conscientious objection; BVerfG 24.02.1971 – 1 BvR 435/68 – BVerfGE 30, 173, 193 –Mephisto; Udo Di Fabio, in: Theodor Maunz and Günter Dürig (eds), *Grundgesetz-Kommentar* (December 2015), Art. 2 para. 246.

consequences result from giving the conflicting principle priority? Practicability reasons must also be taken into consideration.

2. Example of capital markets law: the principle of the rational investment decision

a) Extent of damages: rational investment decision and recession

In capital markets law, there has been rigorous debate about what the relevant damage would be if a company provides an investor with wrong information – for instance, by way of an ad hoc disclosure – and the stock market price has moved to the investor's detriment. In this case, may a claimant only obtain the difference between the accurate price and the incorrect stock market price? Or may the investor also withdraw from the contract and claim restitution in kind, namely the reimbursement of the purchase price in exchange for the securities?

The starting point of the problem was Section 249(1) of the Civil Code (BGB), which establishes the principle of restitution in kind. Accordingly, the condition existing if the harmful event had not occurred has to be established. There was dispute about whether the principle also allows for complete recission of the security transaction. The former prevailing opinion only granted the investor the difference in the market price, because otherwise the market risk of the investor would be unlawfully passed on to the issuer and an excess liability would also arise for the listed company.[78] But this would link the market risk to the alleged protective purpose – an unlawful circular argument.[79] Instead, according to the general right to withdrawal, the tortfeasor causing the other party to withdraw because of the breach of duty bears the risk of deterioration: see Section 346(3) sentence 1 no. 3 of the Civil Code (BGB).[80] Sections 281(5), 283 sentence 2 of the Civil Code provide the link to the law of torts. The Federal Court of Justice (BGH) had to consider the problem in the context of Section 826 of the

78 Thus Holger Fleischer, *Betriebs Berater (BB)* 2002, 1869 (1871); Peter O. Mülbert and Steffen Steup, *Zeitschrift für Wirtschafts- und Bankrecht (WM)* 2005, 1633 (1637).

79 Thomas M.J. Möllers and Franz Clemens Leisch, in: Heribert Hirte and Thomas M.J. Möllers (eds), *Kölner Kommentar zum WpHG* (2nd Edition, 2014), §§ 37b, 37c para. 291.

80 BGH 13.12.2011 – XI ZR 51/10 – BGHZ 192, 90 para. 58 – IKB.

Civil Code, and later for the particular claim to damages pursuant to Sections 37b, 37c of the Securities Trading Act (WpHG). In the IKB decision, the Court stated (in translation):

> "The issue of the scope of the compensation granted by Sections 37b, 37c WpHG seemingly has been focused on only by the District Court in Hamburg (ruling of 10 June 2009 - 329 O 377/08, juris recital 36) and is disputed in academic literature. One opinion only concedes a claim to compensation of the market price difference – in this case between the actual purchase price and the potential price if the defendant had disclosed the inside information in a timely manner – towards the affected investor, according to Sections 37b, 37c WpHG,– (Sethe, in Assmann/Schneider, WpHG, 5th ed. §§ 37b, 37c recital 70 et seqq. m.w.N.; Fuchs, WpHG, §§ 37b, 37c recital 34 et seq.; […]). The contrasting opinion assumes that Sections 37b, 37c WpHG also comprise the recission of the securities business (Möllers/Leisch, in: KK-WpHG, §§ 37b, 37c, recital 240 ff. m.w.N.; […]). The latter view holds true. The starting point of the examination must be Section 249 as a basic rule of the entire tort law that lays down the principle of total reparation […]."[81]

Aside from the aforementioned rules, this resolution can also be justified with a legal principle: the wrongful information leads to the investor's purchase or sale of the security. A rational investment decision was not possible. The reason to view the conclusion of the contract as the relevant damage is that the error prevented a rational investment decision. This is a general principle in capital markets law:[82] the principal of rational investment decision aims to allow the investor to make an autonomous investment decision.[83] The German legislature requires information in the listing prospec-

81 BGH 13.12.2011 – XI ZR 51/10 – BGHZ 192, 90 para. 48 et seqq. – IKB. Before BGH 19.07.2004. – II ZR 402/02 – BGHZ 160, 149, 153 et seq. – Infomatec II; before Thomas M.J. Möllers and Franz Clemens Leisch, *Zeitschrift für Wirtschafts- und Bankrecht (WM)* 2001, 1648 (1655) et seq. See also EuGH (Fn. 132).

82 In detail Thomas M.J. Möllers, in: Thomas M.J. Möllers and Klaus Rotter (eds), *Ad-hoc-Publizität* (2003), § 3 para. 37 et seqq.

83 Heinz-Dieter Assmann, *Zeitschrift für Bankrecht und Bankwirtschaft (ZBB)* 1989, 49 (57) et seqq.; ibid., 'Kapitalmarktrecht - Zur Formation eines Rechtsgebiets in der vierzigjährigen Rechtsentwicklung der Bundesrepublik Deutschland', in: Knut Wolfgang Nörr (ed), *40 Jahre BRD - 40 Jahre Rechtsentwicklung* (1990), 275 (278 et seq.); Thomas M.J. Möllers, 26 (1997) *Zeitschrift für Unternehmens- und Gesellschaftsrecht (ZGR)*, 334 (338); similar Holger Fleischer, *64. Deutscher* Juristentag (DJT) 2002, p. F 27: Principle of the informed transaction decision.

tus and the sales prospectus that allows investors to reach a correct conclusion about financial assets and liabilities.[84] The right to an autonomous investment decision has also been explicitly included in the Securities Acquisition and Takeover Act (WpÜG). The holders of securities of the target company must be 'provided with sufficient information to be able to make a decision on the offer with full knowledge of the facts', Section 11(1) sentence 2 of the Securities Acquisition and Takeover Act[85] which has been positioned at the beginning of the rule, Section 3(2) of the Securities Acquisition and Takeover Act. Therefore, this principle also applies to the ad hoc disclosure according to Section 15 of the Securities Trading Act (WpHG). This cannot be based on the wording, but on the historical intent of the legislature,[86] and is based on the notion that the individual must be able to decide autonomously and that errors caused by a third party must be fully fixed.

b) Conflicting legal principles

Under capital markets law, investors may claim damages if the company disclosed wrongful information and the investor has purchased shares of the company on the basis of this information.[87] Under corporate law, this conflicts *prima facie* with the principle of capital preservation that prohibits a stock corporation from distributing capital to the shareholders unless outside of the statutory regulations, Sections 57, 71 of the Stock Corporation Act (AktG). Subsequently, there was much dispute about whether the protection of investors under capital markets law or the principle of capital maintenance under corporate law has priority.[88] To resolve the conflict, the

---

84 Sec. 5 (1) p. 1 WpPG; Sec. 7 (1) p. 1 VermAnlG; see also Sec. 13 (1) p. 2 WpHG: "consider making his investment decision".

85 WpÜG, Begr. RegE, BT-Drs. 14/7034, p. 29 on General Part and p. 41 on Sec. 11 WpÜG.

86 On ad-hoc publicity, see BT-Drucks. 14/8017, p. 87: "timely possess market sensitive information to be able to make an appropriate investment decision"; Thomas M.J. Möllers (Fn. 82), § 3 para. 49.

87 For example, Sec. 21 et seqq. WpPG, Sec. 12 WpÜG, Sec. 37b, 37c WpHG and Sec. 826 BGB.

88 In detail Thomas M.J. Möllers, *Betriebs Berater (BB)* 2005, 1637 (1639 et seqq.); Eckart Gottschalk, *Das deutsche Steuerrecht (DStR)* 2005, 1648 (1651 et seqq.); *Walter Bayer,* in: Wulf Goette and Mathias Habersack (eds), *Münchener*

classic argumentation constructions need to be taken into account, and the interests of the issuer need to be weighed against the interests of the affected investor.[89]

The relationship between Sections 37b and 37c and Section 826 of the Civil Code (BGB) to Sections 57, 71 of the Stock Corporation Act (AktG) was not explicitly mentioned in the legislative process. However, it cannot be assumed that the legislature adopts standards that from the outset are of no value because of the priority of the principle of capital maintenance.[90] This legislative valuation must be respected: Affected investors are insofar equal to third parties – the claim for damages is not based on the membership rights of the shareholders but on the infliction of damage by the board, which means that the claimants must be considered as third-party creditors.[91] This and the question of whether a 'turnover business' has occurred are decisive for the priority of investor protection.[92] Moreover, in the absence of any deviating regulation, Section 249(1) of the Civil Code (BGB)

Kommentar-AktG (3rd Edition, 2008), § 57 para. 15 et seqq.; Michael Kort, *Neue Zeitschrift für Gesellschaftsrecht (NZG)* 2005, 496 (498); Rolf Sethe, in: Heinz Dieter Assmann and Uwe H. Schneider (eds), *WpHG* (6th Edition, 2012), §§ 37b, 37c para. 6 et seqq.; Daniel Zimmer and Marc Grotheer, in: Eberhard Schwark and Daniel Zimmer (eds), *Kapitalmarktrechts-Kommentar* (4th Edition, 2010), §§ 37b, c para. 11 et seqq.

89 At an early stage already Thomas M.J. Möllers (Fn. 88), 1639 et seqq.; Thomas M.J. Möllers and Franz Clemens Leisch (Fn. 79), §§ 37b, c para. 39 et seqq.

90 Ulf Renzenbrink and Nelson Holzner, *Zeitschrift für Bank- und Kapitalmarktrecht (BKR)* 2002, 434 (438); Thomas M.J. Möllers, in: Thomas M.J. Möllers and Klaus Rotter (eds), *Ad-hoc-Publizität* (2003), § 14 para. 136; Norbert Horn, 'Zur Haftung der AG und ihrer Organmitglieder für unrichtige oder unterlassene Ad-hoc-Informationen', in: Mathias Habersack, Peter Hommelhoff, Uwe Hüffer and Karsten Schmidt, *Festschrift für Peter Ulmer zum 70. Geburtstag* (2003), 817 (827); Sven Keusch and Kerstin Wankerl, *Zeitschrift für Bank-und Kapitalmarktrecht (BKR)* 2003, 744 (746); Rüdiger Veil, 167 (2003) *Zeitschrift für das gesamte Handels- und Wirtschaftsrecht (ZHR)*, 365 (394); Katja Langenbucher, *Zeitschrift für Wirtschaftsrecht (ZIP)* 2005, 239 (241). On Austrian law OGH 15.03.2012 – 6 Ob 28/12d – ÖBA 2012, 548/1828 No. 3.5; Friedrich Rüffler, 'Haftung für Kapitalmarktinformationen nach OGH 7 Ob 77/10i', in: Susanne Kalss and Ulrich Torggler (eds), *Kapitalmarkthaftung und Gesellschaftsrecht* (2013), 1 (7).

91 BGH 09.5.2005 – II ZR 287/02 – NJW 2005, 2450, 2451 – EM.TV; Rolf Sethe (Fn. 88), §§ 37b, 37c para. 6; Holger Fleischer, Stephan Schneider and Marlen Thaten, *Neue Zeitschrift für Gesellschaftsrecht (NZG)* 2012, 801 (802).

92 For a different view Eberhard Schwark, 'Prospekthaftung und Kapitalerhaltung in der AG', in: Karsten Schmidt and Eberhard Schwark (eds), *Unternehmen,*

explicitly allows for compensation for the negative interest also within the framework of Section 21 of the Securities Prospectus Act (WpPG) and Section 826 of the Civil Code (BGB), Section 12 of the Securities Acquisition and Takeover Act (WpÜG)[93] and Section 37b, 37c of the Securities Trading Act (WpHG). Thus however, as the Federal Court of Justice emphasised, the damaged party's obligation to return the shares mainly relies on the notion that, due to the damage inflicted, the claimant should not obtain any benefit exceeding the compensation of the damage (*Bereicherungsverbot*).[94]

Balancing the interests of the company or their creditors with those of the affected shareholders, the Higher Regional Court (OLG) in Frankfurt[95] and the Federal Court of Justice (BGH)[96] are right to emphasise the serious misconduct in relation to an immoral damage according to Section 826 of the Civil Code (BGB). It is not surprising that the civil liability actions are accompanied by criminal convictions of the acting members of the company's board. The priority of company law fails for the simple reason that the capital of a company stems from the deceived shareholders' assets, and because Section 57 of the Stock Corporation Act (AktG) may not be misused as a *carte blanche* for improper activities under the tort law.[97] In other words: for the damaged investors it would be incomprehensible if the company distributed dividends to the other shareholders at the expense of the deceived shareholders.[98] In economic terms, the capital market may not be put at a disadvantage – overemphasising the creditor protection at the expense of the shareholders – because otherwise the willingness to provide

---

Recht und Wirtschaftsordnung: Festschrift für Peter Raisch zum 70. Geburtstag (1995), 269 (288 et seq.).

93 Thomas M.J. Möllers (Fn. 79), § 12 para. 99.

94 BGH 09.05.2005 – II ZR 287/02 – NJW 2005, 2450 under II.2.b) bb) – EM.TV.

95 OLG Frankfurt 17.03.2005 – 1 U 149/04 – ZIP 2005, 710, 713 – Comroad.

96 BGH 09.05.2005 – II ZR 287/02 – NJW 2005, 2450 under II.2.b.bb – EM.TV.

97 Sven Keusch and Kerstin Wankerl (Fn. 90), 746.

98 OLG München 20.04.2005 – 7 U 5303/04 – ZIP 2005, 901, 902 – Comroad; before Ossip Flechtheim, *Juristische Wochenschrift (JW)* 1916, 937; James Breit, 76 (1915) *Zeitschrift für das gesamte Handels- und Wirtschaftsrecht (ZHR)*, 415 (442); Felix Moos, 70 (1911) *Zeitschrift für das gesamte Handels- und Wirtschaftsrecht (ZHR)*, 184; Hartwig Henze, *Neue Zeitschrift für Gesellschaftsrecht (NZG)* 2005, 115 (120).

venture capital would decrease and this would eventually be to the company's disadvantage.[99] Therefore, the priority of issuer liability under capital markets law contributes to allocative efficiency and to an increase in competitiveness towards foreign stock exchanges.[100] Numerous other Member States of the European Union and the USA recognise a claim to damages under the tort law directed against the company if a wrongful capital markets information is intentionally provided.[101]

VI. Formation of principles at the European level

1. Extraction of principles through comparative law

Looking at principles at the European level, one should distinguish between the general principles of primary law, which have priority in cases of doubt, and the principles of European civil law, which have no force of precedence whatsoever, and can (only) be used in the context of teleological considerations.[102]

a) Reference to the general principles of law or constitutional traditions of the Member States

General principles of law also serve to fill in gaps in European law. Reference is thereby often made to the general principles of law that are common to the legal systems. One such provision, for example, is the liability of the Union under Article 340 TFEU. By reference to provisions of the national Member States, the Court of Justice of the European Union (CJEU) can

99 OLG Frankfurt 17.03.2005 – 1 U 149/04 – ZIP 2005, 710, 713 – Comroad; Lutz Krämer and Matthias Baudisch, *Zeitschrift für Wirtschafts- und Bankrecht (WM)* 1998, 1161 (1167); Ulf Renzenbrink and Nelson Holzner (Fn. 90), 437; Sezer Doğan, *Ad-hoc-Publizitätshaftung* (2005), 230.

100 Holger Fleischer (Fn. 83), p. F 73; Eberhard Schwark (Fn. 92), 269, 281 et seqq.; Daniel Zimmer and Grotheer (Fn. 88), §§ 37b, 37c para. 13.

101 Thomas M.J. Möllers and Franz Clemens Leisch (Fn. 79), §§ 37b, c para. 49 et seqq. On the view of the EuGH see below Fn. 126, 132.

102 Bettina Heiderhoff, *Europäisches Privatrecht* (4th Edition, 2016), para. 230.

form a general rule from various provisions by induction.[103] By reference to the constitutional traditions common to the Member States, the CJEU has developed the fundamental rights at a European level,[104] now standardised in Article 6(3) TEU,[105] and established the claim for State liability against the Member States. It has always emphasised the duty to develop the law that the general principles of law have to fulfil.[106] Meanwhile, at the European level, in addition to recognising fundamental rights the Court has also recognised general principles of law[107] – such as legal certainty,[108] protection of legitimate expectations,[109] effective legal protection,[110] *effet utile*, and proportionality.[111]

---

103 For European law, Axel Metzger (Fn. 47), 2009, 25 et seq.; Jürgen Basedow, 'Mangold, Audiolux und die allgemeinen Grundsätze des europäischen Privatrechts', in: Stefan Grundmann, Brigitte Haar, Hanno Merkt et al. (eds), *Festschrift für Klaus J. Hopt zum 70. Geburtstag* (2010), 27 (35).

104 ECJ 14.05.1974 – 4/73 – ECLI:EU:C:1974:51 – ECR 1974, 491, para. 13 – Nold.

105 Meanwhile, however, the fundamental rights were derived broadly from the Charter of Fundamental Rights of the European Union Art 6 (1) TEU.

106 ECJ 05.03.1996 – Case no. C-46/93 inter alia – ECLI:EU:C:1996:79, para. 27 – Brasserie du Pêcheur: Reference to "the fundamental principles of the Community legal system and, where necessary, general principles common to the legal systems of the Member States."; here Werner Schroeder, *Juristische Schulung (JuS)* 2004, 180 (183 et seq.).

107 Generally on the integration of general legal principles in European case law: Peter Häberle, *Europäische Grundrechte-Zeitschrift (EuGRZ)* 1991, 261 et seq.; Peter Christian Müller-Graff and Eibe Riedel (eds), *Gemeinsames Verfassungsrecht in der Europäischen Union* (1998).

108 ECJ 21.09.1983 – 205/85 inter alia – ECLI:EU:C:1983:233, para. 30 – Milchkontor; ECJ 13.02.1996 – Case no. C-143/93 – ECLI:EU:C:1996:45, para. 27 – Van Es Douane Agenten; ECJ 21.02.2006 – C-255/02 – ECLI:EU:C:2006:121, para. 72 – Halifax.

109 ECJ 05.07.1973 – 1/73 – ECLI:EU:C:1973:78, para. 6 et seq.– Westzucker; ECJ 10.09.2009 – C-201/08 – ECLI:EU:C:2009:539, para. 46 – Plantanol.

110 ECJ 15.05.1986 – 222/84 – ECLI:EU:C:1986:206, para. 18 – Johnston; confirmed as an inherent principle in ECJ 13.03.2007 – C-432/05 – ECLI:EU:C:2007:163, para. 37 et seq. – Unibet.

111 ECJ 16.07.1956 – 8/55 – ECLI:EU:C:1956:11 = ECR 1955/1957, 197, 311 – Fédération Charbonnière; ECJ 13.12.1979 – 44/79 – ECLI:EU:C:1979:290, para. 23 – Hauer; Paul Craig and Gráinne de Búrca, *EU Law* (6th Edition, 2015), 15.4(b), 551 et seq.; Uwe Kischel, *Zeitschrift Europarecht (EuR)* 2000, 380 et seq.; Oliver Koch, *Der Grundsatz der Verhältnismäßigkeit in der Rechtsprechung des Gerichtshofs der Europäischen Gemeinschaften* (2003); Jochen A. Frowein, 'Die Herausbildung europäischer Verfassungsprinzipien', in: Arthur

Interestingly, the CJEU has since developed European fundamental rights and general principles of law. To an extent, they afford citizens stronger legal protection than the fundamental rights of individual Member States. For example, broadly beyond the case law of German courts, the CJEU strengthened equal rights – and particularly the rights of women. This covered not only the level of the wage entitlement, but also access to and securing employment.[112] With respect to procedural law, the CJEU has repeatedly stressed that access to the national courts must also be guaranteed,[113] and with this principle of effective legal protection restricted the procedural autonomy of the Member States.[114] The European Court of Human Rights has, for example, set higher standards for the requirement for timely legal protection than the national courts, and therefore declared proceedings of lengthy duration to be unlawful.[115]

Kaufmann, Ernst-Joachim Mestmäcker and Hans F. Zacher (eds), *Rechtsstaat und Menschenwürde: Festschrift für Werner Maihofer* (1988), 149 (151); Manfred Zuleeg and Stefan Kadelbach, 'Individuelle Rechte und Pflichten', in: Reiner Schulze, Manfred Zuleeg and Stefan Kadelbach, *Europarecht* (3rd Edition, 2014), § 8 para. 42 et seq.; The legal competence for the principle of proportionality is found in Art. 5 (4) TEU.

112 ECJ 14.12.1995 – C-317/93 – ECLI:EU:C:1995:438, para. 28– Nolte; ECJ 11.11.1997 – C-409/95 –ECLI:EU:C:1997:533, para. 31 with approving comments, Tobias Lenz, *Neue Juristische Wochenschrift (NJW)* 1998, 1619 – Marschall; Sacha Prechal, 20 (1993) Legal Issues of European Integration, 81 et seq. On the influence of the ECJ on the German Federal Labour Court (BAG) concerning impermissible questions regarding a pregnancy by the ECJ 08.11.1990 – C-177/88 – ECLI:EU:C:1990:383 – ECR 1990, I-3941 para. 24 et seq. – Dekker see BAG 15.10.1992 – 2 AZR 227/92 – BAGE 71, 252, para. 13.

113 ECJ 15.10.1987 – 222/86 – ECLI:EU:C:1987:442, para. 14 – Heylens; ECJ 13.12.1991 – C-18/88 – ECLI:EU:C:1991:474, para. 34 – GB-Inno-BM.

114 Rodríguez Iglesias and Gil Carlos, *Europäische Grundrechte-Zeitschrift (EuGRZ)* 1997, 289 (290); Rupert Scholz, *Die öffentliche Verwaltung (DÖV)* 1998, 261 (262 et seq.); Rigide Kakouris, 34 (1997) *Common Markets Law Review*, 1389, 1407 et seq.; Andreas Cahn, *Zeitschrift für europäisches Privatrecht (ZEuP)* 1998, 969 (975).

115 Wolfgang Frowein and Jochen Peukert, *EMRK-Kommentar* (2009), Art. 6 para. 248 et seq. with further citations. On the requirement for effective legal protection as a common constitutional tradition, see ECJ, 13.03.2007 – C-432/05 – ECLI:EU:C:2007:163, para. 37 et seq. – Unibet; ECJ of 26.11.2013 – C-58/12 P – ECLI:EU:C:2013:770, para. 72 – Groupe Gascogne.

b) Isolated codification of European legal principles

Meanwhile, the European legislature has set out individual fundamental rights in the Amsterdam Treaty, and also included the 1950 European Declaration of Human Rights, Article 6 TEU. Otherwise, general principles of law as found within the German Civil Code (BGB) are only tenuously standardised in the European treaties. This is due to the fact that most principles were first developed by the CJEU before they then found their way into the treaties. In the TEU, for example, one can find the principle of conferral and the principle of subsidiarity (Article 5(1)–(3) TEU) and the principle of proportionality (Article 5(4) TEU). Other principles are also recognised, such as the principle of democracy (Article 2 TEU).

2. General legal principles of European civil law from the classification of European law

a) Difficulties at the European level

If one attempts to extract general legal principles from primary and secondary European law, various disadvantages become evident. Firstly, numerous principles are not standardised at all; secondly, entire areas of law are also only selectively regulated at the European level;[116] and thirdly, there is a danger that the European Union is exceeding its competence by extracting a principle and thus violating the principle of conferral, Article 5(2) TFEU.[117] Finally, one must avoid the risk of exporting one's own prior understanding. Instead, European law is to be interpreted autonomously. As a consequence, the objectives at the European level are not absolutely identical to the objectives in individual Member States.

---

116 Fritz Rittner, 50 (1995) *JuristenZeitung (JZ)*, 849 (851): "An island in the sea of national law"; before Hein Kötz, 50 (1986) *Rabels Zeitschrift für ausländisches und internationales Privatrecht (RabelsZ)*, 1 (5) "pointillist character"; Thomas M.J. Möllers, 59 (2004) *Juristen Zeitung (JZ)*, 1067 et seq.

117 Critical e.g. Martin Schmidt-Kessel, 'Europäisches Vertragsrecht', in: Karl Riesenhuber, *Europäische Methodenlehre* (3rd Edition, 2015), § 17 para. 43.

It is also interesting to note the attempt to develop a European Civil Code, such as the Draft Common Frame of Reference (DCFR)[118] from various research groups or the (withdrawn) proposal from the Commission for a Common European Sales Law (CESL).[119] Some principles and rules from German law are already included in these drafts for European law. However, these are all still not legally binding.

b) Legal principles of European civil law

However, it does not seem hopeless to extract general legal principles at a European level from European law itself without having to resort to the law of the Member States. The examples illustrate this.

In academic literature, attempts have been made to develop general legal principles,[120] such as discerning freedom of contract or contractual fidelity (*pacta sunt servanda*), from European law.[121] This is not straightforward, because neither the treaties nor the Charter of Fundamental Rights directly

118 From Christian Bar, Eric Clive and Hans Schulte-Nölke, *Principles, Definition and Model Rule of European Private Law (Draft Common Frame of Reference – DCFR)* 2009, online edition, accessible at http://ec.europa.eu/justice/policies/civil/docs/dcfr_outline_edition_en.pdf (accessed 12 July 2016); see here, e.g. Martin Schmidt-Kessel (Fn. 117), § 17 para. 47 et seq.; Horst Eidenmüller, Florian Faust, Hans Christoph Grigoleit, Nils Jansen, Gerhard Wagner and Reinhard Zimmermann, 63 (2008) *JuristenZeitung (JZ)*, 529 et seq.; Wolfgang Ernst, 208 (2008) *Archiv für die civilistische Praxis* (AcP), 248 et seq.

119 Proposal for a Regulation of the European Parliament and of the Council on a Common European Sales Law of 11.10.2011, COM (2011) 635 final; here the contributions of the extraordinary meeting of civil law lecturers, published in: 212 (2012) *Archiv für die civilistische Praxis (AcP)*, 467-852.

120 Stefan Grundmann (ed), Systembildung und Systemlücken in Kerngebieten des europäischen Privatrechts (2000); Karl Riesenhuber, System und Prinzipien des Europäischen Vertragsrechts (2003), § 18; generally: Nils Jansen (2005), Zeitschrift für europäisches Privatrecht (ZEuP), 750 et seq.; Alex Metzger, Extra legem, intra ius: Allgemeine Rechtsgrundsätze im Europäischen Privatrecht (2009); Norbert Reich, General Principles of EU Civil Law (2014).

121 See, e.g. Karl Riesenhuber, 'Die Inhaltskontrolle von Vereinbarungen über Hauptleistung und Preis im Europäischen Vertragsrecht', in: Jens Dammann, Wolfgang Grunsky and Thomas Pfeiffer, *Gedächtnisschrift Wolf* (2011), 123 (130) with further citations; Bettina Heiderhoff (Fn. 102), para. 230 et seq.

standardise freedom of contract.[122] There are only a few judgements that address freedom of contract.[123] However, Article 119 TFEU acknowledges the 'principle of an open market economy with free competition'; freedom of contract is an essential requirement for this.[124] Freedom of contract seeks to strengthen the internal market by dismantling different legal rules.

Eventually, also conflict set out above between the principle of protection of investors under capital markets law and the principle of capital preservation is of European origin, because the relevant national rules implement European directives. The Austrian Supreme Court (OGH) was correct to initiate a preliminary ruling procedure to the ECJ, while the German Federal Court of Justice (BGH) misjudged the obligation.[125] In the *Hirmann* case, the CJEU found that numerous European directives on capital markets law require liability, and that even without a specific regulation the requirement of effective sanctions does not prohibit claims for damages.[126]

The principle of rational investment decision, and therefore the right to make an autonomous investment decision, is incorporated in the European directives.[127] The prospectus has to contain information "that enables investors and their advisors to form a well-founded opinion on assets and liabilities, financial situation, gains and losses, and future perspectives".[128] Similarly, the Transparency Directive on the harmonisation of transparency requirements in relation to information about issuers whose securities are admitted to trading on a regulated market requires information that enables

122 Whereas Art. 2 (1) GG standardises freedom of action, and thus also private autonomy, Art. 16 et seq. Charter of Fundamental Rights only contains the protection of freedom to conduct business; critical, therefore Josef Franz Lindner, *Zeitschrift für Rechtspolitik (ZRP)* 2007, 54 (56): incomplete protection of fundamental rights.

123 ECJ 10.07.1980 – 99/79 – ECLI:EU:C:1980:193, para. 16 – Lancôme speaks of "legal certainty in contractual matters".

124 Christian Schmidt-Leithoff, 'Gedanken über die Privatrechtsordnung als Grundlage zum EWG_Vertrag', in: Manfred Löwisch, Christian Schmidt-Leithoff and Burkhard Schmiedel (eds), *Beiträge zum Handels- und Wirtschaftsrecht: Festschrift für Fritz Rittner*, 597 (604); Peter O. Mülbert, 159 (1995) *Zeitschrift für das gesamte Handels- und Wirtschaftsrecht (ZHR),* 2 (8); see also Art. II.-1:101 – II.1:103 DCFR.

125 Therefore, critical Thomas M.J Möllers (Fn. 88), 1641.

126 ECJ 19.12.2013 – C-174/12 – ECLI:EU:C:2013:856, para. 39 et seq. – Alfred Hirmann/Immofinanz AG; before Thomas M.J. Möllers (Fn. 88), 1641.

127 On the following before Thomas M.J. Möllers (Fn. 82), § 3 para. 38.

128 Prospectus Directive 2003/71/EC of 4 November 2003, Art. 5 (1).

investors to buy or sell shares in full knowledge of the changes in the voting structure.[129] Also, under the Takeover Directive, the owner of securities of the target company "must have sufficient time and information to enable them to reach a properly informed decision on the bid".[130] The right to an autonomous investment decision is phrased most clearly in Recital 1 of the former Directive on Securities Sales Prospectus.[131] Therefore, it was only consequent that the CJEU accepted the reversal of the purchase agreement in the *Hirmann* case, arguing that the damaged party is taken back to the situation they were in before the damaging event happened.[132]

3. Limits to legal development at the European level

a) Insufficient justification

As in German law, legal principles – when they are newly devised – must be developed from the applicable law. When the CJEU's decision in the *Mangold* case elevated the prohibition of age discrimination into a legal principle and invoked *inter alia* the common constitutional traditions,[133] it attracted complaints because such a common tradition did not exist in the Member States.[134]

---

129 Transparency Directive 2004/109/EC of 15 December 2004, Recital 18.

130 Directive 2004/25/EC of 21 April 2004 on takeover bids Art. 3 (1) lit. b) and Art. 6 (2).

131 Securities Prospectus Directive 89/298/EEC of 17 April 1989, Recitals 1–3.

132 ECJ 19.12.2013 – C-174/12 – ECLI:EU:C:2013:856, para. 53 – Alfred Hirmann/Immofinanz AG: "The aim of such legislation is, inter alia, to ensure that the injured party is put back in the position he was in before the occurrence of the act which has caused him harm, by requiring, first, repayment to the purchaser of a sum equivalent to the price which he paid for the purchase of the shares, together with interest, and, secondly, the maintenance of those shares in the share capital of the company concerned in the same way as other shares."

133 ECJ 22.11.2005 – C-144/04 – ECLI:EU:C:2005:709, para. 75 – Mangold/Helm.

134 Critical, inter alia, Jan H. Jans, 34 (2007) *Legal Issues of European Integration*, 53 (65); Jürgen Basedow (Fn. 103), 27 (34); Jürgen Basedow, 71 (2016) *JuristenZeitung (JZ)*, 269 (275 et seq.).

b) Conflicting legal principles

As in German law, general principles of law can ultimately conflict with a particular outcome. Here, it is again important to bear in mind the protection of legitimate expectations for the benefit of citizens. Such a protection of legitimate expectations conflicts with the development of the law concerning horizontal direct effect of directives,[135] and also needs to be taken into consideration as part of the development of the law in conformity with the directive.[136] Conversely, the principle of effective legal protection can restrict the principle of legal certainty and protection of legitimate expectations – for example, when the national authorities do not revoke unlawful state aid within a one-year period, and the beneficiary must nevertheless repay the unlawfully acquired aid after this period.[137]

VII. Outlook

The German Civil Code (BGB), marked by the ideas of 19th Century Pandectists,[138] trains German lawyers in systematic thinking and the associated legal doctrine and legal principles. In order to further develop the law,[139] but also to better understand it, a consolidated doctrine of law with legal

---

135 ECJ 08.10.1987 – 80/86 – ECLI:EU:C:1987:431, para. 10 – Kolpinghuis.

136 ECJ 04.07.2006 – C-212/04 – ECLI:EU:C:2006:443, para. 110 et seq. – Adeneler.

137 ECJ 20.03.1997 – C-24/95 – ECLI:EU:C:1997:163, para. 37 et seq. und 48 et seq. – Alcan, reclaiming state aid.

138 To mention, for example Anton Friedrich Justus Thibaut, *System des Pandektenrechts*, 3 Volumes (5th Edition, 1818); Georg Friedrich Puchta, *Pandekten* (5th Edition, 1850); Bernhard Windscheid, *Lehrbuch des Pandektenrechts*, 3 Volumes (7th Edition, 1891); Heinrich Dernburg, *Pandekten*, 3 Volumes (4th Edition, 1894); Ferdinand Regelsberger, *Pandekten* (1893); Reinhard Zimmermann, 'Das Bürgerliche Gesetzbuch und die Entwicklung des Bürgerlichen Rechts', in: Mathias Schmoekel, Joachim Rückert and Reinhard Zimmermann, *Historisch-kritischer Kommentar zum BGB* (2003), § 1 para. 6 et seq.

139 On the role of general legal principles for the filling of gaps see Fn. 13 et seq.

principles is required.[140] The relatively young capital markets law is still at the beginning of the process of forming principles.[141]

Consequently, jurisprudence needs to attempt to develop legal principle at the European level. As shown, there are already initial signs that this is occurring. But due to the gaps in the European legal framework, it faces particular challenges. Aside from the problems depicted above, the concurrency of directives (which need to be implemented in national law) and regulations (which are directly applicable) presents a further challenge for developing principles.[142] The challenges for scholars never cease.

Bibliography

Robert Alexy, 'Rechtsregeln und Rechtsprinzipien' 25 (1985) *Archiv für Rechts- und Sozialphilosophie – Beihefte (ARSP-B)*, 13.

Robert Alexy, 'Rechtssystem und praktische Vernunft' 18 (1987) *Rechtstheorie*, 405.

Robert Alexy, *Theorie der Grundrechte,* (Suhrkamp, Frankfurt am Main 1986).

Robert Alexy, 'Verfassungsrecht und einfaches Recht – Verfassungsgerichtsbarkeit und Fachgerichtsbarkeit' 61 (2002) *Veröffentlichungen der Vereinigung der Deutschen Staatsrechtslehrer (VVDStRL)*, 7.

Heinz-Dieter Assmann, 'Konzeptionelle Grundlagen des Anlegerschutzes' *Zeitschrift für Bankrecht und Bankwirtschaft (ZBB)* 1989, 49.

Heinz-Dieter Assmann, 'Kapitalmarktrecht – Zur Formation eines Rechtsgebiets in der vierzigjährigen Rechtsentwicklung der Bundesrepublik Deutschland', in: Knut Wolfgang Nörr (ed), *40 Jahre BRD – 40 Jahre Rechtsentwicklung* (Mohr Siebeck, Tübingen 1990), 275.

---

140 Legal doctrine is vividly compared with grammar, without which language, here the legal norms, cannot be understood, Maximilian Herberger, *Dogmatik* (1981), 37 et seq., 74 et seq., 119, 257 et seq. with extensive references to Roman law; Nils Jansen, *Zeitschrift für das Europäische Privatrecht (ZEuP)* 2005, 750 (754).

141 Further principles in the law on capital markets are, for example, avoidance of asymmetries of information, or avoidance of conflicts of interest, see Thomas M.J. Möllers, 'Anlegerschutz im System des Kapitalmarktrechts', in: Stefan Grundmann, Brigitte Haar, Hanno Merkt et al. (eds), *Festschrift für Klaus J. Hopt zum 70. Geburtstag* (2010), 2247 et seq.

142 In greater depth recently Thomas M.J. Möllers, *Zeitschrift für Europäisches Privatrecht (ZEuP) 2016*, 325 (355 et seqq.). The "First Financial Market Amendment Act (1. FiMaNoG)" as of 3.6.2016 is a good example for an inconsistent implementation of the European Market Abuse Directive and Regulation into German law.

Heinz Dieter Assmann and Uwe H. Schneider (eds), *Wertpapierhandelsgesetz (WpHG) Commentary* (6th Edition, Otto Schmidt, Cologne 2012).

Marietta Auer, *Materialisierung, Flexibilisierung, Richterfreiheit* (Mohr Siebeck, Tübingen 2005).

Francis Bacon, *Novum Organum*, Book I (England 1620, Issue Joseph Devey (ed), P.F. Collier, New York 1902).

Jack M. Balkin, 'The Crystalline Structure of Legal Thought' 39 (1986) *Rutgers Law Review (Rutgers L. Rev.),* 1.

Christian Bar, Eric Clive and Hans Schulte-Nölke, *Principles, Definition and Model Rule of European Private Law (Draft Common Frame of Reference - DCFR)* 2009, online edition, accessible at http://ec.europa.eu/justice/policies/civil/docs/dcfr_outline_edition_en.pdf.

Jürgen Basedow, 'Das BGB im künftigen europäischen Privatrecht: Der hybride Kodex' 200 (2000) *Archiv für die civilistische Praxis (AcP)*, 445.

Jürgen Basedow, 'Hundert Jahre Rechtsvergleichung – Von wissenschaftlicher Erkenntnisquelle zur obligatorischen Methode der Rechtsanwendung' 71 (2016) *JuristenZeitung (JZ)*, 269.

Jürgen Basedow, 'Mangold, Audiolux und die allgemeinen Grundsätze des europäischen Privatrechts', in: Stefan Grundmann, Brigitte Haar, Hanno Merkt et al. (eds), *Festschrift für Klaus J. Hopt zum 70. Geburtstag* (De Gruyter, Berlin/New York 2010), 27.

Berner Kommentar on Swiss Private Law, Volume 1, Arthur Meier-Hayoz (ed), (Stämpfli, Bern 1962).

Reinhard Bork, *Allgemeiner Teil des Bürgerlichen Gesetzbuchs* (4th Edition, Mohr Siebeck, Tübingen 2016).

James Breit, 'Ansprüche des Aktionärs gegen die Aktiengesellschaft aus dem Erwerb der Aktien' 76 (1915) *Zeitschrift für das gesamte Handels- und Wirtschaftsrecht (ZHR)*, 415.

Winfried Brohm, 'Die Dogmatik des Verwaltungsrechts vor den Gegenwartsaufgaben der Verwaltung' 30 (1972) *Veröffentlichungen der Vereinigung der Deutschen Staatsrechtslehrer (VVDStRL)*, 245.

Franz Bydlinski, *Fundamentale Rechtsgrundsätze* (Springer Verlag, Wien/New York 1988).

Franz Bydlinski, *Juristische Methodenlehre und Rechtsbegriff* (2nd Edition, Springer Verlag, Wien 1991).

Andreas Cahn, 'Gemeinschaftsrecht und nationales Verfahrensrecht' *Zeitschrift für europäisches Privatrecht (ZEuP)* 1998, 969.

Claus Wilhelm Canaris, *Die Feststellung von Lücken im Gesetz* (2nd Edition, Duncker & Humblot, Berlin 1983).

Claus-Wilhelm Canaris, *Die Vertrauenshaftung im deutschen Privatrecht* (C.H. Beck, Munich 1971).

Claus-Wilhelm Canaris, ‚Wandlungen des Schuldvertragsrechts – Tendenzen zu seiner ‚Materialisierung'' 200 (2000) *Archiv für die civilistische Praxis (AcP)*, 273.

Paul Craig and Gráinne de Búrca, *EU Law* (6th Edition, Oxford University Press, Oxford 2015).

Heinrich Dernburg, *System des römischen Rechts*, Volume 1 (8th Edition, H. W. Müller, Berlin 1911).

Heinrich Dernburg, *Pandekten*, 3 Volumes (4th Edition, H. W. Müller, Berlin 1894).

Sezer Doğan, *Ad-hoc-Publizitätshaftung* (Nomos, Baden-Baden 2005).

Ralf Dreier, *Zum Begriff der „Natur der Sache“* (De Gruyter, Berlin 1965).

Ronald Dworkin, *Taking Rights Seriously* (1st and 2nd Edition, Harvard University Press, Cambridge/Mass. 1977 and 1978).

Horst Eidenmüller, Florian Faust, Hans Christoph Grigoleit, Nils Jansen, Gerhard Wagner and Reinhard Zimmermann, 'Der Gemeinsame Referenzrahmen für das Europäische Privatrecht: Wertungsfragen und Kodifikationsprobleme' 63 (2008) *Juristen-Zeitung (JZ)*, 529.

Ludwig Enneccerus and Hans Carl Nipperdey, *Lehrbuch des Bürgerlichen Rechts* (15th Edition, Mohr Siebeck, Tübingen 1957).

Erman Bürgerliches Gesetzbuch. Handkommentar, Vol. 2, Harm-Peter Westermann, Barbara Grunewald, Georg Maier-Reimer (eds) (14th Edition, Otto Schmidt, Cologne 2014).

Wolfgang Ernst, '„Der Common Frame of Reference“ aus juristischer Sicht' 208 (2008) *Archiv für die civilistische Praxis* (AcP), 248.

Josef Esser, *Grundsatz und Norm in der richterlichen Fortbildung des Privatrechts* (4th Edition, Mohr Siebeck, Tübingen 1990).

Josef Esser, 'Realität und Ideologie der Rechtssicherheit in positiven Systemen', in: Siegfried Hohenleitner, Ludwig Linder and Friedrich Nowakowski (eds), *Festschrift für Theodor Rittler* (Verlag Scientia, Aalen 1957), 13.

Josef Esser, *Vorverständnis und Methodenwahl in der Rechtsfindung* (Athenäum-Verlag, Frankfurt am Main 1970).

Wolfgang Fikentscher, *Methoden des Rechts in vergleichender Darstellung*, Volume II and IV (Mohr Siebeck, Tübingen 1975 and 1977).

Ossip Flechtheim, 'Eine wichtige kartellrechtliche Entscheidung' *Juristische Wochenschrift (JW)* 1916, 937.

Holger Fleischer, 'Der Inhalt des Schadensersatzanspruchs wegen unwahrer oder unterlassener unverzüglicher Ad-hoc-Mitteilungen' *Betriebs Berater (BB)* 2002, 1869.

Holger Fleischer, 'Empfiehlt es sich, im Interesse des Anlegerschutzes und zur Förderung des Finanzplatzes Deutschland das Kapitalmarkt- und Börsenrecht neu zu regeln? ' *64. Deutscher* Juristentag (DJT) 2002, Gutachten F.

Holger Fleischer, Stephan Schneider and Marlen Thaten, 'Kapitalmarktrechtlicher Anlegerschutz versus aktienrechtliche Kapitalerhaltung – wie entscheidet der EuGH?' *Neue Zeitschrift für Gesellschaftsrecht (NZG)* 2012, 801.

Werner Flume, *Allgemeiner Teil des Bürgerlichen Rechts, Das Rechtsgeschäft*, Volume 2 (Springer Verlag, Berlin and Heidelberg 1965).

Werner Flume, 'Rechtsgeschäft und Privatautonomie', in: Ernst von Caemmerer, Ernst Friesenhahn and Richard Lange (eds), *Festschrift zum hundertjährigen Bestehen des Deutschen Juristentages 1860-1960* (C.F. Müller, Karlsruhe 1960), 135.

Marie Theres Fögen, 'Schrittmacher des Rechts – Anmerkungen zum Justiz- und Rechtsverweigerungsverbot', in: Heinrich Honsell (ed), *Privatrecht und Methode: Festschrift für Ernst August Kramer* (Helbing & Lichtenhahn, Basel 2004), 3.

Jochen A. Frowein, 'Die Herausbildung europäischer Verfassungsprinzipien', in: Arthur Kaufmann, Ernst-Joachim Mestmäcker and Hans F. Zacher (eds), *Rechtsstaat und Menschenwürde: Festschrift für Werner Maihofer* (Klostermann, Frankfurt am Main 1988), 149.

Wolfgang Frowein and Jochen Peukert, *EMRK-Kommentar* (N.P. Engel Verlag, Berlin 2009).

Hans-Georg Gadamer, *Wahrheit und Methode* (6th Edition, Mohr Siebeck, Tübingen 1990).

Mahatma Gandhi, 'Seven Social Sins' *Young India* No. 43 (October 22, 1925).

Martin Gellermann, *Grundrechte im einfachgesetzlichen Gewand* (Mohr Siebeck, Tübingen 2000).

Eckart Gottschalk, 'Die deliktische Haftung für fehlerhafte Ad-hoc-Mitteilungen' *Das deutsche Steuerrecht (DStR)* 2005, 1648.

Stefan Grundmann (ed), *Systembildung und Systemlücken in Kerngebieten des europäischen Privatrechts* (Mohr Siebeck, Tübingen 2000).

Peter Häberle, 'Gemeineuropäisches Verfassungsrecht' *Europäische Grundrechte-Zeitschrift (EuGRZ)* 1991, 261.

Bettina Heiderhoff, *Europäisches Privatrecht* (4th Edition, C.F. Müller, Heidelberg 2016).

Hartwig Henze, 'Vermögensbindungsprinzip und Anlegerschutz' *Neue Zeitschrift für Gesellschaftsrecht (NZG)* 2005, 115.

Maximilian Herberger, *Dogmatik* (Klostermann, Frankfurt am Main 1981).

Historisch-kritischer Kommentar zum BGB, Mathias Schmoekel, Joachim Rückert and Reinhard Zimmermann (eds) (Mohr Siebeck, Tübingen 2003).

Norbert Horn, 'Zur Haftung der AG und ihrer Organmitglieder für unrichtige oder unterlassene Ad-hoc-Informationen', in: Mathias Habersack, Peter Hommelhoff, Uwe Hüffer and Karsten Schmidt (eds), *Festschrift für Peter Ulmer zum 70. Geburtstag* (De Gruyter, Berlin 2003), 817.

Rodríguez Iglesias and Gil Carlos, 'Zu den Grenzen der verfahrensrechtlichen Autonomie der Mitgliedstaaten bei der Anwendung des Gemeinschaftsrechts' *Europäische Grundrechte-Zeitschrift (EuGRZ)* 1997, 289.

Jan H. Jans, 'The Effect in National Legal Systems of the Prohibition of Discrimination on Grounds of Age as a General Principle of Community Law' 34 (2007) *Legal Issues of European Integration*, 53.

Nils Jansen, *Die Struktur der Gerechtigkeit* (Nomos, Baden-Baden 1998).

Nils Jansen, 'Dogmatik, Erkenntnis und Theorie im europäischen Privatrecht' *Zeitschrift für das Europäische Privatrecht (ZEuP)* 2005, 750.

Matthias Jestaedt, 'Die Abwägungslehre – ihre Stärken und ihre Schwächen', in: Otto Depenheuer, Markus Heintzen and Peter Axer (eds), *Staat im Wort: Festschrift Josef Isensee* (C. F. Müller, Heidelberg 2007), 253.

Matthias Jestaedt, *Grundrechtsentfaltung im Gesetz* (Mohr Siebeck, Tübingen 1999).

Rudolf von Jhering, *Geist des römischen Rechts*, Volume 1 (4th Edition, Breitkopf und Härtel, Leipzig 1878).

Rigide Kakouris, 'Do the Member States Possess Judicial Procedural 'autonomy'?' 34 (1997) *Common Markets Law Review*, 1389.

Kapitalmarktrechts-Kommentar, Eberhard Schwark and Daniel Zimmer (eds) (4th Edition, C.H. Beck, Munich 2010).

Arthur Kaufmann, *Rechtsphilosophie* (2nd Edition, C.H. Beck, Munich 1997).

Duncan Kennedy, 'Form and Substance in Private Law Adjudication' 89 (1976) *Harvard Law Review (Harv.L.Rev.)*, 1685.

Sven Keusch and Kerstin Wankerl, 'Die Haftung der Aktiengesellschaft für fehlerhafte Kapitalmarktinformationen im Spannungsfeld zum Gebot der Kapitalerhaltung' *Zeitschrift für Bank-und Kapitalmarktrecht (BKR)* 2003, 744.

Uwe Kischel, 'Die Kontrolle der Verhältnismäßigkeit durch den Europäischen Gerichtshof' *Zeitschrift Europarecht (EuR)* 2000, 380.

Jan Henrik Klement, 'Schlusswort zu Jan-R. Sieckmann, Erwiderung auf Jan Henrik Klement' 64 (2009) *JuristenZeitung (JZ)*, 560.

Jan Henrik Klement, 'Vom Nutzen einer Theorie, die alles erklärt. Alexys Prinzipientheorie aus der Sicht der Grundrechtsdogmatik' 63 (2008) *JuristenZeitung (JZ)*, 756.

Oliver Koch, *Der Grundsatz der Verhältnismäßigkeit in der Rechtsprechung des Gerichtshofs der Europäischen Gemeinschaften* (Duncker & Humblot, Berlin 2003).

Kölner Kommentar zum WpHG, Heribert Hirte and Thomas M.J. Möllers (eds) (2nd Edition, Carl Heymanns Verlag, Cologne 2014).

Kölner Kommentar zum WpÜG, Heribert Hirte and Christoph von Bülow (eds) (2nd Edition, Carl Heymanns Verlag, Cologne 2010).

Michael Kort, 'Die Haftung der AG nach §§ 826, 31 bei fehlerhaften Ad-hoc-Mitteilungen' *Neue Zeitschrift für Gesellschaftsrecht (NZG)* 2005, 496.

Hein Kötz, 'Rechtsvereinheitlichung - Nutzen, Kosten, Methoden, Ziele' 50 (1986) *Rabels Zeitschrift für ausländisches und internationales Privatrecht (RabelsZ)*, 1.

Ernst August Kramer, 'Funktionen allgemeiner Rechtsgrundsätze – Versuch einer Strukturierung', in: Helmut Koziol, Peter Rummel (eds), *Im Dienste der Gerechtigkeit: Festschrift für Franz Bydlinski* (Springer Verlag, Wien 2002), 197.

Lutz Krämer and Matthias Baudisch, 'Neues zur Börsenprospekthaftung und zu den Sorgfaltsanforderungen beim Unternehmenskauf' *Zeitschrift für Wirtschafts- und Bankrecht (WM)* 1998, 1161.

Friedrich Kübler, 'Traumpfade oder Holzwege nach Europa? Oder: Was wir uns von der Rechtsgeschichte wünschen sollten' 12 (1993) *Rechtshistorisches Journal*, 307.

Katja Langenbucher, 'Kapitalerhaltung und Kapitalmarkthaftung' *Zeitschrift für Wirtschaftsrecht (ZIP)* 2005, 239.

Karl Larenz, *Methodenlehre der Rechtswissenschaft* (6th Edition, Springer Verlag, Berlin/Heidelberg 1991).

Karl Larenz, *Richtiges Recht* (C.H. Beck, Munich 1979).

Tobias Lenz, 'Marschall' *Neue Juristische Wochenschrift (NJW)* 1998, 1619.

Josef Franz Lindner, 'Fortschritte und Defizite im EU-Grundrechtsschutz – Plädoyer für eine Optimierung der Europäischen Grundrechtscharta' *Zeitschrift für Rechtspolitik (ZRP)* 2007, 54.

Josef Franz Lindner, *Theorie der Grundrechtsdogmatik* (Mohr Siebeck, Tübingen 2005).

Neil MacCormick, *Legal Reasoning and Legal Theory* (Oxford University Press, Oxford/New York 1978).

Theodor Maunz and Günter Dürig (eds), *Grundgesetz Kommentar, Band I* (loose-leaf, C.H. Beck, Munich December 2015).

Arthur Meier-Hayoz, 'Strategische und taktische Aspekte der Fortbildung des Rechts' 36 (1981) *JuristenZeitung (JZ)*, 417.

Axel Metzger, *Extra legem, intra ius: Allgemeine Rechtsgrundsätze im Europäischen Privatrecht* (Mohr Siebeck, Tübingen 2009).

Christoph Möllers, 'Methoden', in: Wolfgang Hoffmann-Riem, Eberhard Schmidt-Aßmann and Andreas Voßkuhle (eds), *Grundlagen des Verwaltungsrechts*, Volume 1 (2nd Edition, C.H. Beck, Munich 2012), 123.

Thomas M.J. Möllers, 'Anlegerschutz durch Aktien- und Kapitalmarktrecht' 26 (1997) *Zeitschrift für Unternehmens- und Gesellschaftsrecht (ZGR)*, 334.

Thomas M.J. Möllers, 'Anlegerschutz im System des Kapitalmarktrechts', in: Stefan Grundmann, Brigitte Haar, Hanno Merkt et al. (eds), *Festschrift für Klaus J. Hopt zum 70. Geburtstag* (De Gruyter, Berlin/New York 2010), 2247.

Thomas M.J. Möllers, 'Das Verhältnis der Haftung wegen sittenwidriger Schädigung zum gesellschaftsrechtlichen Kapitalerhaltungsgrundsatz' *Betriebs Berater (BB)* 2005, 1637.

Thomas M.J. Möllers, 'Europäische Gesetzgebungslehre 2.0: Die dynamische Rechtsharmonisierung im Kapitalmarktrecht am Beispiel von MiFID II und PRIIP' *Zeitschrift für Europäisches Privatrecht (ZEuP)* 2016, 325.

Thomas M.J. Möllers, 'Geschichte und Schutzzweck der Ad-hoc-Publizitätspflicht', in: Thomas M.J. Möllers and Klaus Rotter (eds), *Ad-hoc-Publizität* (C.H. Beck, Munich 2003), § 3.

Thomas M.J. Möllers, 'Rezension zu Karl Riesenhuber: System und Prinzipien des Europäischen Vertragsrechts' 59 (2004) *Juristen Zeitung (JZ)*, 1067.

Thomas M.J. Möllers and Franz Clemens Leisch, 'Haftung des Unternehmens gem. den §§ 37b, 37c WpHG bei Verletzung der Ad-hoc-Publizitätspflicht', in: Thomas M.J. Möllers and Klaus Rotter (eds), *Ad-hoc-Publizität* (C.H. Beck, Munich 2003), § 14.

Thomas M.J. Möllers and Franz Clemens Leisch, 'Haftung von Vorständen gegenüber Anlegern wegen fehlerhafter Ad-hoc-Meldungen nach § 826 BGB' *Zeitschrift für Wirtschafts- und Bankrecht (WM)* 2001, 1648.

Felix Moos, 'Die Schadensersatzansprüche des betrogenen Aktienerwerbers gegen die trügerische Aktiengesellschaft' 70 (1911) *Zeitschrift für das gesamte Handels- und Wirtschaftsrecht (ZHR)*, 184.

Peter O. Mülbert, 'Privatrecht, die EG-Grundfreiheiten und der Binnenmarkt' 159 (1995) *Zeitschrift für das gesamte Handels- und Wirtschaftsrecht (ZHR)*, 2.

Peter O. Mülbert and Steffen Steup, 'Emittentenhaftung für fehlerhafte Kapitalmarktinformation am Beispiel der fehlerhaften Regelpublizität' *Zeitschrift für Wirtschafts- und Bankrecht (WM)* 2005, 1633.

Peter Christian Müller-Graff and Eibe Riedel (eds), *Gemeinsames Verfassungsrecht in der Europäischen Union* (Nomos, Baden-Baden 1998).

Münchener Kommentar zum Aktiengesetz, Volume 2, Wulf Goette and Mathias Habersack (eds) (3rd Edition, C.H. Beck, Munich 2008).

Palandt Bürgerliches Gesetzbuch mit Nebengesetzen, Gerd Brudermüller, Jürgen Ellenberger, Isabell Götz, Christian Grüneberg, Sebastian Herrler, Hartwig Sprau, Karsten Thorn, Walter Weidenkaff, Dietmar Weidlich and Hartmut Wicke (eds) (77th Edition, C. H. Beck, Munich 2018).

Sacha Prechal, 'Combatting Indirect Discrimination in Community Law Context' 20 (1993) *Legal Issues of European Integration*, 81.

Georg Friedrich Puchta, *Pandekten* (5th Edition, Leipzig 1850).

Gustav Radbruch, *Grundzüge der Rechtsphilosophie* (8th Edition, Koehler Verlag, Hamburg 1973).

Peter Raisch, *Juristische Methoden: Vom antiken Rom bis zur Gegenwart* (C. F. Müller, Heidelberg 1995).

Ferdinand Regelsberger, *Pandekten* (Duncker & Humblot, Leipzig 1893).

Norbert Reich, *General Principles of EU Civil Law* (Intersentia Ltd, Cambridge 2014).

Ulf Renzenbrink and Nelson Holzner, 'Das Verhältnis von Kapitalerhaltung und Ad-Hoc-Haftung' 10 (2002) *Zeitschrift für Bank- und Kapitalmarktrecht (BKR)*, 434.

Karl Riesenhuber, 'Die Inhaltskontrolle von Vereinbarungen über Hauptleistung und Preis im Europäischen Vertragsrecht', in: Jens Dammann, Wolfgang Grunsky and Thomas Pfeiffer (eds), *Gedächtnisschrift Wolf* (C.H Beck, Munich 2011), 123.

Karl Riesenhuber, *System und Prinzipien des Europäischen Vertragsrechts* (De Gruyter Recht, Berlin 2003).

Fritz Rittner, 'Das Gemeinschaftsprivatrecht und die europäische Integration' 50 (1995) *JuristenZeitung (JZ)*, 849.

Klaus Friedrich Röhl and Hans Christian Röhl, *Allgemeine Rechtslehre* (3rd Edition, Vahlen, Munich 2008).

Anne Röthel, *Normkonkretisierung im Privatrecht* (Mohr Siebeck, Tübingen 2004).

Friedrich Rüffler, 'Haftung für Kapitalmarktinformationen nach OGH 7 Ob 77/10i', in: Susanne Kalss and Ulrich Torggler (eds), *Kapitalmarkthaftung und Gesellschaftsrecht* (Manz, Wien 2013), 1.

Bernd Rüthers, Christian Fischer and Axel Birk, *Rechtstheorie* (8th Edition, C.H Beck, Munich 2015).

Michael Sachs, 'Die Grundrechte als objektives Recht und als subjektives Recht', in: Klaus Stern (ed), *Das Staatsrecht der Bundesrepublik Deutschland*, Volume III/1 (C.H Beck, Munich 1988), § 65.

Karsten Schmidt, 'Der Zivilrichter als Schöpfer und Vollstrecker wirtschaftsrechtlicher Normen' 4 (1977) *Deutsche Richterzeitung (DRiZ)*, 97.

Martin Schmidt-Kessel, 'Europäisches Vertragsrecht', in: Karl Riesenhuber, *Europäische Methodenlehre* (3rd Edition, De Gruyter, Berlin/Munich/Boston 2015), § 17.

Christian Schmidt-Leithoff, 'Gedanken über die Privatrechtsordnung als Grundlage zum EWG_Vertrag', in: Manfred Löwisch, Christian Schmidt-Leithoff and Burkhard Schmiedel (eds), *Beiträge zum Handels- und Wirtschaftsrecht: Festschrift für Fritz Rittner* (C.H. Beck, Munich 1991) 597.

Rupert Scholz, 'Zum Verhältnis von europäischem Gemeinschaftsrecht und nationalem Verwaltungsverfahrensrecht' 7 (1998) *Die öffentliche Verwaltung (DÖV)*, 261.

Werner Schroeder, 'Die Auslegung des EU-Rechts' 3 (2004) *Juristische Schulung (JuS)*, 180.

Reiner Schulze, Manfred Zuleeg and Stefan Kadelbach (eds), *Europarecht* (3rd Edition, Nomos, Baden-Baden 2014).

Ekkehard Schumann, 'Das Rechtsverweigerungsverbot. Historische und methodologische Bemerkungen zur richterlichen Pflicht, das Recht auszulegen, zu ergänzen und fortzubilden' 81 (1968) *Zeitschrift für Zivilprozeß (ZZP)*, 79.

Eberhard Schwark, 'Prospekthaftung und Kapitalerhaltung in der AG', in: Karsten Schmidt and Eberhard Schwark (eds), *Unternehmen, Recht und Wirtschaftsordnung: Festschrift für Peter Raisch zum 70. Geburtstag* (Carl Heymanns Verlag, Cologne/Berlin/Bonn/Munich 1995), 269.

Jan Sieckmann, *Recht als normatives System* (Nomos, Baden-Baden 2009).

Dieter Simon, *Rechtshistorisches Journal*, Volume 11 (Löwenklau Gesellschaft, Frankfurt am Main 1992).

Staudinger Bürgerliches Gesetzbuch (De Gruyter, Berlin edited 2015).

Anton Friedrich Justus Thibaut, *System des Pandektenrechts*, 3 Volumes (5th Edition, Friedrich Mauke, Jena 1818).

Andreas von Thur, *Allgemeiner Teil des Bürgerlichen Rechts*, Volume 1 (Duncker & Humblot, Berlin 1910).

Rüdiger Veil, 'Die Ad-hoc-Publizitätshaftung im System kapitalmarktrechtlicher Informationshaftung' 167 (2003) *Zeitschrift für das gesamte Handels- und Wirtschaftsrecht (ZHR)*, 365.

Uwe Volkmann, 'Veränderungen der Grundrechtsdogmatik' 60 (2005) *Juristenzeitung (JZ)*, 261.

Andreas Voßkuhle, 'Neue Verwaltungswissenschaft', in: Wolfgang Hoffmann-Riem, Eberhard Schmidt-Aßmann and Andreas Voßkuhle (eds), *Grundlagen des Verwaltungsrechts*, Volume 1 (2nd Edition, C.H. Beck, Munich 2012), § 1.

Christian Waldhoff, 'Lob und Kritik der Dogmatik: Rechtsdogmatik im Spannungsfeld von Gesetzesbindung und Funktionenorientierung', in: Gregor Kirchhof, Stefan Magen and Karsten Schneider (eds), *Was weiß Dogmatik?* (Mohr Siebeck, Tübingen 2012), 17.

Wolfgang Wiegand, 'Back to the future?' 12 (1993) *Rechtshistorisches Journal*, 277.

Bernhard Windscheid, *Lehrbuch des Pandektenrechts*, 3 Volumes (7th Edition, Literarische Anstalt Rütten und Loening, Frankfurt am Main 1891).

Manfred Wolf and Jörg Neuner, *Allgemeiner Teil des Bürgerlichen Rechts* (10th Edition, C.H. Beck, Munich 2012).

Christian Wolff, *Grundsätze des Natur- und Völkerrechts* (Regner, Halle 1754).

Reinhard Zimmermann, 'Heard Melodies are Sweet, but those unheard are sweeter…' 193 (1993) *Archiv für die civilistische Praxis (AcP)*, 121.

Reinhard Zimmermann, 'Law of Obligations' 47 (1992) *Juristenzeitung (JZ)*, 8.

Register of Cases

European Court of Justice (ECJ)

ECJ, Case 8/55, 16.07.1956, *Fédération Charbonnière*, ECLI:EU:C:1956:11.

ECJ, Case 1/73, 05.07.1973, *Westzucker*, ECLI:EU:C:1973:78.

ECJ, Case 4/73, 14.05.1974, *Nold*, ECLI:EU:C:1974:51.

ECJ, Case 44/79, 13.12.1979, *Hauer*, ECLI:EU:C:1979:290.

ECJ, Case 205/85, 21.09.1983, *Milchkontor*, ECLI:EU:C:1983:233.

ECJ, Case 222/84, 15.05.1986, *Johnston*, ECLI:EU:C:1986:206.

ECJ, Case 80/86, 08.10.1987, *Kolpinghuis*, ECLI:EU:C:1987:431.

ECJ, Case 222/86, 15.10.1987, *Heylens*, ECLI:EU:C:1987:442.

ECJ, Case 177/88. 08.11.1990, *Dekker*, ECLI:EU:C:1990:383.

ECJ, Case 18/88, 13.12.1991, *GB-Inno-BM*, ECLI:EU:C:1991:474.

ECJ, Case 317/93, 14.12.1995, *Nolte*, ECLI:EU:C:1995:438.

ECJ, Case 143/93, 13.02.1996, *Van Es Douane Agenten*, ECLI:EU:C:1996:45.

ECJ, Case 46/93, 05.03.1996, *Brasserie du Pêcheur*, ECLI:EU:C:1996:79.

ECJ, Case 24/95, 20.03.1997, *Alcan*, ECLI:EU:C:1997:163.

ECJ, Case 409/95, 11.11.1997, *Marschall*, ECLI:EU:C:1997:533.

ECJ, Case 144/04, 22.11.2005, *Mangold/Helm*, ECLI:EU:C:2005:709.

ECJ, Case 255/02, 21.02.2006, *Halifax*, ECLI:EU:C:2006:121.

ECJ, Case 212/04, 04.07.2006, *Adeneler*, ECLI:EU:C:2006:443.

ECJ, Case 432/05, 13.03.2007, *Unibet*, ECLI:EU:C:2007:163.

ECJ, Case 201/08, 10.09.2009, *Plantanol*, ECLI:EU:C:2009:539.

ECJ, Case 58/12 P, 26.11.2013, *Groupe Gascogne*, ECLI:EU:C:2013:770.

ECJ, Case 174/12, 19.12.2013, *Alfred Hirmann/Immofinanz AG*, ECLI:EU:C:2013:856.

German Federal Constitutional Court (BVerfG)

BVerfG 20.02.1952 – 1 BvF 2/51 – BVerfGE 1, 117, 131.

BVerfG 26.05.1970 – 1 BvR 83/69, 244/69, 345/69 – BVerfGE 28, 243, 261 – conscientious objection.

BVerfG 24.02.1971 – 1 BvR 435/68 – BVerfGE 30, 173, 193 – Mephisto.

BVerfG 14.02.1973 – 1 BvR 112/65 – BVerfGE 34, 269, 286 et seq. – Soraya.

BVerfG 08.04.1987 – 2 BvR 687/85 – BVerfGE 75, 223, 243 et seq. – Kloppenburg.

BVerfG 19.05.1992 – 1 BvR 986/91 – BVerfGE 86, 133.

German Federal Court of Justice (BGH)

BGH 29.03.1971 – III ZR 98/69 – BGHZ 56, 57.

BGH 23.06.1952 – III 297/51 – BGHZ 6, 319 – Duty to compensate among drivers.

BGH 13.04.1956 – VI 347/54 – BGHZ 20, 259 – Operational Risk.

BGH 02.12.1974 – II ZR 78/72 – BGHZ 63, 282 – Compulsory admission of a monopoly organization.

BGH 11.01.1977 – VI ZR 261/75 – NJW 1977, 2073.

BGH 20.01.1983 – VII ZR 32/82 – BGHZ 86, 273 – Authority by estoppel.

BGH 18.09.1987 – V ZR 219/85 – NJW-RR 1988, 136.

BGH 15.10.1987 – III ZR 235/86 – BGHZ 102, 60.

BGH 25.02.1993 – VII 24/92 – BGHZ 121, 378.

BGH 18.04.1997 – V ZR 28/96 – BGHZ 135, 235 – roots in the tennis court.

BGH 19.07.2004 – II ZR 402/02 – BGHZ 160, 149 – Infomatec II.

BGH 09.05.2005 – II ZR 287/02 – NJW 2005, 2450 – EM.TV.

BGH 28.11.2005 – II ZR 80/04 – ZIP 2007, 681 – Comroad I.

BGH 11.05.2011 – VIII ZR 289/09 – BGHZ 189, 346 – Usage of another member's eBay account.

BGH 13.12.2011 – XI ZR 51/10 – BGHZ 192, 90 – IKB.

Supreme Court of the German Reich (RG)

RG 07.11.1931 – V 106/31 – RGZ 133, 388 – Theater

RG 10.02.1930 – VI 270/29 – RGZ 127, 218 – gas meter.

Federal Labour Court (BAG)

BAG 15.10.1992 – 2 AZR 227/92 – BAGE 71, 252.

German Higher Regional Court (OLG)

OLG Frankfurt 17.03.2005 – 1 U 149/04 – ZIP 2005, 710 – Comroad.
OLG München 20.04.2005 – 7 U 5303/04 – ZIP 2005, 901 – Comroad.

Austrian Supreme Court (OGH)

OGH 30.03.2011 – Ob 77/10i – GesRZ 2011, 251 No. II.1.1.
OGH 15.03.2012 – 6 Ob 28/12d – ÖBA 2012, 548/1828 No. 3.5.

Comment: "Law Enforcement in Turbulent Times – How to Work with Principles in Capital Markets Law"

*Derek van der Merwe**

The problem addressed in this paper is formulated thus by the authors: 'Question is: If and how legal principles can be called upon in German and European company, capital markets and antitrust law to solve questions of law.' This question is pertinent when there are gaps in the law or the current law is unsatisfactory, either because the law does not provide a just solution in a particular case or it has not kept abreast of modern circumstances.

Their careful analysis of the *nature* of principles, more especially how they are differentiated from rules (or indeed if their normative nature allows for a ready differentiation from rules) and the *sources* of principles (primarily in legal codes, in moral precepts or, in most cases, derived through induction or analogy) leads to the conclusion that principles can indeed be called upon to solve questions where the solution to a particular legal problem is open-ended, i.e., not immediately apparent. They are, then, in their functionality in a legal system, an intermediate something between an attitude and a rule – if one is allowed to misappropriate the sentiment of the English poet, S.T. Coleridge, who called a work of art 'the intermediate somewhat between a thought and a thing'.[1]

How principles are used to solve difficult questions of law is the stuff of what German jurists call *Methodenlehre* or the theory of legal argumentation and is at the heart of this paper.[2]

---

* Derek van der Merwe, *B.A. (Law), LL.B., LL.D*, Emeritus Professor of Law, University of Johannesburg.

1 Henry N Coleridge, *Specimens of the Table Talk of Samuel Taylor Coleridge* (1858), 52 (he made this statement in 1827).

2 Much, but certainly not all, of German *Methodenlehre* is captured in common-law jurisdictions under the title of 'legal interpretation'. The two standard works on juridical *Methodenlehre* that I have most often consulted are Karl Larenz and Claus-Wilhelm Canaris, *Methodenlehre der Rechtswissenschaft* (3rd Edition, 1995) and Hans-Martin Pawlowski, *Methodenlehre für Juristen* (3rd Edition, 1999). On juridical argumentation theory see in particular Robert Alexy, *Theorie der juristischen Argumentation* (2nd Edition, 1991).

When they apply their particular analysis on the role of principles in legal argumentation to immediate problems in current capital markets law, they do so by, among other things, comparing the applicability of two widely-recognised but contradictory principles in this field of law, namely the principle that an investor be allowed to make a rational (i.e., autonomous) investment decision and the principle of capital preservation in respect of corporate entities. The decision which principle should trump the other in the two scenarios they sketch in the paper is guided by considerations of proportionality. Ultimately, however, it is *considerations of economic policy* that decisively influence the decision: creditor protection should not be over-emphasised to the detriment of shareholders, lest a climate conducive to the provision of venture capital is negatively impacted and competitiveness with respect to foreign stock exchanges decreases. Such principled decision-making, embedded ultimately in considerations of public policy, holds not only for German national law, but also for European law, perhaps even more so, given the relative paucity of European legal rules and the concomitant greater need to argue from principle.

The authors use an appropriate metaphor to explain the methodological process involved in the application of principle to develop the law. Principles, they state, are used to build a bridge between the existing law and new law (between, one could add - employing the language of Habermas – the facticity (*Faktizität*) of existing rules and the validity (*Geltung*) of developed law).[3] An elaboration of this metaphor, if one could be so bold, would be that the bridge is built using the materials of then-current social and economic policy.[4]

3 Here I use the title of Habermas's hugely influential work: Jürgen Habermas, *Faktizität und Geltung* (5th Edition, 1997).

4 Another useful metaphor employed by Anglo-American jurists to explain development of the law through development of existing legal constructs and institutions is that of a *rope*, composed of many strands, none of which runs for the entire length of the rope. The strength of the rope lies in the descendancy and continuity caused by the strands intertwining one with another and forming an item of strength and durability. The metaphor belongs to Wittgenstein and was best appropriated to law by Ronald Dworkin: see Ronald Dworkin, *Law's Empire* (1986), 68-73. See, too, Derek van der Merwe, 'Iudicis est ius dicere, non dare: Judicial Law-making by Institutional Development of the Common Law', in: Christa van Wyk and Rena van Oosten (eds), *Nihil Obstat. Essays in Honour of WJ Hosten* (1996), 225 (234).

Their analysis, namely that economic and/or social policy is the final determinant of which of competing principles to apply when judges develop the law (and by legal development is meant the *adaptation*, *improvement*, *modification*, *expansion* and *amelioration* of the law)[5] holds true also for South African law. In the absence of a developed modern *Methodenlehre*, as in German jurisprudence, South African jurists have largely been led by the fruits of centuries of Romanist civil law and English case law in placing less value on defining what exactly a principle *is*, in the sense of drawing a clear distinction between it and a rule. Their approach has largely been that adopted by the compilers of the Roman Emperor Justinian's Digest in the sixth century AD.[6] These Byzantine jurists, in the last title of the Digest (D50 17 *De diversis regulis iuris antiqui*), made a compilation of some 200 of what they deemed the most important *regulae iuris*, a veritable concoction of rules, principles, axioms, maxims, precepts, standards, institutions and presumptions.[7] The pithiness of the formulation or the appositeness to the matter at hand of a particular statement of law seemingly trumped considerations of definitional precision, then as now. South African jurists and, one assumes, most modern jurists operating in post-modern systems of law, are guided by the truism expressed so well by Javolenus, the Roman jurist

5 See Derek van der Merwe, 'Iudicis est ius dicere, non dare: Judicial Law-making by Institutional Development of the Common Law', in: Christa van Wyk and Rena van Oosten (eds), *Nihil Obstat. Essays in Honour of WJ Hosten* (1996), 225 (225-226).

6 Although now largely of interest only to scholars of Roman law, the Digest (*Digesta*) remains, at least in theory, a source of South African law. The most recent English translation of the Digest, based on the text prepared by Theodor Mommsen, was published in 1985: Alan Watson (ed), *The Digest of Justinian* (1985).

7 On *regulae iuris* in Roman and European Romanist law, see, among many, Peter Stein, *Regulae Iuris. From Juristic Rules to Legal Maxims* (1966) *passim*; Bruno Schmidlin, *Die römische Rechtsregeln. Versuch einer Typologie* (1970) *passim*; Derek van der Merwe, *Tydskrif vir die Suid-Afrikaanse Reg (TSAR)* 1987, 286 (287-300) and Derek van der Merwe, *Tydskrif vir die Suid-Afrikaanse Reg (TSAR)* 2002, 76 (103-105). The Digest title is introduced with the following famous definition by the Roman jurist, Paul, of a *regula iuris* (D. 50. 17. 1): 'A rule [*regula*] is a brief exposition of an existing state of affairs: not of such a nature that the law is derived from the rule, but the rule is established by the existing law. A rule, therefore, contains a brief exposition of the point in question and, so says Sabinus, is akin to the procedural *causae coniectio* in the sense that it, too, ceases to function when it is vitiated in any way.'

of the first century AD, that 'every definition in civil law is dangerous, for it is rare for the possibility not to exist of its being overthrown'.[8]

Modern exponents of the South African Roman-Dutch based common law focus rather on the *sources* of the norms of law and on *how* those norms are best utilised (as building-blocks for constructing an appropriate legal solution) to solve a legal problem than on the nature of a particular norm or set of norms being utilised.[9] The assumption has always been that Roman-Dutch law is 'rich in principle, but poor in detail'[10] (much as the authors describe European law). This statement also holds true of the 1994 South African Constitution (as of all constitutions), so in large measure modern South African jurists presume to have a rich storehouse of legal principle on the basis of which problems may be solved. How to characterise the rich assembly of components within that storehouse is of secondary importance.

As the authors of the paper have pointed out in respect of German and European law, the question is and always will be, as it is also for South African jurists, how are principles best applied in the adjudicatory process, in a manner that does not cross the fine line between *adjudication* and *legislation*. The answer, for German and European law and for South African law, lies in the judicious application of policy, of what Ronald Dworkin in *Law's Empire* has called 'dimensions of political value' in the adjudicatory process.[11]

The authors have demonstrated the validity of this insight, by applying it to a branch of law that the non-expert might regard as teeming with a plethora of laws, rules and directives and therefore 'gap-free', not 'open-ended'. The value of this insight for jurisprudence in general becomes apparent

---

8 See D. 50. 17. 202.

9 See Alan Watson, *The Making of the Civil Law* (1981), 41; Derek van der Merwe, *Tydskrif vir die Suid-Afrikaanse Reg (TSAR)* 1987, 286 (300-302) and Derek van der Merwe, 'Iudicis est ius dicere, non dare: Judicial Law-making by Institutional Development of the Common Law', in: Christa van Wyk and Rena van Oosten (eds), *Nihil Obstat. Essays in Honour of WJ Hosten* (1996), 225 (233).

10 See, e.g., Paul Q.R. Boberg, 83 *South African Law Journal (SALJ)* 1986, 150 (175).

11 Ronal Dworkin, *Law's Empire* (1986), vii; Derek van der Merwe, 'Iudicis est ius dicere, non dare: Judicial Law-making by Institutional Development of the Common Law', in: Christa van Wyk and Rena van Oosten (eds), *Nihil Obstat. Essays in Honour of WJ Hosten* (1996), 225 (232-233); and Derek van der Merwe, *Tydskrif vir die Suid-Afrikaanse Reg (TSAR)* 2002, 12 (27-31).

when one transfers one's focus from the system, structure, concepts and institutions of the law to the inevitable gaps that every normative superstructure leaves. Then one recognises, as did the casuistic-minded Roman jurists of two millennia ago, that law is an essentially dialectical, argumentative exercise, a discourse of persuasion. It is the art of the good and the fair (*ius est ars boni et aequi*, as the jurist Celsus stated),[12] it is about what argument among many is most convincing, most persuasive; it is about an essential dialogue between differing conceptions of right in filling the gaps in the law. It is argumentative practice, a practice deployed, according to Roberto Unger, 'in the service of a distinctive family of political projects'.[13]

It is tempting to extend this recognition beyond the scope of the authors' intentions, into a field of *Methodenlehre* that has thus far enjoyed fringe status among legal theorists. This is the field of '*topics*'.[14] The word is derived from Aristotle, who wrote an eponymous book on dialectics devoted to the art of inventing and judging of their validity meant to facilitate the rhetorical art of persuasion. Cicero romanised this work and there is evidence that the Roman jurists were, in their casuistry, 'topically-minded' in their desire to invent arguments to suit particular legal problems, not overly reliant on system or structure. 'Topical' jurisprudence had its hey-day in the sixteenth and seventeenth centuries, in the immediate post-scholastic age, and then lost its appeal among the practitioners of the *usus modernus pandectarum* and the rise of German legal science in the 18th and 19th centuries. It was revived by the German jurist, Theodor Viehweg, in 1953[15] and has enjoyed fringe popularity ever since, in Germany and France in particular. It is *Problemdenken* that emphasises the invention of arguments (within the confines of the available legal norms) and the judgment of their validity (with reference to juridico-political notions of fairness, justice, stability,

12 The definition is found in the opening paragraph of the Digest: D. 1.1.1.

13 Roberto M. Unger, 59 (1996), *The Modern Law Review (MLR)*, 1 (19). See too Derek van der Merwe, 'Roman-Dutch Law: from Virtual Reality to Constitutional Resource', in: Graham Bradfield and Derek van der Merwe (eds), *'Meaning' in Legal Interpretation* (1998), 117 (127-130 and 131-132).

14 See Derek van der Merwe, *Tydskrif vir die Suid-Afrikaanse Reg (TSAR)* 2001, 428 (439-440) and 664 (664-691) and Derek van der Merwe, *Tydskrif vir die Suid-Afrikaanse Reg (TSAR)* 2002, 76 (76-105).

15 Theodor Viehweg, *Topik und Jurisprudenz* (1953). A fifth edition of this book appeared in 1974.

transparency, persuasiveness, prudence and other dimensions of morality).[16] In such a scheme, principles occupy a place as one among many types of norms that allow one to invent arguments. The policy considerations that led to the decisions referenced by the authors can now be seen to occupy a (legitimate) space within an exercise that judges of the validity of those arguments and chooses one as the most persuasive, that produces *optimisation* of the available law, of law and its institutions as 'an approximation to an intelligible and justified scheme of social life … [a scheme for] a society whose arrangements result from individual and collective self-determination'.[17]

The authors are to be commended for a paper that addresses complex issues of legal theory with an admirable breadth of scope and then is able to utilise the theory they discuss to analyse decision-making in national and European courts on matters of commercial significance as exercises that go far beyond rule application and formal interpretation of laws and directives. If a paper is meant to provide food for later thought, this paper has produced a Michelin-star feast.

Bibliography

Robert Alexy, *Theorie der juristischen Argumentation* (2nd Edition, Suhrkamp, Frankfurt am Main 1999).

Henry N.Coleridge, *Specimens of the Table Talk of Samuel Taylor Coleridge* (James Murray, London 1858).

Robert Dworkin, *Law's Empire* (Belknap Press, Cambridge, Massachusetts 1986).

Jürgen Habermas, *Faktizität und Geltung. Beiträge zur Diskurstheorie des Rechts und das demokratischen Rechtsstaats* (5th Edition, Suhrkamp Verlag, Frankfurt am Main 1997).

Karl Larenz and Claus-Wilhelm Canaris, *Methodenlehre der Rechtswissenschaft* (3rd Edition, Springer Verlag, Berlin 1995).

Hans-Martin Pawlowski, *Methodenlehre für Juristen* (3rd Edition, C.F. Müller, Heidelberg 1999).

---

16 See, too, Robert Alexy, *Theorie der juristischen Argumentation* (2nd Edition, 1991), 39 et seqq. (his discussion is largely critical of a 'topical' jurisprudence) and Hans-Martin Pawlowski, *Methodenlehre für Juristen* (3rd Edition, 1999), 76 et seqq. The latter points out that 'topical' jurisprudence has morphed in recent times into 'rhetorical jurisprudence' or 'juridical argumentation theory': 76 n. 69.

17 Roberto M. Unger, 59 (1996) *The Modern Law Review (MLR)*, 1 (10). Unger himself is critical of this approach to legal resolution.

Bruno Schmidlin, *Die römischen Rechtregeln. Versuch einer Typologie* (Böhlau Verlag, Bonn 1970).

Peter Stein, *Regulae Iuris. From Juristic Rules to Legal Maxims* (The University Press, Edinburgh 1966).

Roberto M. Unger, 'Legal Analysis as Institutional Imagination' 59 (1996) *The Modern Law Review (MLR)*, 1.

Derek Van der Merwe, '*Regulae iuris* and the Axiomatisation of the Common Law in the Sixteenth and Early Seventeenth Centuries' *Tydskrif vir die Suid-Afrikaanse Reg (TSAR)* 1987, 286.

Derek Van der Merwe, '*Iudicis est ius dicere, non dare*: Judicial Law-making by Institutional Development of the Common Law', in: Christa van Wyk and Rena van Oosten (eds), *Nihil Obstat. Essays in Honour of WJ Hosten* (Butterworths, Durban 1996).

Derek Van der Merwe, 'Roman-Dutch Law: from Virtual Reality to Constitutional Resource', in: Graham Bradfield and Derek van der Merwe (eds), *'Meaning' in Legal Interpretation* (Juta and Co., Cape Town 1996).

Derek Van der Merwe, 'Constitutional Colonisation of the Common Law: a Problem of Institutional Integrity' *Tydskrif vir die Suid-Afrikaanse Reg (TSAR)* 2000, 12.

Derek Van der Merwe, 'A Rhetorical-dialectical Conception of the Common Law – an Introduction' *Tydskrif vir die Suid-Afrikaanse Reg (TSAR)* 2001, 428.

Derek Van der Merwe, 'A Rhetorical-dialectical Conception of the Common Law – Aristotle's *Topics*' *Tydskrif vir die Suid-Afrikaanse Reg (TSAR)* 2001, 664.

Derek Van der Merwe, 'A Rhetorical-dialectical Conception of the Common Law – Aristotelian Influence on the Genesis of Roman Legal Science' *Tydskrif vir die Suid-Afrikaanse Reg (TSAR)* 2002, 76.

Theodor Viehweg, *Topik und Jurisprudenz* (5th Edition, C.H. Beck Verlag, München 1974).

Alan Watson, *The Making of the Civil Law* (Harvard University Press, Cambridge, Massachusetts 1981).

Alan Watson (ed), *The Digest of Justinian* (University of Pennsylvania Press, Pennsylvania 1985).

Leniency Programmes under US Antitrust Law and EU Competition Law

*Michael Kort**

Abstract: *Leniency programmes are enormously important for the success of antitrust authorities in their fight against restraints of competition across the world. Leniency programmes incentivise companies to tell antitrust authorities about their infringements by offering substantial discounts on fines that would otherwise be imposed on them.*
In most jurisdictions of the world, leniency programmes are open not only to companies involved in a cartel, but also to individuals. Worldwide, leniency programmes have only restricted or even no influence on civil liability. Another recently discussed problem is the delicate question of whether a (potential) claimant in a civil action for cartel damages may gain access to information about the whistleblowing under a leniency programme.
In the USA, leniency programmes in some respects became a blueprint for other countries. The Department of Justice (DOJ) administers the US leniency programmes. The Leniency Policy in the EU has some similarities with the leniency policy in the USA. As in the USA, the relevant leniency policy is contained in self-binding rules made by the relevant antitrust authority, i.e. the European Commission. Undertakings that self-report can receive immunity from fines. The 2006 Leniency Notice is an important tool for the investigation of hardcore cartels. The 2006 Notice clearly stated that the benefit of leniency could not protect a company from the civil law consequences of its participants in an illegal agreement.

* Michael Kort, *Dr. iur.*; Professor, University of Augsburg, Faculty of Law. Chair for Civil Law, Commercial Law, Intellectual Property Law and Labour Law.

I. Introduction: The importance of leniency programmes

Leniency programmes incentivise companies to tell antitrust authorities about their infringements by offering substantial discounts on fines that would otherwise be imposed on them. Companies that give information about a cartel which provides significant added value to what the antitrust authority already knows, and helps the antitrust authority to proceed against others in the cartel, may have their fine reduced. In many jurisdictions, the first whistleblower will be forgiven the entire fine.[1]

Leniency programmes are enormously important for the success of antitrust authorities in their fight against restraints of competition across the world. The European Commissioner for Competition, *Margrethe Vestager*, recently stressed that leniency programmes are a key tool for competition authorities to uncover illegal cartels. They encourage members of a cartel to come forward and tell authorities about cartels – in return for having their fine reduced, or paying no fine at all. Ms. *Vestager* pointed out that cartels often operate across borders, and companies thinking about coming clean need to know that they will benefit from leniency in the same way – whichever competition authority deals with the case.[2]

The importance of whistleblowing under leniency programmes has been demonstrated recently by whistleblowing in the diesel scandal concerning a potential cartel of five large German carmakers that are known worldwide.

1 Valentine Korah, *An Introductory Guide to EC Competition Law and Practice* (9th Edition, 2007), 38.

2 Margrethe Vestager, *Neue Zeitschrift für Kartellrecht* (NZKart) 2017, 205.

II. The scope of leniency programmes

1. Cartels

Competition law across the world distinguishes between restraints on competition in horizontal agreements or concerted practices between competitors, and vertical agreements or concerted practices between firms that are not competitors, but are doing business in the same line of production or distribution – for example, an agreement between a carmaker and its distributors or wholesalers.

Leniency programmes in the US and in the EU only refer to horizontal agreements or concerted practices between competitors (cartels), but not to vertical agreements and concerted practices. However, leniency programmes in force in some EU Member States cover not only horizontal agreements, but vertical agreements as well.

Further, in most of the jurisdictions of the world leniency programmes do not refer to the abuse of a dominant position by a monopolist.

The reason why leniency programmes usually cover only cartels is that they are the form of restraint of competition that are most difficult to uncover due to the secret nature of the arrangements in nearly all cases and because cartels are the most harmful form of restraint of competition.[3]

2. Corporations and individuals

In most jurisdictions of the world, leniency programmes are open not only to companies involved in a cartel, but also to individuals, who have the right to apply for leniency independently from the company. This is more or less the case in every jurisdiction where individuals can be fined separately from the company for cartel activity.[4]

In addition, a leniency application by a company usually also covers individuals – provided that they cooperate with the competition authority in

---

3 Marcin Trepka, Martyna Wurm, *Leniency Programs-The Devil Is In The Details* (2016), 3, https://www.competitionpolicyinternational.com/wp-content/uploads/2016/09/Europe-Column-September-Full.pdf (15-01-2018).

4 Marcin Trepka, Martyna Wurm, *Leniency Programs-The Devil Is In The Details (2016)*, 4, https://www.competitionpolicyinternational.com/wp-content/uploads/2016/09/Europe-Column-September-Full.pdf (15-01-2018).

the course of the investigation. However, a leniency application by an individual will not cover the relevant company involved. [5]

3. Criminal behaviour

In some countries – including South Africa, the USA and some European countries – cartel activity is subject to criminal liability, including imprisonment. Criminal liability is only covered by the leniency programmes for individuals in some of these countries.[6]

4. Limited influence of leniency programmes on civil liability

As a general rule, worldwide leniency programmes have a restricted or even no influence on civil liability. A private party, whether it be a company or an individual, may successfully sue the whistleblower (a company or an individual) by means of a private action for damages caused by the cartel behaviour notwithstanding the fact that the whistleblower may be covered by a leniency programme and may not have to pay a fine or have to pay only a reduced fine.

5. Leniency programmes and information about potential claimants in private actions

Another problem recently discussed worldwide is the delicate question of whether a (potential) claimant in a civil action for cartel damages may gain access to information about the whistleblowing under a leniency programme. Generally, the more information an antitrust authority (or a court dealing with cartel matters) may have to provide a (potential) claimant for cartel damages, the more the success of leniency programmes endangered.

---

5 Marcin Trepka, Martyna Wurm, *Leniency Programs-The Devil Is In The Details (2016)*, 4, https://www.competitionpolicyinternational.com/wp-content/uploads/2016/09/Europe-Column-September-Full.pdf (15-01-2018).

6 Marcin Trepka, Martyna Wurm, *Leniency Programs-The Devil Is In The Details (2016)*, 4, https://www.competitionpolicyinternational.com/wp-content/uploads/2016/09/Europe-Column-September-Full.pdf (15-08-2018).

III. Leniency programmes under South African Law

The South African Competition Act No. 89 of 1998 makes no specific provision for a leniency policy. However, a Corporate Leniency Policy (CLP) published in 2004 is the principal tool employed in cartel investigations by the national competition authority in South Africa, the Competition Commission. The Commission can grant conditional immunity to a leniency applicant who has satisfied the requirements of the Corporate Leniency Policy.

As in the US and in the EU, South Africa's Corporate Leniency Policy is only applicable to cartel conduct and not to the abuse of a dominant position. Further, similarly to the US and in the EU, it is not applicable to the participation of companies in vertical agreements between entities that are in the same line of production or distribution, but only to those in different lines that are not competitors. Like the US and EU leniency programmes, the South African Corporate Leniency Policy is only applicable to the participants in an agreement or concerted practice among competing firms – i.e. to horizontal agreements.

The Corporate Leniency Policy of South Africa permits civil claims to be brought against a leniency applicant. Therefore, the question of confidentiality during a leniency application arises. There are no formal rules regarding identity disclosure and the disclosure of a leniency applicant's identity. The Commission normally protects confidentiality in relation to all information and evidence provided by the applicant on a case-by-case basis. The Commission has recently concluded a Memorandum of Understanding (MoU) with, *inter alia*, the EU, which is expected to provide greater cooperation for common investigations as well as greater information sharing between the respective agencies.

IV. Leniency programmes under US Antitrust Law

1. Main features

In the USA, leniency programmes are enormously important. The Department of Justice (DOJ) is in charge of prosecuting criminal violations of the federal competition laws (antitrust laws)[7] and therefore administers the US

7 Herbert Hovenkamp, *Federal Antitrust Policy* (5th Edition, 2016), 792 et seqq.

leniency programmes. It has to be stressed that in contrast to leniency programmes in other jurisdictions, the US leniency programmes deal only with criminal violations of the main statutory law against cartels in the US – namely Article 1 of the Sherman Act – because the DOJ is principally in charge of prosecuting criminal violations of the federal antitrust laws. Therefore, US leniency programmes do not cover civil antitrust enforcement by the DOJ or the Federal Trade Commission (FTC). As a consequence, nothing in the leniency programmes can protect a company or an individual in a civil action brought by third parties. This is, however, also the case in the EU, even though EU leniency programmes do not involve criminal prosecution, but fines imposed by the EU Commission.[8]

2. Scope of protection

There are two main leniency programmes in the USA: The Corporate Leniency Policy introduced in 1978 and revised in 1993, and the Individual Leniency Policy introduced in 1994. The Corporate Leniency Policy allows for lenient treatment of a corporation that comes forward and reports a violation before the DOJ has begun an investigation and provided the DOJ has not yet received information about the illegal activity from another source. The corporation must also have immediately ceased its participation in the activity. It must report fully and continue to cooperate. The confession must be made in the name of the corporation, and the corporation must make restitution to injured parties if possible. The corporation may not be the leader of the illegal activity.[9]

The Individual Leniency Policy applies to all individuals who approach the DOJ on their own behalf –i.e. not as part of a corporate proffer or confession – to seek leniency for reporting illegal antitrust activity of which the DOJ has not been previously been made aware. The individual must report fully and candidly, and may not have been the leader of the illegal activity.[10]

Leniency programmes were introduced in the USA much earlier than in other parts of the world and in some respects became a blueprint for other

8 Alison Jones, Brenda Sufrin, *EU Competition Law* (6th Edition, 2016), 990.

9 Douglas Broder, *US Antitrust Law and Enforcement* (3rd Edition, 2016), para. 8.33.

10 Douglas Broder, *US Antitrust Law and Enforcement* (3rd Edition, 2016), para. 8.40.

countries.[11] The leniency programmes were enhanced by the Antitrust Criminal Penalty Enhancement and Reform Act of 2004, which increased the maximum penalties for antitrust criminal violations, but also limited the civil antitrust liability of those who take advantage of the leniency programmes to single damages[12] and not to the treble damages that were common in these cases until 2004.[13]

The leniency programmes of the DOJ can save both corporations and its officers from criminal prosecution if they come forward and make full disclosure of cartel behaviour such as price fixing before the DOJ becomes aware of the cartel activities.

3. Procedural aspects

Concerning procedural aspects of leniency programmes, one must distinguish procedural aspects of the application for leniency as such from further procedural aspects of the leniency programme.

The application requires no particular form. The Antitrust Division gives the applicant a 'marker' for a set period of time to hold its place at the front of the line for leniency while the applicant's legal counsel gathers additional information – for example, by means of an internal investigation to perfect the company's leniency application. To obtain a marker, the applicant's counsel must identify the client and industry, report that an alleged antitrust violation is suspected, and disclose the general nature of the conduct discovered so far.[14]

---

11 Valentine Korah, *An Introductory Guide to EC Competition Law and Practice* (9th Edition, 2007), 280.

12 Douglas Broder, *US Antitrust Law and Enforcement* (3rd Edition, 2016), para. 8.32.

13 Valentine Korah, *An Introductory Guide to EC Competition Law and Practice* (9th Edition, 2007), 280.

14 Douglas Broder, *US Antitrust Law and Enforcement* (3rd Edition, 2016), para. 8.33.

4. Important cases in the USA concerning leniency questions

a) Precision Associates, Inc. v. Panalpina World Transport (Holding) Ltd.

A district court held in 2015 in *Precision Associates, Inc. v. Panalpina World Transp. (Holding) Ltd.*[15] that a corporation's leniency application terminated its involvement in the subject conspiracy. As a consequence, this corporation is no longer liable for any damages incurred by the victims of the conspiracy after the date of the application for the leniency programme.

b) Stolt-Nielsen case

The *Stolt-Nielsen* case,[16] decided by a district court in 2007, dealt with the first (and so-far only) attempt by the Department of Justice (DOJ) to revoke a grant of leniency. First, the DOJ granted Stolt conditional leniency for reporting its involvement in an international conspiracy to restrain trade, but later the DOJ concluded that the company had not been truthful about when it had terminated its part in the conspiracy and withdrew its grant of leniency. Further, the DOJ indicted Stolt and some of its executives. The district court agreed with the company that it had not breached the leniency agreement and dismissed the indictment. Although the DOJ did not appeal the dismissal by this district court, it continued to maintain that it had been correct. However, the DOJ stressed that the revocation was exceptional, because it felt that the revocation of its grant of leniency could make companies less willing to seek leniency.

V. Leniency programmes under EU Competition Law

1. History of EU leniency policy

The Leniency Policy in the EU has some similarities with the leniency policy in the USA. As in the USA, the relevant leniency policy is contained in self-binding rules made by the relevant antitrust authority, i.e. the European

15 *Precision Assocs. V. Panalpina World Transp. (Holding) Ltd.*, EDNY No. 1:08cv00042-JG-VVP (2015).

16 *United States v. Stolt-Nielsen* SA., 524 F. Supp. 2d 586, 609 (ED Pa. 2007).

Commission. Although the Commission practiced leniency before 1996 (see the *Cartonboard* decision, below 2.a), the Commission published a Leniency Notice in 1996 putting this practice on a systematic footing. Provided that in the event of cartel participants giving information to the Commission and cooperating with the Commission's investigation, they could expect a reduced fine or even no fine at all. The 2002 Leniency Notice was then replaced by the 2006 Leniency Notice, which is still in force.

2. Important older European cases concerning leniency questions

a) Cartonboard case

Some forms of leniency already existed even before leniency programmes had come into force in Europe (and in the European Union). This is shown by the Commission's *Cartonboard* decision of 1994.[17] The Commission fined the company store just one-third of what it would have done had this company not come to the Commission and given the Commission information about the cartel at a time when the Commission did not know about it. The ringleader of the cartel spontaneously admitted the infringement, and provided detailed evidence to the Commission about the cartel.

b) BASF AG v. Commission cases

The *BASF AG v. Commission* decision of the General Court of 2007[18] dealt with an appeal of the Commission's decision which found a number of companies to have infringed the main EU provision against the restraint of trade (Article 101 TFEU) by engaging in price-fixing and market-sharing agreements. On appeal, the parties challenged the level of fines imposed by the Commission. The Commission's decision was based upon the 1996 leniency notice, an older leniency notice than the 2006 leniency notice in force at that time. The General Court pointed out that a reduction based on the 1996 Leniency Notice can be justified only where the information provided – and, more generally, the conduct of the company concerned – might be considered to demonstrate genuine cooperation on its part. The conduct of

17 *Cartonboard* (COMP/33.833 [1994] OJ L243/1, par. 171.

18 ECJ, Joined Cases T-101/05 and T-111/05, 2007, *BASF AG v Commission,* ECR II-4949.

a company, which responded in an incomplete and misleading way even though it was not required to respond to a question put forward by the Commission, cannot be considered to reflect the spirit of cooperation required in the 1996 Leniency Notice. Further, the General Court stressed that the Commission had a broad discretion in applying the 1996 Leniency Notice.

3. Structure of the 2006 Leniency Notice

a) General approach

Under the current 2006 Leniency Notice, undertakings that self-report can receive immunity from fines. The 2006 Leniency Notice is an important tool for the investigation of hardcore cartels.[19] The Notice only addresses restraints of competition by horizontal agreements under Article 101 TFEU (i.e. cartels), but not by vertical agreements under Article 101 TFEU. The abuse of the position as a monopolist (abuse of a dominant position) is not addressed by the 2006 Leniency Notice.

The 2006 Leniency Notice is consistent with the European Competition Network (EPN) Model Leniency Programme (MLP), which was adopted to deal with the problem of divergences between the national leniency policies of the EU Member States.[20]

The Commission may not depart in an individual case from the rules contained in the 2006 Leniency Notice without giving reasons compatible with the principle of equal treatment.[21]

b) Immunity

In the 1996 Notice, in contrast to the US and Canadian policies the Commission does not guarantee full immunity to the first participant to come forward. Only in an amended Notice of 2002 did the Commission guarantee

---

19 Antoine Colombani, Jindrich Kloub, Ewoud Sakkers, 'Cartels' in: Jonathan Faull, Ali Nikpay (eds), *The EU Law of Competition* (3rd Edition, 2014), para 8.01, para 8.95.

20 Alison Jones, Brenda Sufrin, *EU Competition Law* (6th Edition, 2016), 983.

21 Alison Jones, Brenda Sufrin, *EU Competition Law* (6th Edition, 2016), 983.

immunity to the first company to submit evidence that met certain criteria.[22] The same applies for the current 2006 Notice.[23]

Under Paragraph 8 of the 2006 Notice, an immunity applicant may be granted leniency if the company is the first to submit information and evidence that, in the Commission's view, will enable the Commission either to carry out a target inspection in connection with the alleged cartel (paragraph 8 (a) test[24]), or find an infringement of Article 101 TFEU in connection with the alleged cartel (paragraph 8 (b) test[25]).[26]

The 2006 Notice allows the Commission considerable discretion regarding the question of what amounts to sufficient evidence and information to satisfy paragraphs 8(a) and 8(b), but this discretion is subject to an in-depth review of the law and the facts by the General Court. [27]

In the *Luftfrachtkartell* decision of 2016,[28] the General Court pointed out that the Commission could not grant to other applicants the benefit of immunity from fines on the basis of point 8(b) of that Notice if it had already granted a valid conditional immunity to one applicant on the basis of point 8(a) of that Notice. There can only be one successful immunity applicant per infringement.

c) Reduction of Fees

Companies or other undertakings approaching the Commission after the first company to submit evidence in a cartel case are eligible for a reduction in the fine that would otherwise have been imposed. They are subject to the

---

22 Alison Jones, Brenda Sufrin, *EU Competition Law* (6th Edition, 2016), 983.
23 Alison Jones, Brenda Sufrin, *EU Competition Law* (6th Edition, 2016), 985.
24 For details see Antoine Colombani, Jindrich Kloub, Ewoud Sakkers, 'Cartels' in: Jonathan Faull, Ali Nikpay (eds), *The EU Law of Competition* (3rd Edition, 2014), para 8.01, para 8.134 to 8.137.
25 Antoine Colombani, Jindrich Kloub, Ewoud Sakkers, 'Cartels' in: Jonathan Faull, Ali Nikpay (eds), *The EU Law of Competition* (3rd Edition, 2014), para 8.01, para 8.95.138 to 8.138.
26 Alison Jones, Brenda Sufrin, *EU Competition Law* (6th Edition, 2016), 985.
27 Alison Jones, Brenda Sufrin, *EU Competition Law* (6th Edition, 2016), 985.
28 European General Court, Case T-251/12, 29.02.2016, *Luftfracht-Kartell,* NZKart 2016, 188, para. 177.

same ongoing cooperation requirement as for the immunity applicants, but with the difference that nothing is guaranteed to them. [29]

d) SAV Test

Under the 2006 Notice, for some forms of fine reduction the applicant must, – apart from terminating its involvement in the suspected cartel – provide the Commission with evidence representing 'significant added value' with respect to the evidence the Commission already possesses in relation to the same case. [30] By its very nature and/or its level of detail, evidence of added value must strengthen the Commission's ability to prove the alleged cartel.[31]

Under the 2006 Notice, the Commission has a broad range of discretion on the question of what qualifies as 'significant added value' (SAV), but this discretion is subject to a review of the law and the facts by the General Court. [32]

e) Marker System

Similar to the US leniency policy (see above IV. 3.), under the Commission's 2006 Leniency Notice, a discretionary 'marker' system provides for an applicant for immunity to reserve its first place in line by initially providing only limited information.[33] The applicant then will have some time (set

---

29 Alison Jones, Brenda Sufrin, *EU Competition Law* (6th Edition, 2016), 985.; for details see Antoine Colombani, Jindrich Kloub, Ewoud Sakkers, 'Cartels' in: Jonathan Faull, Ali Nikpay (eds), *The EU Law of Competition* (3rd Edition, 2014), para 8.01, para 8.114, 8.115, 8.175 to 8.209.

30 For details see Antoine Colombani, Jindrich Kloub, Ewoud Sakkers, 'Cartels' in: Jonathan Faull, Ali Nikpay (eds), *The EU Law of Competition* (3rd Edition, 2014), para 8.01, para 8.01.

31 Antoine Colombani, Jindrich Kloub, Ewoud Sakkers, 'Cartels' in: Jonathan Faull, Ali Nikpay (eds), *The EU Law of Competition* (3rd Edition, 2014), para 8.01, para 8.177.

32 Alison Jones, Brenda Sufrin, *EU Competition Law* (6th Edition, 2016), 985.

33 Antoine Colombani, Jindrich Kloub, Ewoud Sakkers, 'Cartels' in: Jonathan Faull, Ali Nikpay (eds), *The EU Law of Competition* (3rd Edition, 2014), para 8.01, para 8.152 and 8.153; Alison Jones, Brenda Sufrin, *EU Competition Law* (6th Edition, 2016), 985.

at the Commission's discretion) to perfect the application by providing additional evidence required to reach the immunity threshold. [34] The marker system is a frequently used tool of the Commission's leniency policy. [35]

f) Amnesty Plus and Penalty Plus Policy

In contrast to the USA, the EU leniency policy does not provide for an 'Amnesty Plus', whereby an applicant for leniency in respect of one cartel is further rewarded if it reveals another cartel in the course of the proceedings.[36]

A similarity to the US concept of 'penalty plus' does exist in the EU. If a company subsequently contested facts in proceedings before the General Court which were formerly uncontested in front of the Commission, the Commission would normally ask the court to increase the fine imposed on that company if the company had benefitted from a leniency programme.

g) Procedural Aspects

The Commission requires that only persons authorized to represent the company for that purpose could apply for leniency on behalf of the company.[37] A company seeking immunity must contact the DG Competition.[38]

As an alternative to a regular application for immunity, the Commission has set up a mechanism allowing for the 'hypothetical application', which allows the company to know whether or not it will satisfy the conditions of

---

34 Alison Jones, Brenda Sufrin, *EU Competition Law* (6th Edition, 2016), 987.

35 Antoine Colombani, Jindrich Kloub, Ewoud Sakkers, 'Cartels' in: Jonathan Faull, Ali Nikpay (eds), *The EU Law of Competition* (3rd Edition, 2014), para 8.01, para 8.152.

36 Alison Jones, Brenda Sufrin, *EU Competition Law* (6th Edition, 2016), 984.

37 Antoine Colombani, Jindrich Kloub, Ewoud Sakkers, 'Cartels' in: Jonathan Faull, Ali Nikpay (eds), *The EU Law of Competition* (3rd Edition, 2014), para 8.01, para 8.120.

38 Antoine Colombani, Jindrich Kloub, Ewoud Sakkers, 'Cartels' in: Jonathan Faull, Ali Nikpay (eds), *The EU Law of Competition* (3rd Edition, 2014), para 8.01, para 8.150.

paragraphs 8(a) or 8(b) (see (b) above) before disclosing its identity to the Commission together with the relevant facts and evidence.[39]

Further, the 2006 Notice provides that the Commission may accept that corporate statements are provided orally.[40]

Concerning applications for a reduction in fines, the 2006 Notice stresses that a company wishing to benefit from a fine reduction must make a formal application to the Commission. This is a new requirement, because the previous 2002 Leniency Notice did not require formal application for the reduction in fines.[41]

h) Confidentiality of, and access to, the information obtained under the 2006 Notice

By providing the Commission with information about a cartel, applicants not only incriminate other cartel members, but also themselves. The cooperation with the Commission under leniency may have negative consequences in the context of other proceedings – for example, concerning investigations by authorities outside the EU, or in follow-on damages litigation in civil courts inside or outside the EU.[42]

The 2006 Notice clearly stated that the benefit of leniency could not protect a company from the civil law consequences of its participants in an illegal agreement, and that each company should be aware that the role it played in the cartel would be described in full in the final decision.[43] However, corporate statements made by companies applying for leniency under

---

39 Antoine Colombani, Jindrich Kloub, Ewoud Sakkers, 'Cartels' in: Jonathan Faull, Ali Nikpay (eds), *The EU Law of Competition* (3rd Edition, 2014), para 8.01, para 8.154.

40 Antoine Colombani, Jindrich Kloub, Ewoud Sakkers, 'Cartels' in: Jonathan Faull, Ali Nikpay (eds), *The EU Law of Competition* (3rd Edition, 2014), para 8.01, para 8.155.

41 Antoine Colombani, Jindrich Kloub, Ewoud Sakkers, 'Cartels' in: Jonathan Faull, Ali Nikpay (eds), *The EU Law of Competition* (3rd Edition, 2014), para 8.01, para 8.184.

42 Antoine Colombani, Jindrich Kloub, Ewoud Sakkers, 'Cartels' in: Jonathan Faull, Ali Nikpay (eds), *The EU Law of Competition* (3rd Edition, 2014), para 8.01, para 8.217.

43 Antoine Colombani, Jindrich Kloub, Ewoud Sakkers, 'Cartels' in: Jonathan Faull, Ali Nikpay (eds), *The EU Law of Competition* (3rd Edition, 2014), para 8.01, para 8.120.

the 2006 Notice are protected from discovery procedures in civil actions for damages.[44]

i) The relationship between EU Competition Law, the EU leniency policy, and the leniency policies of EU Member States

In the *Schenker* decision[45] of 2013, which deals with the relationship of EU competition law to the national leniency programmes of EU Member States, the Court of Justice stressed that a national leniency programme must not undermine the requirement of effective and uniform application of Article 101 TFEU in the European Union. Further, the Court commented on the need to unify the approach of the European Union and the approach of the Member States of the European Union to fines and reductions of fines in order not to jeopardize the effectiveness of European Union law.

There is no EU-wide system of leniency, and an application for leniency to the Commission does not count as an application to a national competition authority of an EU Member State.[46] The EU eniency policy as such is not binding on the EU Member States concerning their own leniency policy.[47]

4. The meaning of the European Competition Network (ECN)

In order to promote coordination of the work of the Commission as the EU Competition Authority and the work of the national competition authorities (NCAs) of the EU Member States, the Commission established the European Competition Network (ECN) in 2004.[48] The ECN has established an

44 Alison Jones, Brenda Sufrin, *EU Competition Law* (6th Edition, 2016), 985.
45 Court of Justice, Case C-681.
46 Alison Jones, Brenda Sufrin, *EU Competition Law* (6th Edition, 2016), 983.
47 Alison Jones, Brenda Sufrin, *EU Competition Law* (6th Edition, 2016), 984.
48 For details, see Antoine Colombani, Jindrich Kloub, Ewoud Sakkers, 'Cartels' in: Jonathan Faull, Ali Nikpay (eds), *The EU Law of Competition* (3rd Edition, 2014), para 8.01, para 8.233 to 8.247; Hellmann, Hans-Joachim, in: Gerhard Wiedemann (ed) KartR (3rd Edition, 2016), § 46 para 66.

ECN Model Leniency Programme (MLP).[49] The Commission's 2006 Leniency Notice is consistent with the MLP.[50]

Under EU Regulation 1/2003 and under the ECN system, one of the advantages for the applicant for immunity or for a reduction in fine is that the opening of proceedings by the Commission in cartel cases automatically deprives national competition authorities of EU Member States of their competence to investigate the case. Thus, if the Commission grants immunity to an applicant and opens proceedings, the company concerned does not run the risk of further proceedings in an EU Member State.[51]

5. The meaning of Implementation Regulation 773/2004, amended in 2015

No explicit legislative provision for the leniency policy was provided under Article 4a (1) of the EU Implementation Regulation 773/2004 amended in 2015 for the first time.[52] The Implementation Regulation was amended in the wake of the Damages Directive (see section 6 below) to expressly provide (in Article 16a) for the limitation of the use of information obtained in the course of Commission proceedings in cartel cases.[53]

6. The meaning of the EU Directive on Rules Governing Actions for Damages of 2014 (Damages Directive)

The Damages Directive of 2014 was designed to facilitate damages actions of private parties, but the Commission does not wish this to jeopardise the effectiveness of the leniency policy.[54] The Damages Directive of 2014 rec-

---

49 For details, see Antoine Colombani, Jindrich Kloub, Ewoud Sakkers, 'Cartels' in: Jonathan Faull, Ali Nikpay (eds), *The EU Law of Competition* (3rd Edition, 2014), para 8.01, para 8.246 to 8.247.

50 Alison Jones, Brenda Sufrin, *EU Competition Law* (6th Edition, 2016), 983.

51 Antoine Colombani, Jindrich Kloub, Ewoud Sakkers, 'Cartels' in: Jonathan Faull, Ali Nikpay (eds), *The EU Law of Competition* (3rd Edition, 2014), para 8.01, para 8.234.

52 Alison Jones, Brenda Sufrin, *EU Competition Law* (6th Edition, 2016), 983.

53 Alison Jones, Brenda Sufrin, *EU Competition Law* (6th Edition, 2016), 934.

54 Alison Jones, Brenda Sufrin, *EU Competition Law* (6th Edition, 2016), 934.

ognizes that disclosure of evidence should not unduly detract from the effectiveness of the public enforcement of competition law in Europe. Therefore, it limits access to certain documents, *inter alia* those obtained as part of leniency application procedures.[55] In order to reach this aim, the Damages Directive stipulates that it is not necessary that every document relating to proceedings under EU competition law be disclosed to a claimant merely on the grounds of the claimant's intended action for damages. This is because it is highly unlikely that the action for damages will need to be based on all the evidence in the file relating to those proceedings.[56]

7. EU case law partially overridden by recent EU statutory law developments

Two recent, prominent decisions of the Court of Justice have been partially overridden by the Damages Directive of 2014 (see above) and by the amendment of the Implementation Regulation in 2015 (see above). These are the *Pfleiderer* case of 2011 and the *Donau AG Chemie* case of 2013.

a) Pfleiderer case

In the *Pfleiderer* case of 2011,[57] the Court of Justice stressed that EU law does not exclude access to leniency documents by an injured party. In this regard, the Court of Justice did not distinguish between the right to access self-incriminating statements and the right to view other documentation, notwithstanding the risk for effective leniency programmes. In the opinion of the Court of Justice – now overridden by EU statutory law – it is up to the national courts of the Member States to balance the interests of the involved parties. In the end, the German court refused access to the leniency documents to safeguard the effectiveness of cartel detection.

---

55 Ariel Ezrachi, *EU Competition Law,* (6th Edition, 2018), 541.
56 Ariel Ezrachi, *EU Competition Law,* (6th Edition, 2018), 541.
57 Court of Justice, Case C-360/09.

b) Donau Chemie AG case

In the *Donau Chemie AG* case of 2013,[58] which is in many respects a decision parallel to the *Pfleiderer* case (see (a) above), the Court of Justice dealt with the legality of a national provision of an EU Member State, which required the consent of all parties to the cartel court proceedings in order to grant third-party prospective-damage claimants access to documents before the cartel court.

The Court of Justice, referring to its decision in the *Pfleiderer* case, pointed out that the national courts of the EU Member States must weigh up the respective interests in favour of disclosure of the information and in favour of the protection of that information. Further, the Court held that EU law precludes a provision of national law of an EU Member State which conditions access to documents concerning the application of Article 101 TFEU and to leniency programmes in this way without leaving any possibility for the national courts to weigh up the interests involved.

Again, it must be stressed that both decisions are partially overridden by the development of EU statutory law since 2014. In particular, the Damages Directive makes it clear that national courts will not be able to give access to leniency statements under national disclosure rules. [59]

8. Important EU cases concerning leniency questions

a) Evonik Degussa case

In the *Evonik Degussa* case of 2014,[60] the General Court pointed out that although the Commission has discretion to reduce the amount of a fine, it must keep to its own rules concerning a reduction of fines. As a consequence, the Commission has to adhere to the wording of its own Leniency Notice.[61]

---

58 Court of Justice, Case C-536/11.

59 Alison Jones, Brenda Sufrin, *EU Competition Law* (6th Edition, 2016), 1070.

60 General Court, ECLI:EU:T:2014:22.

61 Hellmann, Hans-Joachim, in: Gerhard Wiedemann (ed) KartR (3rd Edition, 2016), § 46 para 87.

b) AKZO Nobel case

In the *AKZO Nobel* case of 2015,[62] the General Court appealed the new policy of the European Commission to publish less heavily redacted versions of its cartel decisions. Therefore, claimants that may take civil action for damages can derive information useful for them – derived from leniency statements – from the published decision. As a result, the attractiveness of leniency for companies may decrease.[63]

c) *DHL* case

In the *DHL* decision of 2016,[64] the Court of Justice decided that the leniency programme established by the Commission through its 2006 Leniency Notice is not binding on EU Member States. That conclusion also applied to the ECN Model leniency programme. DHL's argument that the national competition authorities have formerly undertaken to respect the principle set out in the Notice on Cooperation does not – as the Court of Justice stresses – change the legal status of that notice under EU law, nor that of the ENC Model leniency programme.

VI. Conclusion

As has been shown, a worldwide cooperation and coordination concerning leniency programmes is required.

---

62 Case T-345/12.

63 Alison Jones, Brenda Sufrin, *EU Competition Law* (6th Edition, 2016), 990; Andreas Kafetzopoulos *European Competition Law Review (ECLR)* 2015, 295, 296 et seqq.; Christof R.A. Swaak, Rein Wesseling *European Competition Law Review (ECLR)* 2015, 346.

64 ECJ, Case C-428/14.

Bibliography

Douglas Broder, *US Antitrust Law and Enforcement* (3rd Edition, Oxford University Press, Oxford 2016).

Antoine Colombani, Jindrich Kloub and Ewoud Sakkers, 'Cartels', in: Jonathan Faull and Ali Nikpay (eds), *The EU Law of Competition* (3rd Edition, Oxford University Press, Oxford 2014), para 8.01.

Ariel Ezrachi, *EU Competition Law,* (6th Edition, Hart Publishing, Oxford and Portland, OR 2018).

Hans-Joachim Hellmann, in: Gerhard Wiedemann (ed), KartR (3rd Edition, C.H. Beck, Munich 2016).

Herbert Hovenkamp, *Federal Antitrust Policy* (5th Edition, West Academic Publishing, St. Paul, MN 2016).

Alison Jones and Brenda Sufrin, *EU Competition Law* (6th Edition, Oxford University Press, Oxford 2016).

Andreas Kafetzopoulos, 'European Commission policy on publication of cartel decisions: the latest victory of damage claimants against leniency applicants' *European Competition Law Review (ECLR)* 2015, 295.

Valentine Korah, *An Introductory Guide to EC Competition Law and Pratice* (9th Edition, Hart Publishing, Oxford and Portland, OR 2007).

Christof R.A. Swaak and Rein Wesseling 'Reconsidering the leniency option: if not first in, good reasons to stay out' *European Competition Law Review (ECLR)* 2015, 346.

Marcin Trepka and Martyna Wurm, *Leniency Programs-The Devil Is In The Details* (2016), https://www.competitionpolicyinternational.com/wp-content/uploads/2016/09/Europe-Column-September-Full.pdf (15-01-2018).

Margrethe Vestager, ‚Empowering national competition authorities' *Neue Zeitschrift für Kartellrecht* (NZKart) 2017, 205.

Register of cases

Cartonboard (COMP/33.833 [1994] OJ L'243/1).

European Court of Justice, Joined Cases T-101/05 and T-111/05, 2007, *BASF AG v European Commission,* ECR II-4949.

European Court of Justice, Case C-360/09, 14.06.2011, *Pfleiderer AG v Bundeskartellamt*, ECLI EU:C:2011:389.

European Court of Justice, Case C-536/11, 06.06.2013, *Donau Chemie AG and Others v Bundeswettbewerbsbehörde*, ECLI EU:C:2013:366.

European Court of Justice, Case T-345/12, 28.01.2015, *Akzo Nobel NV and Others v European Commission*, ECLI EU:T:2015:50.

European Court of Justice, Case C-681/13, 16.07.2015, *Diageo Brands BV v Simiramida-04 EOOD*, ECLI EU:C:2015:471.

European Court of Justice, Case C-428/14, 20.01.2016, *DHL Express (Italy) Srl, DHL Global Forwarding (Italy) SpA v Autorità Garante della Concorrenza e del Mercato*, ECLI EU:C:2016:27.

European General Court, Case T-391/09, 23.01.2014, *Evonik Degussa and AlzChem v European Commission*, ECLI EU:T:2014:22.

European General Court, Case T-251/12, 29.02.2016, *Luftfracht-Kartell,* NZKart 2016, 188, para. 177.

Precision Assocs. v Panalpina World Transp. (Holding) Ltd., EDNY No. 1:08cv00042-JG-VVP (2015).

United States v Stolt-Nielsen SA., 524 F. Supp. 2d 586, 609 (ED Pa. 2007).

Aspects of the Corporate Leniency Program in South African Competition Law

*Wim Alberts**

Having had the opportunity of reading Professor Kort's paper I would like to share some thoughts on the concept "corporate leniency" in South African competition law, as found in the Corporate Leniency Program (CLP). This program is administered by the relevant body, the Competition Commission, which is similar to the Bundeskartellamt.

This dependency is acknowledged by the Competition Commission itself, which stated:[1]

> "It is envisaged that a leniency of the nature adopted by the Commission in the CLP would lead to detection and expeditious finalisation of cases that otherwise would have been difficult, if not impossible, to crack."

Professor Kort mentioned the case involving the famous German vehicle manufacturers. But one should not be surprised what becomes visible when the spotlight is shone on South African companies. Allow me two examples.

The first relates to Sasol, the petroleum company, which does substantial business in Germany (incidentally, there is also a German connection in South Africa).[2] The European Union's General Court reduced fines for three companies (including Sasol) involved in a paraffin wax cartel. The court reduced Sasol's €318 million fine down to about €149 million.

The size of Sasol's fine (€149 million) is notable when it is borne in mind that there is (only) a €500 million market for the substance. Sasol's fine was the largest in part because it acted as the leader of the arrangement according to the European Commission. Ironically, a year later, Sasol announced a 21 percent jump in attributable earnings.

---

* Riaan W. Alberts, *B.Iur., LLB., LLD.*, Professor of Intellectual Property Law, Faculty of Law, University of Johannesburg.

1 Competition Commission South Africa, *Corporate Leniency Policy pursuant to the Competition Act 89 of 1998* (2014), par 16.7.

2 Information based on Aaron Vehling, 'EU Court Slashes Sasol Wax Cartel Fine In Half', in: *www.law360.com* (11-07-2014). The reverse is also true. German companies like Lurgi and Linde were involved in construction of the Sasol plants, first in Sasolburg in the Free State, and German expertise, such as the Fischer Tropsch process was used there.

Secondly, the South African competition authorities held that there was a cartel in the bread industry, with the companies involved being some of the most prominent South African businesses. They are Tiger Brands' Albany, Premier's Blue Ribbon, Pioneer, and Foodcorp's Sunbake. The fines involved many millions of rands.

I. Corporate leniency policies in Africa

To my knowledge, the African competition jurisdictions that have corporate leniency policies in place include Algeria, Botswana, Egypt, Ethiopia, Gabon, Gambia, Kenya, Mauritius, Morocco, Mozambique, South Africa, Swaziland, Tanzania, Tunisia and Zambia.

II. The CLP derives its legality from the Competition Act

The legality of the CLP has been challenged on occasion. This issue featured in the *Agri Wire* case,[3] which came before our Supreme Court of Appeal:

> "[22] ... The purpose of the [Competition] Act, as set out in section 2 thereof, is to promote competition in South Africa. To that end the Commission is empowered to promote market transparency (section 21(1)(a)) and to investigate and evaluate alleged contraventions of Chapter 2 of the Act, under which cartels fall (section 21(1)(c)). Breaking up cartels serves to promote market transparency, as cartel behaviour is the antithesis of transparency in the market place. Investigating contraventions of the Act must entitle the Commission to put in place measures that will enable it to perform this function. That is the whole purpose of the CLP. Accordingly, and subject only to the argument that follows, the Commission was empowered under the Act to adopt and implement the CLP by giving conditional and total immunity to parties who make disclosure and provide evidence that enables it to pursue cartels and bring them to an end."

> "[24] ... A complaint is initiated under section 49B, either by the Commissioner or by a third party. The complaint is then investigated. If, at the conclusion of the investigation, the Commissioner decides to refer the complaint to the Tribunal, the Act specifically provides that the Commissioner may refer all or some of the particulars of the complaint and may add particulars to the complaint submitted by the complainant. One of the central particulars in respect of cartel conduct is the identity of the members of the cartel. If the complaint is that A and B and C have engaged

3 Agri Wire (Pty) Ltd v Commissioner of the Competition Commission 2013 (5) SA 484 (SCA).

in cartel behaviour the Commissioner may decide to refer only A and B. In that way the Commissioner exercises the express statutory power to exclude certain particulars, namely C, from the referral. Equally, when the Commissioner decides to add D as a participant in the cartel, that is in accordance with the express provisions of the statute."

III. Criminalisation of cartel conduct and the future of the CLP

It is important to note section 73A of the Competition Act[4] which caused the criminalisation of cartel conduct in South Africa in April 2016:

> "Causing or permitting a firm to engage in prohibited practice"
>
> (1) A person commits an offence if, while being a director of a firm or while having engaged or purporting to be engaged by a firm in a position having management authority within the firm, such person –
>
> (a) Caused the firm to engage in a prohibited practice in terms of section 4(1)(b); or
>
> (b) Knowingly acquiesced in the firm engaging in a prohibited practice in terms of section 4(1)(b).[5]
>
> For purposes of subsection (1)(b), knowingly acquiesced means having acquiesced while having actual knowledge of the relevant conduct by the firm."

Subsection (4) also states:

> "The Competition Commission –
>
> (a) may not seek or request the prosecution of a person for an offence in terms of this section if the Competition Commission has certified that the person is deserving of leniency in the circumstances; and
>
> (b) may make submissions to the National Prosecuting Authority in support of leniency for any person prosecuted for an offence in terms of this section, if the Competition Commission has certified that the person is deserving of leniency in the circumstances."

Some relevant questions were considered in regard to the interaction here between competition and prosecution authorities by writers.[6] The basic rationale is of course that the fear of a prison sentence will deter potential offenders from coming forward in terms of the CLP, and the same applies to consent orders. This is said against the background of the fact that the CLP has been very successful in many instances. Even so, on the other hand,

---

4 Competition Act 89 of 1998.

5 This would typically include price collusion.

6 Tsholofelo Letsike, *The criminalising of cartels – How effective will the new Section 73A of the Competition Amendment Act be?* (2013).

one cannot assume that a rational person will always be deterred by the prospect of a prison sentence. An insidious example of where fear of detection did *not* work, was the rigging of bids for the building of stadiums for the 2010 Soccer World Cup. Well-known construction companies such as Group Five, WBHO, Basil Read, Stefanutti Stocks, Aveng, and Murray & Roberts were involved. Collusion on these stadium projects is estimated to have added R14-billion to the construction costs borne by the municipalities.[7] As I said, deterrence does not always work.

It must be borne in mind here that immunity from criminal sanctions cannot be provided by the Commission or the Competition Tribunal – this could deter leniency applications in the realm of *administrative* fines, but whether it will, remains to be seen.[8]

The new system brings about a dual role between the Commission and the National Prosecuting Authority (NPA) by installing the NPA as the body that is responsible for the criminal prosecution. In turn, the Commission's duty is to make submissions to the NPA in support of leniency of a person certified as deserving of leniency.[9] Apprehension exists as to how effective this dual role will be. What works in the United States might not necessarily work in a developing country.[10]

The basic situation is that whilst the NPA has extensive experience in the prosecution of criminal matters, it does not have experience of competition issues. One step that may be taken might be continuous training programs. Talks between the NPA and the Competition Commission to establish a workable criminal regime have not yet produced concrete results. A person may be found guilty in terms of one system, but innocent in terms of the other – which is an unsatisfactory situation.

Let me conclude with a quotation from the Competition Commissioner as a final example of the working of the CLP:[11]

7 Lisa Steyn, 'World Cup stadium construction cartel gets its comeuppance', in: *Mail&Guardian* (04-12-2015).

8 Tsholofelo Letsike, *The criminalising of cartels – How effective will the new Section 73A of the Competition Amendment Act be?* (2013), 13.

9 Tsholofelo Letsike, *The criminalising of cartels – How effective will the new Section 73A of the Competition Amendment Act be?* (2013), 11.

10 Tsholofelo Letsike, *The criminalising of cartels – How effective will the new Section 73A of the Competition Amendment Act be?* (2013), 12.

11 Lameez Omarjee, 'Competition Commission won't take it easy on banks hoping to settle on forex cartel matter', in: *www.fin24.com* (31-08-2017).

> "The commission doesn't rule out any possible settlement discussion with any bank in this litigation – what we are saying is that those who have wasted time and have [sought] to abuse the process must not expect the same as those who settled earlier".

The case mentioned, dealing with a forex cartel, was referred to the Competition Tribunal. Seventeen banks were been implicated.

Bibliography

Tsholofelo Letsike, *The criminalising of cartels – How effective will the new Section 73A of the Competition Amendment Act be?* (2013), http://www.compcom.co.za/wp-content/uploads/2014/09/THE-NEW-SECTION-73A.pdf (03-05-2018).

Lameez Omarjee, 'Competition Commission won't take it easy on banks hoping to settle on forex cartel matter', in: *www.fin24.com* (31-08-2017), http://www.fin24.com/Companies/Financial-Services/competition-commission-wont-take-it-easy-on-banks-hoping-to-settle-on-forex-cartel-matter-20170831-2 (03-05-2018).

Lisa Steyn, 'World Cup stadium construction cartel gets its comeuppance', in: *Mail&Guardian* (04-12-2015*)*, https://mg.co.za/article/2015-12-03-remaining-2010-world-cup-stadium-colluders-face-prosecution (03-05-2018).

Competition Commission South Africa, *Corporate Leniency Policy pursuant to the Competition Act 89 of 1998* (2014), http://www.compcom.co.za/wp-content/uploads/2014/09/CLP-public-version-120520081.pdf (03-05-2018).

Aaron Vehling, 'EU Court Slashes Sasol Wax Cartel Fine In Half', in: *www.law360.com* (11-07-2014), https://www.law360.com/articles/556733/eu-court-slashes-sasol-wax-cartel-fine-in-half (03-05-2018).

Register of cases

Agri Wire (Pty) Ltd v Commissioner of the Competition Commission 2013 (5) SA 484 (SCA).

20 Years after *ARAG/Garmenbeck*: New Considerations on the Impact of Corporate Reputation on Management Board Liability

*Michael Biesinger**

Abstract:
The conference in 2017 marks the 20th anniversary of the ARAG/Garmenbeck ruling of the German Federal Court of Justice (BGH). In this much-discussed case, the court decided, that the supervisory board can refrain from the enforcement of liability claims against the management board for reputational reasons. However, neither the court addresses the concept of corporate reputation without any profound consideration, nor has the aspect been sufficiently investigated at the legal level yet. Considering the academic concept of corporate reputation, its today's importance, and the difficulties in measuring, it is questionable whether the court was right in qualifying the enforcement decision of the supervisory board as a non-entrepreneurial decision. However, non-enforcement merely with reference to corporate reputation runs the risk of developing a silver bullet and abolishing legal justifications for turning away from a legal basic concept. According to his social and economic findings, the general suitability of corporate reputation as a consideration should generally be critically scrutinized.

* Michael Biesinger, *Dipl.-Jur. (Univ.)*, Academic Assistant at the Augsburg Center for Global Economic Law and Regulation (ACELR), University of Augsburg, Faculty of Law.
Citations of German court judgments in this paper have been translated into English from the original German.

I. Introduction

> "It takes 20 years to build a reputation and five minutes to ruin it. If you think about that, you'll do things differently"[1]

Putting this statement by *Warren Buffet* into a company law context, the American business magnate, investor and philanthropist addresses three crucial points: (1) What is corporate reputation, and why is corporate reputation important for any company? (2) What is the actual impact of corporate reputation on organisational performance? And (3) how does corporate reputation influence corporate governance?

A quick glance through recent newspaper headlines shows a whole slew of incidents at internationally operating companies where business conduct can be a risk factor for the company's reputation (even regardless of an actual violation of legal provisions), and which in turn influences corporate behaviour. Corporate reputation has thus recently been moving more into the spotlight.

A quite remarkable case started in 2015 after the German car manufacturer *Volkswagen* admitted the use of software that could be used to cheat on emissions tests, and affecting around eleven million diesel cars worldwide.[2] The non-compliance with emission rules that was uncovered was particularly embarassing, since *Volkswagen* had been promoting a new era of 'clean diesel' that should have been in compliance with even stricter emission limits in the United States.[3] So far, 'Dieselgate' has had a tremendous economic and legal impact. Shortly after the scandal came to light, the Volkswagen share price dropped by 41%.[4] After operational losses of €3.5 billion in the third quarter of 2015,[5] the 2016 consolidated financial state-

1 Brad Tuttle, 'Warren Buffett's Boring, Brilliant Wisdom', in: *TIME online* (01-03-2010). A similar thought can be found in Sabrina Helm, 'Corporate Reputation: An Introduction to a Complex Construct', in: Sabrina Helm, Kerstin Liehr-Gobbers and Christopher Storck (eds), *Reputation Management* (2011), 3.

2 Jack Ewing, 'Volkswagen Says 11 Million Cars Worldwide Are Affected in Diesel Deception', in: *The New York Times* (22-09-2015).

3 Taras Grescoe, 'The Dirty Truth About 'Clean Diesel'', in: *The New York Times* (02-01-2016).

4 Martin Hock, 'VW-Aktionäre in unbekannten Gewässern', in: *Frankfurter Allgemeine Zeitung – FAZ* (30-09-2015), 23.

5 N.N., 'Milliardenverlust für Volkswagen', in: *Süddeutsche.de* (28-10-2015).

ments disclosed sales revenues declining 0.6% year on year to €105.7 billion, and operational profits dropped from €2.1 billion to €1.9 billion.[6] Even though business figures appear to recover more recently,[7] risk factors still exist: On one hand, there are rather short-term financial risks from various pending compensation claims.[8] On the other hand – often not noted and perhaps even worse – the scandal imposes the risk of tremendous reputational damage. For Germany, an intracompany study detected that the reputation value of Volkswagen has dropped drastically,[9] but the loss of trust in Volkswagen and its products is also noticeable worldwide.[10] Almost three years later, the diesel scandal still weighs heavily on the company and imposes further financial burdens.[11]

Even though the factual framework is still not completely clarified, recent investigations have raised suspicions about the extent to which members of the management board might have been involved in the manipulation.[12] This gives reason to focus on a possible liability of them under Section 93(2) of the Stock Corporation Act (*Aktiengesetz* – AktG) in terms of corporate reputation. Twenty years after the famous ARAG/Garmenbeck ruling of the Federal Court of Justice (BGH), this paper addresses the question of whether or to what extent the company's reputation should affect the enforcement of liability claims of the supervisory board against the management board.

---

6 Carsten Germis, 'Volkswagen überrascht mit hohem Gewinn', in: *FAZ.net* (18-04-2017).

7 Carsten Germis, 'Volkswagen überrascht mit hohem Gewinn', in: *FAZ.net* (18-04-2017).

8 Corinna Budras, 'VW, das wird teuer!', in: *Frankfurter Allgemeine Zeitung – FAZ* (20-03-2016), 28.

9 N.N., 'Image von VW schlechter als das von Hyundai', in: *FAZ.net* (28-05-2017).

10 N.N., 'Vertrauen in VW schwer erschüttert', in: *boerse.ard.de* (06-04-2016); some analyses even listed Volkswagen as top of the list of worst company reputations: Douglas McIntyre, 'Volkswagen tops list of worst company reputations', in: *24/7 Wall St.* (13-05-2016); Evan Comen and Michael B. Sauter, 'Companies With the Best (and Worst) Reputations', in: *24/7 Wall St.* (12-05-2016).

11 Stefan Menzel, 'VW kann die Dieselaffäre nicht abschütteln', in: *Handelsblatt.com* (11-12-2017).

12 Volker Votsmeier and Sönke Iwersen, 'Brisante Dokumente belasten Ex-VW-Chef Martin Winterkorn', in: *Handelsblatt.com* (28-02-2018).

For this purpose, part II.2 reviews the economic debate about corporate reputation and seeks to explain the term 'corporate reputation' in greater depth, to make it accessible for legal considerations by distinguishing it from other economic constructs. In part II.3, we conclude that there are various business-related reasons why a company cannot underestimate its reputation, especially regarding company leaders, before part II.5 turns to the topic of corporate reputation and the board of directors' liability in light of the ARAG/Garmenbeck case.

II. The Impact of Corporate Reputation on Corporate Governance

1. Corporate Reputation – A Brief History

The relevance of reputation has been detected in light of the economic competition mechanism.[13] Economic relationships between humans never follow the conditions of perfect competition.[14] In fact, imperfect consumer information[15] is often supplemented by subjective values and personal relationships.

First considerations about the reputation of a company were published in the early 1960s. *Sandig* described corporate reputation as the recognised capability (to be understood as the result of every single activity of a company to which a third-party assessment can tie) adhering to a company.[16] However, the field of corporate reputation remained as a "relatively understudied"[17] part of economic science before it moved into academic focus in

---

13 Friedrich A. Hayek, *Individualismus und wirtschaftliche Ordnung* (Reproduction, 1976), 128.

14 George J. Stigler, *The Theory of Competitive Price* (1942), 24: "Economic relationships are never perfectly competitive if they involve any personal relationships between economic units".

15 Friedrich A. Hayek, *Individualismus und wirtschaftliche Ordnung* (Reproduction 1976), 126 (128); Klaus Spremann, 58 (1988) *Zeitschrift für Betriebswirtschaft (ZfB)*, 613.

16 Curt Sandig, *Der Ruf der Unternehmung* (1962), 10 (12): „Die anerkannte Leistungsfähigkeit, [...] die an der Unternehmung haftet; [...] Unter dem Begriff Leistung verstehe ich [...] nicht allein das verkaufsreife Ergebnis, sondern das Ergebnis jeder einzelnen Tätigkeit der Unternehmung, an die die Anerkennung der Leistungsfähigkeit durch Dritte anzuknüpfen vermag".

17 Charles J. Fombrun and Cees van Riel, 1 (1997) *Corporate Reputation Review (CRR)*, 5.

the 1990s. After being "rediscovered by scholars in different disciplines",[18] it has recently become a much more prevalent academic focus of management science.[19] Moreover, since 1997 the *Corporate Reputation Review*, a journal solely dealing with corporate reputation issues, has published 588 articles,[20] and academic institutes have created special research centres dedicated to the economic importance of corporate reputation.[21]

So far, only a few efforts have been made to approach the topic thoroughly from a legal perspective.[22] The starting point of the question to be discussed here – the ARAG case – addresses the concept of corporate reputation without any profound consideration.[23]

2. Corporate Reputation: A Definition

One of the reasons why there has been little legal consideration of corporate reputation is certainly the universally recognised statement that the difficulties in working with corporate reputation are still "a problem of definition."[24]

---

18 John F. Mahon, 41 (2002) *Business & Society (Bus. Soc.)*, 415.

19 Charles J. Fombrun, 'The Building Blocks of Corporate Reputation: Definitions, Antecedents, Consequences', in: Michael L. Barnett and Timothy G. Pollock (eds), *The Oxford Handbook of Corporate Reputation* (2012), 94 (95); Michael L. Barnett, John Jermier and Barbara Lafferty, 9 (2006) *Corporate Reputation Review (CRR)*, 26 et seq.; Matteo Tonello, *Reputation Risk: A Corporate Governance Perspective* (2007), 5 illustrates that between the years 2000 and 2007 the publications containing catchphrases like "corporate reputation" or "reputation risk" in their title or abstract more than doubled.

20 See the statistical information as of September 2018, https://link.springer.com/journal/41299 (26-09-2018).

21 The Centre for Corporate Reputation was established as an independent research center within Oxford University's Saïd Business School in 2008, see https://www.sbs.ox.ac.uk/faculty-research/reputation/news/oxford-university-establishes-centre-corporate-reputation (01-05-2018).

22 See, for example Lars Klöhn and Klaus Ulrich Schmolke, *Neue Zeitschrift für Gesellschaftsrecht (NZG)* 2015, 689; Christoph H. Seibt, *Der Betrieb (DB)* 2015, 171.

23 BGH 21.04.1997 – II ZR 175/95 – BGHZ 135, 244 (255). For more details on the ruling see pp. 236 et seqq.

24 Charles J. Fombrun and Cees van Riel, 1 (1997) *Corporate Reputation Review (CRR)*, 5; similarly Kent Walker, 12 (2010) *Corporate Reputation Review (CRR)*, 357 (358): "the need for a comprehensive and well-accepted definition".

In general German language use, "reputation" is used interchangeably with other terms, such as *guter Ruf* (good standing) and *Ansehen*[25] (esteem) or *Renommé*.[26] These synonym definitions show that it is not enough to rely solely on a common language understanding of reputation, since it commonly has a positive connotation.[27] Some dictionaries take both positive and negative aspects into consideration by describing reputation as "the opinion people have of somebody/something, based on what has happened in the past" and the like.[28] Of course, in certain contexts, every individual can intuitively deduce a meaning from those words. Nevertheless, reputation as such is subject to multi-disciplinary research. Efforts in social sciences, psychology, communication research and other disciplines – as well as several (economic) perspectives from which "reputation" is conceptualised – resulted in different approaches for a definition.[29] The "conceptual

25 *Duden: Das große Fremdwörterbuch* (11th Edition, 2015), "Reputation"; Carolin Hümmer, *Die Reputation interner Dienstleister in Konzernen* (2015), 39.

26 Curt Sandig, *Der Ruf der Unternehmung* (1962), 9, with a critical consideration in light of the etymological background of the French words "*le renom*" and "*la renommé*".

27 Similarly Klaus Spremann, 58 (1988) *Zeitschrift für Betriebswirtschaft (ZfB)*, 613 (619): „Der gute Ruf und das Ansehen ist, solange die Reputation unangegriffen besteht […]".

28 Della Summers (ed), *Business English Dictionary* (3rd Edition 2007); according to the *Oxford English Dictionary (www.oed.com)*, "reputation" is "the general opinion or estimate of a person's character or other qualities; the relative esteem in which a person or thing is held"; according to *The American Heritage Dictionary of the English Language (www.ahdictionary.com)*, it is "the general opinion or judgment of the public about a person or thing"; for further attempts of definition see also Sabrina Helm, 'Corporate Reputation: An Introduction to a Complex Construct', in: Sabrina Helm, Kerstin Liehr-Gobbers and Christopher Storck (eds), *Reputation Management* (2011), 3 (5).

29 Charles J. Fombrun and Cees van Riel, 1 (1997) *Corporate Reputation Review (CRR)*, 5; Manfred Schwaiger and Sascha Raithel, 64 (2014) *Management Review Quarterly (MRQ)*, 225 (228); Viola P. Rindova and Luis L. Martins, 'Show me the Money: A Multidimensional Perspective on Reputation as an Intangible Asset', in: Michael L. Barnett and Timothy G. Pollock (eds), *The Oxford Handbook of Corporate Reputation* (2012), 16 et seqq.; Tom J. Brown, Peter A. Dacin, Michael G. Pratt and David A. Whetten, 34 (2006) *Journal of the Academy of Marketing Science (J. Acad. Mark. Sci.)*, 99; an overview of selected existing definitions in both English and German literature can be found in Kent Walker, 12 (2010) *Corporate Reputation Review (CRR)*, 357 (368).

confusion" even increased, since different economic disciplines often interchangeably use other economic concepts, such as prestige, goodwill, identity, and image.[30]

For purposes of legal consideration, however, a precisely contoured construct (at least in the sense of a least definitional common denominator) is absolutely necessary.[31]

a) What Corporate Reputation is not

Since other economic concepts are likely mixed up with the concept of corporate reputation, an "important component leading to the definition of any construct is differentiating it from related terms".[32] Various recent publica-

30 Oded Shenkar and Ephraim Yuchtman-Yaar, 50 (1997) *Human Relations*, 1361 (1362): "In sociology, *prestige* is the preferred term, in economics, it is *reputation*, in marketing, *image*, and in accounting and law, *goodwill*"; see also Michael L. Barnett, John M. Jermier and Barbara A. Lafferty, 9 (2006) *Corporate Reputation Review (CRR)*, 26 (28); Kent Walker, 12 (2010) *Corporate Reputation Review (CRR)*, 357 (363); Steven L. Wartick, 41 (2002) *Business & Society (Bus. Soc.)*, 371 (373).

31 Michael L. Barnett, John M. Jermier and Barbara A. Lafferty, 9 (2006) *Corporate Reputation Review (CRR)*, 26 (35) also promote the necessity of a precise language in economic science. According to them, merely referring to the concept of reputation as it is given by everyday language is not constructive since the term more relates to the reputation of an individual than it does to the idea of corporate reputation and its multi-dimensional characteristics.

32 Kent Walker, 12 (2010) *Corporate Reputation Review (CRR)*, 357 (363).

tions have been anxious to define the scope of corporate reputation in contrast to related concepts such as corporate identity, corporate image and the concept of legitimacy,[33] celebrity,[34] organisational status,[35] and stigma.[36]

For a better understanding, a brief overview of the concepts of identity and image, most commonly associated with reputation, will be given.

(i) Corporate Identity

Identity commonly refers to what is most central, enduring, and distinctive.[37] For an organisation, that means the "self-definitional beliefs of members regarding the character or essence of the organization".[38] These core considerations about an entity shape its own fundamental character and understanding about who or what a company believes it is.[39] Corporate identity thus tends to refer to internal stakeholders and their desired or actual identity only,[40] and can be understood as the internal basis for business action and organisational functions of the firm. As internal stakeholders occupy a special position from which they view the organisation, their more

---

33 See for example Peter O. Foreman, David A. Whetten and Alison Mackey, 'An Identity-Based View of Reputation, Image, and Legitimacy: Clarifications and Distinctions among Related Constructs', in: Michael L. Barnett and Timothy G. Pollock (eds), *The Oxford Handbook of Corporate Reputation* (2012), 179 et seqq.

34 See for example Michael D. Pfarrer, Timothy G. Pollock and Violina P Rindova, 53 (2010) *Academy of Management Journal (Acad. Manag. J.)*, 1131 (1133).

35 See for example David N. Barron and Meredith Rolfe, 'It Ain't What You Do, It's Who You Do It With: Distinguishing Reputation and Status', in: Michael L. Barnett and Timothy G. Pollock (eds), *The Oxford Handbook of Corporate Reputation* (2012), 160 et seqq.

36 See for example Yuri Mishina and Cynthia E. Devers, 'On Being Bad: Why Stigma is not the Same as a Bad Reputation', in: Michael L. Barnett and Timothy G. Pollock (eds), *The Oxford Handbook of Corporate Reputation* (2012), 201 et seqq.

37 David A. Whetten and Alison Mackey, 41 (2002) *Business & Society (Bus. Soc.)*, 393 (394, 401).

38 Peter O. Foreman, David A. Whetten and Alison Mackey, 'An Identity-Based View of Reputation, Image, and Legitimacy: Clarifications and Distinctions among Related Constructs', in: Michael L. Barnett and Timothy G. Pollock (eds), *The Oxford Handbook of Corporate Reputation* (2012), 179 (181).

39 David A. Whetten, 1 (1997) *Corporate Reputation Review (CRR)*, 26 (27).

40 Kent Walker, 12 (2010) *Corporate Reputation Review (CRR)*, 357 (363).

detailed knowledge of the entity justifies a distinct category, separating the perceptions of organizational insiders from those of outsiders.[41]

(ii) Corporate Image

Differentiating corporate reputation from corporate image is particularly difficult, since the concept of organisational image "suffers from extreme definitional plurality".[42] The three main ways of framing this concept are briefly presented here:

(1) Projected/Intended Image

Whereas corporate identity is a solely internal feature, corporate image addresses external stakeholders: Corporate image may therefore be conceptualised as "a projection focus on messages sent out from the organization on how they want to be viewed externally"[43] – namely, the attributes and characteristics that the organisation wants various stakeholders to associate with.[44] More vividly, corporate image answers the question: "What or who do we want others to think we are?"[45] Hence, the image is intentional, and strategically crafted to reflect the company's identity.[46] According to this

---

41 Tom J. Brown, Peter A. Dacin, Michael G. Pratt and David A. Whetten, 34 (2006) *Journal of the Academy of Marketing Science (J. Acad. Mark. Sci.)*, 99 (102 et seq.).

42 Peter O. Foreman, David A. Whetten and Allison Mackey, 'An Identity-Based View of Reputation, Image, and Legitimacy: Clarifications and Distinctions among Related Constructs', in: Michael L. Barnett and Timothy G. Pollock (eds), *The Oxford Handbook of Corporate Reputation* (2012), 179 (183).

43 Peter O. Foreman, David A. Whetten and Alison Mackey, 'An Identity-Based View of Reputation, Image, and Legitimacy: Clarifications and Distinctions among Related Constructs', in: Michael L. Barnett and Timothy G. Pollock (eds), *The Oxford Handbook of Corporate Reputation* (2012), 179 (183).

44 Tom J. Brown, Peter A. Dacin, Michael G. Pratt and David A. Whetten, 34 (2006) *Journal of the Academy of Marketing Science (J. Acad. Mark. Sci)*, 99 (103).

45 David A. Whetten, 1 (1997) *Corporate Reputation Review (CRR)*, 26 (27).

46 Peter O. Foreman, David A. Whetten and Alison Mackey, 'An Identity-Based View of Reputation, Image, and Legitimacy: Clarifications and Distinctions

interpretation, the image of an entity does not emanate from the perception of external stakeholders – it is an "intended image"[47] given by the company itself.

(2) Perceived Image

The prevailing[48] opinion considers corporate image as the "externally perceived self-view"[49] or "perceived image". Whereas the intended image is closely linked to the organisation's identity, the perceived image is often filtered and therefore not completely congruent with the actual identity, since the distortion by third parties makes it only indirectly capable of being influenced by the company through its communication process.[50]

(3) Reflected Image

Another dimension of the concept of corporate image is the 'reflected image' – the insider's perception of how external stakeholders think about the organisation. The reference point of the organisational reflected image is either how the identity of a firm is actually seen or how it should be seen.

---

among Related Constructs', in: Michael L. Barnett and Timothy G. Pollock (eds), *The Oxford Handbook of Corporate Reputation* (2012), 179 (183).

47 Tom J. Brown, Peter A. Dacin, Michael G. Pratt and David A. Whetten, 34 (2006) *Journal of the Academy of Marketing Science (J. Acad. Mark. Sci)*, 99 (103 et seq.).

48 According to Kent Walker, 12 (2010) *Corporate Reputation Review (CRR)*, 357 (366), who did a systematic review of corporate reputation literature by analysing and comparing over 50 well-cited articles published in high-quality journals. Also Peter O. Foreman, David A. Whetten and Alison Mackey, 'An Identity-Based View of Reputation, Image, and Legitimacy: Clarifications and Distinctions among Related Constructs', in: Michael L. Barnett and Timothy G. Pollock (eds), *The Oxford Handbook of Corporate Reputation* (2012), 179 (183): The "external perception-oriented notion is what is most frequently meant by the term 'organizational image'".

49 Peter O. Foreman, David A. Whetten and Alison Mackey, 'An Identity-Based View of Reputation, Image, and Legitimacy: Clarifications and Distinctions among Related Constructs', in: Michael L. Barnett and Timothy G. Pollock (eds), *The Oxford Handbook of Corporate Reputation* (2012), 179 (183).

50 Michael L. Barnett, John M. Jermier and Barbara A. Lafferty, 9 (2006) *Corporate Reputation Review (CRR)*, 26 (34).

(iii) Summary of Corporate Identity and Corporate Image

Even though all three definitions of corporate image successively veer away from the concept of corporate identity and, in this respect, form their own definitional group, all three dimensions still find certain roots in the internal corporate identity. In fact, all three concepts of corporate image reflect a dimension of how an organisation's identity is supposed to be seen (intended image), is actually seen (perceived image), or appears to be seen (reflected image). However, the common distinction is made by considering the roots of both concepts: "Corporate image resides in the heads of the stakeholders, whereas corporate identity resides in the organization."[51]

b) What is Corporate Reputation?

In contrast to the concepts of corporate image, corporate reputation is uncoupled from the corporate identity and indisputably refers to *actual* stakeholder perceptions of the firm and its business conduct.[52] It therefore answers the question: "What do stakeholders actually think of thc organisation?"[53].Whereas corporate image is often influenced by the firm's promotion efforts, corporate reputation is a stakeholder-controlled perception of an organisation[54] and therefore "difficult to manipulate".[55]

---

51 Nuno Zarco da Camara, 'Identity, Image and Reputation', in: Sabrina Helm, Kerstin Liehr-Gobbers and Christopher Storck (eds), *Reputation Management* (2011), 47 (49).

52 Kent Walker, 12 (2010) *Corporate Reputation Review (CRR)*, 357 (367).

53 Tom J. Brown, Peter A. Dacin, Michael G. Pratt and David A. Whetten, 34 (2006) *Journal of the Academy of Marketing Science (J. Acad. Mark. Sci)*, 99 (100).

54 Tom J. Brown, Peter A. Dacin, Michael G. Pratt and David A. Whetten, 34 (2006) *Journal of the Academy of Marketing Science (J. Acad. Mark. Sci)*, 99 (104).

55 Charles J. Fombrun, *Reputation: Realizing Value from the Corporate Image* (1996), 59.

(i) Key Elements

Over the past decades, the "definitional landscape"[56] has been constantly reviewed in search of a definitional consensus – yet without a definition being commonly agreed.[57] The search for the lowest common denominator, distilled out of those definitions, resulted in the following key elements:

- Reputation is the result of the perception of an organisation's past performance actually held by external stakeholders.[58] Consequently, it requires having experience with the company, whereas it is possible to have an image of an organisation through the organisation's marketing and communication campaigns. Since perceptions are not directly under the firm's control, it defines reputation in contrast to above-mentioned concepts of identity and image. A reputation, therefore, is subjective and not purely factual.
- Reputation is not solely based on the cognitive perception, but also determined by affective elements.[59] Shared indirect experiences by others are also relevant. In all likelihood, "not all of the information conveyed is accurate".[60] This communicative aspect has to be taken into account for the analysis of the importance of corporate reputation.
- It is a social/collective concept and based on the perceptions of all (internal and external) stakeholders.[61]

56 See only the tile of the article by Michael L. Barnett, John M. Jermier and Barbara A. Lafferty, 9 (2006) *Corporate Reputation Review (CRR)*, 26: "Corporate Reputation: The Definitional Landscape".

57 Most recently and with a very comprehensive analysis of over 50 approaches to definition given in the literature since the 1990s: Kent Walker, 12 (2010) *Corporate Reputation Review (CRR)*, 357.

58 Kent Walker, 12 (2010) *Corporate Reputation Review (CRR)*, 357 (369); Sabrina Helm, 'Corporate Reputation: An Introduction to a Complex Construct', in: Sabrina Helm, Kerstin Liehr-Gobbers and Christopher Storck (eds), *Reputation Management* (2011), 3 (5) with further reference.

59 Manfred Schwaiger and Sascha Raithel, 64 (2014) *Management Review Quarterly (MRQ)*, 225 (229 et seq.).

60 Charles J. Fombrun, *Reputation: Realizing Value from the Corporate Image* (1996), 70.

61 Kent Walker, 12 (2010) *Corporate Reputation Review (CRR)*, 357 (369). The limitation on external stakeholders only in Tom J. Brown, Peter A. Dacin, Mi-

- Stakeholders are broadly defined as persons or entities whose general welfare may be affected by the firm's management decisions and conduct.[62] As such, there are various different types of stakeholders,[63] such as customers, suppliers, creditors, owners, investors, other contractual partners, the community, employees, trade unions and the government. Each stakeholder group has its own definition of welfare and therefore different – but sometimes overlapping (and not solely economic) – interests in the corporation, which also may vary in the degree of importance from stakeholder group to stakeholder group.[64] However, within one group the ideal reputation regarding one interest will be more or less similar. Thus it is now broadly accepted that corporate reputation cannot be defined as a uni-dimensional aggregated perception of all stakeholders. Instead, corporate reputation is issue specific,[65] with the potential varying for each issue. A firm does not have one reputation but multiple reputations, depending on the specific group of stakeholders and depending on the issues that are in focus.[66] 'Reputation' has therefore to be specified by asking the questions 'for what?' and according 'to whom?'.[67]

---

chael G. Pratt and David A. Whetten, 34 (2006) *Journal of the Academy of Marketing Science (J. Acad. Mark. Sci.)*, 99 (104) apparently does not find consent among the majority of scholars.

62 Thomas Noe, 'A Survey of the Economic Theory of Reputation: Its Logic and Limits', in: Michael L. Barnett and Timothy G. Pollock (eds), *The Oxford Handbook of Corporate Reputation* (2012), 114 (115); Lars Klöhn and Klaus Ulrich Schmolke, *Neue Zeitschrift für Gesellschaftsrecht (NZG)* 2015, 689 (690).

63 Lars Klöhn and Klaus Ulrich Schmolke, *Neue Zeitschrift für Gesellschaftsrecht (NZG)* 2015, 689 (690).

64 Lars Klöhn and Klaus Ulrich Schmolke, *Neue Zeitschrift für Gesellschaftsrecht (NZG)* 2015, 689 (690); Carolin Hümmer, *Die Reputation interner Dienstleister in Konzernen* (2015), 45.

65 E.g. profitability, environmental responsibility, social responsibility, employee treatment, corporate governance, product quality, longevity, liquidity, etc; see Samuel C. Certo and S. Trevis Certo, *Modern Management* (14th Edition, 2016), 56 et seqq.

66 Thomas Noe, 'A Survey of the Economic Theory of Reputation: Its Logic and Limits', in: Michael L. Barnett and Timothy G. Pollock (eds), *The Oxford Handbook of Corporate Reputation* (2012), 114 (116).

67 Patsy G. Lewellyn, 41 (2002) *Business & Society (Bus. Soc.)*, 446 (451); Lars Klöhn and Klaus Ulrich Schmolke, *Neue Zeitschrift für Gesellschaftsrecht (NZG)* 2015, 689 (690): "multidimensional concept".

- The perceptions result in a collective assessment of the company's attractiveness.[68] The attractiveness is a result of the forecasted future behaviour of the firm.[69] A positive forecast is the expectation of delivering valued outcomes to multiple stakeholders.[70] This forecast of future prospects is the representation of a company's past actions and corporate performance.[71]
- The level of attractiveness between companies is a competitive setting due to the value of the reputation as an intangible asset.[72]

Walker also views the findings that a reputation can be both positive and negative, and that it is a relatively stable and enduring worth to be a definitional element.[73] However, it is doubtful whether there is any additional benefit by doing so. She even explicitly pointed out that there is a possibility for reputations to also change quickly.[74] Hence, using the stability of a company's reputation, supplemented by the restriction 'relatively', as a definitional element does not seem necessary. Its stability appears neither to be an obligatory definitional element, nor to contribute to any kind of definitional certainty.

Indeed, the time factor is implicitly referred to insofar as the basis for reputation building is the firm's past actions. It is also intended by using the word 'perception', which terminologically requires some kind of experience with the company. The time factor mostly distinguishes the long-term perspective of reputation from the concept of image, which may be created and changed relatively quickly.[75]

---

68 Charles J. Fombrun, 'The Building Blocks of Corporate Reputation: Definitions, Antecedents, Consequences', in: Michael L. Barnett and Timothy G. Pollock (eds), *The Oxford Handbook of Corporate Reputation* (2012), 94 (100).

69 Sabrina Helm, 'Corporate Reputation: An Introduction to a Complex Construct', in: Sabrina Helm, Kerstin Liehr-Gobbers and Christopher Storck (eds), *Reputation Management* (2011), 3 (6) with further references.

70 Charles J. Fombrun and Cees van Riel, 1 (1997) *Corporate Reputation Review (CRR)*, 5 (10).

71 Charles J. Fombrun, *Reputation: Realizing Value from the Corporate Image* (1996), 72.

72 See p. 229.

73 Kent Walker, 12 (2010) *Corporate Reputation Review (CRR)*, 357 (370).

74 Kent Walker, 12 (2010) *Corporate Reputation Review (CRR)*, 357 (370).

75 Nuno Zarco da Camara, 'Identity, Image and Reputation', in: Sabrina Helm, Kerstin Liehr-Gobbers and Christopher Storck (eds), *Reputation Management* (2011), 47 (50).

Even though 'reputation' commonly has a positive connotation,[76] from a scientific point of view there is no actual dispute that reputations may be either rather positive or rather negative.[77] This already implies the competitive setting in which reputation is relevant. The inclusion of the terms positive and negative as a definitional element, however, calls for a clear delineation between both terms. That requires defining a zero point – a point at which reputation is completely neutral. However, it is doubtful if the comparative concept of reputation allows a reputation to be neutral. Secondly, 'positive' and 'negative' refer to a dimension that exceeds the aim of a mere definitional conception, but is rather result-oriented. The outcome should not be part of a definition, but the result of it. Therefore, it seems to be appropriate to view reputation as definitionally neutral. That reputation serves as a benchmark for a positive or negative outcome is already expressed by the element "level of attractiveness".

The call to avoid an overly narrow definitional scope of the construct corporate reputation by over-defining is consistent with the finding of *Fombrun*, who suggests concentrating on key elements by removing all reference to antecedents and consequences from the definition.[78]

(ii) Summarizing: Clusters of Meaning

The above key elements of corporate reputation can be categorised into three "clusters of meaning":[79]

(1) Awareness

Corporate reputation is a construct based on cognitive and affective perceptions. The starting point is therefore the mere passive stakeholder action. At

76 See p. 219

77 Kent Walker, 12 (2010) *Corporate Reputation Review (CRR)*, 357 (367, 370); Carolin Hümmer, *Die Reputation interner Dienstleister in Konzernen* (2015), 39.

78 Charles J. Fombrun, 'The Building Blocks of Corporate Reputation: Definitions, Antecedents, Consequences', in: Michael L. Barnett and Timothy G. Pollock (eds), *The Oxford Handbook of Corporate Reputation* (2012), 94 (100).

79 See Michael L. Barnett, John M. Jermier and Barbara A. Lafferty, 9 (2006) *Corporate Reputation Review (CRR)*, 26 (32 et seq.).

this stage, the general awareness of a firm has not caused stakeholders to make any judgements.

(2) Assessment

An active evaluation is carried out from the perceptions in stage two. Here, stakeholders compare their perceptions, knowledge and emotions about a company with their own demands and expectations. Reputation as an assessment refers to a judgmental nature. Resulting aspects may be reliability, expertise, appreciation, and appraisal.[80] In particular, the reference point may be the firm's current level of reputation.

(3) Asset

The assessment of the stakeholder's perceptions results in a parameter, which is "something of value and significance to the firm".[81] It can be positive or negative – or in other words more or less advantageous – and reflects the level of attractiveness. Whereas reputation at the assessment level is a rather subjective attitude towards a firm, the asset level captures the idea of a company's reputation having an objective economic value. Insofar, it is consistent with the consequences of corporate reputation and must not be a dominating part of a definition. However, it is characteristic to compare the dissimilarity of reputations in a competitive setting. Otherwise, the concept of reputation would be meaningless. This justifies the asset stage to be a definitional element in as far as it describes the reputational character.

80 Charles J. Fombrun, 'The Building Blocks of Corporate Reputation: Definitions, Antecedents, Consequences', in: Michael L. Barnett and Timothy G. Pollock (eds), *The Oxford Handbook of Corporate Reputation* (2012), 94 (100).

81 Michael L. Barnett, John M. Jermier and Barbara A. Lafferty, 9 (2006) *Corporate Reputation Review (CRR)*, 26 (33).

(iii) Towards a definition

Taking the findings obtained into account, a definition – largely following *Fombrun*[82] – should consist of the following components:

> Corporate reputation is the (1) collective assessment (2) of a company's attractiveness (3) to a specific group of stakeholders (4) relative to a reference group of companies with which the company competes for resources, (5) based on cognitive and affective perceptions of the relevant individual.

Only adding the perception-based nature to the definition makes it congruent with the above findings. The use of the hypernym 'attractiveness' allows involvement of a generalised emotional response to a company's reputation, which is congruent with the subjective nature of perceptions.

c) Reference Point of Corporate Reputation

Contrary to *van der Linde's* objection at the conference, the concept of corporate reputation, as it is understood here, should not only refer to the individual reputations that exist about individual divisions of a company or persons working there. It is an abstraction clinging to the name of an institution that in public objectively appears as a discrete economic entity.[83] A separation from the reputation of the entire institution therefore only seems to be possible if individual products in the market become independent under their own name and build their own reputation.[84] However, the decisive factor is that there is no external discernible connection to the manufacturing company. Nowadays, this hardly appears to be admissible for a well-informed general public.

This, however, does not preclude that individual persons or divisions by their own reputation contribute significantly to the reputation of the entire company if they appear prominently in public.[85] In this respect, they are to be understood as representatives of the overall corporate reputation.[86]

---

82 Charles J. Fombrun, 'The Building Blocks of Corporate Reputation: Definitions, Antecedents, Consequences', in: Michael L. Barnett and Timothy G. Pollock (eds), *The Oxford Handbook of Corporate Reputation* (2012), 94 (100).

83 Curt Sandig, *Der Ruf der Unternehmung* (1962), 10, 19 et seq.

84 Curt Sandig, *Der Ruf der Unternehmung* (1962), 20.

85 For the impact of CEO reputation see p. 235.

86 Curt Sandig, *Der Ruf der Unternehmung* (1962), 10 et seq.

3. Corporate Reputation and the Market: What Makes Corporate Reputation so Important?

a) Social and Market Developments

Among both company executives and consumers, product quality is still the first-ranked factor that affects the consumer's decision to buy a product, and therefore is promoted by companies most often.[87] However, due to radical changes in consumer behaviour in recent times, the company behind the product or the brand has become at least as – or even more – important as the individual product or brand itself.[88] Meanwhile, the focus has turned more to the producing company, since the company's goals and behaviour in various aspects are gaining increasing attention from customers making purchase decisions.[89]

New developments in market relationships, driven by consumers who are either overwhelmed by the ever-exploding number of choices[90] and the unlimited information opportunity via the internet[91] or the continuing product homogenisation[92], means that a purely cognitive decision not always possible.

---

87 Weber Shandwick, *The Company Behind the Brand: In Reputation We Trust* (2012), 14.

88 According to a study conducted by public relations firm Weber Shandwick, product reputation and corporate reputation become nearly "indivisible", see Weber Shandwick, *The Company Behind the Brand: In Reputation We Trust* (2012), 1, 3, 21.

89 Weber Shandwick, *The Company Behind the Brand: In Reputation We Trust* (2012), 7. The study concludes that consuming in a modern interpretation is not only a matter of getting a product to the best price available, but also matter of selected and purposeful supporting an idea or a concept the producing company is connected with.

90 Manfred Schwaiger and Sascha Raithel, 64 (2014) *Management Review Quarterly (MRQ)*, 225 (238).

91 Christopher A. Runge and Anabel Ternès, 'Reputationsmarketing – Unternehmensführung 2.0: Warum der gute Ruf in der globalen und digitalisierten Welt ein erfolgskritischer Geschäftsfaktor ist', in: Anabel Ternès and Ian Towers (eds), *Internationale Trends in der Markenkommunikation – Was Globalisierung, neue Medien und Nachhaltigkeit erfordern* (2014), 59.

92 Christopher A. Runge and Anabel Ternès, 'Reputationsmarketing – Unternehmensführung 2.0: Warum der gute Ruf in der globalen und digitalisierten Welt ein erfolgskritischer Geschäftsfaktor ist', in: Anabel Ternès and Ian Towers

If the information asymmetry prevents stakeholders putting their decision to have any kind of business relationship with the company on an adequate factual basis, reputation may be also supportive for decision-making.[93] In such an uncertain environment, the corporate reputation provides an "anchor of trust and credibility"[94] for all kinds of stakeholders. Consumers, particularly, may also draw a conclusion about product quality.[95]

Moreover, increasing social awareness and activism, combined with increasing value-based stakeholder behaviour[96] and an overall more demanding and critical general public,[97] are leading people to have greater interest in utilising their (consumer) behaviour as a political statement. To mention just a few aspects, to a greater extent than it was the case in the past, consumers want to give a directional impulse towards more ethical, employee- and environmental friendly and honest business conduct.[98]

In times where there is "erosion of public confidence in business organisations and securities markets", [99] consumers and investors generally appear

(eds), *Internationale Trends in der Markenkommunikation – Was Globalisierung, neue Medien und Nachhaltigkeit erfordern* (2014), 60.

93 Klaus Spremann, 58 (1988) *Zeitschrift für Betriebswirtschaft (ZfB)*, 613; Manfred Schwaiger and Sascha Raithel, 64 (2014) *Management Review Quarterly (MRQ)*, 225 (238 et seq.); see also p. 222, fn. 15.

94 Weber Shandwick, *The Company behind the Brand: In Reputation We Trust* (2012), 4.

95 Weber Shandwick, *The Company behind the Brand: In Reputation We Trust* (2012), 9: A well-rated reputation provides assurance that the company's product reflects the same level of quality. It is therefore that consumers look for "assurance". As a general concept, the finding appears to be generalizable to all stakeholders of a company, see Manfred Schwaiger and Sascha Raithel, 64 (2014) *Management Review Quarterly (MRQ)*, 225 (237 et seqq.).

96 Weber Shandwick, *The Company behind the Brand: In Reputation We Trust* (2012), 1, 7.

97 Manfred Schwaiger and Sascha Raithel, 64 (2014) *Management Review Quarterly (MRQ)*, 225 (227); Weber Shandwick, *The Company behind the Brand: In Reputation We Trust* (2012), 1.

98 Edelman, Inc., *Edelman Trust Barometer – Special Report: Institutional Investors* (2017), 7; Weber Shandwick, *The Company behind the Brand: In Reputation We Trust* (2012), 7, 14 et seq.

99 Matteo Tonello, *Reputation Risk: A Corporate Governance Perspective* (2007), 5.

to be less trusting. Instead, market participants seek a more stable and enduring indicator on which a long-lasting reputation has been based.[100]

b) Corporate Reputation as an Asset

Studies have explored corporate reputation having a share of up to 60% of the whole market value of a firm.[101] Various reasons on both the expenditure and the spending side contribute to such a high number:[102]

- Good reputations attract more potential customers. If their expectations correspond with their experience with a certain company, this leads to a higher level of customer satisfaction, which again may result in a better reputation and attract even more customers. The greater demand of the company's service allows for premium pricing. A good reputation therefore is in direct proportionality to the company's profit.
- Investors in the capital markets especially are confronted with a high level of uncertainty and a volume of information that often is too much to process in time.[103] A company's reputation may thus be utilised as a risk minimiser, indicating the security of an investment and the subjective profit from it. Since investments in companies with a good reputation are expected to be low-risk, the majority of investors are more likely to hold shares from a company with a good reputation than from a competitor having a less excellent reputation.[104] In other words: the better the reputation, the easier is it for companies to raise funds through the capital market. Consequently, share prices increase. Studies also

---

100 Weber Shandwick, *The Company behind the Brand: In Reputation We Trust* (2012), 20.

101 Weber Shandwick, *The Company behind the Brand: In Reputation We Trust* (2012), 18.

102 Manfred Schwaiger and Sascha Raithel, 64 (2014) *Management Review Quarterly (MRQ)*, 225 (238 et seqq.).

103 Thomas M.J. Möllers and Eva Kernchen, 40 (2011) *Zeitschrift für Unternehmens- und Gesellschaftsrecht (ZGR)*, 1, 11.

104 Edelman, Inc., *Edelman Trust Barometer – Special Report: Institutional Investors* (2017), 3 et seqq.

found out that bad news has less negative effects when a company's reputation is better; reputation may serve as a buffer.[105]

- It is easier for companies to find well-educated experts as employees. Similar to the premium pricing effect, companies with a good reputation may attract high potentials even if they earn less. A good reputation might compensate salary losses of up to 19% compared to competitors.[106]
- Companies pay a lower interest rate on debt financing.

Since reputation is directly connected with a certain company and almost impossible to imitate by a competitor, it gives a clear competitive advantage and is one of the "key drivers of corporate competitiveness and profitability".[107]

c) Corporate Reputation in Practice

A rising interest in building and maintaining reputation in management practice has been noted over recent decades. This is documented by the assessment of executives who voted damage to reputation as the number one risk for an enterprise in 2017,[108] and is in line with an increasing demand for new reputation risk insurance products.[109]

Despite this confirmation of the importance of corporate reputation, a survey found that only 19% of all companies questioned have a formal system to measure their corporate reputation value and act accordingly.[110] This demonstrates the failure to properly explore corporate reputation in the field of corporate governance. While the existing literature is primarily manage-

105 Michael D. Pfarrer, Timothy G. Pollock and Violina P. Rindova, 53 (2010) *Academy of Management Journal (Acad Manage J)*, 1131 (1142).

106 Manfred Schwaiger and Sascha Raithel, 64 (2014) *Management Review Quarterly (MRQ)*, 225 (242).

107 Ann Svendsen, *The Stakeholder Strategy: Profiting From Collaborative Business Relationships* (1998), 19.

108 AON, *Global Risk Management Survey* (2017), 17 et seq.

109 N.N., 'Top 10 Hot New Markets', in: *insurancejournal.com* (25-03-2013).

110 Burson-Marsteller, *CEO Reputation Study* (2003), cited in: Kim Harrison, 'Why a good corporate reputation is vital to your organization', in: *cuttingedgepr.com*.

ment focused, there is at best little examination and discussion on the impacts of corporate reputation on corporate governance[111] and the respective legal aspects.[112]

4. The Impact of CEO Reputation on Corporate Reputation

While corporate reputation can be affected by almost uncountable influencing factors, company's leaders contribute largely to the overall corporate reputation. With a growing general scepticism towards corporate leaders, 66% of consumers think that their perceptions of a company is highly, or at least moderately, influenced by the persons on the management board – especially the CEO – and what executives communicate and how they behave.[113] Even 84% of the executives questioned concede that the CEO highly or at least moderately affects the stakeholders' opinion about the company.[114] On average, 49% of a company's reputation is attributable to the reputation of corporate leaders.[115] An even higher percentage emerges from studies with German stakeholders.[116] It follows that the CEO may influence business success merely by his or her reputation.

Particularly bad reputational effects result from legal actions against members of the management board.[117]

---

111 Matteo Tonello, *Reputation Risk: A Corporate Governance Perspective* (2007), 8.

112 Specifically for Germany see Lars Klöhn and Klaus Ulrich Schmolke, *Neue Zeitschrift für Gesellschaftsrecht (NZG)* 2015, 689.

113 Weber Shandwick, *The Company Behind the Brand: In Reputation we Trust – CEO Spotlight*, 3.

114 Weber Shandwick, *The Company Behind the Brand: In Reputation we Trust – CEO Spotlight*, 3.

115 Weber Shandwick, *The Company Behind the Brand: In Reputation we Trust – CEO Spotlight*, 2.

116 Burson Marsteller, *CEO Reputation Study* (2003), 3 reveals a percentage of 64% in Germany compared to the average of 48% (which also reflects their result for the U.S.); similar Maike Telgheder, 'Manager bestimmen das Firmenimage mit', in: *Handelsblatt.com* (23-03-2004).

117 Maike Telgheder, 'Manager bestimmen das Firmenimage mit', in: *Handelsblatt.com* (23 March 2004).

5. Framing the Problem: The ARAG/Garmenbeck Case

The direct proportionality between CEO reputation and the reputation of the company throws up a particular problem in matters of internal liability of members of the management board against the company pursuant to Section 93(2) sentence 1 of the Stock Corporation Act (AktG).

This corporate claim is generally asserted through the company's representatives only. Whereas the management board usually represents the company (Section 78(1) sentence 1 AktG), under the German two-tier system Section 112 sentence 1 AktG explicitly entitles the supervisory board to represent the company vis-à-vis members of the management board.[118] This exception from the general principle laid down in Section 78(1) sentence 1 AktG follows the aim of the legislature to avoid any conflicts of interest that would derive from a form of self-dealing.[119] Others view the competence to enforce in light of the duty to supervise, pursuant to Section 111(1) AktG,[120] or a combination of both.[121]

In the past, however, there have been cases in which the supervisory board refused to enforce even existing claims of the company, since the available action alternatives were considered to present a no-win situation – either reputation-wise, or from a social or economic perspective.[122]

---

118 Marcus Lutter, Gerd Krieger and Dirk Verse, *Rechte und Pflichten des Aufsichtsrats* (6th Edition, 2014), § 3 para. 61: "most important, permanent and indispensable task"; Hartmut Oetker, 'Vorstand, Aufsichtsrat und ihr Zusammenwirken aus rechtlicher Sicht', in: Peter Hommelhoff, Klaus J. Hopt and Axel v.Werder (eds), *Handbuch Corporate Governance* (2nd Edition, 2009), 277 (281); Michael Kort, in: Heribert Hirte, Peter O. Mülbert and Markus Roth (eds), *AktG Großkommentar* (5th Edition, 2015), § 76 para. 9.

119 BGH 08.02.1988 – II ZR 159/87 – BGHZ 103, 213 (216); BGH 26.06.1995 – II ZR 122/94 – BGHZ 130, 108 (111 et seq.); Mathias Habersack, in: Wulf Goette, Mathias Habersack and Susanne Kalss (eds), *Münchener Kommentar zum Aktiengesetz* (4th Edition, 2014), § 112 para. 1; Uwe Hüffer and Jens Koch (eds), *Aktiengesetz* (12th Edition, 2016) § 112 para. 1.

120 Detlef Kleindiek, Entscheidungen zum Wirtschafts- und Bankrecht (WuB), II A § 112, AktG 1.88.

121 BGH 21.04.1997 – II ZR 175/95 – BGHZ 135, 244 (252); Mathias Habersack, in: Wulf Goette, Mathias Habersack and Susanne Kalss (eds), *Münchener Kommentar zum Aktiengesetz* (4th Edition, 2014), § 111 para. 34.

122 OLG Düsseldorf 22.06.1995 – 6 U 104/94 – AG 1995, 416, 420.

At such a case, the Federal Court of Justice (BGH) took a closer look in its prominent *ARAG/Garmenbeck* judgment [123] in 1997. The court pointed out what requirements the supervisory board has to fulfil in light of the right to enforcement and his duty to supervise and support current and control past management measures. Therefore, the court developed a two-part test:[124]

a) Step One: Factual Investigation and Legal Assessment

As soon as there is an indication that management has acted contrary to its duties,[125] the supervisory board has to investigate the factual basis on which the management board might be liable. This fact-finding follows a thorough legal analysis as to whether or not the management board complied with its duties to manage the company diligently and conscientiously[126] at the time of decision-making (Section 93(1) sentence 1 of the Stock Corporation Act, AktG). This must be aligned with the broad scope of action and the therefrom-following wide standard of fault[127] of the management board pursuant

123 BGH 21.04.1997 – II ZR 175/95 – BGHZ 135, 244 et seqq. For a general analysis of the background, outcome and effects of this case, see Jens Koch, 'Die ARAG/Garmenbeck-Entscheidung des BGH (BGHZ 135, 244) – Geschichte und Wirkungsgeschichte', in: Susanne Kalss, Holger Fleischer and Hans-Ueli Vogt (eds), *Bahnbrechende Entscheidungen – Gesellschafts- und Kapitalmarktrechtsgeschichten* (2016), 91 et seqq.

124 A compareable procedure is required unter South African Law, see below Van der Linde, p. 266.

125 BGH 16.02.2009 – II ZR 185/07 – BGHZ 180, 9 (21); Mathias Habersack, in: Wulf Goette, Mathias Habersack and Susanne Kalss (eds), *Münchener Kommentar zum Aktiengesetz* (4th Edition, 2014), § 111 para. 35; Uwe Hüffer and Jens Koch (eds), *Aktiengesetz* (12th Edition, 2016), § 111 para. 8: To what degree a violation of the management board's duty must be indicated to create the supervisory board's duty to investigation should be viewed flexibly, particularly considering the reasonableness of the suspicion and the severity of the alleged accusation.

126 In leading the company and conducting the day-to-day business, the management board "shall employ the care of a diligent a conscientious manager" (translation taken from Norton Rose Fulbright, *German Stock Corporation Act (Aktiengesetz) – English Translation as at May 10, 2016*).

127 BGH 21.04.1997 – II ZR 175/95 – BGHZ 135, 244 (253); Uwe Hüffer and Jens Koch (eds), *Aktiengesetz* (12th Edition, 2016), § 111 para. 8.

to the business-judgement-rule under Section 93(1) sentence 2 AktG.[128] At the same time, the supervisory board also has to examine the risk of litigation and whether the claim is actually enforceable against the management board. At this stage, the supervisory board's duty to perform an objective legal examination is subject to the principle of legality and therefore it is not given any leeway in assessing those points and it is subject to full judicial control.[129]

b) Step Two: Enforcement of Existing Claims

In a second step, the court acknowledged that it was possible for the supervisory board to refrain from the enforcement of claims against the management board that had been assessed as existing in step one.[130] In order to make such a decision, the supervisory board has to give the matter thorough consideration.

According to the court, however, this does not give the supervisory board any entrepreneurial discretion, which would consequently result in a limitation of judicial review.[131] Such entrepreneurial discretion falls solely within the competence of the management board,[132] whose competences

128 The management board did not violate its duty "if, at the time of taking the entrepreneurial decision, they had good reason to assume that they were acting on the basis of adequate information for the benefit of the company." (translation taken from Norton Rose Fulbright, *German Stock Corporation Act (Aktiengesetz) – English Translation as of May 10, 2016*). Sec. 93 para. 1 sentence 2 AktG has been added by the Gesetz zur Unternehmensintegrität und Modernisierung des Anfechtungsrechts (UMAG) of September 22nd, 2005, BGBl. I, 2802. Prior to the legislative amendment already BGH 21.04.1997 – II ZR 175/95 – BGHZ 135, 244 (253) in ARAG/Garmenbeck.

129 BGH 21.04.1997 – II ZR 175/95 – BGHZ 135, 244 (254); Uwe Hüffer and Jens Koch (eds), *Aktiengesetz* (12th Edition, 2016), § 111 para. 8; differing view OLG Düsseldorf 22.06.1995 – 6 U 104/94 – AG 1995, 416 (418 et seqq.) (previous instance).

130 BGH 21.04.1997 – II ZR 175/95 – BGHZ 135, 244 (254).

131 BGH 21.04.1997 – II ZR 175/95 – BGHZ 135, 244 (254); dissenting from OLG Düsseldorf 22.06.1995 – 6 U 104/94 – AG 1995, 416 (418 et seqq.) (previous instance), that considered the supervisory board's work as subject to "autonomous entrepreneurial decision" and therefore includes allowance at discretion, not completely under judicial control.

132 BGH 21.04.1997 – II ZR 175/95 – BGHZ 135, 244 (254 et seq.).

may only be delegated to the supervisory board when it supports the entrepreneurial activity of the management board in the sense of preventive control. In this regard, the court considers the enforcement of liability claims as a purely retroactive controlling task.[133] The court strictly referenced the concept of the two-tier system, with a controlling body overseeing the management body.[134]

Moreover, the enforcement of liability claims against the management board is designed to avoid damages for the company and to contribute only to the company's welfare. The enforcement of the damage claim would at least restore the damaged corporate financial assets, which is a clear positive effect. However, at this point the court allows the supervisory board to also take account of other disadvantages, in line with the enforcement. For the purpose of a thorough consideration, the decision about whether to enforce liability claims must again be based on the company's welfare.[135] Having that in mind, the court continued that arguments against the enforcement of the damage claim must either "predominate or […] at least be almost equivalent".[136] In this context, the court especially mentioned the "company's public reputation"[137] as a counter-argument.

Based on what has been outlined above, the court concluded that the supervisory board is "generally obligated to enforce damage claims against members of the management board", whereas otherwise "substantial counter arguments" must exist.[138]

---

133 Mathias Habersack, in: Wulf Goette, Mathias Habersack and Susanne Kalss (eds), *Münchener Kommentar zum Aktiengesetz* (4th Edition, 2014), § 111 para. 29: next to future-oriented supervision, controlling past actions is the predominately part of the supervisory board's duties.

134 See fn.118.

135 BGH 21.04.1997 – II ZR 175/95 – BGHZ 135, 244 (255); Uwe Hüffer and Jens Koch (eds), *Aktiengesetz* (12th Edition, 2016), § 111 para. 10; Mathias Habersack, in: Wulf Goette, Mathias Habersack and Susanne Kalss (eds), *Münchener Kommentar zum Aktiengesetz* (4th Edition, 2014), § 111 para. 37.

136 BGH 21.04.1997 – II ZR 175/95 – BGHZ 135, 244 (255).

137 BGH 21.04.1997 – II ZR 175/95 – BGHZ 135, 244 (255).

138 BGH 21.04.1997 – II ZR 175/95 – BGHZ 135, 244 (256): „Die vorstehenden Überlegungen führen zu der Schlussfolgerung, dass die Verfolgung der Schadensersatzansprüche gegenüber einem Vorstandsmitglied die Regel sein muss. Hingegen bedarf es gewichtiger Gegengründe […], von einer – voraussichtlich – aussichtsreichen Anspruchsverfolgung […] abzusehen.".

6. Subsequent Problems

This ruling has always been subject to further disputes among scholars.[139] The reputational aspect addressed by the court and its consistency with the overall ruling raises undiscussed questions. Therefore, the court's relevant arguments in step two of the *ARAG/Garmenbeck* ruling need to be examined in greater detail, with special regard to the possibility of non-enforcement on grounds of reputation.

a) The Weight of Counter-Arguments

The court concluded that counter-arguments have to be "substantial".[140] What is meant exactly by this may be deduced from the standard the court required earlier – "predominant or a least almost equivalent arguments".[141] This involves some definitional controversies.

The wording allows reasons for non-enforcement to be relevant even if they do not meet or exceed a 50% threshold compared to those points that speak for enforcement. In other words: Even if "mathematically" the reasons for enforcement still predominate (and this is supposed to be standard after the *ARAG/Garmenbeck* ruling), the supervisory board could deviate from that with reasons, and not only reputational reasons.

Furthermore, the court sets up a requirement that is not as strict as intended by the legislature for the enforcement of claims for damages by a shareholders' minority. Section 148(1) sentence 2 no. 4 of the Stock Corporation Act (AktG) requires that this action does not face "*überwiegend*" (overriding) counter-arguments regarding the company's best interests. This caused disputes among scholars. While some even question whether "overriding" requires something more than 'substantial',[142], others interpret

139 See for an overview of the different views: Jens Koch, *Neue Zeitschrift für Gesellschaftsrecht (NZG)* 2014, 934.

140 BGH 21.04.1997 – II ZR 175/95 – BGHZ 135, 244 (256): „gewichtige Interessen und Belange".

141 BGH 21.04.1997 – II ZR 175/95 – BGHZ 135, 244 (255): „überwiegen oder zumindest gleichwertig".

142 Wilhelm Happ, 'Das Klagezulassungsverfahren des § 148 AktG auf dem Prüfstand', in: Lutz Aderhold, Barbara Grunewald, Dietgard Klingberg et al. (eds), *Festschrift für Harm Peter Westermann* (2008), 971 (990).

– on the basis of the official explanatory memorandum[143] – the tightened requirements in Section 148(1) sentence 2 no. 4 AktG to be applicable only to the enforcement by a minority of shareholders.[144] A third group sees no point in applying two different criteria for enforcing damage claims, depending on who appears as the plaintiff. Due to the chronology of the legislation, they advocate a uniform standard of overriding counter-arguments.[145]

Neither approach, however, lessens the relevance of corporate reputation in this regard.[146] First, the original wording of the case mentioned corporate reputation immediately after setting up the requirement of "predominant or at least almost equivalent" counter-arguments.[147] This indicates that the court in *ARAG/Garmenbeck* accepted arguments based on the concept of corporate reputation to have the potential of being of sufficient importance. This is strongly supported by the importance of good corporate reputation as an organisational asset as outlined above, and its tremendous importance for a company's business success and its overall market value.[148] It indicates that the reputation of a company might even make a greater contribution to the company's welfare than the mere right to financial compensation does. Thus, *a fortiori,* corporate reputation has the potential to be "predominant" in individual cases.

---

143 Entwurf eines Gesetzes zur Unternehmensintegrität und Modernisierung des Anfechtungsrechts (UMAG) of 14-03-2005, BT-Drucks. 15/5092, 22 (right column).

144 Matthias Casper, 176 (2012) *Zeitschrift für das gesamte Handels- und Wirtschaftsrecht (ZHR)*, 617 (629).

145 Uwe Hüffer and Jens Koch (eds), *Aktiengesetz* (12th Edition, 2016), § 111 para. 9; Jens Koch, 35 (2006) *Zeitschrift für Unternehmens- und Gesellschaftsrecht (ZGR)*, 769 (776).

146 Also recognizing corporate reputation as a generally relevant factor: Matthias Casper, 176 (2012) *Zeitschrift für das gesamte Handels- und Wirtschaftsrecht (ZHR)*, 617 (632); Wulf Goette, 'Zur ARAG/Garmenbeck-Doktrin' in: Michael Hoffmann-Becking, Uwe Hüffer and Jochen Reichert (eds), *Liber amicorum für Martin Winter* (2011), 153, (165 et seq.).

147 BGH 21.04.1997 – II ZR 175/95 – BGHZ 135, 244 (255).

148 See above B.III.Corporate Reputation as an Asset

b) Measuring the Weight of Counter Arguments

In its decision, the Federal Court of Justice calls for a comparison of the counter-arguments with the basic need for damage compensation.

However, a true comparison, as laid down in the *ARAG/Garmenbeck* case, only appears conclusive if the conceivable damage can be clearly quantified and compared at the time of consideration. Enormous difficulties in dealing with corporate reputation are still encountered in the exact financial determination of corporate reputational damage.[149] Here, in particular, the problem of the intangibility of corporate reputation arises.
Furthermore, it is unclear at what time the reputation damage is finally certain. Long-term disadvantages are particularly associated with the loss of reputation, which might not be clearly foreseeable at the time the supervisory board makes its decision. The consequence would be a continuing danger of the occurrence of considerably higher damages in the future, which can still be traced back to the loss of reputation.

At this stage, much is still unclear. Although the actual existence of reputational damage is diagnosable, there seems to be a certain lack of quantification of reputational damage to provide a sufficient basis for decision-making within the meaning of the *ARAG/Garmenbeck* case.

c) Discretional Power of the Supervisory Board

Whereas the actual power of the supervisory board to weigh up the issues is basically undisputed,[150] controversies mainly arose regarding the discretional power of the supervisory board and the intensity of judicial control of the supervisory board's decision.[151] Although this question often appears

---

149 Manfred Schwaiger and Sascha Raithel, 64 (2014) *Management Review Quarterly (MRQ)*, 225 (230 et seqq.); Kent Walker, 12 (2010) *Corporate Reputation Review (CRR)*, 357 (370 et seqq.).

150 Matthias Casper, 176 (2012) *Zeitschrift für das gesamte Handels- und Wirtschaftsrecht (ZHR)*, 617 (628); Klaus J. Hopt and Markus Roth, in: Klaus J. Hopt and Herbert Wiedemann (eds), *Großkommentar zum Aktiengesetz* (4th Edition, 2005), §111 paras 356 et seqq.

151 Below Heterogeneous Range of Opinion in Legal Literature; see for a comprehensive overview of the divergent opinions Jens Koch, *Neue Zeitschrift für Gesellschaftsrecht (NZG)* 2014, 934; Jens Koch, 'Die ARAG/Garmenbeck-Entscheidung des BGH (BGHZ 135, 244) – Geschichte und Wirkungsgeschichte',

in the context of the rather practical consideration of either too strict,[152] but in any case too burdensome,[153] consequences for the management board, it is also relevant for dealing with the hardly manageable reputation construct.

(i) Restrictive Opinion of the Federal Court of Justice

The discussion finds its roots in a possibly misleading wording in the ruling. Regarding the requirements under which the supervisory board may refrain from enforcement, the Court explained:

> Contrary to the opinion of the Court of Appeal, the **supervisory board does not have any autonomous entrepreneurial discretion** in this decision. The entrepreneurial freedom to act is a part and necessary counterpart of the management task assigned to the management board but not to the supervisory board. Thereto, the supervisory board contributes only to an extent to that the law explicitly assigned it entrepreneurial tasks, such as the appointment and dismissal of members of the management board or in the context of Section 111(4) sentence 2 AktG; generally, this applies wherever the law allows it to shape the entrepreneurial decisions in the sense of preventive control. The decision whether to enforce damage claims against members of the management board violating their duties, however, is part of its retrospective monitoring task, which aims to urge to management board to fulfil its obligations and to prevent damage to the company [...]. When assessing whether the management board acted unlawfully, the supervisory board particularly has to take the entrepreneurial freedom of the management board [...] into account. For its own decision, however, the supervisory board **cannot avail itself of an entrepreneurial discretion** in the sense adopted by the appeal court.[154]

---

in: Susanne Kalss, Holger Fleischer and Hans-Ueli Vogt (eds), *Bahnbrechende Entscheidungen – Gesellschafts- und Kapitalmarktrechtsgeschichten* (2016), 91 (102 et seqq.).

152 Jens Koch, *Neue Zeitschrift für Gesellschaftsrecht (NZG)* 2014, 934 (935).

153 Gregor Bachmann, 'Reform der Organhaftung? Materielles Haftungsrecht und seine Durchsetzung in privaten und öffentlichen Unternehmen', in: Ständige Deputation des Deutschen Juristentages (ed), *Verhandlungen des 70. Deutschen Juristentages, Vol. 1 – Gutachten*, (2014), E9 (E16).

154 BGH 21.04.1997 – II ZR 175/95 – BGHZ 135, 244 (254 et seq.). This has been translated from the original German wording, and the highlights are the author's own. The original wording is: „*Entgegen der Ansicht des Berufungsgerichts steht dem Aufsichtsrat auch bei dieser Entscheidung kein autonomer unternehmerischer Ermessensspielraum zu. Die unternehmerische Handlungsfreiheit ist Teil und notwendiges Gegenstück der dem Vorstand und nicht dem Aufsichtsrat obliegenden Führungsaufgabe. An ihr hat der Aufsichtsrat nur insoweit Anteil,*

Completing the demand to weigh up between the "restoration of the damaged corporate assets" and other "important interests and issues of the corporation", [155] the Court concludes:

> Only within these **narrow limits**, the supervisory board [...] can be **granted discretional power** as to whether to refrain from enforcing damage claims due to overriding reasons contributing to the company's best interests, despite the prospect of the damage claim's success.[156]

The tension between "no autonomous entrepreneurial discretion" on the one hand and "discretional power within narrow limits" is the driving force behind an ongoing debate on the scope of the discretion to be employed by the supervisory board and the scope of judicial review available.

(ii) Heterogeneous Range of Opinion in Legal Literature

Whereas academic authors were initially quite reluctant to grant the supervisory board any discretional power,[157] the vast majority of newer publications advocate granting quite a considerable margin of discretion when

---

wie das Gesetz auch ihm unternehmerische Aufgaben überträgt, wie z.B. bei der Bestellung und Abberufung von Vorstandsmitgliedern oder im Rahmen des § 111 Abs. 4 Satz 2 AktG, d.h. überhaupt überall dort, wo er die unternehmerische Tätigkeit des Vorstands im Sinne einer präventiven Kontrolle begleitend mitgestaltet. Die Entscheidung über die Geltendmachung von Schadenersatzansprüchen gegen pflichtwidrig handelnde Vorstandsmitglieder ist dagegen Teil seiner nachträglichen Überwachungstätigkeit, deren Ziel darauf gerichtet ist, den Vorstand zur Erfüllung seiner Pflichten anzuhalten und Schäden von der Gesellschaft abzuwenden [...]. Bei dieser Kontrolltätigkeit hat der Aufsichtsrat zwar die dem Vorstand zustehende unternehmerische Handlungsfreiheit [...] im Rahmen seiner Prüfung des Vorliegens eines pflichtwidrigen Vorstandshandelns zu berücksichtigen. Für seine eigene Entscheidung kann der Aufsichtsrat aber ein unternehmerisches Ermessen in dem vom Berufungsgericht angenommenen Sinne nicht in Anspruch nehmen."

155 The conflict between substantial and predominant, see above The Weight of Counter-Arguments

156 BGH 21.04.1997 – II ZR 175/95 – BGHZ 135, 244 (256). Original wording: *„Nur in diesen engen Grenzen kann dem Aufsichtsrat [...] ein Entscheidungsermessen für die Frage zuzubilligen sein, ob er trotz Erfolgsaussicht einer Haftungsklage aus übergeordneten Gründen des Unternehmenswohles ausnahmsweise von der Durchsetzung des Schadenersatzanspruchs absehen möchte."*

157 Thomas Raiser, *Neue Juristische Wochenschrift (NJW)* 1996, 552 (554); Hartwig Henze, *Neue Juristische Wochenschrift (NJW)* 1998, 3309 (3311); Uwe

making the enforcement decision, and agree with the limitation of scope for judicial review.[158]

This result is partly advocated by convenient correction of the *ARAG/Garmenbeck* case.[159] Others even argue that the classification as an entrepreneurial decision already results from a correct understanding of the ARAG case.[160] This is in part achieved by classifying the act of weighting up by the supervisory board as an entrepreneurial decision, and subsequently applying the scope of the business judgement rule (Sections 116 sentence 1 and 93(1) sentence 2 AktG) – at first glance in complete contrast to the findings of the court in *ARAG/Garmenbeck*.[161]

(iii) Dealing with Corporate Reputation as an Entrepreneurial Decision

Considering the findings on corporate reputation, it seems questionable whether it is justifiable to classify the decision about whether to refrain from enforcement on grounds of reputation as categorically non-entrepreneurial.

Hüffer, 10 (2007) *Neue Zeitschrift für Gesellschaftsrecht (NZG)*, 47 (48); today: Jens Koch, 17 (2014) *Neue Zeitschrift für Gesellschaftsrecht (NZG)*, 934 (938 et seqq.); Uwe Hüffer and Jens Koch (eds), *Aktiengesetz* (12th Edition, 2016), § 111 para. 11 with further references.

158 Wulf Goette, 'Zur ARAG/GARMENBECK-Doktrin' in: Michael Hoffmann-Becking, Uwe Hüffer and Jochem Reichert (eds), *Liber amicorum für Martin Winter* (2011), 153 (161); Gregor Bachmann, 'Reform der Organhaftung? Materielles Haftungsrecht und seine Durchsetzung in privaten und öffentlichen Unternehmen', in: Ständige Deputation des Deutschen Juristentages (ed), *Verhandlungen des 70. Deutschen Juristentages, Vol. 1 – Gutachten*, (2014), E9 (E80 et seq.); Walter G. Paefgen, *Die Aktiengesellschaft (AG)* 2014, 554, 571 et seqq.; Walter G. Paefgen, *Die Aktiengeselschaft (AG)* 2008, 761, 762 et seqq.

159 Mathias Habersack, in: Wulf Goette, Mathias Habersack and Susanne Kalss (eds), *Münchener Kommentar zum Aktiengesetz* (4th Edition, 2014), § 111 para. 38.; Gregor Bachmann, 'Reform der Organhaftung? Materielles Haftungsrecht und seine Durchsetzung in privaten und öffentlichen Unternehmen', in: Ständige Deputation des Deutschen Juristentages (ed), *Verhandlungen des 70. Deutschen Juristentages, Vol. 1 – Gutachten*, (2014), E9 (E44).

160 Wulf Goette, 'Zur ARAG/Garmenbeck-Doktrin' in: Michael Hoffmann-Becking, Uwe Hüffer and Jochem Reichert (eds), *Liber amicorum für Martin Winter* (2011), 153 (159 et seq.); Wulf Goette, 176 (2012) Zeitschrift für das gesamte Handels- und Wirtschaftsrecht (ZHR), 588.

161 Walter G. Paefgen, *Die Aktiengesellschaft (AG)* 2008, 761 (762).

On the issue of whether the supervisory board makes an entrepreneurial decision, the Court only distinguishes between past-oriented, repressive decisions from preventive control.[162] It is only with respect to the latter that qualification as an entrepreneurial decision may come into question. However, the Court concluded that acts associated with the enforcement of damage claims fall only within the first category.[163] The application of entrepreneurial freedom in accordance with the business judgement rule pursuant to Sections 116 sentence 1 and 93(1) sentence 2 AktG would thus be generally excluded.[164]

However, the Court in *ARAG* did not completely preclude the supervisory board from exercising any autonomous discretion – however, "only to an extent to that the law explicitly assigned it to entrepreneurial tasks".[165] Particularly in the context of a company's reputation, it is the question whether the differentiating mechanism applies to the true and economic nature of the supervisory board's decision.[166] Rather, assessing the granted exception for reputational risks could actually require an entrepreneurial decision.

Dealing with aspects of corporate reputation, it seems hardly conceivable that with an enforcement decision one could strictly differentiate between solely past monitoring of the management board and future-oriented measures. The enforcement of claims for damages does not primarily serve the mere civil liability of members of the management board, but is designed to restore the reduced corporate assets.[167] Logically, the court con-

---

162 BGH 21.04.1997 – II ZR 175/95 – BGHZ 135, 244 (255) following the opinion of Thomas Raiser, *Neue Juristische Wochenschrift (NJW)* 1996, 552 (553); earlier applying the same distinguishing criteria: BGH 25.03.1991 – II ZR 188/89 – BGHZ 114, 127 (129 et seq.).

163 BGH 21.04.1997 – II ZR 175/95 – BGHZ 135, 244 (255).

164 Uwe Hüffer and Jens Koch (eds), *Aktiengesetz* (12th Edition, 2016), § 116 para. 5; Walter G. Paefgen, *Die Aktiengesellschaft (AG)* 2008, 761 (762).

165 BGH 21.04.1997 – II ZR 175/95 – BGHZ 135, 244 (254). Original wording: „[a]n ihr hat der Aufsichtsrat nur insoweit Anteil, wie das Gesetz auch ihm unternehmerische Aufgaben überträgt […]".

166 Walter G. Paefgen, *Die Aktiengesellschaft (AG)* 2008, 761 (763 et seq.); Matthias Casper, 176 (2012) *Zeitschrift für das gesamte Handels- und Wirtschaftsrecht (ZHR)*, 617 (635).

167 Matthias Casper, 176 (2012) *Zeitschrift für das gesamte Handels- und Wirtschaftsrecht (ZHR)*, 617 (628 et seq.).

cluded explicitly that the supervisory board should take account of all effects of its decision on corporate best interests. In doing so, the supervisory board must inevitably make a forward-looking, prognostic and therefore genuinely entrepreneurial decision.[168] In other words: if the court demands a balancing act in step two, it automatically demands a decision based on entrepreneurial aspects. The entrepreneurial quality results from different aspects that come up during the decision-making process. In this sense, every entrepreneurial decision inherits a selection element that is based on economic considerations with particularly sound knowledge of the market situation of a company. The decision concerning scope and/or risk has a significant impact on the future development of the company. Nevertheless, the decision itself is so complex that an unambiguous prediction of its effects can usually not be expected.[169]

The entrepreneurial quality is particularly evident when assessing the company's reputation. After all, its tremendous economic importance has been demonstrated. In exercising economic vision, the supervisory board actively participates in the development of the company and its future wellbeing. As a high-impact but also intangible asset, risk-taking is a decisive characteristic when dealing with reputation in the decision-making process. On the one hand, the supervisory board is faced with the task of identifying an impending loss of reputation and, on the other, has to quantify the financial impacts to make it possible to compare it to the material damage that has already occurred. Since reputation is based on perceptions and is due to subjective uncertainties at the time of the supervisory board's decision, neither the determination of an actual reputational loss nor an exact quantification of financial consequences is always possible. It requires knowledge

---

168 Walter G. Paefgen, *Die Aktiengesellschaft (AG)* 2008, 761 (763); Walter G. Paefgen, *Die Aktiengesellschaft (AG)* 2014, 554 (571).

169 For the aspects of an entrepreneurial decision, see in detail: Gerald Spindler, 'Die Haftung von Vorstand und Aufsichtsrat für fehlerhafte Auslegung von Rechtsbegriffen', in: Andreas Heldrich and Ingo Koller et al. (eds), *Festschrift für Claus-Wilhelm Canaris* (2007), Vol. 2, 403 (413 et seqq.); Bruno Kropff, 'Informationspflichten des Aufsichtsrats', in: Reinhard Damm, Peter W. Heermann and Rüdiger Veil (eds), *Festschrift für Thomas Raiser* (2005), 225 (229); Peter W. Heermann, *Die Aktiengesellschaft (AG)* 1998, 201 (203); a detailed definition on the "entrepreneurial" aspect is given in: Stefan Mutter, *Unternehmerische Entscheidungen und Haftung des Aufsichtsrats der Aktiengesellschaft* (1994), 23.

of the market position of the company, just like a management board member would have to have in day-to-day management of the business.

The decision is future-oriented. Contrary to what the court indicated, the supervisory board's task is not only the restoration of already damaged assets. It is not only to oversee the inflow of money, but the supervisory board is then obligated to take medium-term and even long-term consequences into account when it decides to raise a claim.[170]

Thus, based on current facts, the supervisory board is obligated to make a prognosis as accurate as possible. This uncertainty in future-oriented decisions, combined with the risk of high damages, is the legislative basis for implementation and application of the business judgement rule.[171]

The contrary view in academic literature refers to the basic legislative motives, which allegedly do not support the qualification as an entrepreneurial decision.[172] The business judgment rule is based on the consideration that excessively severe sanctioning would stifle readiness to take risks, which are desirable from an entrepreneurial and economic point of view. With the business judgment rule, the legislature aims to avoid the exercise of exaggerated *ex-post* control by the courts, which might not take sufficient account that the actual consequences were not clearly foreseeable from the supervisory board's perspective at the time of decision (hindsight bias). Insofar, the law wants to replace the duty to act successfully by the duty to act for the comprehensible welfare of the company, based on a rational basis for decision-making. Additionally, full judicial control might not be reasonable since the decision is greatly influenced by the entrepreneurial background. Judges who are not familiar with entrepreneurial decision-making might not be able to comprehend the economic subtleties of the decision-making.

These objectives can also be applied to the handling of corporate reputation. There are also liability risks for the supervisory board (Sections 116, 93(2) sentence 1 AktG). By adopting an entrepreneurial decision, the threat of sanctions could already be met at the level of fact.

Dealing with corporate reputation is particularly difficult with respect to its intangibility. With regard to the difficulties in measuring the stakeholder-specific, perception-based phenomenon, the supervisory board is faced with

---

170 Matthias Casper, 176 (2012) *Zeitschrift für das gesamte Handels- und Wirtschaftsrecht (ZHR)*, 617 (629).

171 Jens Koch, *Die Aktiengesellschaft (AG)* 2009, 93 (94) referring to Entwurf eines Gesetzes zur Unternehmensintegrität und Modernisierung des Anfechtungsrechts (UMAG) of 14-03-2005, BT-Drucks. 15/5092, 11.

172 Jens Koch, *Die Aktiengesellschaft (AG)* 2009, 93 et seqq.

the difficult task of determining the indirect financial consequences of the loss of reputation for individually defined stakeholders, and weighing it against each other and the total sum. A safe prognosis by the supervisory board may be highly unlikely even if external experts are consulted. Nevertheless, the supervisory board is expected to make unpopular and risky decisions on such an uncertain basis.

Usually, the supervisory board may not be able to make such decisions without consulting external experts if it wishes to avoid the allegation that it did not act on the basis of reasonable and appropriate information (Section 93(1) sentence 2 AktG). If the complexity of such a decision leads the board of a company to work together with external partners to come to a – at best – correct decision, it is not expectable that a court will have sufficient economic and PR-competence to assess the issue accordingly.

In an *ex-post* review, the imponderables that the supervisory board faces at the time of its decision cannot be simulated. This runs the risk that from its *ex-post* perspective the court might rate the likelihood of a concrete damage sequence more severely than it would have appeared to the supervisory board in the immediate decision-making situation.

Hence, qualifying the supervisory board's decision as an entrepreneurial act and applying the business judgement rule also seems to be justifiable from a practical standpoint. The task of the supervisory board is approximated to that of the management board. In the assessment of corporate reputation, a different treatment can hardly be justified. Consequently, the supervisory board's task at step two is to be judged pursuant to the business judgment rule in Sections 116, 93(1) and (1) sentence 2 AktG.

At the same time, the general obligation to enforce liability claims against members of the management board would be annulled if the decision to not enforce the claim is only subject to full judicial control if there is an irresponsible misjudgement.[173] In light of the hardly tangible and complex construct of corporate reputation, this seems particularly dangerous.

d) The Relevance of Corporate Reputation as a Counter-Argument against the Enforcement of Damage Claims

If the intensity of judicial review is reduced to a degree to that only the irresponsible misjudgement by the supervisory board is a relevant breach of duty, this vague legal term should be concretised in light of the reputation

173 Jens Koch, *Neue Zeitschrift für Gesellschaftsrecht (NZG)* 2014, 934 (936).

aspect. It always seems possible to extract reputational risks from any kind of behaviour. The mere generalised reference to imminent reputational damage is thus to be rejected as an argumentative silver bullet.[174]

Insofar as the Federal Court of Justice, with its reference to corporate reputation, focuses solely on the general risk of reputational damage through public disclosure of the failings of the management board or the general involvement of the company in a recourse procedure, even this is questionable in view of the results presented here.[175] It may be doubtful whether refraining from the enforcement of damage claims really contributes to the company's welfare. In light of the general scepticism about CEOs and social sensitivity regarding the impact of CEO (or the management board as the corresponding equivalent) reputation on the corporation,[176] the reverse appears to be a possible scenario. It could even be conductive to the reputation of a firm if there is a consequent reaction to drawbacks by laying claims against the responsible party.[177]

In any case, account should only be taken of those damages which do not arise directly from the assertion of a claim, but as a side effect.[178] The public disclosure of further internal information through public trials might impose a relevant reputational risk.[179] For this, however, a very detailed assessment of the reputational risks with regard to the respective stakeholder group will be essential. In doing so, it is necessary to ascertain their current level of

174 Matthias Casper, 176 (2012) *Zeitschrift für das gesamte Handels- und Wirtschaftsrecht (ZHR)*, 617 (633); On the danger of a gradual erosion of the requirement to state reasons Lars Klöhn and Klaus Ulrich Schmolke, *Neue Zeitschrift für Gesellschaftsrecht (NZG)* 2015, 689 (694).

175 Likewise: Johannes Semler, 'Überlegungen zur Praktikabilität der Organhaftungsvorschriften', in: Mathias Habersack and Peter Hommelhof (eds), *Festschrift für Wulf Goette* (2011), 499 (507); Heinrich Götz, *Neue Juristische Wochenschrift (NJW)* 1997, 3275, 3277.

176 See above The Impact of CEO Reputation on Corporate Reputation.

177 Likewise: Mathias Habersack, in: Wulf Goette, Mathias Habersack and Susanne Kalss (eds), *Münchener Kommentar zum Aktiengesetz* (4th Edition, 2014), § 111 para. 37; Heinrich Götz, *Neue Juristische Wochenschrift (NJW)* 1997, 3275, 3277; Michael Fischer, *Betriebsberater (BB)* 1996, 225, 228.

178 Johannes Semmler, 'Überlegungen zur Praktikabilität der Organhaftungsvorschriften', in: Mathias Habersack and Peter Hommelhof (eds), *Festschrift für Wulf Goette* (2011), 499 (507).

179 Hartwig Henze, *Neue Juristische Wochenschrift (NJW)* 1998, 3309, 3311.

information[180] and the hypothetical effects, as well as to contrast the different expectations of each stakeholder group. Then the respective stakeholder-dependent effects would have to be balanced against each other.

From the perspective of an already difficult position fixing in the field of corporate reputation, the question of practicability of this approach arises. This is not least because such reputational questions would be decisive in any enforcement decision, and not only – as the wording of the verdict might suggest – by way of exception. Thus, indirectly, the supervisory board would be required to work very closely with external experts.

Nevertheless, because a consistently reliable impact assessment does not seem possible – in questions of reputation in any case – a predominant reputational risk compared to the financial advantages of the enforcement of the claim must be demanded. In doing so, the ongoing uncertainties in the assessment could possibly be minimised.

III. Conclusion

The court's suggestion in *ARAG/Garmenbeck* that the supervisory board can refrain from filing a legal action for reputational reasons is now twenty years old. Since then, questions of reputational research have not yet been sufficiently investigated at the legal level. This paper has given first consideration to dealing with the *obiter dictum* of the Federal Court of Justice.

Indeed, one can say with certainty: Reputation matters.[181] The reputation of a company is a significant corporate asset, contributing in a major way to the company's financial situation.

For a meaningful legal debate, the concept of reputation needs a definition consensus. A proposal has been outlined in this paper. However, uncertainties continue to arise regarding the exact measurability – and thus also the comparability – of the aspects to be weighed against each other. At this point, much is still unclear and requires further (interdisciplinary) research work.

The considerable financial risks associated with a loss of reputation and the unclear basis for consideration make the decision of the supervisory

---

180 This line of argument, however, does not apply where the public already knows the relevant facts: Mathias Habersack, in: Wulf Goette, Mathias Habersack and Susanne Kalss (eds), *Münchener Kommentar zum Aktiengesetz* (4th Edition, 2014), § 111 para. 37.

181 Likewise: Lars Klöhn and Klaus Ulrich Schmolke, *Neue Zeitschrift für Gesellschaftsrecht (NZG)* 2015, 689 (697) ("main finding").

board essentially a future-oriented one. It seems quite plausible to grant the supervisory board the quality of an entrepreneurial decision with the appropriate discretionary powers.

When reputational risk is sufficiently high and which conditions must be met for the supervisory board to reasonably assume that it is acting in the best interests of the company remains questionable. Rather, it is the task of jurisprudence to identify more precise criteria and factors in interdisciplinary research. To date, according to the previous social and economic findings, a rash justification by reference to the company's reputation should be disregarded, and the general suitability of corporate reputation as consideration criteria should generally be critically scrutinised.

Bibliography

AON, *Global Risk Management Survey* (AON Empower Results, 2017),

http://www.aon.com/2017-global-risk-management-survey/pdfs/2017-Aon-Global-Risk-Management-Survey-Full-Report-062617.pdf (22-10-2018).

Gregor Bachmann, 'Reform der Organhaftung? Materielles Haftungsrecht und seine Durchsetzung in privaten und öffentlichen Unternehmen', in: Ständige Deputation des Deutschen Juristentages (ed), *Verhandlungen des 70. Deutschen Juristentages*, Vol. 1 – Gutachten (C.H. Beck, Munich 2014), E9.

Michael L. Barnett, John M. Jermier and Barbara A. Lafferty, 'Corporate Reputation: The Definitional Landscape' 9 (2006) *Corporate Reputation Review (CRR)*, 26.

David N. Barron and Meredith Rolfe, 'It ain't what you do, it's who you do it with: Distinguishing Reputation and Status', in: Michael Barnett and Timothy Pollock (eds), *The Oxford Handbook of Corporate Reputation* (Oxford University Press, Oxford 2012), 160.

Tom J. Brown, Peter A. Dacin, Michael G. Pratt and David A. Whetten, 'Identity, Intended Image, Construed Image, and Reputation: An Interdisciplinary Framework and Suggested Terminology' 34 (2006) *Journal of the Academy of Marketing Science (J. Acad. Mark. Sci.)*, 99.

Corinna Budras, 'VW, das wird teuer!', in: *Frankfurter Allgemeine Zeitung – FAZ* (20-03-2016), 28. also online: http://www.faz.net/aktuell/wirtschaft/vw-abgasskandal/vw-skandal-schadensforderung-in-milliardenhoehe-14135356.html (10-02-2018).

Burson-Marsteller, *CEO Reputation Study* (2003), cited in: Kim Harrison, 'Why a good corporate reputation is vital to your organization', in: *cuttingedgepr.com*,

https://cuttingedgepr.com/free-articles/reputation-trust-stakeholder-relations/good-corporate-reputation-important-organization/ (22-10-2018).

Matthias Casper, 'Hat die grundsätzliche Verfolgungspflicht des Aufsichtsrats im Sinne des ARAG/Garmenbeck-Urteils ausgedient?' 176 (2012) *Zeitschrift für das gesamte Handels- und Wirtschaftsrecht (ZHR)*, 617.

Samuel C. Certo and S. Trevis Certo, *Modern Management* (Pearson Education Limited, Harlow, United Kingdom, 2015).

Evan Comen and Michael B. Sauter, 'Companies With the Best (and Worst) Reputations', in: *24/7 Wall St.* (12-05-2016),

https://247wallst.com/special-report/2016/05/12/companies-with-the-best-and-worst-reputations-4/ (22-10-2018).

Duden: Das große Fremdwörterbuch, Volume 5 (11th Edition, Dudenverlag, Berlin 2015).

Edelman, Inc., *Edelman Trust Barometer – Special Report: Institutional Investors* (Edelman, 2017), https://www.edelman.com/trust2017/institutional-investors/ (28-05-2018).

Jack Ewing, 'Volkswagen Says 11 Million Cars Worldwide Are Affected in Diesel Deception', in: *The New York Times* (22-09-2015),

https://www.nytimes.com/2015/09/23/business/international/volkswagen-diesel-car-scandal.html (22-10-2018).

Michael Fischer, 'Der Entscheidungsspielraum des Aufsichtsrats bei der Geltendmachung von Regreßansprüchen gegen Vorstandsmitglieder' *Betriebsberater (BB)* 1996, 225.

Charles J. Fombrun, *Reputation: Realizing Value from the Corporate Image* (Harvard Business School, Boston 1996).

Charles J. Fombrun and Cees B.M. van Riel, 'The Reputational Landscape' 1 (1997) *Corporate Reputation Review (CRR)*, 5.

Charles Fombrun, 'The Building Blocks of Corporate Reputation: Definitions, Antecedents, Consequences', in: Michael Barnett and Timothy Pollock (eds), *The Oxford Handbook of Corporate Reputation* (Oxford University Press, Oxford 2012), 94.

Peter O. Foreman, David A. Whetten and Alison Mackey, 'An Identity-Based View of Reputation, Image, and Legitimacy: Clarifications and Distinctions among Related Constructs', in: Michael Barnett and Timothy Pollock (eds), *The Oxford Handbook of Corporate Reputation* (Oxford University Press, Oxford 2012), 179.

Norton Rose Fulbright, *German Stock Corporation Act (Aktiengesetz) – English Translation as at May 10, 2016*, http://www.nortonrosefulbright.com/files/german-stock-corporation-act-147035.pdf (22-10-2018).

Carsten Germis, 'Volkswagen überrascht mit hohem Gewinn', in: *FAZ.net* (18-04-2017), http://www.faz.net/aktuell/wirtschaft/unternehmen/sanierung-der-marke-vw-volkswagen-ueberrascht-mit-gewinn-14977018.html (22-10-2018).

Wulf Goette, 'Zur ARAG/Garmenbeck-Doktrin', in: Michael Hoffmann-Becking and Uwe Hüffner and Jochen Reichert (eds), *Liber Amicorum für Martin Winter* (Dr. Otto Schmidt, Cologne 2011), 153.

Heinrich Götz, 'Die Pflicht des Aufsichtsrats zur Haftbarmachung von Vorstandsmitgliedern. Besprechung des ARAG-Urteils des BGH' *Neue Juristische Wochenschrift (NJW)* 1997, 3275.

Taras Grescoe, 'The Dirty Truth About 'Clean Diesel'', in: *The New York Times* (02-01-2016), https://www.nytimes.com/2016/01/03/opinion/sunday/the-dirty-truth-about-clean-diesel.html (22-10-2018).

Großkommentar zum Aktiengesetz, Klaus J. Hopt and Markus Roth (eds) (4th Edition, de Gruyter, Berlin 2006).

Friedrich A. Hayek, *Individualismus und wirtschaftliche Ordnung* (2nd Edition, Neugebauer, Salzburg 1976).

Peter W. Heermann, 'Wie weit reicht die Pflicht des Aufsichtsrats zur Geltendmachung von Schadensersatzansprüchen gegen Mitglieder des Vorstands' *Die Aktiengesellschaft (AG)* 1998, 201.

Sabrina Helm, 'Corporate Reputation: An Introduction to a Complex Construct', in: Sabrina Helm, Kerstin Liehr-Gobbers and Christopher Storck (eds), *Reputation Management* (Springer, Berlin 2011), 3.

Hartwig Henze, 'Prüfungs- und Kontrollaufgaben des Aufsichtsrates in der Aktiengesellschaft – Die Entscheidungspraxis des Bundesgerichtshofes' *Neue Juristische Wochenschrift (NJW)* 1998, 3309.

Heribert Hirte, Markus Roth and Peter O. Mülbert (eds), *Aktiengesetz (AktG) Volume 4/1*, Commentary (5th Edition, De Gruyter, Berlin 2015).

Martin Hock, 'VW-Aktionäre in unbekannten Gewässern', in: *Frankfurter Allgemeine Zeitung – FAZ* (30-09-2015), 23.also online: http://www.faz.net/aktuell/finanzen/aktien/abgas-skandal-vw-aktionaere-brauchen-gute-nerven-13829928.html (22-10-2018)

Uwe Hüffer, 'Die leitungsbezogene Verantwortung des Aufsichtsrats' *Neue Zeitschrift für Gesellschaftsrecht (NZG)* 2007, 47.

Carolin Hümmer, *Die Reputation interner Dienstleister in Konzernen* (Springer Fachmedien, Wiesbaden 2015).

Detlef Kleindiek, 'Vertretungsbefugnis des Aufsichtsrats einer AG, BGH, Urt. v. 8.2.1988', *Entscheidungen zum Wirtschafts- und Bankrecht (WuB)*, II A § 112, AktG 1.88.

Lars Klöhn and Klaus Ulrich Schmolke, 'Ökonomische Erkenntnisse und ihre Bedeutung im Gesellschafts- und Kapitalmarktrecht' *Neue Zeitschrift für Gesellschaftsrecht (NZG)* 2015, 689.

Jens Koch, 'Die schleichende Erosion der Verfolgungspflicht nach ARAG/Garmenbeck' *Neue Zeitschrift für Gesellschaftsrecht (NZG)* 2014, 934.

Jens Koch, 'Das Gesetz zur Unternehmensintegrität und Modernisierung des Anfechtungsrechts (UMAG)' 35 (2006) *Zeitschrift für Unternehmens- und Gesellschaftsrecht (ZGR)*, 769.

Jens Koch, 'Keine Ermessensspielräume bei der Entscheidung über die Inanspruchnahme von Vorstandsmitgliedern' *Die Aktiengesellschaft (AG)*, 2009, 93.

Jens Koch, 'Die ARAG/Garmenbeck-Entscheidung des BGH (BGHZ 135, 244) Geschichte und Wirkungsgeschichte', in: Susanne Kalss, Holger Fleischer and Hans-Ueli Vogt (eds), *Bahnbrechende Entscheidungen – Gesellschafts- und Kapitalmarktrechtsgeschichten* (Mohr Siebeck, Tübingen 2016), 91.

Jens Koch and Uwe Hüffer (eds), *Aktiengesetz (AktG)*, Commentary (12th Edition, C.H. Beck, Munich 2016).

Bruno Kropff, 'Informationspflichten des Aufsichtsrats', in: Reinhard Damm, Peter W. Heermann and Rüdiger Veil (eds), *Festschrift für Thomas Raiser* (de Gruyter, Berlin 2005),225.

Patsy G. Lewellyn, 'Corporate Reputation' 41 (2002) *Business and Society (Bus. Soc.)*, 446.

Marcus Lutter, Gerd Krieger and Dirk Axel Verse, *Rechte und Pflichten des Aufsichtsrats* (6th Edition, Dr. Otto Schmidt, Cologne 2014).

John F. Mahon, 'Corporate Reputation' 41 (2002) *Business and Society (Bus. Soc.)*, 415.

Douglas McIntyre, 'Volkswagen Tops List of Worst Company Reputations', in: *24/7 Wall St.* (13-05-2016), http://247wallst.com/autos/2016/05/13/volkswagen-tops-list-of-worst-company-reputations/ (22-10-2018).

Stefan Menzel, 'VW kann die Dieselaffäre nicht abschütteln', in: *Handelsblatt.com* (11-12-2017), http://www.handelsblatt.com/unternehmen/industrie/volkswagen-bilanz-vw-kann-die-dieselaffaere-nicht-abschuetteln/20697510.html (22-10-2018).

Yuri Mishina and Cynthia E. Devers, 'On Being Bad: Why Stigma is not the Same as a bad Reputation', in: Michael Barnett and Timothy Pollock (eds), *The Oxford Handbook of Corporate Reputation* (Oxford University Press, Oxford 2012), 201.

Thomas M.J. Möllers and Eva Kernchen, 'Information Overload am Kapitalmarkt – Plädoyer zur Einführung eines Kurzfinanzberichts auf empirischer, psychologischer und rechtsvergleichender Basis' 40 (2011) *Zeitschrift für Unternehmens- und Gesellschaftsrecht (ZGR)*, 1.

Münchener Kommentar zum Aktiengesetz, Volume 2, Wulf Goette, Mathias Habersack and Susanne Kalss (eds) (4th Edition, C.H. Beck, Munich 2014).

Stefan Mutter, *Unternehmerische Entscheidungen und Haftung des Aufsichtsrats der Aktiengesellschaft* (Dr. Otto Schmidt, Cologne 1994).

N.N., 'Image von VW schlechter als das von Hyundai', in: *FAZ.net* (28-05-2017), http://www.faz.net/aktuell/wirtschaft/vw-abgasskandal/konzernbericht-image-von-vw-schlechter-als-das-von-hyundai-15036010.html (22-10-2018).

N.N., 'Milliardenverlust für Volkswagen', in: *Süddeutsche.de* (28-10-2015), http://www.sueddeutsche.de/wirtschaft/-abgas-skandal-bringt-vw-konzern-milliarden-euro-quartalsverlust-1.2703892 (22-10-2018).

N.N., 'Top 10 Hot New Markets', in: insurancejournal.com (25-03-2013), https://www.insurancejournal.com/magazines/features/2013/03/25/285532.htm (22-10-2018).

N.N., 'Vertrauen in VW schwer erschüttert', in: *boerse.ard.de* (06-04-2016), http://boerse.ard.de/aktien/vertrauen-in-vw-schwer-erschuettert100.html (01-05-2018).

Thomas H. Noe, 'A Survey of the Economic Theory of Reputation: Its Logic and Limits', in: Michael Barnett and Timothy Pollock (eds), *The Oxford Handbook of Corporate Reputation* (Oxford University Press, Oxford 2012), 114.

Hartmut Oetker, 'Vorstand, Aufsichtsrat und ihr Zusammenwirken aus rechtlicher Sicht', in: Peter Hommelhoff, Klaus J. Hopt and Axel v.Werder (eds), *Handbuch Corporate Governance* (2nd Edition, Schäffer Poeschel, Stuttgart 2009), 277.

Walter G. Paefgen, 'Die Inanspruchnahme pflichtvergessener Vorstandsmitglieder als unternehmerische Ermessensentscheidung des Aufsichtsrats' *Die Aktiengesellschaft (AG)* 2008, 761.

Walter G. Paefgen, 'Organhaftung: Bestandsaufnahme und Zukunftsperspektiven' *Die Aktiengesellschaft (AG)* 2014, 554.

Michael D. Pfarrer, Timothy G. Pollock and Violina P Rindova, 'A Tale of Two Assets: The Effects of Firm Reputation and Celebrity on Earnings Surprises and Investors' Reactions' 53 (2010) *Academy of Management Journal (Acad. Manag. J.)*, 1131.

Thomas Raiser, 'Pflicht und Ermessen von Aufsichtsratsmitgliedern – Zum Urteil des OLG Düsseldorf im Fall ARAG/Garmenbeck', *Neue Juristische Wochenschrift (NJW)* 1996, 552.

Viola Rindova and Luis Martins, 'Show me the Money: A Multidimensional Perspective on Reputation as an Intangible Asset', in: Michael Barnett and Timothy Pollock (eds), *The Oxford Handbook of Corporate Reputation* (Oxford University Press, Oxford 2012), 16.

Christopher A. Runge and Anabel Ternès, 'Reputationsmarketing – Unternehmensführung 2.0: Warum der gute Ruf in der globalen und digitalisierten Welt ein erfolgskritischer Geschäftsfaktor ist', in: Anabel Ternès and Ian Towers (eds), *Internationale Trends in der Markenkommunikation – Was Globalisierung, neue Medien und Nachhaltigkeit erfordern* (Springer Fachmedien, Wiesbaden 2014), 59.

Curt Sandig, *Der Ruf der Unternehmung* (Kohlhammer, Stuttgart 1962).

Manfred Schwaiger and Sascha Raithel, 'Reputation und Unternehmenserfolg' 64 (2014) *Management Review Quarterly (MRQ)*, 225.

Christoph H. Seibt, 'Corporate Reputation Management: Rechtsrahmen für Geschäftsleiterhandeln' *Der Betrieb (DB)* 2015, 171.

Johannes Semler, 'Überlegungen zur Praktikabilität der Organhaftungsvorschriften', in: Mathias Habersack, Wulf Goette (eds), *Festschrift für Wulf Goette* (C.H. Beck, Munich 2011), 499.

Weber Shandwick, *The Company behind the Brand: In Reputation We Trust* (Weber Shandwick, Munich 2012), http://www.webershandwick.com/uploads/news/files/InRepWeTrust_ExecutiveSummary.pdf (28-05-2018).

Oded Shenkar and Ephraim Yuchtman-Yaar, 'Reputation, Image, Prestige, and Godwill: An Interdisciplinary Approach to Organizational Standing' 50 (1997) *Human Relations*, 1361.

Gerald Spindler, 'Die Haftung von Vorstand und Aufsichtsrat für fehlerhafte Auslegung von Rechtsbegriffen', in: Andreas Heldrich and Ingo Koller et al. (eds), *Festschrift für Claus-Wilhelm Canaris zum 70. Geburtstag* (C. H. Beck, Munich 2007), 403.

Klaus Spremann, 'Reputation, Garantie, Information' 58 (1988) *Zeitschrift für Betriebswirtschaft (ZfB)*, 613.

George J. Stigler, *The Theory of Competitive Price* (Macmillan, New York 1942).

Della Summers (ed), *Business English Dictionary* (3rd Edition, Longman, Harlow 2007).

Ann Svendsen, *The Stakeholder Strategy: Profiting From Collaborative Business Relationships* (Berrett-Koehler, San Francisco 1998).

Maike Telgheder, 'Manager bestimmen das Firmenimage mit', in: *Handelsblatt.com* (23-03-2004), http://www.handelsblatt.com/unternehmen/management/ceo-reputations-studie-manager-bestimmen-das-firmenimage-mit/2315344.html (22-10-2018).

Matteo Tonello, *Reputation Risk: A Corporate Governance Perspective* (Conference Board, New York 2007).

Brad Tuttle, 'Warren Buffett's Boring, Brilliant Wisdom', in: *TIME online* (01-03-2010), http://business.time.com/2010/03/01/warren-buffetts-boring-brilliant-wisdom/ (22-10-2018).

Volker Votsmeier and Sönke Iwersen, 'Brisante Dokumente belasten Ex-VW-Chef Martin Winterkorn', in: Handelsblatt.com (28-02-2018), http://www.handelsblatt.com/my/unternehmen/industrie/dieselskandal-bei-volkswagen-brisante-dokumente-belasten-ex-vw-chef-martin-winterkorn/21012870.html (22-10-2018).

Kent Walker, 'Reputation and Supportive Behavior: Moderating Impacts of Foreignness, Industry and Local Exposure' 12 (2010) *Corporate Reputation Review (CRR)*, 357.

Steven Wartick, 'Measuring Corporate Reputation' 41 (2002) *Business and Society (Bus. Soc.)*, 371.

David A. Whetten and Alison Mackey, 'A Social Actor Conception of Organizational Identity and Its Implications for the Study of Organizational Reputation' 41 (2002) *Business and Society (Bus. Soc.)*, 393.

David A. Whetten, 'Part II: Where Do Reputations Come From? Theory Development and the Study of Corporate Reputation' 1 (1997) *Corporate Reputation Review (CRR)*, 26.

Nuno Zarco da Camara, 'Identity, Image and Reputation', in: Sabrina Helm, Kerstin Liehr-Gobbers and Christopher Storck (eds), *Reputation Management* (Springer, Heidelberg 2011), 47.

Register of Cases

BGH 08.02.1988 – II ZR 159/87 – BGHZ 103, 213.

BGH 25.03.1991 – II ZR 188/89 – BGHZ 114, 127.

BGH 26.06.1995 – II ZR 122/94 – BGHZ 130,108.

BGH 21.04.1997 – II ZR 175/95 – BGHZ 135, 244.

BGH 16.02.2009 – II ZR 185/07 – BGHZ 180, 9.

OLG Düsseldorf 22.06.1995 – 6 U 104/94 – AG 1995, 416.

The Impact of Corporate Reputation on Board Liability

*Kathleen van der Linde**

Mr Biesinger's contribution considers the nature of a supervisory board's decision whether or not to litigate against members of the management board who have breached their duties to the company. It asks whether the supervisory board can rely on the company's reputation as justification to refrain from instituting a damages claim. This response provides a brief South African law perspective on this issue.

South Africa adheres to a unitary board structure. The board in its entirety is the focal point of corporate governance.[1] The board can comprise executive and non-executive directors and certain companies are by law required to have directors on their board who are not involved in the "day-to-day management of the company's business". This is the case for companies that are required to have an audit committee[2] or a social and ethics committee.[3] The King Code on Corporate Governance[4] recommends a majority of

* Kathleen E. van der Linde, *B. Juris, LL.B., Hons. B.A. (Latin), LL.M., LL.D.*, Professor of Corporate Law and Head of the Department of Mercantile Law, Faculty of Law, University of Johannesburg.

1 Companies Act of 2008, s 66(1); see also the Code on Corporate Governance contained in Institute of Directors in Southern Africa *King IV Report on Corporate Governance in Southern Africa* (2016), (hereafter King IV Code), principle 1, recommended practice 1.c.i.

2 The Companies Act of 2008, s 94(2), prescribes audit committees for public companies, state-owned companies, as well as any other company required by its own memorandum of incorporation to have such a committee. The audit committee comprises of at least three members, all of whom must be non-executive directors, s 94(4)(*b*)(i).

3 These are listed public companies, state-owned companies and other companies based on their public interest score, regulation 43(1) of the Companies Regulations of 2011. The social and ethics committee comprises at least three directors of which at least one must be a non-executive director, regulation 43(4).

4 Although the Code applies on a voluntary basis, certain of its practices are incorporated in the JSE Limited Listings Requirements (see 3,84) and listed companies are obliged to disclose their application of the Code's recommended practices (see 8.63).

non-executive directors, the majority of which should in turn be independent.[5]

The board's role is to manage or direct the management of the company.[6] It is expressly empowered to delegate authority to one or more board committees.[7] The King IV Code in fact recommends delegation of management functions and confirms the supervisory role of the collective board.[8] On a functional level it would thus be possible, for example, to have an executive committee comprising of only the executive directors. Likewise, there could be a committee consisting of all the non-executive directors, perhaps even termed a "supervisory committee". Such a structure could approximate the German two-tier board, but there will still be a principled distinction in that both these committees would be accountable to the unified board.[9]

In *South African Broadcasting Corporation Ltd and Another v. Mpofu*[10] the court stated that although the non-executive directors could meet separately, any resolutions had to be adopted by the full board.[11] The purported resolution by the non-executive directors to suspend one of the executive directors was declared invalid because all three the executive directors had been excluded from the meeting.

This matter confirms that in the absence of a specific delegation to a board committee, the decision to institute proceedings against a director who has breached his or her duties[12] will have to be taken by the full board. The particular director against whom proceedings are being considered can

5 principle 7 recommended practices 7 and 8.

6 Companies Act of 2008, s 66(1).

7 Companies Act of 2008, s 72(1).

8 See King IV Code, principle 4, recommended practices 1 - 8; principle 8, recommended practice 49, and the recommended practices under principle 10 on the delegation of functions to management and the supervisory role of the board.

9 Delegation cannot detract from the accountability of the full board, see Companies Act of 2008, s 72(3) and King IV Code, principle 1, recommended practice 1.d.

10 [2009] 4 All SA 169 (GJ) para. 30.

11 The SABC is a state-owned broadcasting company and the Broadcasting Act of 1999, s 12 prescribes a board comprising 12 or more non-executive directors and 3 executive directors.

12 The overarching duties are to act in good faith and for a proper purpose, in the best interests of the company, and with care, skill and diligence, Companies Act of 2008, s 76(3)(*a*)-(*c*).

be seen as having a material personal financial interest[13] in the matter and will thus be excluded from the decision-making process.[14]

Although there is no direct statutory obligation on the board to ensure that the company proceeds against the wrongdoers, the directors will have to consider whether the company's best interests dictate that steps should be taken against the wrongdoer. As the existence of corporate reputation is recognized in South African law,[15] the likely reputational impact on the company can certainly be taken into account.

While it is not altogether clear whether the German supervisory board will enjoy the protection of the business judgement rule in respect of a decision to not institute proceedings[16], the South African rule[17] is wide enough to offer protection also when the board decides that the company's interests would be better served by not bringing a claim for damages. This is because it applies "in respect of any particular matter arising in the exercise of the powers or the performance of the functions of director".[18] Any director who has made a decision or supported a decision of the board or of a board committee can invoke the rule to show that he or she did not breach the duty to act in the best interests of the company or to display the required care, skill and diligence.[19] Thus no distinction is made between executive and non-executive directors or between "entrepreneurial" and "supervisory decisions".

If, for whatever reason, the board does not pursue a claim against the director, stakeholders can use the mechanism of the derivative action to bring proceedings on the company's behalf. This option is available to shareholders, directors, prescribed officers and trade unions or other employee representatives.[20] The procedure involves formally demanding from

---

13 See the definition of "personal financial interest" and of "material" in Companies Act of 2008, s 1.

14 Companies Act of 2008, s 75(2).

15 See, eg, *Media 24 v. SA Taxi Securitisation* 2011 (5) SA 329 (SCA), in the context of defamation.

16 See Biesinger, pp. 242 et seqq.

17 As codified in Companies Act of 2008, s 76(4).

18 Companies Act of 2008, s 76(4) introductory words.

19 Companies Act of 2008, s 76(4)(*a*)(iii).

20 Companies Act of 2008, s 165(2)(*a*)-(*c*). In addition, the court can grant leave to any other person to institute proceedings on this basis if it is necessary or expedient to do so in order to protect a legal right of that person, Companies Act of 2008, s 165(2)(*d*).

the company that it takes steps to protect its legal interests. Unless the company successfully applies to have the demand set aside,[21] the company is obliged to appoint an impartial person or committee to investigate the matter and report to the board whether there appears to be a cause of action, the likely costs of pursuing it and whether it would be in the best interests of the company to pursue the cause of action. The report thus comprises an assessment of the facts and legal position as well as an evaluation of the wisdom of pursuing any claim the company is found to have. This is comparable to the two-step approach prescribed by the German federal court for the supervisory board in ARAG/Garmenbeck. Although it is the investigator or committee that has to deal with these issues, the board will eventually have to consider the report in order to decide on the way forward. The costs of litigating are expressly recognized as relevant, but there is as yet no judicial guidance on other factors that may be taken into account and on the relative weighting of such factors.

If the company fails to act in accordance with the recommendations in a reasonable report,[22] the person who served the demand may approach the court for permission to proceed on behalf of the company.[23] The court can grant permission if it is satisfied that the applicant is acting in good faith, that the proposed proceedings involve a serious question of material consequence to the company and that it is in the best interests of the company that the applicant should proceed on its behalf.[24] The court will thus again consider the best interests of the company. Although the court retains a controlling discretion whether or not to grant permission,[25] there is a degree of deference to the board's assessment of the company's best interests. This is articulated in a rebuttable presumption that applies in respect of proceedings

---

21 This can be done on the basis that it is frivolous, vexatious or without merit, see Companies Act of 2008, s 165(3).

22 Or if it fails to properly comply with the demand, see Companies Act of 2008, s 165(5)(a) for a list of failures.

23 Companies Act of 2008, s 165(5)(*a*).

24 Companies Act of 2008, s 165(5)(*b*).

25 *Mbethe v. United Manganese of Kalahari* 2017 (6) SA 409 (SCA).

against third parties. Directors are regarded as third parties[26] for this purpose.[27] If the company decided not to bring proceedings, it is presumed that it will not be in the company's best interests to grant leave to the applicant to institute proceedings.[28] For this presumption to apply, the court must be satisfied that all the directors who took part in the decision acted in good faith and for a proper purpose; did not have a personal financial interest and were not related to anyone with a personal financial interest in the decision; informed themselves about the subject matter of the decision; and reasonably believed that the decision was in the best interests of the company. This presumption is thus based on a dedicated test resembling the business judgement rule.[29]

The prerequisites for the presumption are, however, stricter than the elements of the general business judgement rule in two respects. Firstly, in addition to the absence of a personal financial interest, it requires the establishment of good faith and acting for a proper purpose. This element is particularly appropriate for the context under consideration, as board members might be influenced by their relationship with the infringing director or perhaps by apprehension about their own future exposure to liability. Secondly, and more importantly, it requires a "reasonable" as opposed to just a "rational" basis for the belief that the decision is in the best interests of the company. Although the presumption is envisaged to be rebuttable, it is difficult to see how a court could simultaneously be satisfied that despite the existence of objectively reasonable grounds to believe that litigation is not in the company's best interests, such litigation is, after all, in the company's best interests. Perhaps this might be the case if circumstances changed between the time the board made its initial decision and the time the court is considering the issue.

---

26 A third party is someone who is not "related" to the company as envisaged in Companies Act of 2008, s 2. Under this provision an individual is related to a company if he or she can exercise the majority of the shareholder voting rights or can elect or appoint directors who control the majority of the board voting rights.

27 This position is criticised by Maleka F. Cassim, *The New Derivative Action under the Companies Act* (2016), 13-14, as directors can be expected to be the usual defendants in derivative proceedings and should not enjoy the benefit of the presumption.

28 Companies Act of 2008, s 165(7).

29 Companies Act of 2008, s 165(7)(*c*).

While South Africa has not had a matter comparable to the ARAG/Garmenbeck decision,[30] the court in *Lewis Group Limited v. Woollam and Others*[31] may appear to have been somewhat ambivalent on the relevance of corporate reputation in the context of proceedings against directors. An activist shareholder attempted to force the company, which was listed on the JSE Ltd, to institute proceedings against four of its directors,[32] but the company succeeded in having the demand set aside as frivolous, vexatious or without merit.[33] The court remarked that the company would have an interest in setting aside a demand because an early exit would protect it from the prejudicial effect of the publicity attendant on the protracted derivative action procedure that could otherwise follow.[34] In a subsequent matter between the same parties,[35] after the shareholder had served a second demand but then withdrew it, the company applied to have that demand set aside, arguing that the withdrawal was incompetent. It desired a court order setting aside the second demand on the merits so as to help repair the harm of the adverse publicity caused by the demand.[36] The same judge held that while redressing bad publicity might be an incidental effect of the setting aside remedy, it could not be a purpose in itself.[37] In assessing these remarks, it must be remembered that they were made in the context of applications for the setting aside of a demand. At that stage it is not yet relevant whether litigation would indeed be in the best interests of the company.

---

30 BGH 21.04.1997 - II ZR 175/95 - BGHZ 135, 244ff.

31 2017 (2) SA 547 (WCC) and subsequently in [2017] ZAWCHC 15 (01.03.2017).

32 He wanted to force the company to apply for an order declaring each of the directors delinquent under the Companies Act of 2008, s 162. As the opportunity to apply for such an order is also directly available to shareholders and certain other parties, the court found derivative proceedings to be inappropriate - this was a public interest matter and not a question of protecting a legal right of the company, see *Lewis Group Limited v. Woollam and Others* 2017 (2) SA 547 (WCC) para. 43, 48-49.

33 This is in terms of Companies Act of 2008, s 165(3).

34 *Lewis Group Limited v. Woollam and Others* 2017 (2) SA 547 (WCC), para. 89. The court mentioned that the share price had indeed been negatively influenced by the allegations, see para. 86.

35 See *Lewis Group Limited v. Woollam and Others* [2017] ZAWCHC 15 (01.03.2017).

36 See *Lewis Group Limited v. Woollam and Others* [2017] ZAWCHC 15 (01.03.2017), para. 3.

37 The court held the withdrawal to be valid and refused to set aside the demand as that would amount to deciding a moot point, see *Lewis Group Limited v. Woollam and Others* [2017] ZAWCHC 15 (01.03.2017), para. 13.

The best interests of the company will ultimately determine whether proceedings should be instituted against directors who breached their duties. This is the case regardless of whether the board considers proceedings by the company itself or whether the court decides whether someone else should be allowed to litigate in the name of and on behalf of the company. In both instances a business judgement rule is relevant, although I have illustrated important differences in detail between the two contexts. While nothing precludes the consideration of corporate reputation when the open-ended best interests concept is applied, there is as yet no judicial guidance on the weight it should enjoy.

Bibliography

Maleka F. Cassim, *The New Derivative Action under the Companies Act* (Juta, Cape Town 2016).

Institute of Directors in Southern Africa, *King IV Report on Corporate Governance for South Africa* (2016).

Register of Cases

Lewis Group Limited v. Woollam and Others 2017 (2) SA 547 (WCC).

Lewis Group Limited v. Woollam and Others [2017] ZAWCHC 15 (01.03.2017).

Mbethe v. United Manganese of Kalahari 2017 (6) SA 409 (SCA).

Media 24 v. SA Taxi Securitisation 2011 (5) SA 329 (SCA).

South African Broadcasting Corporation Ltd and Another v. Mpofu [2009] 4 All SA 169 (GJ).

BGH 21.04.1997 – II ZR 175/95 – BGHZ 135, 244 et seqq.

The Constitutionalization of Public Policy in Private International Law

*Wolfgang Wurmnest**
*Maximilian Kübler-Wachendorff***

Abstract: *The impact of constitutionally protected values shape the reach of the public policy reservation in German and European private international law. Historically, this process began in Germany with the 1971 "Spaniard case", which led to many changes in German private international law to implement the principle of gender equality. Over time, courts used constitutional values increasingly to discard the application of foreign law. Consequently, public policy violations are particularly numerous in the areas of family and succession law. Around the world, these areas of law are shaped by very different cultural and religious influences. Analysing the European regulations on private international law reveals that the concept of public policy is still, to a large extent, defined by national values. However, recent actions of the European legislator threaten to abandon established principles of private international law as Art. 10 Rome III Regulation can be interpreted as an abstract control of foreign divorce rules to protect gender equality. We argue that an abstract control may have unwarranted consequences for the parties involved. Looking at the future of the public policy reservation, we argue that its importance will surely diminish given that the connecting factors of European private international law ensure in many cases that the law of the forum (and not a foreign law) applies. As far as courts still have to apply foreign laws, we believe that these laws should not be controlled too tightly on constitutional grounds.*

* Wolfgang Wurmnest, *Dr. iur., LL.M. (Berkeley)*; Professor, University of Augsburg, Faculty of Law. Chair for Private Law, Commercial Law, International Private and Comparative Law.

** Maximilian Kübler-Wachendorff, Academic Assistant at the Chair of Wolfgang Wurmnest.

I. Introduction

The public policy reservation (*ordre public*) is a cornerstone of modern Private International Law. It is not only German conflict-of-law rules which contain a provision on public policy (Art. 6 of the German Introductory Act to the Civil Code, hereafter: EGBGB).[1] All European Regulations on private international law, such as the Rome I Regulation,[2] the Rome II Regulation,[3] the Rome III Regulation[4] or the Succession Regulation,[5] and other country's choice-of-law rules[6] also do so. These provisions allow courts to disregard foreign laws that would otherwise apply. The reason why every legal order contains such a safety net is that traditional private international law rules are designed to find the law with the closest connection to a case.[7] However, applying this law might violate fundamental values of the forum and create tensions within a jurisdiction, a situation that should be avoided.[8]

Yet, from the perspective of private international law, public policy remains an "*enfant terrible*".[9] Disregarding the applicable foreign law, the public policy reservation undermines the principle of closest connection and endangers the international consistency of decision-making. Excessively

---

1 Einführungsgesetz zum Bürgerlichen Gesetzbuch, English translation available at: http://www.gesetze-im-internet.de/englisch_bgbeg/englisch_bgbeg.html.

2 Art. 21 Rome I Regulation (Regulation (EC) No 593/2008 of the European Parliament and of the Council of 17 June 2008 on the law applicable to contractual obligations (Rome I), OJ L 177, 4.7.2008, 6).

3 Art 26 Rome II Regulation (Regulation (EC) No 864/2007 of the European Parliament and of the Council of 11 July 2007 on the law applicable to non-contractual obligations (Rome II), OJ L 199, 31.7.2007, 40).

4 Art. 12 Rome III Regulation (Council Regulation (EU) No 1259/2010 of 20 December 2010 implementing enhanced cooperation in the area of the law applicable to divorce and legal separation, OJ L 343, 29.12.2010, 10).

5 Art. 35 Succession Regulation (Regulation (EU) No 650/2012 of the European Parliament and of the Council of 4 July 2012 on jurisdiction, applicable law, recognition and enforcement of decisions and acceptance and enforcement of authentic instruments in matters of succession and on the creation of a European Certificate of Succession, OJ L 201, 27.7.2012, 107).

6 See, e.g., Art. 21 Belgian Private International Law Act of 2004 (English translation in 70 (2006) *Rabels Zeitschrift für ausländisches und internationales Privatrecht (RabelsZ)*, 358–397; Art. 16 Italian Private International Law Act of 1995.

7 Gerhard Kegel and Klaus Schurig, *Internationales Privatrecht* (9th Edition, 2004), § 2 I; Wolfgang Wurmnest, 'Ordre Public (Public Policy)', in: Stefan Leible (ed), *General Principles of European Private International Law* (2016), § 14.03 [C], 319 et seq.

8 Christian von Bar and Peter Mankowski, *Internationales Privatrecht* (2nd Edition, 2003) Vol. 1, § 7 para. 258.

9 Pierre Mayer and Vincent Heuzé, *Droit international privé* (11th Edition, 2014), para. 206.

applied, the doctrine would destroy the system of private international law. As *Christian von Bar* and *Peter Mankowski* put it:

> "Very much like distinguishing between medicine and poison, the question of the effect of public policy depends foremost on the quantity. Only the application in the right amount will have the desired positive effect."[10]

Against this background, German doctrine and courts have developed the following prerequisites for invoking the *ordre public* reservation:

- Courts may only set aside the application of foreign law if it produces a result that is incompatible with fundamental German values. It is not the abstract rule or provision at issue which is subject to control, but rather the result of its application ("result control").[11] Consequently, a foreign rule abstractly incompatible with values of German law nonetheless must be applied to a case whenever that concrete application produces an acceptable result. Hence, a foreign law awarding custody of a child that has reached a certain age to the father without considering the child's best interest would apply nevertheless, if the father's custody was in the best interest of the child (for example because the mother cannot take care of the child because of severe drug problems).
- To reject the application of foreign law, the result must further be manifestly incompatible with fundamental values.[12] The term "manifestly" refers to the severity of the breach of principles and values. Rejecting the foreign law solution requires not only a breach of domestic values but rather a severer incompatibility with these.[13]

---

10 Christian von Bar and Peter Mankowski, *Internationales Privatrecht* (2nd Edition, 2003) Vol. 1, § 7 para. 258: „Wie die Abgrenzung von Arznei vom Gift, so ist deshalb auch die Frage der Wirkungsweise des ordre public-Vorbehalts ein Problem der Menge. Positiv wirkt er sich nur aus, wenn er in richtig dosierter Menge zur Anwendung gelangt".

11 Bernd von Hoffmann and Karsten Thorn, *Internationales Privatrecht* (9th Edition, 2007), § 6 para. 150; Jan Kropholler, *Internationales Privatrecht* (6th Edition, 2006), § 36 II.

12 Christian von Bar and Peter Mankowski, *Internationales Privatrecht* (2nd Edition, 2003) Vol. 1, § 7 para. 259; Jan Kropholler, *Internationales Privatrecht* (6th Edition, 2006), § 36 II.

13 Michael Stürner, in: Christine Budzikiewicz, Marc-Philippe Weller and Wolfgang Wurmnest (eds), *BeckOGK* (March 2018), Art. 6 EGBGB para. 263.

- Furthermore, there is a form of relativity to the *ordre public*: Weak ties to the forum demand more serious breaches of public policy to disregard the foreign law.[14] The degree of the domestic relations (*Inlandsbeziehung)* matters for an *ordre public* analysis.[15] This prerequisite is necessary to prevent the public policy doctrine from becoming an abstract control mechanism of foreign law.[16]

The rejection of a foreign rule leaves a gap in need of filling. Instead of the foreign rule, one could simply be tempted to apply the law of the forum.[17] However, public policy does not allow courts to disregard the foreign law entirely.[18] Bearing the principle of closest connection in mind, one should primarily turn to the foreign law which would otherwise be applicable. Courts should thus try to fill the gap which has emerged either by applying different rules of the foreign law or modifying the offending rule.[19] Recourse to the law of the forum is only permissible as a last resort, in circumstances where applying a different or modified rule of the foreign law is impossible.[20]

---

14 Christian von Bar and Peter Mankowski, *Internationales Privatrecht* (2nd Edition, 2003) Vol. 1, § 7 para. 263; Wolfgang Wurmnest, 'Ordre Public (Public Policy)', in: Stefan Leible (ed), *General Principles of European Private International Law* (2016), § 14.03 [D], 323.

15 BGH 20.12.1972 – IV ZB 20/72 – BGHZ 60 (68 and 79) = NJW 1973, 417 (419); Jan Kropholler, *Internationales Privatrecht* (6th Edition, 2006), § 36 II; on the difficulties to apply this criterion to violations of the *Grundgesetz* see Dirk Looschelders, 65 (2001) *Rabels Zeitschrift für ausländisches und internationales Privatrecht (RabelsZ)*, 461 (475 et seq.).

16 Jan Kropholler, *Internationales Privatrecht* (6th Edition, 2006), § 36 II.

17 Christian von Bar and Peter Mankowski, *Internationales Privatrecht* (2nd Edition, 2003) Vol. 1, § 7 para. 285 et seq.

18 Michael Stürner, *Zeitschrift für das Privatrecht der Europäischen Union (GPR)* 2014, 317 (324); Wolfgang Wurmnest, 'Ordre Public (Public Policy)', in: Stefan Leible (ed), *General Principles of European Private International Law* (2016), § 14.04, 327.

19 Jan Kropholler, *Internationales Privatrecht* (6th Edition, 2006), § 36 V; Michael Stürner, *Zeitschrift für das Privatrecht der Europäischen Union (GPR)* 2014, 317 (324); Wolfgang Wurmnest, 'Ordre Public (Public Policy)', in: Stefan Leible (ed), *General Principles of European Private International Law* (2016), § 14.04, 327 et seq.

20 Michael Stürner, *Zeitschrift für das Privatrecht der Europäischen Union (GPR)* 2014, 317 (324); Jan Kropholler, *Internationales Privatrecht* (6th Edition, 2006), § 36 V.

In German law, fundamental values are enshrined in the German constitution (*Grundgesetz,* GG).[21] Over the last few decades, German courts have relied more and more on provisions of the *Grundgesetz* to disregard the application of foreign law. This article discusses the implications of this development. It will first recall the landmark "Spaniard" judgment of the Federal Constitutional Court of Germany, which introduced constitutional aspects to the field of private international law (II.) and explain the consequences of this judgment leading to the reform of the German rules of private international law in 1986 (III.). It then examines case law in various areas of law to demonstrate the impact of the Constitution on the application of the *ordre public* (IV.) and assesses the influence of European legislation on public policy (V.). Finally, future developments of the *ordre public* will be assessed and evaluated (VI.).

II. How it all started: the Spaniard case of the Federal Constitutional Court

The 1971 ruling in the Spaniard case[22] of the Federal Constitutional Court (*Bundesverfassungsgericht*) marks the beginning of the constitutionalization process. German authorities had refused to marry a German-Spanish couple because Spanish marriage law determining the conditions of marriage for the catholic Spanish fiancé, applicable under the German rules of private international law, did not recognise the (German) fiancée's divorce from her former husband under German law. From the perspective of the applicable Spanish marriage law, the German fiancée was still married to her former spouse and thus unable to enter into a second marriage with the Spanish fiancé. When the case came before the *Bundesverfassungsgericht*, the Court upheld their complaint and ruled that the German authorities were to marry the couple. This was the first case in which the Court had the opportunity to rule on the relationship of the GG and the rules of private international law. The Court made clear that not only the rules of German private international law but also the application of foreign law on the basis of these rules must be measured against the basic rights enshrined in the

---

21 Basic Law for the Federal Republic of Germany, English translation available at: https://www.gesetze-im-internet.de/englisch_gg/.

22 BVerfG 4.5.1971 – 1 BvR 636/68 – BVerfGE 31, 58 = NJW 1971, 1509.

German constitution.[23] The Court held that refusing to marry the claimants on the ground that the home law of the Spanish fiancée did not recognise the German fiancée's divorce violated the couple's right to enter into a marriage, protected by Art. 6 GG of the German Constitution.[24]

The Court's ruling presented a significant volte-face in how the Constitution's effect on the field of private international law was perceived. The prevailing opinion prior to this decision among German courts[25] and scholars[26] saw this field of law largely excluded from the scope of constitutional provisions. Private international law was seen as a "neutral" and rather "technical" area which called for the application of the law with the closest connection to a case.[27] The operation of these rules was not to be hindered by a thorough constitutional review. It was accepted that a review was possible when rules led to the application of German law. And it was also widely agreed upon that the German conflict-of-law rules had to be in conformity with constitutional requirements,[28] although different views existed as to how to achieve this result. If, however, a foreign law was to be applied, the *ordre public* (then Art. 30 EGBGB) only required a foreign rule to be disregarded if "fundamental principles of the German constitution, which are an unmovable basis of the public or social life in Germany, are violated. Only in such severe cases could foreign rules incompatible with the

23 BVerfG 4.5.1971 – 1 BvR 636/68 – BVerfGE 31, 58 = NJW 1971, 1509 Leitsatz 2: „Die Vorschriften des deutschen Internationalen Privatrechts und die Anwendung des durch sie berufenen ausländischen Rechts im Einzelfall sind an den Grundrechten zu messen."

24 BVerfG 4.5.1971 – 1 BvR 636/68 – BVerfGE 31, 58 (80 et seq.) = NJW 1971, 1509 (1512).

25 BGH 12.2.1964 – IV AR (VZ) 39/63 – BGHZ 41, 136 (150 et seq.) = NJW 1964, 976 (979); BGH 29.4.1964 – IV ZR 93/63 – BGHZ 42, 7 (12 et seq.) = NJW 1964, 2013 (2014). For further references see Jan Kropholler, *Gleichberechtigung durch Richterrecht. Erfahrungen im Familienrecht – Perspektiven im internationalen Privatrecht* (1975), 81 et seq.

26 Murad Ferid, 'Wechselbeziehungen zwischen Verfassungsrecht und Kollisionsnormen', in: Ernst von Caemmerer, Arthur Nikisch and Konrad Zweigert (eds), *Vom deutschen zum europäischen Recht – Festschrift für Hans Dölle* (1963) Vol. 2, 119 (143 et seq.).

27 On this debate see Dieter Henrich, *Zeitschrift für das gesamte Familienrecht (FamRZ)* 1974, 105; Jan Kropholler, *Gleichberechtigung durch Richterrecht. Erfahrungen im Familienrecht – Perspektiven im internationalen Privatrecht* (1975), 82 et seq.

28 Hans Dölle, *Internationales Privatrecht* (2nd Edition, 1972), 20.

Grundgesetz not be applied".[29] In other words, a violation of constitutional rights was only considered incompatible with public policy if the essential content of a given right was affected.[30] This confined the reach of the *ordre public* to severe violations of constitutional rights.

In overruling this case law, the Federal Constitutional Court reminded the ordinary courts that according to Art. 1(3) GG all German authorities are bound by the basic rights set out in the Constitution.[31] The basic rights enshrined in the Constitution are the foundation of a "free and democratic order in Germany."[32] The reach of these rights must therefore not depend on the rules of the EGBGB; it must be determined directly and solely on the basis of these rights.[33] A limited control to protect parties against foreign rules is not justifiable. Thus, violations of rights enshrined in the Constitution must lead to courts disregarding the foreign law.[34]

III. The aftermath of the Spaniard case I: reforming the EGBGB at last

Even though it is undisputed that the Spaniard case of 1971 marked a turning point in the conception of the constitution's effect on the field of private international law, it was a while before the full force of this decision was felt. This is well illustrated by the existence of conflict-of-law rules in the

29 BGH 29.4.1964 – IV ZR 93/63 – NJW 1964, 2013 (2014): „Auf Grund des Art. 30 EGBGB ist auch die Anwendung eines ausländischen Gesetzes ausgeschlossen, wenn dadurch wesentliche Verfassungsgrundsätze, die eine unverrückbare Grundlage des deutschen staatlichen oder sozialen Lebens bilden, verletzt werden. Nur in derartig schwerwiegenden Fällen scheidet die Anwendung ausländischer Vorschriften, die sich mit dem GG nicht vereinbaren lassen, aus."

30 BGH 29.4.1964 – IV ZR 93/63 – NJW 1964, 2013 (2014) with reference to Karl Heinz Neumayer, 'Zur positiven Funktion der kollisionsrechtlichen Vorbehaltsklausel', in: Ernst von Caemmerer, Arthur Nikisch and Konrad Zweigert (eds), *Vom deutschen zum europäischen Recht. Festschrift für Hans Dölle* (1963) Vol. 2, 179 (202).

31 BVerfG 4.5.1971 – 1 BvR 636/68 – BVerfGE 31, 58 (72 et seq.) = NJW 1971, 1509 (1510 et seq.).

32 BVerfG 4.5.1971 – 1 BvR 636/68 – BVerfGE 31, 58 (73) = NJW 1971, 1509 (1511): „freiheitlich-demokratischen Ordnung des staatlichen Lebens".

33 BVerfG 4.5.1971 – 1 BvR 636/68 – BVerfGE 31, 58 (73) = NJW 1971, 1509 (1511).

34 BVerfG 4.5.1971 – 1 BvR 636/68 – BVerfGE 31, 58 (73 et seq.) = NJW 1971, 1509 (1511).

EGBGB which did not comply with the constitutionally protected principle of equality of men and women (Art. 3(2) GG). The conflict rules in family law used the nationality of the husband as the connecting factor to determine the applicable law in many family matters such as the law of divorce or of the property regime. This discrimination against wives was defended by scholars arguing that the application of conflict-of-law rules "is merely a technical process [...] by which neither the husband nor the wife receives preferential treatment." [35] And given the possibility that the law of the husband would be more favourable to the wife than the law of her nationality, she might have an interest in the application of the law of the husband.[36] Even though this view was not undisputed,[37] courts were reluctant to deviate from the traditional approach for a significant period, hoping that the legislature would step in to alter the law.[38] It was only in the 1980s when the *Bundesgerichtshof* (BGH),[39] i.e. the highest court in civil and commercial matters, and again the *Bundesverfassungsgericht* made clear that such a connecting factor violated the principle of equal treatment of men and women. Such a connecting factor generally subordinated a wife – unlike her

---

35 Hans Dölle, *Internationales Privatrecht* (2nd Edition, 1972), 21: „[Eine Verfassungswidrigkeit ist [n]ach herrschender Ansicht [zu verneinen], da die Anknüpfung primär ein technischer Vorgang ist, durch den in materieller Hinsicht weder der Mann noch die Frau bevorzugt wird ...". This view was also shared by the *Bundesgerichtshof*, see BGH 18.1.1954 – IV ZR 144/53 – NJW 1954, 837.

36 Hans Dölle, *Internationales Privatrecht* (2nd Edition, 1972), 57: „Man mag fragen, ob diese Bevorzugung des Mannesrechts angesichts der heute in Deutschland anerkannten Gleichberechtigung von Mann und Frau noch Verfassungsmäßig ist .... Das IPR hat zwar mit materiellrechtlichen Wertungen wenig zu tun. Allein, die Frau kann u.U. ein Interesse haben, nicht dem Recht des Mannes unterworfen zu sein, sondern ihrem eigenen. Die Gleichberechtigung ist hier jedoch zumindest einer unter mehreren Gesichtspunkten der besonderen ‚Anknüpfungsgerechtigkeit' des IPR ...".

37 Alexander N. Makarov, 17 (1952) *Rabels Zeitschrift für ausländisches und internationales Privatrecht (RabelsZ)*, 382 (385); see also Dieter Henrich, *Zeitschrift für das gesamte Familienrecht (FamRZ)* 1974, 105 (106 et seq.) (with regard to certain albeit not all conflict rules that used the husband's nationality as connecting factor); Jan Kropholler, *Zeitschrift für das gesamte Familienrecht (FamRZ)* 1976, 316.

38 See OLG Stuttgart 22.5.1978 – 17 UF 20/78 G – IP-Rechtsprechung 1978, No. 54, 117 (118). For further references see Paul Heinrich Neuhaus, *Grundbegriffe des Internationalen Privatrechts* (2nd Edition, 1976), 46 et seq.

39 BGH 8.12.1982 – IVb ZR 334/81 – BGHZ 86, 57 (61 et seq.) = NJW 1983, 1259 (1260).

husband – to a law different from her home law and did so in such a way that she could also not change the applicable law, even by acquiring another nationality.[40] The *Bundesverfassungsgericht* thus declared the rules determining the law applicable to the matrimonial property regime (Art. 15 EGBGB old version)[41] and to divorces (Art. 17 EGBGB old version)[42] void.

These decisions placed the legislature under strong pressure to act. As consequence, in 1986 a new EGBGB was promulgated.[43] In so doing, conflict-of-law rules were provided with a new basis, aligning them with constitutional requirements. Three changes deserve attention.

First, the newly formed Art. 6 EGBGB expressly refers to basic rights (*Grundrechte*) of the German constitution as values protected by public policy. Applications of foreign law resulting in the violation any of these protected human rights must not be implemented by a German court.[44] By introducing this reference, the German legislature sent a clear signal that the public policy doctrine must be open to constitutional values.

Second, the legislature created special clauses to ensure that constitutional rights are not violated,[45] such as Art. 13(2) EGBGB.[46] Art. 13(2) EGBGB mandates the application of the law of the forum when applying foreign marriage law violates the individual freedom to marry, protected by

40 Alexander N. Makarov, 17 (1952) *Rabels Zeitschrift für ausländisches und internationales Privatrecht (RabelsZ)*, 382 (385); Michael Sachs, *Grenzen des Diskriminierungsverbots* (1987), 279.

41 BVerfG 22.2.1983 – 1 BvL 17/81 – BVerfGE 63, 181 (194) = NJW 1983, 1968 (1970).

42 BVerfG 8.1.1985 – 1 BvR 830/83 – BVerfGE 68, 384 (390) = NJW 1985, 1282.

43 Art. 1 Gesetz zur Neuregelung des Internationalen Privatrechts of 25 July 1986, BGBl. I, 1142, 1143. For an overview see Jürgen Basedow, *Neue Juristische Wochenschrift (NJW)* 1986, 2971 et seq.

44 Regierungsbegründung zum Gesetz zur Neuregelung des IPR, BT-Drucksache 10/504 of 20 October 1983, 44; see also Dirk Looschelders, 65 (2001) *Rabels Zeitschrift für ausländisches und internationales Privatrecht (RabelsZ)*, 461 (478).

45 Michael Stürner, in: Christine Budzikiewicz, Marc-Philippe Weller and Wolfgang Wurmnest (eds), *BeckOGK* (March 2018), Art. 6 EGBGB para. 121 et seq.; specifically regarding the creation of Art. 13(2) no. 3 EGBGB: Regierungsbegründung zum Gesetz zur Neuregelung des IPR, BT-Drucksache 10/504 of 20 October 1983, 53.

46 Regierungsbegründung zum Gesetz zur Neuregelung des IPR, BT-Drucksache 10/504 of 20 October 1983, 53.

Art. 6 GG, provided that the following provisions are met: one of the persons engaged to be married is a German national or has his habitual residence in Germany (no. 1), both persons have taken necessary and reasonable steps to set aside the obstacle (no. 2) and refusing to marry the engaged would violate their freedom of marriage, for example because the home state law of one the fiancés does not recognise a German divorce decree or a foreign divorce decree recognised in Germany (no. 3).[47] Thus, in cases having sufficient connections with Germany, a foreign law preventing one of the fiancés from marrying may be replaced by German law if the constitutionally protected freedom of marriage demands so and the parties have taken all reasonable steps to overcome the obstacle of the home state law – for example by trying to have a divorce decree in their home jurisdiction recognised. Recently, Art. 13 EGBGB was amended even further to tighten the control over marriages officiated abroad if one of the parties had not reached the age of 16 at the time of marriage (see below section IV. 3. a)).

Finally, since the 1986 reform of the EGBGB, the provisions regarding the general effects of marriage, the matrimonial property regime as well as divorces (Art. 14-17 EGBGB) no longer refer to the home state law of the husband. Instead, they followed a cascade approach, according to which different factors apply starting from the common home state law of both spouses leading to the principle of closest connection (so called "*Kegel'sche Leiter*"). Meanwhile some of these provisions have been replaced by EU law (Art. 17 EGBGB) or will be replaced soon (Art. 15 EGBGB).

IV. The aftermath of the Spaniard case II: controlling the application of foreign law by recourse to the Grundrechte

Since the 1986 reform, it has fallen to the judiciary to decide quite a number of cases in which violations of the Constitution called for the invocation of the public policy reservation. The following overview analyses important cases in different areas of the law. The survey will show that the frequency

---

47 Article 13(2) no. 3 EGBGB states: If under this [foreign] law, a requirement is not fulfilled, German law shall apply to that extent, if it is incompatible with the freedom of marriage to refuse the conclusion of the marriage; in particular, the previous marriage of a person engaged to be married shall not be held against him or her if it is nullified by a decision issued or recognised here or the spouse of the person engaged to be married has been declared dead. (translation by Juliana Moersdorf-Schulte, available at: http://www.gesetze-im-internet.de/englisch_bgbeg/ englisch_bgbeg.html).

with which the public policy exception has been successfully applied differs depending on the area of law. It further reveals that in some areas courts have recently tightened the grip by resorting to constitutional values.

1. Contract law

In the field of contract law, the *ordre public* reservation does not play a major role. The judiciary has found violations of public policy mainly in very special circumstances.

The BGH, for instance, ruled that claiming payment out of a directly enforceable suretyship violates public policy if the creditor (a bank) is controlled by a foreign state that has previously disowned the surety of all the shares it held in the chief debtor.[48] The BGH considered such a claim a dispossession without compensation of the surety, violating the constitutionally protected right of ownership of Art. 14 GG.[49]

Excessively high contractual penalties may also violate the *ordre public* reservation, allowing courts to reduce the penalties.[50] Foreign legal orders not containing provisions for objecting contractual obligations on the grounds of abuse of law may also contradict public policy.[51] Nowadays, the

---

48 BGH 28.4.1988 – IX ZR 127/87 – NJW 1988, 2173 (2174).

49 BGH 28.4.1988 – IX ZR 127/87 – NJW 1988, 2173 (2175). For details on the question of whether foreign surety law is compatible with public policy if the foreign law imposes an excessively heavy financial burden on the surety see Michael Stürner, in: Christine Budzikiewicz, Marc-Philippe Weller and Wolfgang Wurmnest (eds), *BeckOGK* (March 2018), Art. 21 Rom I VO para. 60 et seq.

50 This finding is commonly traced back to OLG Hamburg 23.12.1902 – II. ZS – summarised in OLGE 6 (1903), 231; see Rupert Doehner, in: Rainer Hüßtege and Heinz-Peter Mansel (eds), *NomosKommentar BGB* (2nd Edition, 2015), Art. 21 Rom I VO para. 12; Gerhard Hohloch, in: Harm-Peter Westermann and Georg Maier-Reimer (eds), *Erman BGB* (15th Edition, 2017), Art. 21 Rom I VO para. 5; Dieter Martiny, in: Jan von Hein (ed), *Münchener Kommentar BGB* (7th Edition, 2018), Art. 21 Rom I VO para. 4; Michael Stürner, in: Christine Budzikiewicz, Marc-Philippe Weller and Wolfgang Wurmnest (eds), *BeckOGK* (March 2018), Art. 21 Rom I VO para. 56.

51 LG Frankfurt 11.12.1979 – 3/10 O 123/79 – NJW 1981, 56 (58); Rupert Doehner, in: Rainer Hüßtege and Heinz-Peter Mansel (eds), *NomosKommentar BGB* (2nd Edition, 2015), Art. 21 Rom II VO para. 12; Gerhard Hohloch, in: Harm Peter Westermann and Georg Maier-Reimer (eds), *Erman BGB* (15th Edition, 2017), Art. 21 Rom I VO para. 5; Dieter Martiny, in: Jan von Hein (ed),

public policy reservation for most contractual obligations is found in Art. 21 Rome I Regulation, which has superseded Art. 6 EGBGB in the scope of application of the Rome I Regulation.[52]

2. Tort law

In tort law, the impact of the public policy reservation has been a little larger but not of great importance. There is a wide consensus that punitive damages (U.S. style) might violate German public policy.[53]

Accordingly, the BGH has, in 1992, declined the possibility of recognising punitive damages awarded in an American judgment to a claimant who had suffered sexual abuse and battery by the tortfeasor.[54] According to the BGH, the general yardstick of German law is the principle of adequate compensation, and the aim of punishment of the tortfeasor is a matter to be dealt with by criminal law. The recognition and enforcement of punitive damages

Münchener Kommentar BGB (7th Edition, 2018), Art. 21 Rom I VO para. 4; Michael Stürner, in: Christine Budzikiewicz, Marc-Philippe Weller and Wolfgang Wurmnest (eds), *BeckOGK* (March 2018), Art. 21 Rom I VO para. 47; Karsten Thorn, in: Peter Bassenge, Jürgen Ellenberger, Christian Grüneberg et al. (eds), *Palandt BGB* (77th Edition, 2018), Art. 21 Rom I VO para. 5.

52 Rupert Doehner, in: Rainer Hüßtege and Heinz-Peter Mansel (eds), *NomosKommentar BGB* (2nd Edition, 2015), Art. 21 Rom I VO para. 12; Gerhard Hohloch, in: Harm-Peter Westermann and Georg Maier-Reimer (eds), *Erman BGB* (15th Edition, 2017), Art. 21 Rom I VO para. 5.

53 Matteo Fornasier, in: Christine Budzikiewicz, Marc-Philippe Weller and Wolfgang Wurmnest (eds), *BeckOGK* (March 2018), Art. 40 EGBGB para. 144; Gerhard Hohloch, in: Harm-Peter Westermann and Georg Maier-Reimer (eds), *Erman BGB* (15th Edition, 2017), Art. 26 Rom II VO para 7; Dominique Jakob and Peter Picht, in: Thomas Rauscher (ed), *Europäisches Zivilprozessrecht und Kollisionsrecht Kommentar* (4th Edition, 2016), Art. 26 Rom II VO para. 24; Abbo Junker, in: Jan von Hein (ed), *Münchener Kommentar BGB* (7th Edition, 2018), Art. 26 Rom II VO para. 25; Michael Stürner, in Christine Budzikiewicz, Marc-Philippe Weller and Wolfgang Wurmnest (eds), *BeckOGK* (March 2018), Art. 26 Rom II VO para. 44 and 46; Karsten Thorn, in: Peter Bassenge, Jürgen Ellenberger, Christian Grüneberg et al. (eds), *Palandt BGB* (77th Edition, 2018), Art. 26 Rom II VO para. 2 et seq., all referring to the judiciary practice under Art. 6 EGBGB before the enactment of the Rome II Regulation.

54 BGH 4.6.1992 – IX ZR 149/91 – NJW 1992, 3096 (3103). On the prerequisites of recognition and enforcement of money judgments from States outside the European judicial area in Germany see Wolfgang Wurmnest, 23 (2005) *Berkeley Journal of International Law (Berk. J. Int'l Law)*, 175 et seq.

awards bare the danger of circumventing the procedural protection of defendants under criminal law and are thus incompatible with public policy.[55] Nevertheless, such damages are compatible with public policy according to the BGH as far as they do serve a purpose different from punishment, for example by awarding the claimant a general compensation for legal fees or losses that are hard to prove or quantify.[56] Regarding the application of a foreign law calling for non-compensatory damages, it is important to note that, in 1999, the German legislature introduced Art. 40(3) nos. 1 and 2 EGBGB with the intention of preventing German courts from awarding punitive and multiple damages.[57] This provision bars damage claims under foreign tort law as far as they serve a purpose other than compensating the plaintiff for losses suffered.[58] Today, Art. 40(3) EGBGB (and also Art. 6 EGBGB) are mostly superseded by the Rome II Regulation as far as delictual obligations in civil and commercial matters are concerned.[59] Although the Rome II Regulation takes a softer stance towards non-compensatory damages[60] as some EU Member States as well as EU law permit non-compensatory damages, many authors argue that U.S. style punitive damages remain incompatible with German public policy.[61] Other European jurisdiction, however, take a much softer stance towards such damages and a dis-

---

55 BGH 4.6.1992 – IX ZR 149/91 – NJW 1992, 3096 (3103).

56 BGH 4.6.1992 – IX ZR 149/91– NJW 1992, 3096 (3103).

57 Regierungsbegründung zum Gesetz zum Internationalen Privatrecht für außervertragliche Schuldverhältnisse und für Sachen, BT-Drucksache 14/343 of 1 February 1999, 12.

58 Matteo Fornasier, in: Christine Budzikiewicz, Marc-Philippe Weller and Wolfgang Wurmnest (eds), *BeckOGK* (March 2018), Art. 40 EGBGB para. 136.

59 Michael Stürner, in: Christine Budzikiewicz, Marc-Philippe Weller and Wolfgang Wurmnest (eds), *BeckOGK* (March 2018), Art. 6 EGBGB para. 322.

60 See Angelika Fuchs, in: Peter Huber (ed), *Rome II Regulation - Pocket commentary* (2011), Art. 26 Rome II para. 28.

61 Gerhard Hohloch, in: Harm Peter Westermann and Georg Maier-Reimer (eds), *Erman BGB* (15th Edition, 2017), Art. 26 Rom II VO para. 7; Dominique Jakob and Peter Picht, in: Thomas Rauscher (ed), *Europäisches Zivilprozessrecht und Kollisionsrecht Kommentar* (4th Edition, 2016), Art. 26 Rom II VO para. 24; Abbo Junker, in: Jan von Hein (ed), *Münchener Kommentar BGB* (7th Edition, 2018), Art. 26 Rom II VO para. 25; Michael Stürner, in: Christine Budzikiewicz, Marc-Philippe Weller and Wolfgang Wurmnest (eds), *BeckOGK* (March 2018), Art. 26 Rom II VO para. 44 and 46; Art. 26 Rom II VO para. 2 et seq; Jan von Hein, in: Gralf–Peter Calliess (ed), *Rome Regulations Commentary* (2nd Edition, 2015), Art. 26 Rome II Regulation para. 20.

cussion has emerged as to what extent the Rome II Regulation may influence national concepts of public policy.[62] Without touching upon this debate, it is apparent that especially European private law (but also German law) has in some areas of law strongly embraced the idea that claims for damages can also serve preventive purposes.[63] It is therefore not possible to reject *per se* the application of foreign rules awarding damages that (from a traditional perspective) go beyond mere compensation for public policy reasons. Against this background it is very doubtful that the 1992 judgment of the BGH on recognition and enforcement of punitive damages would be handed down as straightforwardly today as it was done nearly 30 years ago.[64]

3. Family law

In this area of law, *ordre public* violations have been much more frequent. German courts have found public policy violations in numerous cases where foreign laws were considered incompatible with constitutional values. The following will provide a short overview of the most important cases.

---

62 On this discussion see Thomas Ackermann, 'Antitrust Damages Actions under the Rome II Regulation', in: Mielle Bulterman, Leigh Hancher, Alison McDonnell et al. (eds), *Liber Amicorum Piet Jan Slot* (2009), 109 (118); Jan von Hein, 'Punitive Damages in European and Domestic Private International Law', in: Alexander Bruns and Masabumi Suzuki (eds), *Preventive Instruments of Social Governance* (2017), 143 (151 et seq.); Cedric Vanleenhove, *Punitive Damages in Private International Law* (2016), 80 et seq. (241).

63 For a detailed analysis of the European rules see Christian Heinze, *Schadensersatz im Unionsprivatrecht* (2017).

64 Astrid Stadler, in: Hans-Joachim Musielak and Wolfgang Voit (eds), *Zivilprozessordnung* (15th Edition, 2018), § 328 ZPO Rn. 25.

a) Validity of foreign marriages

Various courts have found a number of different minimum marriageable ages imposed by foreign marriage laws incompatible with national values.[65] Most of the German judiciary seems to have conceded that a marriageable age of 14 years or younger violates public policy, as sexual intercourse of any sort with minors below the age of 14 years is a criminal offence pursuant to § 176 of the German Criminal Code.[66] The intended protection of these minors has to apply to international cases, as it safeguards their right to physical integrity protected by Art. 2(2) GG.[67] Very recently, the German legislature has, however, introduced a new form of reservation clause in Art. 13(3) EGBGB for minimum marriageable ages,[68] which will alter the existing findings of the judiciary. Art. 13(3) no. 1 EGBGB now declares all marriages concluded after a certain point of time null and void under German law if one of the parties has not reached the age of 16 at the time of marriage – irrespective of the law applicable and the facts of the case. Further, any marriage shall be annulled under German law, if one of the parties has reached the age of 16 but not 18 at the time of marriage, Art. 13(3) no. 2 EGBGB. This new piece of legislation has already led to controversies and many questions regarding the application of these new reservation clauses and their constitutionality remain unanswered for now.[69]

---

65 AG Hannover 7.1.2002 – 616 F 7355/00 – BeckRS 2002, 1869 (15 years); AG Offenbach 30.10.2009 – 314 F 1132/09 – BeckRS 2010, 23013 (16 years); declining a violation at the age 15: KG 7.6.1989 – 18 U 2625/88 – BeckRS 1989, 2838.

66 OLG Köln 4.9.1996 – 16 Wx 181/96 – NJWE-FER 1997, 55 (Iranian law: 10 years); KG 21. 11. 2011 – 1 W 79/11 – FamRZ 2012, 1495 (Lebanese law: 14 years); leaving the question of a public policy violation unanswered OLG Bamberg 12.5.2016 – 2 UF 58/16 – BeckRS 2016, 09621: appeal to the BGH pending: XII ZB 292/16.

67 Jennifer Antomo, *Neue Juristische Wochenschrift (NJW)* 2016, 3558 (3561 et seq.); Michael Stürner, in: Christine Budzikiewicz, Marc-Philippe Weller and Wolfgang Wurmnest (eds), *BeckOGK* (March 2018), Art. 6 EGBGB para. 344; Jan von Hein, in: Jan von Hein (ed), *Münchener Kommentar BGB* (7th Edition, 2018), Art. 6 EGBGB para. 259.

68 Gesetz zur Bekämpfung von Kinderehen of 17 July 2017, BGBl. I, 2429 et seq.

69 See for more details: Jennifer Antomo, 50 (2017) *Zeitschrift für Rechtspolitik (ZRP)*, 79 (81 et seq.); Christian Friedrich Majer, *Neue Zeitschrift für Familienrecht (NZFam)* 2017, 537 (540 et seq.); Lena-Maria Möller and Nadjma Yassari, *Kritische Justiz (KJ)* 2017, 269 et seq. The authors criticise especially the fact

Apart from the minimum marriageable age, different impediments to marriage imposed by foreign laws have been considered to violate public policy. The BGH found a foreign law obstructing a marriage due to different religious affiliations of the engaged incompatible with constitutionally guaranteed legal principles.[70] The constitution guarantees equal access to civil duties, rights, and privileges of a general nature regardless of religious affiliation. This includes equal access to marriage. Foreign laws implementing such obstacles cannot be applied.[71]

Public policy has not only made courts disregard certain foreign impediments to marriage; it has also forced courts to restrict certain forms of marriages permissible under foreign law. Foreign marriage laws permitting polygamy, for example, have been disregarded where German authorities were to marry the parties and one partner was already married.[72] The special protection Art. 6 GG granted to the institution of marriage prohibits such unions in Germany. The recognition of polygamous marriages officiated abroad, on the other hand, does not violate national public policy.[73]

b) Divorce

The legal institute of divorce itself has experienced an increase in protection by the German judiciary over the last few decades. Initially, the BGH found that foreign laws not providing any means of divorce accorded with German values and principles.[74] A more recent decision of the BGH shows that the court has changed its view on that matter and that it is willing to protect access to divorce before German courts.[75] The court held foreign laws treating marriage as inseparable for life incompatible with the freedom of marriage, Art. 6 GG, and thus a public policy violation.[76]

---

that marriages are declared null and void without regarding the circumstances of each case.

70 BGH 12. 5. 1971 – IV AR (Vz) 38/70 – NJW 1971, 1519.

71 BGH 12. 5. 1971 – IV AR (Vz) 38/70 – NJW 1971, 1519 (1521).

72 BVerwG 30.4.1985 – 1 C 33/81 – NJW 1985, 2097.

73 Michael Stürner, in: Christine Budzikiewicz, Marc-Philippe Weller and Wolfgang Wurmnest (eds), *BeckOGK* (March 2018), Art. 6 EGBGB para. 357.

74 BGH 12.2.1964 – IV AR (Vz) 39/63 – NJW 1964, 976; BGH 29.4.1964 – IV ZR 93/63 – NJW 1964, 2013.

75 BGH 11.10.2006 – XII ZR 79/04 – NJW-RR 2007, 145 (148 et seq.).

76 BGH 11.10.2006 – XII ZR 79/04 – NJW-RR 2007, 145 (149).

Foreign laws providing the possibility of "unilateral" divorce for one spouse only (usually the husband, whereas the wife can demand a divorce only on certain grounds) have also been problematic on public policy grounds. Such divorces are allowed, for example, in countries whose divorce laws are based on the tradition of Islamic law (so-called "ṭalaq divorces"). Courts have found such divorces adverse to the *ordre public* in cases in which their application led to results discriminating against women and thus violating Art 3 GG.[77] However, it is not the divorce as such that is held incompatible with national values and principles. Rather, the BGH has found divorce rules in line with public policy whenever applying these rules did not discriminate against the wife – for example because the wife agreed to the divorce[78] – or because the divorce was permissible under the law of the forum as well.[79]

c) Custody

In this area, for example, the laws of countries with strict distribution of custody according to gender and religion have been prone to violate public policy. For example, Courts have disregarded foreign rules that made transferring any kind of custody dependant on religious affiliation with Islam.[80]

---

77 OLG Frankfurt a. M. 18.1.2001 – 1 UF 251/00 – BeckRS 2001, 30156129; OLG Hamm 11.10.2010 – 6 UF 59/10 – BeckRS 2011, 18163 (public policy violation because wife had no possibility of divorcing her husband). BayObLG 29.11.1982 – BReg. 1 Z 54/82 – BayObLGZ 1982, 389; OLG Stuttgart 3.12.1998 – 17 VA 6/98 – BeckRS 1998, 13578 (public policy violation because the wife had no knowledge of her husband's unilateral divorce intent and did not accept the divorce afterwards). See for further details: Michael Stürner, in: Christine Budzikiewicz, Marc-Philippe Weller and Wolfgang Wurmnest (eds), *BeckOGK* (March 2018), Art. 6 EGBGB para. 373.

78 BGH 6.10.2004 – XII ZR 225/01 – NJW-RR 2005, 81 (84).

79 BGH 6.10.2004 – XII ZR 225/01 – NJW-RR 2005, 81 (84); similarly: OLG Frankfurt a. M. 11.5.2009 – 5 WF 66/09 – BeckRS 2009, 2441; Tobias Helms, *Zeitschrift für das gesamte Familienrecht (FamRZ)* 2011, 1765 (1772) with further references.

80 OLG Düsseldorf 23.3.1993 – 6 UF 4/92, NJW-RR 1994, 7; OLG Hamm 8.2.1990 – 2 UF 216/89, BeckRS 2010, 26684; Recently most Islamic countries have introduced the principle of the best interests of the child in their custody rules, see for a comparative analysis the contributions in Nadjma Yassari, Lena-

This dependency on religious belief has been considered incompatible with the discrimination prohibition in Art. 3 GG. Furthermore, foreign legal orders transferring custody of minors to one parent, e.g. the father, without considering the minor's well-being violate public policy.[81] The BGH concluded that neglecting the child's well-being breaches its constitutionally guaranteed rights of physical integrity as well as free development of the personality protected by Art. 1 and 2 GG.[82]

4. Succession law

In the area of succession law, the issue of public policy has only recently become of importance,[83] as the reported judgments confirming violations of public policy were essentially handed down in the last 10 years.[84] Problems have arisen particularly regarding foreign laws that, based on religious provisions, contained discriminatory provisions on the allocation of the inheritance.[85]

In 2010, the OLG Frankfurt a.M. disregarded Egyptian succession law because its application resulted in an unequal treatment of men and women.[86] It contained a provision in terms of which wives inherited less

---

Maria Möller and Imen Gallala-Arndt (eds), *Parental Care and the Best Interests of the Child in Muslim Countries* (2017).

81 BGH 14.10.1992 – XII ZB 18/92 – NJW 1993, 848.

82 BGH 14.10.1992 – XII ZB 18/92 – NJW 1993, 848 (850).

83 See Gerhard Hohloch, 'Internationales Erbrecht und Ordre public – Stand, Bedeutung und Perspektiven', in: Rolf Stürner, Hiroyuki Matsumoto, Wolfgang Lüke and Masahisa Deguchi (eds), *Festschrift für Dieter Leipold zum 70. Geburtstag* (2009), 997 et seq.

84 OLG Hamm 28.2.2005 – 15 W 117/04 – ZEV 2005, 436 (439); OLG Düsseldorf 19.12.2008 – 3 Wx 51/08 – NJW-RR 2009, 732; OLG Frankfurt a. M. 10.5. 2010 – 20 W 4/10 – ZEV 2011, 135; OLG München 16.4.2012 – 31 Wx 45/12 – NJW-RR 2012, 1096.

85 Anatol Dutta, in: Jan von Hein (ed), *Münchener Kommentar BGB* (7th Edition, 2018), Art. 35 EuErbVO para. 9; Dirk Looschelders, in: Rainer Hüßtege and Heinz-Peter Mansel (eds), *NomosKommentar BGB* (2nd Edition, 2015), Art. 35 EuErbVO para. 19; Michael Stürner, in: Christine Budzikiewicz, Marc-Philippe Weller and Wolfgang Wurmnest (eds), *BeckOGK* (March 2018), Art. 6 EGBGB para. 404.

86 OLG Frankfurt a. M. 10.5. 2010 – 20 W 4/10 – ZEV 2011, 135. Criticising this decision: Thomas Rauscher and Steffen Pabst, *Neue Juristische Wochenschrift (NJW)* 2011, 3547 (3350).

than husbands on the death of their spouse. In 2012, the OLG München ruled similarly regarding Iranian succession law, which equally discriminated against women.[87] Both court decisions show that the breach of gender equality subject to the protection of Art. 3 GG may violate the *ordre public*. Other decisions show that courts have also rejected foreign succession laws excluding family members from the inheritance because they had different religious beliefs from the deceased.[88] Such a discrimination is adverse to Art. 3(3) GG and was considered incompatible with public policy.

5. Analysis

The overview reveals significant differences with regard to the frequency of public policy violations in the areas of the law that we have adumbrated. While violations in the areas of family and succession law have been relatively numerous, only very few cases concern the application of foreign contract and tort law. In the following we try to explain this imbalance.

a) Special connecting factors

One reason for the imbalanced application can be found in the varying usage of special connecting factors in the different areas of private international law.

The rules on international contract and tort law provide special connecting factors for overriding mandatory provisions that lead to the application of the law of the forum (Art. 9 Rome I Regulation and Art. 16 Rome II Regulation). These rules ensure that important provisions of German law are enforced regardless of the law that otherwise applies. Thus, the choice of law rules already respect a forum's sensitivity to certain areas of law, making recourse to public policy largely unnecessary.[89] The protection granted by these rules goes further than the protection by public policy as

87 OLG München 16.4.2012 – 31 Wx 45/12 – NJW-RR 2012, 1096.

88 OLG Hamm 28.2.2005 – 15 W 117/04 – ZEV 2005, 436 (439); OLG Düsseldorf 19.12.2008 – 3 Wx 51/08 – NJW-RR 2009, 732; OLG Frankfurt a. M. 10.5.2010 – 20 W 4/10 – ZEV 2011, 135.

89 Christian von Bar and Peter Mankowski, *Internationales Privatrecht* (2nd Edition, 2003) Vol. 1, § 7 para. 278.

the application of mandatory overriding provisions does not depend on a result control. In addition, the multitude of special connecting factors ensures that certain standards and values are maintained and not circumvented by the application of a foreign, less protective rule, thereby making recourse to public policy largely obsolete.[90]

By contrast, the situation in family and succession law is somewhat different. There are no rules on overriding mandatory provisions. Therefore, recourse to public policy is more important for protecting fundamental German values.

b) Cultural differences and religious influences

Moreover, it seems that in contract and tort law there is – despite significant differences – more agreement on certain basic principles around the globe than in the fields of family and succession law that are shaped by very different cultural and religious influences. Therefore, public policy violations are more likely especially when courts protect the principle of access to marriage, as partly protected by Art. 6 GG, or the principle of non-discrimination, as enshrined in Art. 3 GG, with heightened scrutiny. An early example of this development was the extension of the *ordre public* in the area of marriage law leading to the increased possibility of fiancés being able to get married as a consequence of the Federal Constitutional Court's Spaniard ruling (see supra section II.). Later foreign divorce laws came under closer scrutiny and the possibility of the spouses to obtain a divorce was strengthened (see supra section III.). Another example of this trend may be found in the area of succession law where most judgements finding public policy violations are of recent origin.[91] While courts have been reluctant to interfere with foreign succession law in the past, the decisions show that courts have lately become more willing to do so. For example, the OLG Hamm found provisions of Iranian succession law that discriminated against

90 Christian von Bar and Peter Mankowski, *Internationales Privatrecht* (2nd Edition, 2003) Vol. 1, § 7 para. 278; Moritz Renner, in: Gralf–Peter Calliess (ed), *Rome Regulations Commentary* (2nd Edition, 2015), Art. 9 Rome I Regulation para. 1.

91 The oldest one stems from 2005: OLG Hamm 28.2.2005 – 15 W 117/04 – ZEV 2005, 436 (439).

women to be compatible with public policy back in 1992.[92] Only a few years later, courts have found many discriminatory provisions of religiously inspired foreign succession rules incompatible with the public policy of the forum.[93] In sum, enforcing constitutional values has led the German judiciary to find public policy violations more readily, making rules differing from German law less likely to be tolerated. Naturally, this increases the frequency of public policy violations in the areas of family and succession law.

V. The Europeanisation of the public policy doctrine

1. Defining the content of the public policy: National or European concept

The *ordre public* is also a key element of the European conflict-of-law rules. All European regulations on private international law allow courts to disregard foreign law if an application is contrary to the forum's public policy. The question arises whether the European reservation clauses are to be interpreted according to autonomous European standards. A closer look at the wording of the provisions reveals that this cannot be the case. All of the European choice-of-law Regulations state that the application of foreign law is to be denied "if such application is manifestly incompatible with the public policy (*ordre public*) [...] *of the forum*".[94] The wording emphasising the values of the forum shows that, in general, public policy is still defined

92 OLG Hamm 29.4.1992 – 15 W 114/91 – IPRax 1994, 49 (53).

93 OLG Hamm 28.2.2005 – 15 W 117/04 – ZEV 2005, 436 (439); OLG Frankfurt a. M. 10.5. 2010 – 20 W 4/10 – ZEV 2011, 135; OLG München 16.4.2012 – 31 Wx 45/12 – NJW-RR 2012, 1096; similarly: OLG Düsseldorf 19.12.2008 – 3 Wx 51/08 – NJW-RR 2009, 732. These cases concerned the application of foreign laws inspired by "Islamic law" (which is of course a very heterogenic source of law). On the succession law in Egypt, Tunisia and Morocco, see Andreas Pattar, *Islamisch inspiriertes Erbrecht und deutscher Ordre public* (2007), 281 et seq.

94 Art. 21 Rome I Regulation, Art. 26 Rome II Regulation, Art. 12 Rome III Regulation, Art. 35 Succession Regulation (emphasis added).

by national, not European values. As a national concept, it preserves and protects the values of the forum, which may differ across Europe.[95]

The observation that the *ordre public* is still governed by national values does not mean, however, that its content may not be shaped by recourse to European values. European law is an integral part of each Member State's legal system and penetrates the legal orders of its Member States.[96] This influence of European law has also extended to the field of public policy, enriching formerly purely national doctrines.[97] By supplementing the existing national values, public policy now also serves in the protection of European values and standards incorporated into German law.[98] The following four sources are the primary sources of the European values protected by national courts throughout Europe:[99] The Charter of Fundamental Rights of the European Union,[100] the European Convention on Human Rights

95 Dieter Martiny, 'Die Zukunft des europäischen ordre public im Internationalen Privat- und Zivilverfahrensrecht', in: Michael Coester, Dieter Martiny, Karl August von Sachsen Gessaphe (eds), *Privatrecht in Europa: Vielfalt, Kollision, Kooperation. Festschrift für Hans Jürgen Sonnenberger zum 70. Geburtstag* (2004), 523 (531 et seq.); Götz Schulze, in: Rainer Hüßtege and Heinz-Peter Mansel (eds), *NomosKommentar BGB* (2nd Edition, 2015), Art. 26 Rom II VO para. 2; Michael Stürner, in: Christine Budzikiewicz, Marc-Philippe Weller and Wolfgang Wurmnest (eds), *BeckOGK* (March 2018), Art. 21 Rom I VO para. 19; Susanne Gössl, in: Christine Budzikiewicz, Marc-Philippe Weller and Wolfgang Wurmnest, *BeckOGK* (December 2017), Art.12 Rom III VO para. 3.

96 Pietro Franzina, in: Ulrich Magnus and Peter Mankowski (eds), *European Commentaries of Private International Law* (2015), Art. 21 Rome I Regulation para. 28.

97 Michael Stürner, 'Europäisierung des (Kollisions-)Rechts und nationaler ordre public', in: Herbert Kronke and Karsten Thorn (eds), *Grenzen überwinden – Prinzipien bewahren. Festschrift für Bernd von Hoffmann zum 70. Geburtstag* (2011), 463 (464).

98 Pietro Franzina, in: Ulrich Magnus and Peter Mankowski (eds), *European Commentaries of Private International Law* (2015), Art. 21 Rome I Regulation para. 28; Christian von Bar and Peter Mankowski, *Internationales Privatrecht* (2nd Edition, 2003) Vol. 1, § 7 para. 271.

99 See Wolfgang Wurmnest, 'Ordre Public (Public Policy)', in: Stefan Leible (ed), *General Principles of European Private International Law* (2016), § 14.03 [B], 316.

100 Cf. Recital 58 of the Succession Regulation; Recital 54 Matrimonial Property Regulation.

(ECHR),[101] the four fundamental freedoms of the EU[102] and the general legal principles developed by the Court of Justice of the European Union (ECJ).[103] In addition, the contours of European private law shape the reach of the public policy reservation.

Simultaneously, European values also set boundaries to the application of the *ordre public*. Disregarding foreign law may not contravene European law. The content of national public policy is not excluded from the scrutiny of European law; invoking the public policy exception must always be in line with European provisions.[104] The steadily increasing number of European private law and choice of law rules are likely to advance the influence of European values on the concept of public policy.[105] Limiting the application of different national *ordre public* reservations, this corrective function of the European influence will steadily increase the consistency of public policy applications by national courts. In the long term, there will be an

---

101 Dieter Martiny, 'Die Zukunft des europäischen ordre public im Internationalen Privat- und Zivilverfahrensrecht', in: Michael Coester, Dieter Martiny, Karl August von Sachsen Gessaphe (eds), *Privatrecht in Europa: Vielfalt, Kollision, Kooperation. Festschrift für Hans Jürgen Sonnenberger zum 70. Geburtstag* (2004), 523 (533 et seq.); Karsten Thorn, in: Peter Bassenge, Jürgen Ellenberger, Christian Grüneberg et al. (eds), *Palandt BGB* (77th Edition 2018), Art. 21 Rom I VO para. 4. Pursuant to Art. 6(3) of the EU Treaty, the fundamental rights, as guaranteed by the ECHR and as they result from the constitutional traditions common to the Member States, are regarded as general principles of EU law.

102 Stefan Leible and Matthias Lehmann, *Recht der Internationalen Wirtschaft (RIW)* 2007, 721 (734) (regarding the Rome II Regulation); Götz Schulze, in: Rainer Hüßtege and Heinz-Peter Mansel (eds), *NomosKommentar BGB* (2nd Edition, 2015), Art. 26 Rom II VO para 2; Karsten Thorn, in: Peter Bassenge, Jürgen Ellenberger, Christian Grüneberg et al. (eds), *Palandt BGB* (77th Edition, 2018), Art. 21 Rom I VO para. 4.

103 Erik Jayme, *Ein internationales Privatrecht für Europa* (1991), 37. For further European influences, see Michael Stürner, 'Europäisierung des (Kollisions-) Rechts und nationaler ordre public', in: Herbert Kronke and Karsten Thorn (eds), *Grenzen überwinden – Prinzipien bewahren. Festschrift für Bernd von Hoffmann zum 70. Geburtstag* (2011), 463 (464 et seq.).

104 Christian von Bar and Peter Mankowski, *Internationales Privatrecht* (2nd Edition, 2003) Vol. 1, § 7 para. 272.

105 For details see Wolfgang Wurmnest, 'Ordre Public (Public Policy)', in: Stefan Leible (ed), *General Principles of European Private International Law* (2016), § 14.03 [B], 317 et seq.

ever-increasing overlap between European values and national public policy doctrines.[106] So for example, where Member State introduces punitive damages when transposing a European directive calling for dissuasive sanctions to safeguard Community rights, German courts cannot reject the application of these rules even though – from a traditional national perspective – they are not in line with principles of German law (see supra section IV. 2.), as setting aside the foreign rules would impair the effective enforcement of Community law.[107]

In short, national courts must disregard foreign laws violating European values, even if the result of the foreign law accords with the traditional concept of national public policy. Correspondingly, courts wishing to decline the application of foreign law on the grounds of national public policy must verify if doing so accords with European law. Hence, the primacy of European law may force a national court to apply the law of another EU state contrary to its national values.[108]

2. Art. 10 Rome III Regulation: European paternalism

European law has not only given the *ordre public* a "European dress".[109] It is also capable of overriding fundamental concepts of private international law, as a closer look at Art. 10 Rome III Regulation reveals. This special reservation clause for divorce cases sits beside the "general" (and traditional) public policy reservation in Art. 12 Rome III Regulation. Art. 10

---

106 Michael Stürner, 'Europäisierung des (Kollisions-)Rechts und nationaler ordre public', in: Herbert Kronke and Karsten Thorn (eds), *Grenzen überwinden - Prinzipien bewahren. Festschrift für Bernd von Hoffmann zum 70. Geburtstag* (2011), 463 (472).

107 Jan von Hein, 'Punitive Damages in European and Domestic Private International Law', in: Alexander Bruns and Masabumi Suzuki (eds), *Preventive Instruments of Social Governance* (2017), 143 (156).

108 For example Recital 58 of the Succession Regulation states that recourse to public policy to disregard or alter a foreign law of a Member State is impermissible "when doing so would be contrary to the Charter of Fundamental Rights of the European Union, and in particular Article 21 thereof, which prohibits all forms of discrimination."

109 Stefan Leible, *Rom I und Rom II: Neue Perspektiven im europäischen Kollisionsrecht* (2009), 72 (public policy is "europäisch aufgeladen"); Christian von Bar and Peter Mankowski, *Internationales Privatrecht* (2nd Edition, 2003) Vol. 1, § 7 para. 271 (public policy is "europäisch angereichert").

Rome III states: "Where the law applicable pursuant to Article 5 or Article 8 makes no provision for divorce or does not grant one of the spouses equal access to divorce or legal separation on grounds of their sex, the law of the forum shall apply." This special reservation clause demands the application of the law of the forum in two circumstances: First, the law of the forum applies if the foreign law applicable does not contain any provisions for divorce. Second, the law of the forum must also be applied if the possibility of becoming divorced under the foreign law depends on the sex of the spouse.

The first alternative of Art. 10 Rome III Regulation was enacted with Maltese law in mind,[110] which did not provide any divorce provisions up until 1st October 2011.[111] Courts should not have been compelled to refuse to divorce the spouses just because Maltese law was applicable.[112] The second example seeks to prevent any gender based discrimination against a spouse willing to file for divorce.[113] Such a discrimination is particularly common not only in some jurisdictions which have a divorce law based on

110 Maarit Jänterä-Jareborg, 'Jurisdiction and Applicable Law in Cross-Border Divorce Cases in Europe', in: Jürgen Basedow, Harald Baum and Yuko Nishitani (eds), *Japanese and European Private International Law in Comparative Perspective* (2008), 317 (338).

111 After a referendum that took place after the Rom III Regulation was adopted, Malta has enacted rules on divorce. For details on the new divorce law see Peter Pietsch, *Zeitschrift für das gesamte Familienrecht (FamRZ)* 2012, 426 et seq.

112 Christine Budzikiewicz, in: Rainer Hüßtege and Heinz-Peter Mansel (eds), *NomosKommentar BGB* (2nd Edition, 2015), Art. 10 Rom III VO para. 2; Maarit Jänterä-Jareborg, 'Jurisdiction and Applicable Law in Cross-Border Divorce Cases in Europe', in: Jürgen Basedow, Harald Baum and Yuko Nishitani (eds), *Japanese and European Private International Law in Comparative Perspective* (2008), 317 (338); Tobias Helms, *Zeitschrift für das gesamte Familienrecht (FamRZ)* 2011, 1765 (1771).

113 Christine Budzikiewicz, in: Rainer Hüßtege and Heinz-Peter Mansel (eds), *NomosKommentar BGB* (2nd Edition, 2015), Art. 10 Rom III VO para. 3; Proposal for a Council Regulation (EU) implementing enhanced cooperation in the area of the law applicable to divorce and legal separation of 24 March 2010, COM (2010) 105 final, 8 (Comment on Art. 5).

Islamic tradition[114] but under Jewish "get" divorce law as well,[115] as both systems differentiate the grounds for divorce according to the sex of the spouses.

As much as the intent of Art. 10 Rome III Regulation is clear, the modalities of its application are not. Whereas Art. 12 Rome III Regulation follows the traditional approach of public policy only examining the result of the application of a foreign rule (see supra section I.), and not the foreign rule itself, the wording of Art. 10 Rome III Regulation stipulates just that.[116] According to its wording, disregarding a foreign law does not depend on the result being unacceptable to the forum. The recitals also contain no limitation of the reservation clause to unacceptable results of foreign law.[117] Hence, Art. 10 Rome III Regulation seems to allow courts to refuse the application of foreign law as soon as a foreign rule is incompatible with the protected values – i.e. gender-neutral divorce provisions.[118] The legislative history of the rule also favours this understanding: The introduction of Art. 10 Rome III Regulation can be traced back to some Member States exercising pressure on the legislative process. Those states wanted to "fend off"

114 Marc Philippe Weller, Irene Hauber and Alix Schulz, *Praxis des Internationalen Privat- und Verfahrensrechts (IPRax)* 2016, 123 (124); Christine Budzikiewicz, in: Rainer Hüßtege and Heinz-Peter Mansel (eds), *NomosKommentar BGB* (2nd Edition, 2015), Art. 10 Rom III VO para. 4. See section IV. 3. b) for details on talaq divorces.

115 Eva Lein, in: Gralf–Peter Calliess (ed), *Rome Regulations Commentary* (2nd Edition, 2015), Art. 10 Rome III Regulation para. 26 et seq. with further references; for details on the Jewish "get" law see Christoph Herfarth, *Die Scheidung nach jüdischem Recht im internationalen Zivilverfahrensrecht* (2000), 22 et seq.; Walter Homalka, *Das jüdische Eherecht* (2009), 113 et seq.; Marc Philippe Weller, Irene Hauber and Alix Schulz, *Praxis des Internationalen Privat- und Verfahrensrechts (IPRax)* 2016, 123 (124 et seq.).

116 Marc Philippe Weller, Irene Hauber and Alix Schulz, *Praxis des Internationalen Privat- und Verfahrensrechts (IPRax)* 2016, 123 (127); Peter Winkler von Mohrenfels, 'Art. 10 Rom III-VO: Kollisionsrechtliche Eingriffsnorm oder Spezialfall des ordre public?', in: Normann Witzleb, Reinhard Ellger, Peter Mankowski, Hanno Merkt and Oliver Remien (eds), *Festschrift für Dieter Martiny zum 70. Geburtstag* (2014), 595 (599).

117 See recital 24 Rome III Regulation. See also the opinion of the advocate general Saugmandsgaard Øe, C-372/16, 14.9.2017, *Soha Sahyouni v. Raja Mamisch*, ECLI:EU:C:2017:686, para. 74.

118 Marc Philippe Weller, Irene Hauber and Alix Schulz, *Praxis des Internationalen Privat- und Verfahrensrechts (IPRax)* 2016, 123 (129 et seq.).

sexually discriminatory rules of religious origin. Consequently, the application of the special reservation would be a lot broader than that of public policy.[119] Many scholars therefore argue that an abstract discrimination is sufficient to trigger the application of Art. 10 Rome III.[120] This conclusion was shared by the advocate general at the ECJ Saugmandsgaard Øe in his opinion he delivered on 9 September 2016 on the case *Soha Sahyouni v. Raja Mamisch.*[121]

However convincing the wording, systematic position[122] and legislative history may seem, these arguments cannot conceal the unwanted consequences of such an interpretation of Art. 10 Rome III Regulation. This is true especially for the more relevant case of unequal access to divorce on grounds of sex, protected by Art. 10 2nd alt. Rome III Regulation. Before the enactment of the Rome III regulation, German courts held that an Islamic "talaq divorce" does not violate German public policy if the wife agrees to the divorce.[123] An abstract control of foreign law would change this significantly. Art. 10 Rome III Regulation would bar courts from applying discriminatory foreign divorce laws regardless of whether the result is acceptable to the forum or not.

---

119 Marc Philippe Weller, Irene Hauber and Alix Schulz, *Praxis des Internationalen Privat- und Verfahrensrechts (IPRax)* 2016, 123 (127).

120 Marc Philippe Weller, Irene Hauber and Alix Schulz, *Praxis des Internationalen Privat- und Verfahrensrechts (IPRax)* 2016, 123 (129); Peter Winkler von Mohrenfels, 'Art. 10 Rom III-VO: Kollisionsrechtliche Eingriffsnorm oder Spezialfall des ordre public?', in: Normann Witzleb, Reinhard Ellger, Peter Mankowski, Hanno Merkt and Oliver Remien (eds), *Festschrift für Dieter Martiny zum 70. Geburtstag* (2014), 595 (599, 615).

121 Opinion of the advocate general Saugmandsgaard Øe, Case C-372/16, 14.9.2017, *Soha Sahyouni v. Raja Mamisch*, ECLI:EU:C:2017:686, para. 89. In its final judgement, the ECJ did not elaborate on this question. Instead, this question turned out to be irrelevant in the specific case as the ECJ found the Rome III Regulation inapplicable to private divorces in general, which was the main question asked, see ECJ, Case C-372/16, 20.12.2017, *Soha Sahyouni v. Raja Mamisch*, ECLI:EU:C:2017:988, para. 50.

122 If Art. 10 were to be understood as a special public policy provision, the general public policy clause of Art. 12 Rome III Regulation would completely absorb its scope of application, rendering it redundant, see Peter Winkler von Mohrenfels, *Zeitschrift für Vergleichende Rechtswissenschaft (ZVglRWiss)* 2016, 650 (658).

123 See IV) 3) b).

This approach is contrary to the established principles of private international law and violates the principle of international consistency of decision-making, the principle of closest connection and the assumption of general equality of all legal orders.[124] It also makes matters more difficult for the divorced spouses. A divorce effected under the law of an EU state might face more trouble being recognised and enforced in the spouses' home country.

Imposing an abstract result control does not make sense. Hence, the only sensible approach to Art. 10 Rome III Regulation is to interpret the rule in line with other public policy reservations and limit the application to a result control only.[125]

VI. The future of public policy

After focussing on various aspects that shaped the current public policy doctrine, it is now appropriate to try to evaluate the future of this *Vorbehaltsklausel*. Two aspects are important in this regard.

1. Diminishing importance

First of all, it seems clear that the importance of the public policy reservation will diminish. As shown above, the rules regarding mandatory overriding provisions of the forum and other special connecting factors have already limited the application of public policy in contract and tort law.[126] Special connecting factors have also been included in new European choice

---

124 Christine Budzikiewicz, in: Rainer Hüßtege and Heinz-Peter Mansel (eds), *NomosKommentar BGB* (2nd Edition, 2015), Art. 10 Rom III VO para. 27; Tobias Helms, *Zeitschrift für das gesamte Familienrecht (FamRZ)* 2011, 1765 (1772); Lena-Maria Möller, *Journal of Private International Law (JPrivIntL)* 2014, 461 et seq.

125 Christine Budzikiewicz, in: Rainer Hüßtege and Heinz-Peter Mansel (eds), *NomosKommentar BGB* (2nd Edition, 2015), Art. 10 Rom III VO para. 27; Tobias Helms, *Zeitschrift für das gesamte Familienrecht (FamRZ)* 2011, 1765 (1772); Eva Lein, in: Gralf–Peter Calliess (ed), *Rome Regulations Commentary* (2nd Edition, 2015), Art. 10 Rome III Regulation para. 27.

126 See the analysis in section IV. 5. a).

of law rules, like Art. 30 of the Matrimonial Property Regime Regulation[127] and Art. 30 of the Property Consequences of Registered Partnerships Regulation.[128] More special connecting factors will limit the necessity of public policy control.

Moreover, in the fields of succession and family law, EU Regulations replacing nationality as the principal connecting factor with habitual residence will further limit the application of the *ordre public* since the rules of jurisdiction support the alignment of forum and *ius* to a large extent. A glimpse at some of the recently adopted European Regulations may serve to demonstrate this point.

Art. 21(2) Succession Regulation determines that the law of the State in which the deceased had his or her habitual residence governs all aspects of the succession.[129] Prior to that, many EU Member States regarded nationality[130] as the relevant connecting factor. In addition, the Succession Regulation contains provisions for establishing the international jurisdiction of courts. The general rule of Art. 4 Succession Regulation states that "the courts of the Member State in which the deceased had his habitual residence at the time of his death shall have jurisdiction […]." Using the same connecting factor for determining the jurisdiction and the applicable law synchronises forum and law. This means that an authority dealing with succession will regularly be applying its own law.[131] Thus, the issue of public policy usually does not arise.[132] Violations of the *ordre public* remain possible only in the rare case that the forum will not be applying its own law, for

127 Council Regulation (EU) 2016/1103 of 24 June 2016 implementing enhanced cooperation in the area of jurisdiction, applicable law and the recognition and enforcement of decisions in matters of matrimonial property regimes, OJ L 183, 8.7.2016, 1.

128 Council Regulation (EU) 2016/1104 of 24 June 2016 implementing enhanced cooperation in the area of jurisdiction, applicable law and the recognition and enforcement of decisions in matters of the property consequences of registered partnerships, OJ L 183, 8.7.2016, 30.

129 Whether or not the law specified by the Succession Regulation is the law of a Member State is irrelevant for the application, Art. 20 Succession Regulation.

130 The nationality of the deceased was the connecting factor set out in Art. 25 EGBGB (old version).

131 Recital 27 Succession Regulation

132 Michael Stürner, *Zeitschrift für das Privatrecht der Europäischen Union (GPR)* 2014, 317 (321).

example if the prorogation of the forum according to Art. 5 Succession Regulation is invalid or jurisdiction is based on Art. 10 (subsidiary jurisdiction) or Art. 11 Succession Regulation (*forum necessitatis*), if the deceased had no habitual residence within the EU.[133]

In divorce matters, in the absence of a choice of law, Art. 8 Rome III Regulation primarily refers to the spouses' common habitual residence at the time the court is seized with the application of the divorce (subsection (a)) to determine the applicable law. Even if the spouses no longer have a common habitual residence, the law of that state applies provided that one spouse still resides therein and "the period of residence did not end more than one year before the court was seized" (subsection (b)).[134] The common nationality of the spouses is no longer the primary connecting factor as it used to be under Art. 17(1), 14(1) no. 1 EGBGB (Art. 17(1) EGBGB has been abrogated after the coming into force of the Rome III Regulation). Jurisdiction for these divorce cases is - inter alia - also established by reference to the spouses' habitual residence (Art. 3(1) Brussels IIa Regulation).[135] The rules of private international law thus often lead to the application of the *lex fori* as intended by the Commission,[136] thereby diminishing the importance of the *ordre public*.

The situation is somewhat similar in the area of maintenance law, although the Europeanisation of private international law did not bring significant changes to the prior rules in force in Germany. Art. 3(1) of the Proto-

---

133 Michael Stürner, *Zeitschrift für das Privatrecht der Europäischen Union (GPR)* 2014, 317 (320).

134 If these requirements are not met one has to apply the law of the common nationality of the spouses or, failing that, the lex fori of the court seized (Art. 8 subsection (c), (d) Rome III Regulation).

135 Council Regulation (EC) No 2201/2003 of 27 November 2003 concerning jurisdiction and the recognition and enforcement of judgments in matrimonial matters and the matters of parental responsibility, repealing Regulation (EC) No 1347/2000, OJ L 338, 12.12.2003, 1.

136 Katharina Hilbig-Lugani, in: Rainer Hüßtege and Heinz-Peter Mansel (eds), *NomosKommentar BGB* (2nd Edition, 2015), Art. 8 Rom III para. 4; Proposal for a Council Regulation (EU) implementing enhanced cooperation in the area of the law applicable to divorce and legal separation of 24 March 2010, COM (2010) 105 final, 7 (Comment on Art. 4).

col of 23 November 2007 on the Law Applicable to Maintenance Obligations[137] now determines the law of the habitual residence of the maintenance creditor applicable. Art 3 of the Maintenance Regulation[138] provides four alternative connecting factors for establishing the international jurisdiction of courts, one of which being the habitual residence of the maintenance creditor (Art. 3 (b) Maintenance Regulation), which will often be chosen by the creditor. Hence, it is possible, to a certain extent, to perceive an alignment of the connecting factors in this area as well.

These synchronised connecting factors for determining jurisdiction and the law applicable ensure that courts will be applying the law of the forum more often, or even in most cases. As public policy violations are out of the question in such cases, the importance of public policy in these areas of law will diminish significantly.

2. Overtight control of foreign law?

Second, there is the danger that the constitutionalization of the *ordre public* might lead to an overtight control of foreign law. The most recent developments indicate an expansion of public policy: In the area of succession law, asserting gender equality has prompted German courts to disregard more foreign laws in recent years.[139] With regard to Art. 10 Rome III Regulation there are voices advocating that this rule stipulates an abstract control to enforce the principle of gender equality and recital 58 of the Succession Regulation emphasises the importance of the European ban on discrimination[140] when applying public policy.

This development must be viewed critically. The public policy reservation should not "fend off" rules simply because they differ from local rules. It is a means of last resort to protect fundamental values of the forum and

137 Council decision of 30 November 2009 on the conclusion by the European Community of the Hague Protocol of 23 November 2007 on the Law Applicable to Maintenance Obligations, OJ L 331, 16.12.2009, 17.

138 Council Regulation (EC) No 4/2009 of 18 December 2008 on jurisdiction, applicable law, recognition and enforcement of decisions and cooperation in matters relating to Maintenance obligations, OJ L 7, 10.1.2009, 1.

139 See supra section IV. 5. b).

140 Art. 21 of the Charter of Fundamental Rights of the European Union.

must, therefore, be confined to exceptional cases.[141] Denying the application of foreign law too often undermines the principle of closest connection and endangers the international consistency of decision-making.[142] Finding the most suitable law to resolve a legal dispute is not only necessary to find the most appropriate solution to the conflict, but also to ensure that the judgement will be recognised abroad. Rejecting foreign laws too readily makes the whole process of searching for the best suited law obsolete. One could simply apply national law to all disputes instead. The outcome of a dispute depending solely on the forum chosen and the resulting judgment not being recognised abroad would, however, not serve any party to a conflict.

It is therefore imperative that the principle of result control is not watered down. Moreover, courts should always look for solutions which confine the application of the *ordre public* as far as possible. A good example of such a cautious approach is the case law of German courts regarding the application of foreign succession rules designating only those relatives as heirs that possess the same religion as the testator. German courts have found that such rules may possibly violate the German *ordre public* as they discriminate against potential heirs on religious grounds (Art. 3(3) GG).[143] But, under German law a testator is free to allocate his property as he wishes (and

---

141 Paul Torremans and James J. Fawcett, *Cheshire/North/Fawcett Private International Law* (15th Edition, 2017), 133 and 140 et seq.; Jan Kropholler, *Internationales Privatrecht* (6th Edition, 2006), § 36 II („zurückhaltende Handhabung"); Paul Vlas, 'Public Policy in Private International Law and its Continuing Importance', in: The Permanent Bureau of the Hague Conference on Private International Law (ed), *A Commitment to Private International Law: Essays in Honour of Hans van Loon* (2013), 621 (624) ("ultimum remedium").

142 Christian von Bar and Peter Mankowski, *Internationales Privatrecht* (2nd Edition, 2003) Vol. 1, § 7 para. 258; Patrick Kinsch, 'La 'sauvegarde de certaines politiques législatives', cas d'intervention de l'ordre public international?', in: Tristan Azzi et al. (eds), *Liber amicorum Hélène Gaudemet-Tallon. Vers de nouveaux équilibres entre ordres juridiques* (2008), 447.

143 OLG Hamm 28.2.2005 – 15 W 117/04 – ZEV 2005, 436 (437 et seq.); OLG Düsseldorf 19.12.2008 – 3 Wx 51/08 – NJW-RR 2009, 732 (733); OLG Frankfurt a. M. 10.5. 010 – 20 W 4/10 – ZEV 2011, 135 (136).

can therefore discriminate against one of his children, for example, by allocating more of the inheritance to one of them than to another).[144] This freedom is also protected by the German constitution (Art. 14(1) GG).[145] So, if it can be proven that the testator wanted the "discriminatory" foreign rule to apply, courts must apply it and not invoke the *ordre public*.[146]

Such a cautious approach also needs to be applied with regard to forced heirship rights (*Pflichtteilsrecht*). Under German law, forced heirship rights guarantee, under certain conditions, direct descendants of a testator and his surviving spouse a minimum part of the inheritance, enforceable against the actual heir in the form of a money claim. German law does not make these claims dependent on the needs of these family members. In 2005, the German Federal Constitutional Court granted some constitutional protection to those rights stressing that the participation of children in the inheritance is protected irrespective of their needs.[147] This decision must be mirrored when deciding under which conditions foreign rules not containing such a right or similar rights may constitute a public policy violation.[148] Views differ on this issue, given that the reach of the judgment of the Federal Constitutional Court is disputed and the older case law of the ordinary courts accepted that the testator could partly circumvent these rights without violating the *ordre public*.[149] For some, the judgement states that forced heirship rights promote a right of the descendants of the deceased to partake in a

---

144 OLG Hamm 28.2.2005 – 15 W 117/04 – ZEV 2005, 436 (439); OLG Düsseldorf 19.12.2008 – 3 Wx 51/08 – NJW-RR 2009, 732 (734); OLG Frankfurt a. M. 10.5. 2010 – 20 W 4/10 – ZEV 2011, 135 (137).

145 Wolfgang Wurmnest, *Praxis des Internationalen Privat- und Verfahrensrechts (IPRax)* 2016, 447 (451).

146 OLG Hamm 28.2.2005 – 15 W 117/04 – ZEV 2005, 436 (437 et seq.); OLG Düsseldorf 19.12.2008 – 3 Wx 51/08 – NJW-RR 2009, 732 (733); OLG Frankfurt a. M. 10.5. 2010 – 20 W 4/10 – ZEV 2011, 135 (136); Anatol Dutta, in: Jan von Hein (ed), *Münchener Kommentar BGB* (7th Edition, 2018), Art. 35 EuErbVO para. 9; Dirk Looschelders, in: Rainer Hüßtege and Heinz-Peter Mansel (eds), *NomosKommentar BGB* (2nd Edition, 2015), Art. 35 EuErbVO para. 8.

147 BVerfG 19.4.2005 – 1 BvR 1644/00 – BVerfGE 112, 332 = NJW 2005, 1561.

148 See KG 26. 2. 2008 – 1 W 59/07 – ZEV 2008, 440 (441) (considered invoking the *ordre public* because of the Constitutional Court's judgment, but leaving the question undecided in the end).

149 BGH 21.4.1993 – XII ZR 248/91 – NJW 1993, 1920 (1921); OLG Köln 26. 6. 75 – 10 U 215/74 – FamRZ 1976, 170 (172).

minimum part of the inheritance regardless of their actual needs.[150] Foreign laws falling short of that absolute minimum are incompatible with German public policy regardless of other compensating schemes they may provide – such as maintenance claims, which depend on the descendants being in need of support. Others read the judgment of the Federal Constitutional Court more narrowly when assessing its impact on the *ordre public*.[151]

In our opinion the latter view is correct. It is incorrect to derive from the Constitutional Court's judgement that children must always be guaranteed a minimum inheritance. Even under German law, the minimum participation in the inheritance is not guaranteed[152] and awarding a minimum share is therefore not completely independent of any prerequisites.[153] Thus, the judgment of the Constitutional Court must not be interpreted as guaranteeing the descendants an absolute right to participate in the inheritance regardless of any need. Instead, the participation in the inheritance is granted only "generally" and "structurally"[154] regardless of any need.[155] This interpretation of the *ordre public* remains feasible because the Constitutional

---

150 KG 26. 2. 2008 – 1 W 59/07 – ZEV 2008, 440 (441); Dirk Looschelders, *Praxis des Internationalen Privat- und Verfahrensrechts (IPRax)* 2006, 462 (465): „Das Pflichtteilsrecht soll … nicht nur den Bedarf minderjähriger Kinder absichern, sondern die Kinder des Erblassers generell vor unverhältnismäßiger Zurücksetzung schützen. Billigt das Erbstatut den Abkömmlingen überhaupt kein Pflichtteilsrecht zu, so dürfte dies daher mit dem deutschen ordre public unvereinbar sein."; Tobias Pfundstein, *Pflichtteil und ordre public* (2010), 247 et seq, who postulates a "constitutional right to inherit" (*Grundrecht zu erben*) and develops a detailed analysis to safeguard this right.

151 Anatol Dutta, in: Jan von Hein (ed), *Münchener Kommentar BGB* (7th Edition, 2018), Art. 35 EuErbVO para. 9; Anne Röthel, 'Englische family provision und ordre public', in: Herbert Kronke and Karsten Thorn (eds), *Grenzen überwinden – Prinzipien bewahren. Festschrift für Bernd von Hoffmann zum 70. Geburtstag* (2011), 348 (361).

152 § 2333 of the German Civil Code provide certain grounds to bar direct descendants from forced heirship rights.

153 Anne Röthel, 'Englische family provision und ordre public', in: Herbert Kronke and Karsten Thorn (eds), *Grenzen überwinden – Prinzipien bewahren. Festschrift für Bernd von Hoffmann zum 70. Geburtstag* (2011), 348 (361).

154 BVerfG 19.4.2005 – 1 BvR 1644/00 – BVerfGE 112, 332 (349 and 355) = NJW 2005, 1561 (1563 et seq.): „Bedarfsunabhängige wirtschaftliche Mindestbeteiligung der Kinder am Nachlass ist tragendes Strukturprinzip des Pflichtteilsrechts".

155 Anne Röthel, 'Englische family provision und ordre public', in: Herbert Kronke and Karsten Thorn (eds), *Grenzen überwinden – Prinzipien bewahren. Festschrift für Bernd von Hoffmann zum 70. Geburtstag* (2011), 348 (360).

Court only dealt with the question under which conditions children or the surviving spouse are excluded from claiming a minimum share of the estate because they are unworthy to inherit (§ 2333 of the German Civil Code). It did not draw a strict line delineating the requirements foreign succession laws have to meet in enabling a minimum participation of the direct descendants in the inheritance. In fact, it did not even do so concerning German forced heirship rights.

While the Federal Constitutional Court stated that descendants had to be granted an adequate proportion of the inheritance regardless of any need, it did not state how this goal was to be achieved or how high such a proportion might be.[156] The current design of forced heirship rights in form of money claims is not compulsory; other participation possibilities would also be in line with the Constitutional provisions.[157] Against this background, any foreign law providing some means to compensate the testator's children, for example through maintenance claims, remains applicable – even after the judgment of the German Constitutional Court.[158] Thus, if – as it is the case under the English concept of family provision – a judge decides on the allocation and opines that the children (because they are adult and have own sources of income) do not need to be compensated, the *ordre public* is not violated.[159]

These examples demonstrate that courts should not hastily discard the application of foreign law but rather only do so if national values protected by the constitution are violated. As the safety net of last resort, the *ordre*

---

156 Reinhard Gaier, 'Pflichtteil und grundrechtliche Freiheit', in: Anne Röthel (ed), *Reformfragen des Pflichtteilsrechts* (2007), 161 (163).

157 Reinhard Gaier, 'Pflichtteil und grundrechtliche Freiheit', in: Anne Röthel (ed), *Reformfragen des Pflichtteilsrechts* (2007), 161 (163).

158 Heinrich Dörner, in: Jan Kropholler (ed), *Staudinger BGB* (2007), Art. 25 EGBGB para. 726; Gerhard Hohloch, 'Internationales Erbrecht und Ordre public – Stand, Bedeutung und Perspektiven', in: Rolf Stürner, Hiroyuki Matsumoto, Wolfgang Lüke and Masahisa Deguchi (eds), *Festschrift für Dieter Leipold zum 70. Geburtstag* (2009), 997 (1005); Michael Stürner, *Zeitschrift für das Privatrecht der Europäischen Union (GPR)* 2014, 317 (323).

159 Heinrich Dörner, in: Jan Kropholler (ed), *Staudinger BGB* (2007), Art. 25 EGBGB para. 726; Anatol Dutta, in: Jan von Hein (ed), *Münchener Kommentar BGB* (7th Edition, 2018), Art. 35 EuErbVO para. 8; Anne Röthel, 'Englische family provision und ordre public', in: Herbert Kronke and Karsten Thorn (eds), *Grenzen überwinden – Prinzipien bewahren. Festschrift für Bernd von Hoffmann zum 70. Geburtstag* (2011), 348 (361 et seq.); Michael Stürner, in: Christine Budzikiewicz, Marc-Philippe Weller and Wolfgang Wurmnest (eds), *BeckOGK* (March 2018), Art. 6 EGBGB para. 408.

public must only apply when other measures fail to deliver an acceptable result to the forum.

VII. Conclusion

(1) Public policy is a reservation clause of private international law allowing courts to disregard foreign laws that violate fundamental values of the forum.

(2) The application of the public policy reservation depends on the result of foreign law being unacceptable to the protected values of the forum.

(3) In Germany, the public policy reservation rightly protects constitutional provisions as fundamental values of the forum; the basic rights of the *Grundgesetz* define the content of the *ordre public* to a large extent.

(4) The Spaniard decision of the Federal Constitutional Court of Germany started the process of constitutionalizing the content of public policy. This process has forced the German legislator to change many conflict-of-law rules to implement the principle of equal treatment of men and women. Moreover, courts imposed a tighter control over foreign law which has been further and further extended over the last decades.

(5) While courts have, since the reforms of the EGBGB, regularly found the public policy reservation to apply in the area of family and succession law, the application of the *ordre public* is of less importance in the fields of contract and tort law. One explanation for this divergence is the existence of special connecting factors that make recourse to public policy largely redundant in the areas of contract and tort law. Another explanation is that family and succession laws across the globe are shaped by very different cultural and religious influences whereas there is more agreement on basic principles in the area of contract and tort law.

(6) European law has also influenced the content of public policy. While the concept of public policy still remains a national concept, European values have supplemented the existing content and introduced boundaries to the application of public policy by national courts. Thus, national courts must disregard foreign rules contradicting European values on public policy grounds. On the other hand, courts may not disregard a foreign law if doing so violates European values.

(7) Art. 10 Rome III Regulation should be interpreted as a special public policy reservation even though its wording, systematic position, and legislative history suggest an abstract control of foreign divorce law.

(8) The importance of public policy will diminish significantly in the future: More special connecting factors enforcing the application of the law of the forum in sensitive legal areas will reduce public policy violations. Most importantly, changing the connecting factors for the determination of the applicable law from nationality to habitual residence, thereby aligning it with the factor establishing international jurisdiction, will reduce public policy violations significantly in family and succession law. Thus, public policy violations will be reduced as courts will be applying the law of the forum more regularly.

(9) Courts and also the legislature should be careful to implement an overtight control of foreign law. Disregarding foreign rules by recourse to public policy has to remain an extraordinary remedy to safeguard the most important values of the forum.

Bibliography

Thomas Ackermann, 'Antitrust Damages Actions Under the Rome II Regulation', in: Mielle Bulterman, Leigh Hancher and Alison McDonnell et al. (eds), *Liber Amicorum Piet Jan Slot* (Kluwer Law International, Alphen aan den Rijn, 2009), 109.

Jennifer Antomo, 'Kinderehen, ordre public und Gesetzesreform' *Neue Juristische Wochenschrift (NJW)* 2016, 3558.

Jennifer Antomo, 'Verbot von Kinderehen?' *Zeitschrift für Rechtspolitik (ZRP)* 2017, 79.

Christian von Bar and Peter Mankowski, *Internationales Privatrecht Vol. 1: Allgemeine Lehren* (2nd Edition, C. H. Beck, München 2003).

Jürgen Basedow, 'Die Neuregelung des Internationalen Privat- und Prozeßrechts' *Neue Juristische Wochenschrift (NJW)* 1986, 2971.

beck-online.GROSSKOMMENTAR, Rom I-VO/EGBGB, Christine Budzikiewicz, Marc-Philippe Weller and Wolfgang Wurmnest (eds) (C. H. Beck, München 2018).

Hans Dölle, *Internationales Privatrecht* (2nd Edition, C. F. Müller, Karlsruhe 1972).

Erman Bürgerliches Gesetzbuch. Handkommentar, Vol. 2, Harm-Peter Westermann, Barbara Grunewald, Georg Maier-Reimer (eds) (15th Edition, Otto Schmidt Verlag, Köln 2017).

Europäisches Zivilprozess- und kollisonsrecht EuZPR/EulPR – Kommentar, Vol. 3, Thomas Rauscher (ed) (4th Edition, Otto Schmidt Verlag, Köln 2016).

European Commentaries on Private International Law ECPIL, Vol. 2, Ulrich Magnus and Peter Mankowski (eds) (Otto Schmidt Verlag, Köln 2017).

Murad Ferid, 'Wechselbeziehungen zwischen Verfassungsrecht und Kollisionsnormen', in: Ernst von Caemmerer, Arthur Nikisch and Konrad Zweigert (eds), *Vom deutschen zum europäischen Recht - Festschrift für Hans Dölle Vol. 2,* Internationales Recht, Kollisionsrecht und internationales Zivilprozessrecht – Europäisches Recht (Mohr Siebeck, Tübingen 1963), 119.

Reinhard Gaier, 'Pflichtteil und grundrechtliche Freiheit', in: Anne Röthel (ed), *Reformfragen des Pflichtteilsrechts: Symposium vom 30.11.–2.12.2006 in Salzau* (Nomos, Baden-Baden 2007), 161.

Jan von Hein, 'Punitive Damages in European and Domestic Private International Law', in: Alexander Bruns and Masabumi Suzuki (eds), *Preventive Instruments of Social Governance* (Mohr Siebeck, Tübingen 2017), 143.

Christian Heinze, *Schadensersatz im Unionsprivatrecht* (Mohr Siebeck, Tübingen 2017).

Tobias Helms, 'Reform des internationalen Scheidungsrechts durch die Rom III-Verordnung' Zeitschrift für das gesamte Familienrecht (FamRZ) 2011, 1765.

Dieter Henrich, 'Gleichberechtigung im internationalen Privat- und Staatsangehörigkeitsrecht' *Zeitschrift für das gesamte Familienrecht (FamRZ)* 1974, 105.

Christoph Herfarth, *Die Scheidung nach jüdischem Recht im internationalen Zivilverfahrensrecht* (Winter, Heidelberg 2000).

Bernd von Hoffmann, Karsten Thorn and Karl Firsching, *Internationales Privatrecht* (9th Edition, C. H. Beck, München 2007).

Gerhard Hohloch,'Internationales Erbrecht und Ordre public – Stand, Bedeutung und Perspektiven', in: Rolf Stürner, Hiroyuki Matsumoto, Wolfgang Lüke and Masahisa Deguchi (eds), *Festschrift für Dieter Leipold zum 70. Geburtstag* (Mohr Siebeck, Tübingen 2009), 997.

Walter Homalka, *Das jüdische Eherecht* (De Gruyter, Berlin 2009).

Maarit Jänterä-Jareborg, 'Jurisdiction and Applicable Law in Cross-Border Divorce Cases in Europe', in: Jürgen Basedow, Harald Baum and Yuko Nishitani (eds), *Japanese and European Private International Law in Comparative Perspective* (Mohr Siebeck, Tübingen 2008), 317.

Erik Jayme, *Ein internationales Privatrecht für Europa* (Decker & Müller, Heidelberg 1991).

Gerhard Kegel and Klaus Schurig, *Internationales Privatrecht* (9th Edition, C. H. Beck, München 2004).

Patrick Kinsch, 'La 'sauvegarde de certaines politiques législatives', cas d'intervention de l'ordre public international?', in: Tristan Azzi et al. (eds), *Liber amicorum Hélène Gaudemet-Tallon. Vers de nouveaux équilibres entre ordres juridiques* (Dalloz-Sirey, Paris 2008), 447.

Jan Kropholler, *Gleichberechtigung durch Richterrecht. Erfahrungen im Familienrecht – Perspektiven im internationalen Privatrecht* (Gieseking, Bielefeld 1975).

Jan Kropholler, *Internationales Privatrecht* (6th Edition, Mohr Siebeck, Tübingen 2006).

Jan Kropholler, 'Gleichberechtigung und Aufenthaltsprinzip' *Zeitschrift für das gesamte Familienrecht (FamRZ)* 1976, 316.

Stefan Leible, *Rom I und Rom II: Neue Perspektiven im europäischen Kollisionsrecht*, Vorträge und Berichte des Zentrums für Europäisches Wirtschaftsrecht No. 173 (Zentrum für Europäisches Wirtschaftsrecht, Bonn 2009).

Stefan Leible and Matthias Lehmann, 'Die neue EG-Verordnung über das auf außervertragliche Schuldverhältnisse anzuwendende Recht ("Rom II")' *Recht der Internationalen Wirtschaft (RIW)* 2007, 721.

Dirk Looschelders, 'Die Ausstrahlung der Grund- und Menschenrechte auf das Internationale Privatrecht' 65 (2001) *Rabels Zeitschrift für ausländisches und internationales Privatrecht (RabelsZ)*, 461.

Dirk Looschelders, 'Grundrechtliche Diskriminierungsverbote, Pflichtteilsrechte und Testierfreiheit im internationalen Erbrecht' *Praxis des Internationalen Privat- und Verfahrensrechts (IPRax)* 2006, 462.

Christian Friedrich Majer, 'Das Gesetz zur Bekämpfung von Kinderehen' *Neue Zeitschrift für Familienrecht (NZFam)* 2017, 537.

Alexander N. Makarov, 'Die Gleichberechtigung der Frau und das Internationale Privatrecht' 17 (1952) *Rabels Zeitschrift für ausländisches und internationales Privatrecht (RabelsZ)*, 382.

Dieter Martiny, 'Die Zukunft des europäischen ordre public im Internationalen Privat- und Zivilverfahrensrecht', in: Michael Coester, Dieter Martiny, Karl August von Sachsen Gessaphe (eds), *Privatrecht in Europa: Vielfalt, Kollision, Kooperation. Festschrift für Hans Jürgen Sonnenberger zum 70. Geburtstag* (C. H. Beck, München 2004), 523.

Pierre Mayer and Vincent Heuzé, *Droit international privé* (11th Edition, LGDJ, Issy-les-Moulineaux 2014).

Lena-Maria Möller, 'No Fear of Ṭalāq: A Reconsideration of Muslim Divorce Laws in Light of the Rome III Regulation' *Journal of Private International Law (JPrivIntL)* 2014, 461.

Lena-Maria Möller and Nadjma Yassari, 'Wenn Jugendliche heiraten. Die Minderjährigenehe aus rechtsvergleichender und international-privatrechtlicher Sicht' *Kritische Justiz (KJ)* 2017, 269.

Hans-Joachim Musielak and Wolfgang Voit (eds), *Zivilprozessordnung. Kommentar* (15th Edition, Franz Vahlen, München 2018).

Münchener Kommentar zum Bürgerlichen Gesetzbuch, Vol. 11, Jan von Hein (ed) (7th Edition, C. H. Beck, München 2018).

Münchener Kommentar zum Bürgerlichen Gesetzbuch, Vol. 12, Jan von Hein (ed) (7th Edition, C. H. Beck, München 2018).

Karl Heinz Neumayer, 'Zur positiven Funktion der kollisionsrechtlichen Vorbehaltsklausel', in: Ernst von Caemmerer, Arthur Nikisch and Konrad Zweigert (eds), *Vom deutschen zum europäischen Recht - Festschrift für Hans Dölle Vol. 2,* Internationales Recht, Kollisionsrecht und internationales Zivilprozessrecht - Europäisches Recht (Mohr Siebeck, Tübingen 1963), 179.

NomosKommentar BGB. Rom-Verordnungen, Vol. 6, Rainer Hüßtege, Heinz-Peter Mansel (eds) (2nd Edition, Nomos, Baden-Baden 2015).

Palandt Bürgerliches Gesetzbuch. mit Nebengesetzen, Gerd Brudermüller, Jürgen Ellenberger Isabell Götz, Christian Grüneberg, Sebastian Herrler, Hartwig Sprau, Karsten Thorn, Walter Weidenkaff, Dietmar Weidlich and Hartmut Wicke (eds) (77th Edition, C. H. Beck, München 2018).

Andreas Kurt Pattar, *Islamisch inspiriertes Erbrecht und deutscher Ordre public: Die Erbrechtsordnungen von Ägypten, Tunesien und Marokko und ihre Anwendbarkeit im Inland* (Duncker & Humblot, Berlin 2007).

Tobias Pfundstein, *Pflichtteil und ordre public* (C. H. Beck, München 2010).

Peter Pietsch, 'Scheidungsrecht in Malta' *Zeitschrift für das gesamte Familienrecht (FamRZ)* 2012, 426.

Thomas Rauscher and Steffen Pabst, 'Die Rechtsprechung zum Internationalen Privatrecht 2010-2011' *Neue Juristische Wochenschrift (NJW)* 2011, 3547.

Rome Regulations Commentary, Gralf-Peter Calliess (ed) (2nd Edition, Kluwer Law International, Alphen aan den Rijn 2015).

Rome II Regulation: Pocket Commentary – Pocket Commentaries on European Regulations and International, Vol. 1, Peter Huber (ed) (Sellier, München 2011).

Anne Röthel, 'English family provision und ordre public', in: Herbert Kronke and Karsten Thorn (eds), *Grenzen überwinden - Prinzipien bewahren. Festschrift für Bernd von Hoffmann zum 70. Geburtstag* (Gieseking, Bielefeld 2011), 348.

Michael Sachs, *Grenzen des Diskriminierungsverbots: Eine Untersuchung zur Reichweite d. Unterscheidungsverbots nach Art. 3 Abs. 2 u. 3 Grundgesetz* (Vahlen, München 1987).

Staudinger BGB – EGBGB, Jan Kropholler (ed) (De Gruyter, Berlin 2007).

Michael Stürner, 'Europäisierung des (Kollisions-)Rechts und nationaler ordre public', in: Herbert Kronke and Karsten Thorn (eds), *Grenzen überwinden - Prinzipien bewahren. Festschrift für Bernd von Hoffmann zum 70. Geburtstag* (Gieseking, Bielefeld 2011), 463.

Michael Stürner, 'Die Bedeutung des ordre public in der EuErbVO' *Zeitschrift für das Privatrecht der Europäischen Union (GPR)* 2014, 317.

Paul Torremans and James J. Fawcett, *Cheshire/North/Fawcett Private International Law* (15th Edition, Oxford University Press, Oxford 2017).

Cedric Vanleenhove, *Punitive Damages in Private International Law* (Intersentia, Cambridge 2016).

Paul Vlas, 'Public Policy in Private International Law and its Continuing Importance', in: The Permanent Bureau of the Hague Conference on Private International Law (ed), *A Commitment to Private International Law: Essays in Honour of Hans van Loon* (Intersentia, Cambridge 2013), 621.

Marc Philippe Weller, Irene Hauber and Alix Schulz, 'Gleichstellung im Internationalen Scheidungsrecht – talaq und get im Licht des Art. 10 Rom III-VO' *Praxis des Internationalen Privat- und Verfahrensrechts (IPRax)* 2016, 123.

Peter Winkler von Mohrenfels, 'Art. 10 Rom III-VO: Kollisionsrechtliche Eingriffsnorm oder Spezialfall des ordre public?', in: Normann Witzleb, Reinhard Ellger, Peter Mankowski, Hanno Merkt and Oliver Remien (eds), *Festschrift für Dieter Martiny zum 70. Geburtstag* (Mohr Siebeck, Tübingen 2014), 595.

Peter Winkler von Mohrenfels, 'Die Rom III- und Brüssel IIa-Verordnungen in der deutschen Rechtspraxis' *Zeitschrift für Vergleichende Rechtswissenschaft (ZVglRWiss)* 2016, 650.

Wolfgang Wurmnest, 'Ordre Public (Public Policy)', in: Stefan Leible (ed), *General Principles of European Private International Law* (Kluwer Law International, Alphen aan den Rijn 2016), 305.

Wolfgang Wurmnest, 'Der Anwendungsbereich des deutsch-iranischen Niederlassungsabkommens bei erbrechtlichen Streitigkeiten und deutscher ordre public' *Praxis des Internationalen Privat- und Verfahrensrechts (IPRax)* 2016, 447.

Wolfgang Wurmnest, 'Recognition and Enforcement of U.S. Money Judgments in Germany' 23 (2005) *Berkeley Journal of International Law (Berk. J. Int'l Law)*, 175.

Nadjma Yassari, Lena-Maria Möller and Imen Gallala-Arndt (eds), *Parental Care and the Best Interests of the Child in Muslim Countries* (Asser Press, The Hague 2017).

Register of Cases

BVerfG 4.5.1971 – 1 BvR 636/68 – BVerfGE 31, 58–87.

BVerfG 22.2.1983 – 1 BvL 17/81 – BVerfGE 63, 181–196.

BVerfG 8.1.1985 – 1 BvR 830/83 – BVerfGE 68, 384–391.

BVerfG 19.4.2005 – 1 BvR 1644/00 – BVerfGE 112, 332–363.

BVerwG 30.4.1985 – 1 C 33/81 – BVerwGE 71, 228–234.

BGH 18.1.1954 – IV ZR 144/53 – NJW 1954, 837.

BGH 12.2.1964 – IV AR (Vz) 39/63 – BGHZ 41, 136.

BGH 29.4.1964 – IV ZR 93/63 – BGHZ 42, 7–16.

BGH 12. 5. 1971 – IV AR (Vz) 38/70 – BGHZ 56, 180–192.

BGH 20.12.1972 – IV ZB 20/72 – BGHZ 60, 68–84.

BGH 8.12.1982 – IVb ZR 334/81 – BGHZ 86, 57–71.

BGH 28.4.1988 – IX ZR 127/87 – BGHZ 104, 204–246.

BGH 4.6.1992 – IX ZR 149/91 – BGHZ 118, 312–351.

BGH 14.10.1992 – XII ZB 18/92 – BGHZ 120, 29–38.

BGH 21.4.1993 – XII ZR 248/91 – NJW 1993, 1920–1921.

BGH 6.10.2004 – XII ZR 225/01 – BGHZ 160, 332–354.

BGH 11.10.2006 – XII ZR 79/04 – BGHZ 169, 240–255.

BayObLG 29.11.1982 – BReg. 1 Z 54/82 – BayObLGZ 1982, 389–395.

KG 7.6.1989 – 18 U 2625/88 – BeckRS 1989, 2838.
KG 26. 2. 2008 – 1 W 59/07 – ZEV 2008, 440–442.
KG 21. 11. 2011 – 1 W 79/11 – FamRZ 2012, 1495–1497.
OLG Bamberg 12.5.2016 – 2 UF 58/16 – BeckRS 2016, 09621.
OLG Düsseldorf 23.3.1993 – 6 UF 4/92 – NJW-RR 1994, 7–8.
OLG Düsseldorf 19.12.2008 – 3 Wx 51/08 – NJW-RR 2009, 732–735.
OLG Frankfurt a. M. 18.1.2001 – 1 U 209/99 UF 251/00 – BeckRS 2001, 30156129.
OLG Frankfurt a. M. 11.5.2009 – 5 WF 66/09 – BeckRS 2009, 24414.
OLG Frankfurt a. M. 10.5. 2010 – 20 W 4/10 – ZEV 2011, 135–137.
OLG Hamburg 23.12.1902 – II. ZS – OLGE 6 (1903), 231.
OLG Hamm 8.2.1990 – 2 UF 216/89 – BeckRS 2010, 26684.
OLG Hamm 29.4.1992 – 15 W 114/91 – IPRax 1994, 49–55.
OLG Hamm 28.2.2005 – 15 W 117/04 – ZEV 2005, 436–440.
OLG Hamm 11.10.2010 – 6 UF 59/10 – BeckRS 2011, 18163.
OLG Köln 26.6.1975 – 10 U 215/74 – FamRZ 1976, 170.
OLG Köln 4.9.1996 – 16 Wx 181/96 – NJWE-FER 1997, 55.
OLG München 16.4.2012 – 31 Wx 45/12 – NJW-RR 2012, 1096–1097.
OLG Stuttgart 22.5.1978 – 17 UF 20/78 G – FamRZ 1978, 507–508.
OLG Stuttgart 3.12.1998 – 17 VA 6/98 – BeckRS 1998, 13578.
LG Frankfurt 11.12.1979 – 3/10 O 123/79 – NJW 1981, 56–58.
AG Hannover 7.1.2002 – 616 F 7355/00 – BeckRS 2002, 01869.
AG Offenbach 30.10.2009 – 314 F 1132/09 – BeckRS 2010, 23013.

European Court of Justice, Case C-372/16, 20.12.2017, *Soha Sahyouni v. Raja Mamisch*, ECLI:EU:C:2017:988.

The Various Roles of Public Policy in Private International Law: Exclusion, Inclusion and Reform on the Basis of Constitutional Values

*Jan L. Neels**
*Eesa A. Fredericks***

As is the case in German private international law,[1] the device of public policy may also be used in the South African conflict of laws to exclude the application of so-called 'unwelcome' foreign law.[2] It is accepted in South African doctrine that foreign law should be excluded when it is manifestly, patently or severely in conflict with internal (national / domestic) public policy; only then will it infringe on external or international public policy.[3]

* Jan L. Neels, *B.Com. (Law), LL.B., LL.M., Dr. Jur.*, Professor of Private International Law and Director of the Research Centre for Private International Law in Emerging Countries, Faculty of Law, University of Johannesburg.

** Eesa A. Fredericks, *B.A. (Law), LL.B., LL.M., Dr. Jur.*, Associate Professor in the Department of Mercantile Law, Head of the Department of Practical Business Law and Deputy Director of the Research Centre for Private International Law in Emerging Countries, Faculty of Law, University of Johannesburg.

1 See WolfgangWurmnest and Maximilian Kübler-Wachendorff, 'The constitutionalization of public policy in private international law' p. 267 in this volume.

2 For this terminology, see T. M. de Boer, 'Unwelcome foreign law: Public policy and other means to protect the fundamental values and public interests of the European Community', in: Alberto Malatesta, Stefania Barriati and Fausto Pocar (eds), *The External Dimension of EC Private International Law in Family and Succession Matters* (2008), 295.

3 Jan L. Neels, *Tydskrif vir die Suid-Afrikaanse Reg / Journal of South African Law (T.S.A.R.),* 1991, 694 (696); Jan L. Neels, 'External public policy, the incidental question properly so-called and the recognition of foreign divorce orders', in: Katharina Boele-Woelki, Talia Einhorn, Daniel Girsberger and Symeon Symeonides (eds), *Convergence and Divergence in Private International Law. Liber amicorum Kurt Siehr* (2010), 331 (347-350); Jan L. Neels, *South African Journal for Human Rights (S.A.J.H.R.),* 28 (2012), 219 (221-222, 225-226); and J. C. W. van Rooyen, *Die Kontrak in die Suid-Afrikaanse Internasionale Privaatreg* (1972), 161-162.

For instance, a *pactum successorium* is invalid in terms of domestic South African law (unless included in an ante-nuptial contract),[4] but if the contract is valid in terms of its proper law it will not be excluded on the basis of public policy, as the agreement is not manifestly or severely in conflict with internal policy (and therefore not in conflict with external public policy). This was decided by the Transvaal High Court already in 1943, in a case known as *Berman v Winrow*.[5]

Where do constitutional values fit in? Is an unjustifiable infringement of a fundamental right in the South African Constitution[6] automatically in conflict with external public policy? In other words: is the Bill of Rights[7] necessarily also applicable to foreign law?

This issue has not pertinently been considered by the South African courts, but *dicta* in case law strongly suggest that there is indeed a direct link between constitutional values and external public policy. These decisions were not delivered in the field of family or succession law (the most important field of application of public policy in German private international law),[8] but in the areas of the international law of delict and in marine insurance law. The reason for this may indeed be (as has been suggested in a different context)[9] that domicile (and not nationality) is the leading connecting factor in South African international family and succession law.[10] The relevant decisions are both from 2010.

Burchell v Anglin,[11] a decision of the Eastern Cape High Court in Grahamstown, deals with cross-border defamation in a commercial context. The plaintiff (who ran a game reserve and a hunting safari business in the

---

4 M. J. de Waal and M. C. Schoeman-Malan, *Law of Succession* (4th Edition, 2008), 212-219; and Juanita Jamneck and Christa Rautenbach (eds) *The Law of Succession in South Africa* (2011), 223-232.

5 1943 TPD 213.

6 Constitution of the Republic of South Africa of 1996.

7 Chapter 2 of the Constitution.

8 Wurmnest and Kübler-Wachendorff (fn. 1) para. IV, VI and VII.

9 See Wurmnest and Kübler-Wachendorff (fn. 1) para. VI and VII (in respect of habitual residence). According to the authors, the replacement in European Regulations of nationality as a connecting factor with habitual residence will lead to an increased 'alignment of *forum* and *ius*' (para. VI).

10 See, in general, Christopher F. Forsyth, *Private International Law. The Modern Roman-Dutch Law including the Jurisdiction of the High Courts* (5th Edition, 2012), ch. 5, 7 and 9.VI.

11 2010 3 SA 48 (ECG).

vicinity of Grahamstown) alleged that the defendant made defamatory statements about him to a booking agent in Nebraska (United States of America). Most of his safari clients originated from this agent. However, the bookings suddenly and dramatically decreased and, according to the plaintiff, this was due to defamatory statements made by the defendant to the agent. Accordingly, he instituted action for general damages and loss of profit.

Crouse AJ decided that the *lex loci delicti* was the law of Nebraska as the defamatory statements were heard and read in that state.[12] Yet, although '[weighing] heavily in the balancing scale',[13] the place of the delict was in final instance 'only to be used as a factor in a balancing test to decide which jurisdiction would have the most real or significant relationship with the defamation and the parties'.[14] Nevertheless, taking into account the other connecting factors,[15] the judge decided that the law of Nebraska would *prima facie* be applicable.[16]

However, she also indicated that the defamation laws of Nebraska needed to comply with local constitutional values to be applied by a South African court:

> 'In South Africa the highest test for our public policy is our Constitution. Just as all South African law is under public scrutiny, so any foreign law which a court intends to apply in South Africa should be placed under constitutional scrutiny. I must therefore decide whether the law of Nebraska passes constitutional muster in South Africa before deciding I can apply [the] same.'[17]

The court was therefore of the opinion that South African constitutional norms are always, and automatically, to be applied to foreign law in a direct sense.

---

12 Para. 118.
13 Para. 124.
14 Para. 128.
15 As listed in para. 124.
16 Paras. 130 and 147.3.1 (but not necessarily in respect of the quantification of damages: paras. 112, 129 and 130).
17 Para. 127. Also see paras. 128 and 130.

The issue of conflict with constitutional norms was left open for decision at the end of the trial.[18] Unfortunately, the final case, if any, was never reported.[19] It might have been an interesting decision, as American defamation law is perceived to be pro-defendant (the defendant indeed alleged that his statements were protected under the American Constitution),[20] while South African defamation law is, in comparison, more favourable to the plaintiff, also due to constitutional provisions.[21]

In *Representative of Lloyds v Classic Sailing Adventures (Pty) Ltd*[22] the South African Supreme Court of Appeal decided that sections 53 and 54 of the South African Short-Term Insurance Act[23] constitute rules of immediate application that cannot be excluded by a choice of law. English law was chosen as the proper law of the marine insurance contract. The court held that, in as far as the United Kingdom's Marine Insurance Act of 1906 was in conflict with the South African provisions, it would not be applied. Section 53 deals with the effect of non-disclosure and misrepresentations and 'is designed to protect insured parties who are ignorant, careless or uneducated from unscrupulous insurers who attempt to escape liability'.[24] Section 54 'ensures that a policy is not avoided because the insured has contravened a law'.[25]

Although the case deals with the overriding mandatory rules of the forum, Lewis JA indicated in an important *obiter dictum* that constitutional norms are invariably of direct application. She referred to overriding mandatory rules as follows:

> 'These norms are of direct application, much as the values of the Constitution are. Counsel for Lloyds was constrained to concede that parties cannot contract out of provisions – and thus the norms and values – of the Constitution. The protection

---

18 Para. 127.

19 See, however, *Anglin v Burchell* (1134/2005) [2010] ZAECGHC 79 (22 Sept 2010); and *Anglin v Burchell* (1134/2005) [2011] ZAECGHC 34 (22 July 2011) (both available at www.saflii.org).

20 Para. 121.

21 See sec. 10 ('human dignity'), 14 ('privacy'), 16 ('freedom of expression') and 36 ('limitation of rights') of the Constitution.

22 2010 5 SA 90 (SCA). Also see the critical discussion by J. P. van Niekerk, *Tydskrif vir die Suid-Afrikaanse Reg / Journal of South African Law (T.S.A.R.)*, 2011, 159.

23 53 of 1998.

24 Para. 24.

25 *Ibid.*

> afforded to insured persons by the Short-Term Insurance Act, on this basis, can likewise not be avoided.'[26]

The Constitution will therefore be directly applicable to all foreign law and, as such, constitute external public policy.

The view in case law that constitutional norms are always of direct application seems to be in accordance with the provision in section 8(1) of the Constitution that the Bill of Rights applies to 'all law', which phrase is sufficiently wide to include foreign law. The provision does not distinguish, as is customary in German law,[27] between the application of a foreign rule in the abstract and the concrete results in the particular case. An unwelcome foreign rule will be excluded, even if the result *in casu* does not *per se* contravene constitutional values.

Doctrine also considers the exclusion of foreign law on the basis of constitutional values in the field of international family and succession law. For instance, if the applicable foreign law of intestate succession would provide the deceased's daughter with 75% and the son with 25% of the estate, both children would each inherit half of the estate on the basis of the equality principle in the Constitution.[28]

However, the foreign law is only excluded in as far as it is in conflict with local constitutional values. Of course, the foreign law does not have to be the same as the local law.[29] Assume that the foreign law of intestate succession provides 50% of the estate to the surviving children and 50% to the surviving siblings of the deceased, the foreign law is not excluded on the basis that internal South African law would allocate the whole estate to the surviving children.[30]

On the other hand, if the foreign law provides that the male siblings of the deceased inherit half and the children of the deceased the other half of the estate, and the deceased is survived by a brother, a sister and a daughter, the brother and sister should inherit 25% each and the daughter 50%.[31]

---

26 Para. 25.

27 Wurmnest and Kübler-Wachendorff (fn. 1) para. I, VI and VII (*cf.* para. V).

28 See sec. 9.

29 See *Bell v Bell* 1991 4 SA 195 (W) 198I; and Jan L. Neels, *Tydskrif vir die Suid-Afrikaanse Reg /Journal of South African Law (T.S.A.R.)*, 1992, 336 (344).

30 Sec. 1(1)(b) of the Intestate Succession Act 81 of 1987.

31 See sec. 9 of the Constitution ('equality'). The examples are based on the text of a series of lectures entitled 'Cultural diversity, constitutional values and social justice in the conflict of laws', delivered by the first author at the summer school

So far, the discussion pertained to the *exclusion* of foreign law on the basis of constitutional public policy. However, doctrine in South Africa makes a distinction between the negative and the positive function of public policy in private international law.[32] For instance, it has been suggested that foreign religious marriages, perhaps invalid in terms of the law of the country of conclusion, may be recognised in South Africa in as far as these marriages would be recognised in this country.[33] Hindu and Muslim marriages are recognised in South African law in as far as intestate succession is concerned,[34] even though the marriage is possibly not registered in terms of the Marriage Act.[35] The suggestion in doctrine is that the non-recognition of such foreign religious marriages would be in conflict with the constitutional values of cultural diversity and freedom of religion.[36] They must therefore be recognised irrespective of their invalidity in terms of the otherwise applicable legal system.[37]

Of course, public policy also underlies the re-formulation of conflicts rules in line with the Constitution. Roman-Dutch law had the law of the country of the domicile of the husband (at the conclusion of the marriage) govern the proprietary consequences of marriage.[38] The courts have indicated that this rule is now unconstitutional, being in conflict with the equal-

---

of the Hague Academy of International Law in 2011. Also see Neels (fn. 3 (2010)) 343.

32 Neels (fn. 3 (2012)).

33 *Ibid.*

34 *Daniels v Campbell NO* 2005 5 SA 331 (CC); *Hassam v Jacobs NO* 2009 5 SA 572 (CC); *Govender v Ragavayah NO* 2009 3 SA 178 (D). See Jan L. Neels, *Tydskrif vir die Suid-Afrikaanse Reg / Journal of South African Law (T.S.A.R.)*, 2012, 486 (491; 504-506).

35 25 of 1961.

36 See sec. 15 ('freedom of religion'), 30 ('language and culture') and 31 ('cultural, religious and linguistic communities') of the Constitution.

37 Neels (fn. 3 (2012)).

38 *Frankel's Estate v The Master* 1950 1 SA 220 (A); *Sperling v Sperling* 1975 3 SA 707 (A).

ity principle, and because it does not make provision for same-sex marriages.[39] The leading proposal in South African doctrine,[40] as directly influenced by developments in German private international law,[41] contains a so-called ladder of connecting factors, referring to a choice of law by the parties, the law of the common domicile of the parties, the law of common habitual residence, the law of common nationality and the law of closest connection.[42]

Unlike in Germany,[43] no reservations have been expressed in South African case law or in doctrine about the increasing influence of the Constitution in South African private international law. Indeed, such influence has been unanimously welcomed.[44]

---

39 *Fourie v Minister of Home Affairs* 2005 1 All SA 273 (SCA) 315d-g; *Minister of Home Affairs v Fourie (Doctors for Life International); Lesbian and Gay Equality Project v Minister of Home Affairs* 2006 1 SA 524 (CC) 536-537 n 24; *Sadiku v Sadiku* (30498/06) [2007] ZAGHPC 1 (26 Jan 2007) (available at www.saflii.org) para. 10; *AS v CS* 2011 2 SA 360 (WCC) para. 55; *Lenferna v Lenferna* (120/13) [2013] ZASCA 204 (02 Dec 2013) (available at www.saflii.org) para. 10.

40 H. Stoll and P. J. Visser, *De Jure*, 1989, 330.

41 See Jan L. Neels, 'The law applicable to the proprietary consequences of marriage in South Africa – the influence of German private international law', in: Charl Hugo and Thomas M. J. Möllers (eds), *Transnational Impacts on Law: Perspectives from South Africa and Germany* (2017), 115; Elsabe Schoeman, *Tydskrif vir die Suid-Afrikaanse Reg / Journal of South African Law (T.S.A.R.)*, 2004, 115; and Wurmnest and Kübler-Wachendorff (fn.1) paras. II and III.

42 Stoll and Visser (fn. 40).

43 Wurmnest and Kübler-Wachendorff (fn. 1) paras. II, VI and VII.

44 See, for instance, Forsyth (fn. 10) 19-20, 295-296 and 300-303; Neels (fn. 3 (2010)) 339-343 and 347-355; Neels (fn. 3 (2012)); Jan L. Neels and Eesa A. Fredericks, *Tydskrif vir die Suid-Afrikaanse Reg / Journal of South African Law (T.S.A.R.)*, 2015, 918; J. L. Neels and Marlene Wethmar-Lemmer, *Tydskrif vir die Suid-Afrikaanse Reg / Journal of South African Law (T.S.A.R.)*, 2008, 587; Schoeman (fn. 40); Elsabe Schoeman *Praxis des Internationalen Privat- und Verfahrensrecht (IPRax)*, 24 (2004) 65; Elsabe Schoeman, Christa Roodt and Marlene Wethmar-Lemmer, *Private International Law in South Africa* (2014), 17, 42-43 and 84.

Bibliography

De Boer, T. M., 'Unwelcome foreign law: Public policy and other means to protect the fundamental values and public interests of the European Community', in: Alberto Malatesta,, Stefania Barriati and Fausto Pocar, (eds), *The External Dimension of EC Private International Law in Family and Succession Matters* (Cedam, Padova 2008), 295.

De Waal, M. J. and Schoeman-Malan, M. C., *Law of Succession* (4th Edition, Juta, Cape Town 2008).

Forsyth, Christopher F., *Private International Law. The Modern Roman-Dutch Law including the Jurisdiction of the High Courts* (5th Edition, Juta, Cape Town 2012).

Jamneck, Juanita and Rautenbach, Christa (eds), *The Law of Succession in South Africa* (Oxford University Press Southern Africa, Cape Town 2011).

Neels, Jan L., 'Constitutional aspects of the Muslim Marriages Bill' *Tydskrif vir die Suid-Afrikaanse Reg / Journal of South African Law (T.S.A.R.)*, 2012, 486.

Neels, Jan L., 'External public policy, the incidental question properly so-called and the recognition of foreign divorce orders' in: Katharina Boele-Woelki, Talia Einhorn, Daniel Girsberger and Symeon Symeonides (eds), *Convergence and Divergence in Private International Law. Liber amicorum Kurt Siehr* (Eleven International Publishing - Schulthess, The Hague – Zurich, 2010), 331.

Neels, Jan L., 'Geoorloofdheid van 'n kontrak en openbare beleid in die internasionale privaatreg' *Tydskrif vir die Suid-Afrikaanse Reg / Journal of South African Law (T.S.A.R.)*, 1991, 694.

Neels, Jan L., 'Die internasionale privaatreg en die herverdelingsbevoegheid by egskeiding' *Tydskrif vir die Suid-Afrikaanse Reg /Journal of South African Law (T.S.A.R.)*, 1992, 336.

Neels, Jan L., 'The law applicable to the proprietary consequences of marriage in South Africa – the influence of German private international law' in: Hugo, Charl and Möllers, Thomas M. J. (eds), *Transnational Impacts on Law: Perspectives from South Africa and Germany* (Nomos, Juta, Baden-Baden 2017), 115.

Neels, Jan L., 'The positive role of public policy in private international law and the recognition of foreign Muslim marriages' *South African Journal for Human Rights (S.A.J.H.R.),* 28 (2012), 219.

Neels, Jan L. and Fredericks, Eesa A., 'The proper law of the proprietary consequences of marriage: Mauritian law in the South African Supreme Court of Appeal' *Tydskrif vir die Suid-Afrikaanse Reg / Journal of South African Law (T.S.A.R.)*, 2015, 918.

Neels, Jan L. and Wethmar-Lemmer, Marlene, 'Constitutional values and the proprietary consequences of marriage in private international law – introducing the *lex causae proprietatis matrimonii*' *Tydskrif vir die Suid-Afrikaanse Reg / Journal of South African Law (T.S.A.R.)*, 2008, 587.

Schoeman, Elsabe, 'The South African conflict rule for proprietary consequences of marriage: learning from the German experience' *Tydskrif vir die Suid-Afrikaanse Reg / Journal of South African Law (T.S.A.R.)*, 2004, 115.

Schoeman, Elsabe, 'The South African conflict rule for proprietary consequences of marriages: the need for reform' *Praxis des Internationalen Privat- und Verfahrensrecht (IPRax)*, 24 (2004), 65.

Schoeman, Elsabe, Roodt, Christa and Wethmar-Lemmer, Marlene, *Private International Law in South Africa* (Kluwer, Alphen-aan-den-Rijn, 2014).

Stoll, H. and Visser, P. J., 'Aspects of the reform of German (and South African) private international family law' *De Jure*, 1989, 330.

Van Niekerk, J. P., 'Choice of foreign law in a South African marine insurance policy: An unjustified limitation of party autonomy?' *Tydskrif vir die Suid-Afrikaanse Reg / Journal of South African Law (T.S.A.R.)*, 2011, 159.

Van Rooyen, J. C. W., *Die Kontrak in die Suid-Afrikaanse Internasionale Privaatreg* (Juta, Cape Town, 1972).

Wurmnest, Wolfgang and Maximilian Kübler-Wachendorff, M., 'The constitutionalization of public policy in private international law' (in this volume, p. 271).

Register of Cases

Anglin v Burchell (1134/2005) [2010] ZAECGHC 79 (22 Sept 2010) (available at www.saflii.org)

Anglin v Burchell (1134/2005) [2011] ZAECGHC 34 (22 July 2011) (available at www.saflii.org)

AS v CS 2011 2 SA 360 (WCC)

Bell v Bell 1991 4 SA 195 (W)

Burchell v Anglin 2010 3 SA 48 (ECG)

Daniels v Campbell NO 2005 5 SA 331 (CC)

Fourie v Minister of Home Affairs 2005 1 All SA 273 (SCA)

Frankel's Estate v The Master 1950 1 SA 220 (A)

Govender v Ragavayah NO 2009 3 SA 178 (D)

Hassam v Jacobs NO 2009 5 SA 572 (CC)

Lenferna v Lenferna (120/13) [2013] ZASCA 204 (02 Dec 2013) (available at www.saflii.org)

Minister of Home Affairs v Fourie (Doctors for Life International); Lesbian and Gay Equality Project v Minister of Home Affairs 2006 1 SA 524 (CC)

Representative of Lloyds v Classic Sailing Adventures (Pty) Ltd 2010 5 SA 90 (SCA)

Sadiku v Sadiku (30498/06) [2007] ZAGHPC 1 (26 Jan 2007) (available at www.saflii.org)

Sperling v Sperling 1975 3 SA 707 (A)

External Trade Agreements of the European Union and South Africa – Association Agreements versus Economic Partnership Agreements?

*Stefan Lorenzmeier**
*Hennie Strydom***

Abstract: *The European Union (EU) enjoys legal personality and is very active in concluding international trade agreements. This contribution will analyse two basic forms of the Union's external trade actions, Association Agreements (AA) and Economic Partnership Agreements (EPA) by using the agreement with Ukraine and the SADC with South Africa respectively as examples. Both types of agreements are meant to deepen and broaden the trade between the partners, which is in line with the EU's strategic goals. The rather disputed AA with Ukraine was novel in establishing a deep and comprehensive free trade area between the EU and Ukraine whereas the EPA with the SADC can be regarded as a more traditional free trade agreement and distinguishes between South Africa and the other members of the SADC due to their very different economic development. Thirdly, the rules of the new ACFTA will be explored and analysed. The comparison will show the strengths and weaknesses of each approach and the paper seeks to make a proposal to improve trade agreements.*

* Stefan Lorenzmeier, *Dr. iur., LL.M.*; senior research and teaching position, University of Augsburg, Faculty of Law.
** Hennie Strydom, *B Iuris, LLB, LLM, LLD*, Professor in Public International Law and holder of the South African Research Chair in International Law, University of Johannesburg.

I. Introduction

The European Union is very active in concluding international agreements and is now a partner to more than 1200 bi- or multilateral treaties.[1] Its external actions mainly, but not exclusively, cover trade issues which is due to the Union's special competence in the field of the Common Commercial Policy generally, and Art. 207 TFEU specifically, regulating the Union's

1 European External Action Service, *EU Treaties Office Database* (2018).

power to conclude international agreements falling within the ambit of the provision[2]. This contribution will therefore concentrate on two types of special trade agreements pursued by the EU, Association Agreements concluded in accordance with Art. 217 TFEU[3] on the one hand and Economic Partnership Agreements as they are concluded with the Sub-Sahara African countries, on the other. Both types will be illustrated by using the agreements with Ukraine[4] and the SADC-countries[5], respectively. Thirdly, the rules of the recently established African Continental Free Trade Area (ACFTA) will be explored, which will be relevant for South Africa.

1. EU Trade Strategies

By establishing free trade areas between the partners and creating special trade relations, the Union intends to foster world trade and the well-being of persons. Both EU agreements analysed here establish preferential trade zones among the partners. In 2015, the EU adopted a new trade strategy, aptly named "Trade for all"[6], developing further the 2006 "Global Europe strategy"[7] according to which the agreements with Ukraine and the SADC-countries were largely modelled.

---

2 See, for example, European Court of Justice, Opinion 2/15, 16.05.2017, *Free Trade Agreement with Singapore*, ECLI:EU:C:2017:376; Treaty on the Functioning of the European Union (TFEU), Art. 207(1) reads: "The common commercial policy shall be based on uniform principles, particularly with regard to changes in tariff rates, the conclusion of tariff and trade agreements relating to trade in goods and services, and the commercial aspects of intellectual property, foreign direct investment, the achievement of uniformity in measures of liberalization, export policy and measures to protect trade such as those to be taken in the event of dumping and subsidies. [...]".

3 Treaty on the Functioning of the European Union (TFEU) Art. 217 reads: "The Union may conclude with one or more third countries or international organizations agreements establishing an association involving reciprocal rights and obligations, common action and special procedure".

4 Association Agreement between the European Union and its Member States, of the one part, and Ukraine, of the other part, OJ 2014 L 161/1.

5 Economic Partnership Agreement between the European Union and its Member States, of the one part, and the SADC EPA states, of the other part, OJ 2016 L 350/3, not yet in force, only provisionally applicable.

6 European Commission, *Trade for all* (2015).

7 European Commission, *Global Europe competing in the world* (2006).

The 2006 Global Europe strategy stated that "Free Trade Agreements (FTAs), if approached with care, can build on WTO and other international rules by going further and faster in promoting openness and integration, by tackling issues which are not ready for multilateral discussion and by preparing the ground for the next level of multilateral liberalization".[8] Yet, the new free trade agreements should be developed further and cover more areas. Content-wise,

> "the new FTAs would need to be comprehensive and ambitious in coverage, aiming at the highest possible degree of trade liberalisation, including far-reaching liberalisation of services and investment. A new, ambitious model EU investment agreement should be developed in close coordination with Member States.[9] Where our partners have signed FTAs with other countries that are competitors to the EU, we should seek full parity at least. Quantitative import restrictions and all forms of duties, taxes, charges and restrictions on exports should be eliminated."

In addition, the EU Commission also identified non-tariff barriers as an obstacle to trade. Thus, according to the 2006 strategy, the new

> "[…] FTAs should also tackle non-tariff barriers through regulatory convergence wherever possible and contain strong trade facilitation provisions. FTAs should include stronger provisions for IPR and competition, including for example provisions on enforcement of IP rights along the lines of the EC Enforcement Directive. We (the EU-Commission) will seek to include provisions on good governance in financial, tax and judicial areas where appropriate. We should also ensure Rules of Origin in FTAs are simpler and more modern and reflect the realities of globalisation. We will put in place internal mechanisms to monitor the implementation and the results of new FTAs."[10]

Stemming from the 2006 strategy, the trade relations of the European Union are intended to be deepened and widened at the same time. "Deepening" means that trade agreements shall go beyond the traditional removal of tariff barriers and quotas by focusing on other issues such as regulatory convergence. Additionally, the scope of the trade agreements should be extended by covering areas such as services, investment and so on. The "widening" part of the 2006 strategy meant that the respective free trade agreement had to be embedded into the EU's wider policy goals, as laid down in Articles

---

8 European Commission, *Global Europe competing in the world* (2006), 10.

9 This is due to the EU's limited competence in this regard as stated in the Singapore opinion by the Court of Justice, see European Court of Justice, Opinion 2/15, 16.05.2017, *Free Trade Agreement with Singapore*, ECLI:EU:C:2017:376, paras. 243 et seq.

10 European Commission, *Global Europe competing in the world* (2006), 11.

2, 3 and 21 TEU. The 2015 "trade for all"-strategy put more emphasis on the development policy and intents to create a more responsible trade and investment policy of the Union, which will not be dealt with in this contribution.

Instead, this contribution intends to show how the aims of the Union have been achieved in the course of the negotiations of the Association Agreement with Ukraine and the Economic Partnership Agreement with the SADC-countries.[11] Due to the extensive volume of the agreements, this can only be done in using parts of the treaties as examples. By way of introduction, a brief section will be devoted to the structure of the European Union's external (trade) actions.

2. South Africa

South Africa, as one of the leading economies on the African continent, has traditionally strong ties with some member states of the European Union, for instance Germany and the Netherlands. Moreover. It is economically also closely linked together with its African partners by the Southern African Development Cooperation (SADC). The economic relations with other African economies will be improved by the African Continental Free Trade Area, which is also explored infra.

II. External (Trade) Actions of the European Union

The European Union is a special international organisation. According to Article 47 TEU, the European Union had been entrusted with legal personality, which means that the Union is considered by its members to be a subject under Public International Law. As such, the EU can enter into international agreements as far as it is competent to do so, which is a function of its internal division of competences laid down in the EU treaties and in the Article 2 et seq. TFEU.

In this context, the notion of the Union's limited attribution of powers has special relevance in that the EU can only act if the member states have

11 OJ 2016 L 250/1. The Agreement was signed in 2016, but has not yet been ratified.

granted her the said power in the EU-treaties.[12] For instance, the power to conclude international trade agreements, like the EU-SADC agreement, is conferred in Article 207 (3) TFEU[13], and the power to conclude association agreements, like the one with Ukraine, is laid down in Article 217 TFEU. Trade agreements of the European Union usually do establish a free trade area which is accompanied by other considerations such as respect for human rights and democracy.[14] Association agreements have similar but more characteristic features. Besides the intention to establish close political and economic cooperation, paritary bodies concerning the management of the agreement are established which leads in essence to a special, privileged link between the two partners.[15]

International agreements are concluded in all areas of Union competence. However, in only a few instances the respective competences of a to be concluded agreement are fully and exclusively in the hands of the Union alone.[16] In these cases, not only the European Union but also the member states become parties to the agreement with the third party. Hence, the external agreement of the Union assumes a "mixed" character.[17] Both agreements at stake have been concluded as mixed agreements. Mixed agreements, which are peculiar to the Union's legal order and unknown in other facets of international law, are extremely complex[18] and a breeding ground

---

12 The principle of conferral, see Treaty on European Union (TEU), Art. 5(1).

13 For the EU competence in matters of commercial policy, see Piet Eeckhout, *EU External Relations Law* (2nd Edition, 2011), 12 et seq.

14 For the SADC agreement: Southern African Development Community (SADC), Art. 20 establishes a free trade area, while the first part of the agreement covers issues of sustainable development and other parts of cooperation, OJ 2016 L 250/5 ff.

15 European Court of Justice, Case 12/86, 30.09.1987, *Demirel v. Stadt Schwäbisch Gmünd*, ECLI:EU:C:1987:400.

16 Bart Van Vooren, Ramses Wessels, *EU External Relations Law* (2014), 55.

17 On mixed agreements, see Joni Heliskoski, *Mixed Agreements as a Technique for Organizing the International Relations of the European Community and its Member States*, (2001); Christophe Hillion, Panos Koutrakos, *Mixed Agreements revisited* (2010); Piet Eeckhout, *EU External Relations Law* (2nd Edition, 2011), 212 et seqq.; Pieter Kuijper, Jan Wouters, Frank Hoffmeister, Gert De Baere and Thomas Ramopoulos, *The Law of EU External Relations* (2013), 105 et seqq. One of the unresolved issues is, for instance, the effect of Brexit on the mixed agreements concluded by the EU.

18 Bart Van Vooren, Ramses Wessels, *EU External Relations Law* (2014), 56 with examples.

for internal legal conflicts[19] due to the interwoven Union and Member States competences. Hence, the EU-organs' political idea is to conclude more EU only agreements in the future[20] to avoid these problems.

III. The Association Agreement with Ukraine

Rather unexpectedly, the Association Agreement with Ukraine became one of the most disputed agreements ever concluded by the Union which entered into force on September 1, 2017 after a long negotiation and ratification history.[21]

1. Political Issues

It led to a change of government in Ukraine, a war with one of its neighbours and the loss of control of parts of its territory. This became especially problematic in respect of the territorial scope of the agreement, which applies to the full territory of Ukraine as accepted under Public International Law.[22] Products stemming from the occupied areas are covered by the agreement but need an official Ukrainian export permit, which is impossible to obtain for products from Crimea and the Donbass region.

---

19 See, for example, the conflict about the ratification of the agreement with Ukraine or the CETA-agreement with Canada.

20 See, for example, the signed Economic Partnership Agreement with Japan falling solely within the competence of the EU, which will be accompanied by a Strategic Partnership Agreement of a more mixed character, see European Commission, *EU-Japan economic partnership agreement* (2017).

21 On the entry into force: European Union, *EU-Ukraine Association Agreement enters fully into force* (2017). Regarding the history see Guillaume Van der Loo, *The EU-Ukraine Association Agreement and Deep and Comprehensive Free Trade Area* (2016), 104 et seqq.

22 On these issues: Stefan Lorenzmeier, 'Territorialer Anwendungsbereich von Assoziierungsabkommen – Im Hinblick auf umstrittene Gebiete', in: Stefan Lorenzmeier and Hans-Peter Folz (eds), *Recht und Realität* (2017), 336 (352 et seqq).

a) Eastern Partnership of the European Union

The agreement with Ukraine is part of the European Union's Eastern Partnership initiative, which aims at establishing good relations with the Union's eastern partner countries.[23] As a policy tool, the Eastern Partnership had been developed by the EU Commission in 2004 as a result of its enlargement process and now forms part of Article 8 TEU, according to which the Union shall seek to establish good relations with its neighbours.[24] It is part of the Union's Neighborhood Policy and shall accelerate political association and further economic integration between the EU and its eastern partners[25], which in the current instance means Ukraine.[26]

b) Integration (Without Membership) Agreement

From a legal point of view the Association Agreement with Ukraine can be considered the most ambitious agreement the European Union has ever offered to a non-Member State.[27] It includes provisions with the whole array of EU activities, including cooperation in areas like common foreign and security policy and the areas of freedom, security and the law. Most importantly, it creates a deep and comprehensive free trade area between the partners, covering substantially all trade between the EU and Ukraine.[28] Article 1 lit. (d) AA states that Ukraine shall be gradually integrated into the EU market. The main tool for achieving such integration is the obligation

23 See, for example, Peter Van Elsuwege, Roman Petrov (eds), *Legislative Approximation and Application of EU Law in the Eastern Neighbourhood of the European Union* (2016).

24 The European Neighborhood Policy (ENP) is analysed by Bart Van Vooren, *EU External Relations Law and the European Neighborhood Policy* (2012), 225 et seqq.

25 European Commission, *Eastern Partnership*, COM (2008) 823 final, 3 December 2008.

26 Other partners are Georgia and Moldova, which have ratified similar, but not so advanced agreements with the EU as Ukraine.

27 Herman Van Rompuy, *Remarks of the President of the European Council at the press conference of the European Summit in Vilnius* (2013). A clear indicator for this is its sheer size with over 2100 pages. Now, the CETA can be regarded as a similar agreement.

28 Guillaume Van der Loo, *The EU-Ukraine Association Agreement and Deep and Comprehensive Free Trade Area* (2016), 3.

to apply or integrate into the Ukrainian legal order a (far-reaching) selection of the EU acquis[29] which makes it an EU integration agreement. [30] The peculiarity of this approach can be seen in the fact that the partner country of the Union has to apply the acquis directly in its legal order as in the case of an EU member state, which goes far beyond a mere approximation of its own laws to EU standards.[31] As a result, the Association Agreement creates a common legal space between the EU and Ukraine[32] causing Ukraine to become integrated, without membership, in the single European market[33], which is, admittedly, one of the main goals of the agreement.

This goal can only be achieved by establishing a uniform application of the respective European legal act in the European as well as in the legal order of the third state. Unfortunately, the application of the said principles is anything but uniform throughout the agreement. In the chapters of the EU – Ukraine agreement, where a far-reaching integration into the EU market is envisaged, the procedures to achieve uniformity of the Ukrainian with the European legal order are very elaborate. In other chapters this is not the case. For instance, in some chapters of the DCFTA an obligation to incorporate the case-law of the Court of Justice of the European Union can be found, whereas this obligation is absent in other chapters.

The same is true for the update of the acquis. In some chapters an obligation to update the acquis can be found, in others such a provision is missing. Consequently,, the agreement is rather difficult to understand and apply and may fail the objective of establishing clear legal rules. Secondly, it

---

29 Guillaume Van der Loo, *The EU-Ukraine Association Agreement and Deep and Comprehensive Free Trade Area* (2016), 23.

30 Marc Maresceau, 'Les accords d'intégration dans les relations de proximité de l'Union Europeénne', in: Claude Blumann (ed), *Les frontiers de l'Union Europeénne* (2013), 151 (152 et seqq.).

31 See, for example, Adam Lazowski, 'Box of Chocolates Integration: The European Economic Area and the Swiss Model Revisited', in: Steven Blockmans and Sacha Prechal (eds), *Reconciling the Deepening and the Widening of the European Union* (2008), 87 (89); Marc Maresceau, *Bilateral Agreements concluded by the European Community* (2006), 317.

32 Adam Lazowski, 45 (2008) *Common Market Law Review (CMLRev)*, 1433 (1437).

33 To the concept: Adam Lazowski, 45 (2008) *Common Market Law Review (CMLRev)*, 1433. Especially for the EU – Ukraine Agreement: Guillaume Van der Loo, *The EU-Ukraine Association Agreement and Deep and Comprehensive Free Trade Area* (2016), 3.

should be noted that different terms[34] are used to establish an obligation to approximate the Ukrainian legal order. However, despite the use of different terms, their meaning is identical. In any case, Ukraine is obligated to act and the approximation is not merely voluntary, as in other trade agreements.[35]

2. Deep and Comprehensive Free Trade Area

The cornerstone of the Association agreement with Ukraine is the establishment of a deep and comprehensive free trade area. As a free trade instrument, the agreement eliminated almost all tariffs on goods[36], although the agreement is asymmetrical in the sense that the EU will remove the trade barriers faster than Ukraine.[37]

a) Deep Free Trade Area

A "deep" free trade area does not only focus on the removal of traditional obstacles to trade but also entails regulatory convergence and goes beyond trade in goods by focusing on other areas like services, intellectual property, competition etc. as well.[38] As a consequence, its telos can be considered to be the removal of non-tariff barriers through legislative approximation between the partners[39] which means in reality the approximation of the Ukrainian legal order to the EU acquis. Unfortunately, the EU is using an incoherent terminology for achieving this result by using terms such as "alignment with EU standards", "regulatory convergence", "progressive

---

34 The used terms are 'alignment', 'convergence', '(regulatory) approximation' and 'adoption'.

35 This raises critical issues for the internal Ukrainian legal order, see Roman Petrov, *European Public Law (EPL)* 2015, 241 et seqq.

36 About 99.1% of the duties in trade volume will be eliminated; European Commission, *EU-Ukraine Deep and Comprehensive Free Trade Area* (2013).

37 This shall give Ukrainian producers more time to adept to competition from the European Union.

38 Karel De Gucht, *Trade as a cornerstone for the EU Eastern Partnership* (23 January 2012).

39 Guillaume Van der Loo, *The EU-Ukraine Association Agreement and Deep and Comprehensive Free Trade Area* (2016), 222.

approximation of EU rules and practices" and "regulatory alignment", without providing a clear indication of the reason for the use of different terms for the same principle. The long term goal is that Ukrainian exporters must meet EU standards by respecting their own rules and regulations.[40] In this way the Ukrainian market would open up to foreign investors and Ukraine would be integrated into the EU market. Seemingly, such an ambitious form of market integration and liberalisation of markets can only work with economically weaker partners who do not have the leverage to export their own rules.[41] As TTIP and CETA show, such an approach is not feasible with stronger trade partners. This is true for the provisions on market access conditionality as well, which will be dealt with below.

b) Comprehensive Free Trade Area

A widening of areas, the comprehensive part of the free trade area, is part of this policy too. As a result, Ukraine commits itself on regulatory approximation in trade-related areas, which will lead to its gradual integration into the EU market[42] without being a member of it. The comprehensive character of the agreement implies that the agreement covers a broad range of subject matters, signifying an evolution from the already existing traditional free trade agreements which usually cover only goods.[43] For instance, the EU – Ukraine DCFTA consists of 15 chapters entailing e. g. rules on national treatment and market access for goods, trade remedies, technical barriers to trade, sanitary and phytosanitary measures, establishment, trade in services, movement of capital, public procurement, competition, trade and sustainable development and dispute settlement.

---

40 Karel De Gucht, *Trade as a cornerstone for the EU Eastern Partnership* (23 January 2012).

41 See also Guillaume Van der Loo, *The EU-Ukraine Association Agreement and Deep and Comprehensive Free Trade Area* (2016), 223.

42 See Frank Hoffmeister, 'The Deep and Comprehensive Free Trade Areas of the European Union – Concept and Challenges', in: Marise Cremona and Tamara Takács (eds), *Trade liberalisation and standardisation – new directions in the low politics of EU foreign politics* (2013), 11.

43 Guillaume Van der Loo, *The EU-Ukraine Association Agreement and Deep and Comprehensive Free Trade Area* (2016), 221.

Moreover, it also has a chapter on trade-related energy issues, which is of special relevance for Ukraine due to its position as a gas trading intermediary. In respect of goods, the agreement is rather ambitious too, and goes further than most other free trade areas of the EU when it comes to agriculture. For instance, the DCFTA establishes, after burdensome and difficult negotiations, close to full liberalisation of trade in agricultural and agro-related goods.[44] Concerning trade in industrial goods, raw materials and textiles, tariffs will be removed for most products.[45] In both cases there is an asymmetry in respect of the market opening; the EU has to open its markets sooner than Ukraine in that the transitional period is usually seven years for the EU and ten years for Ukraine.

The obligation on Ukraine to implement a predetermined selection of European legislation into its own legal order makes the agreement an "integration agreement"[46] causing a third party to become integrated into the European legal order which is then secured from the union side by the concept of conditionality (see infra), which is absent in other far-reaching agreements such as the Agreement on the European Economic Area (EEA-Agreement).[47]

3. Conditionality Principles

As already stated, the conditionality-clauses of the Association Agreement with Ukraine are of special relevance for the execution and implementation of the agreement and constitute a very special layer of the legal system established by the EU – Ukraine Association Agreement. In the agreement conditionality exists in two different, but related forms, namely a value and market-related conditionality. This will be addressed in turn.

---

44 See the table in Guillaume Van der Loo, *The EU-Ukraine Association Agreement and Deep and Comprehensive Free Trade Area* (2016), 230 et seq.

45 With the notable exception of the automotive sector and worn clothing.

46 See supra and Guillaume Van der Loo, *The EU-Ukraine Association Agreement and Deep and Comprehensive Free Trade Area* (2016), 212.

47 The EEA-Agreement entails in Art. 6 EEA a homogeneity clause, which is not accompanied by a security mechanism, see Finn Arnesen, 'Homogeneity and Disparity', in: Stefan Lorenzmeier and Hans-Peter Folz (eds), *Recht und Realität* (2017), 257 et seqq.; Pål Wennerås, in: Finn Arnesen, Halvard Fredriksen, Hans Graver, Ola Mestad and Christoph Vedder (eds), *Agreement on the European Economic Area – A Commentary* (2018), art. 6 EEA.

a) Common Values Conditionality

First, there is the concept of common values conditionality, whereby the European Union exports its key values as laid down in Article 2 TEU, like full respect for democratic principles, the rule of law, good governance, human rights and fundamental freedoms, to an external legal order.[48] Also important is Article 6 AA which states that the EU and Ukraine shall cooperate in order to ensure that their internal policies are based on principles common to the Parties, in particular stability and effectiveness and democratic institutions and the rule of law […]. This political conditionality can lead, for instance, to a visa free regime in accordance with Article 19 (3) AA.

b) Market Access Conditionality

The second layer can be described as market access conditionality, whereby it shall be ensured that Ukraine's integration in the market will be in accordance with EU rules. It can only be found in the DCFTA and is an unprecedented mechanism, which comes in various forms.[49] In effect, the principle is intertwined with the additional principle of legislative approximation of the Ukrainian legal order to the EU acquis, as explained earlier on. This means that the more integrated a sector of the economy is, the stronger will be the supervisory mechanism, in this instance the principle of market access conditionality. It is a *conditio sine qua non* to obtain additional access to the EU market and it is a part of the EU Policy of the deepening of trade agreements.[50]

---

48 Association Agreement (AA), Art. 2 states explicitly: "Respect for democratic principles, human rights and fundamental freedoms, as defined in particular in the Helsinki Final Act of 1975 of the CSCE and the Charter of Paris for a new Europe of 1990, and other relevant human rights instruments, among them the UN Universal Declaration of Human Rights and the ECHR, and respect for the principle of the rule of law shall form the basis of the domestic and external policies of the Parties and constitute essential elements of this Agreement. [...]". To note is also Art. 14 AA on justice, freedom and security, which attaches special importance to the principles of Art. 2 AA.

49 Guillaume Van der Loo, *The EU-Ukraine Association Agreement and Deep and Comprehensive Free Trade Area* (2016), 210.

50 Guillaume Van der Loo, *The EU-Ukraine Association Agreement and Deep and Comprehensive Free Trade Area* (2016), 210 et seq.

Moreover, in some chapters of the DCFTA[51] a special form of market access is granted to Ukraine which can be described as a two-tier system. As a first step, Ukraine has to apply a part of the EU acquis, which is usually annexed to the agreement. This will be strictly monitored by the EU through different mechanisms, like drafting progress reports or "on-the spot-missions".[52] Following this, the results of the monitoring process are to be discussed within the joint bodies established by the AA. Only after a positive assessment of these bodies, further market access can be granted to Ukraine. In addition, the decisions of these bodies are not covered by the agreement's dispute settlement mechanism.[53] In essence, the mechanisms establish an asymmetrical market access conditionality which is difficult to reconcile with the idea of an equal partnership between two treaty partners.[54]

The main point of a conditionality is that it is granting a party to the Association Agreement the right to take appropriate measures immediately when an essential element of the Association Agreement is violated by the other party. Presumably, the EU will trigger this mechanism which is provided for in Article 478 AA. Also noteworthy is the fact that in the case of a violation of a common value, the EU is entitled to suspend trade advantages granted under the DCFTA as well, due to the extensive scope of the provision.

4. Intermediate Results

The EU – Ukrainian Association Agreement is an asymmetric legal instrument and severely limits Ukraine's sovereignty in respect of law-making in the areas covered by the DCFTA. This is achieved through the legal principle of conditionality, which shall ensure that Ukraine is following the required EU rules for gaining extensive access to the EU market.

The disadvantage of market access conditionality is that, in light of the extensive drafting history of the agreement, the to be applied rules of the EU acquis become outdated over time and not in all chapters is the reference to the EU acquis an evolutionary one. For instance, the references to the secondary financial markets law of the Union are not evolutionary since

51 The mechanism applies to the 'new' sectors like services and public procurement, not for the traditional trade in goods part.

52 See Ukraine Association Agreement (AA), Art. 475.

53 Ukraine Association Agreement (AA), Art. 475(6).

54 Guillaume Van der Loo, *The EU-Ukraine Association Agreement and Deep and Comprehensive Free Trade Area* (2016), 213.

they actually refer to the EU acquis of the pre-financial crisis. This runs counter to the idea of market access conditionality as a tool for supervising the application of EU law in the Ukrainian legal order because Ukraine would only be obliged to implement outdated secondary law of the Union. Thus, for future agreements it would be better to have active implementation clauses which are relying on still valid Union law.

The Association Agreement with Ukraine can only work in a situation of the third partner's clear economic dependence on the EU. However, it has to be stated, too, that the Union does not seem to exploit its much stronger position by exporting its own political and market rules to a third country. This is because of the advantages of the approach taken by the Ukraine, namely that its exporters automatically comply with EU regulations.

IV. The Economic Partnership Agreement with the SADC

The not yet ratified Economic Partnership Agreement (EPA) with the SADC-countries (SADC-Agreement) has a long negotiating history as well. Its incubator is the Trade, Development and Co-Operation_Agreement with South Africa from 1999[55], which regulates the trade relations between the EU and South Africa at the moment. The Trade, Development and Co-Operation-Agreement has established a preferential free trade area between the partners, applicable to about 90% of the bilateral trade between the European Union and South Africa.[56] It has increased trade with South Africa to about 120% of its pre-application level.

As part of its development strategy for Africa[57], the European Union decided to renew and change its trade relations with South Africa and to include the SADC-countries in a general, trade promotional environment as well. This happened especially in light of the Union's special trade relations with the SADC-countries, mostly former colonies of EU member states. Additionally, according to Art. 2 (1) SADC-A the SADC-Agreement builds upon the already existing treaty relations between the partners, namely the Cotonou Agreement and other agreements concluded with the ACP-countries.

---

55 OJ 1999 L 311/1.

56 See European Commission, *Country Report South Africa* (2018).

57 See e. g. European Commission, *Communication on a new Africa –Europe Alliance for Sustainable Investment and Jobs: Taking our partnership for investment and jobs to the next level*, COM(2018) 643 final.

1. The Agreement – Political and Market Access Provisions

Like the Association Agreement with Ukraine, the SADC-Agreement can also be divided into a political and a market access-part, whereas both parts are much shorter and cover less subjects than the DCFTA in the case of Ukraine. Hence, and by comparison, the SADC-Agreement can be regarded as a more traditional trade agreement. However, the SADC-Agreement also entails rules on conditionality, although these differ from the ones laid down in the Association Agreement with Ukraine. It is also a very extensive agreement, covering more than 2100 pages including the annexes.

a) Political Provisions

The SADC-Agreement has a political part as well, which is laid down in the opening parts of the agreement.[58] In respect of the political provisions, Article 2 (1) SADC-A states clearly that the EPA is based on the principles of human rights, democracy and rule of law. If one of these fundamental principles is violated by any-one party to the agreement, appropriate retaliation measures can be taken, including, as a matter of last resort and in conformity with the provisions of the Cotonou agreement, the suspension of trade benefits.

Additionally, the parties are obligated to comply with international labour and environmental standards if they enact new or modify legislation in the fields mentioned. As a result, the parties are barred from weakening labour and environmental standards to increase trade. In addition, the provisions of the Cotonou Agreement from 2000[59] on human rights, sustainable development and civil/parliamentary dialogue continue to apply in the case of the SADC-Agreement. This creates a very comprehensive protection in the said areas, which is rather special for international agreements establishing an economic partnership.

---

58 Southern African Development Community (SADC) Art. 2–19.

59 On the Cotonou Agreement see: European Commission, *ACP – The Cotonou Agreement* (2018).

b) Market Access Provisions

The European Union is the SADC-countries' strongest trading partner with South Africa being the strongest trade partner in the group of the SADC member states. The signed, but not yet ratified agreement aims at promoting trade and fostering development by opening the EU market through eliminating tariffs for all products except arms and ammunition coming from Botswana, Lesotho, Mozambique and Swaziland, and about 99% of goods from South Africa. The SADC-countries do not have to respond with the same openness in areas sensitive to international competition. For instance, South Africa removes customs duties on about 86% of EU goods imported into South Africa. This makes the agreement an instrument of asymmetric liberalisation unknown outside of Economic Partnership Agreements for development purposes. It is also the first EU agreement prohibiting EU export subsidies for agricultural products.

(i) Regional Integration

An additional layer of the agreement is the strengthening of regional integration in southern Africa by extending every advantage granted by the EU to other members of the SADC-countries to the other member states as well (Article 3 SADC-A). As such, it is expected by the European Union that, over time, the existing obstacles to trade between the SADC members will be abolished or at least reduced.

A further feature in this respect is the harmonisation of customs rules established by the Southern African Customs Union (SACU). The SACU, consisting of Botswana, Lesotho, Namibia, South Africa and Swaziland, thus the majority of the SADC states, is the world's oldest customs union. Unfortunately, the SACU members are applying different tariffs to imports from the European Union, which lead, in effect, to an imbalanced customs union. With the entry into force of the SADC-Agreement, the different customs regimes will be redeemed by a uniform one creating greater unity among the SACU partners.

(ii) Special Rules for South Africa

South Africa is by far the biggest economy in the SADC region and the SADC EPA distinguishes strongly between South Africa and other members of SADC by laying down special rules in an additional protocol to the agreement. The "old" Trade, Development and Cooperation Agreement with South Africa[60], concluded in 2000, only opened the markets between the parties partially.[61] The new SADC EPA can be regarded as a next step in relations between the European Union and South Africa, because it opens the respective markets for additional, mostly agricultural products and protects, in particular, traditional product names, also called geographical indications, which include special provisions for South African wines and spirits. Hence, only South African producers can produce "Rooibos" teas. Most South African products do enjoy preferential customs duties by entering the EU market.

(iii) Trade in accordance with WTO-rules

A final issue of the agreement is that EU trade with the SADC countries will now be fully in line with WTO rules which further strengthens the international, rule-based system of international trade. In light of recent protectionist developments on the global stage this feature can hardly be overstated. In effect, the SADC EPA is a classic trade agreement envisaged in the European Union's 2006 Global Strategy.

c) Conditionality

As stated above, the conditionality aspect is limited in the SADC-Agreement. Article 4 SADC-A mentions only the continuous monitoring of the agreement's implementation by the parties. If a problem occurs in this respect, the parties are obliged to consult each other and the matter can be regulated by the Joint Council, a common institution established under the agreement. If consultation does not prove to be successful in a given case, the general rules of Public International Law regarding the suspension or termination of an agreement will apply in line with the Cotonou-principles

---

60 See Southern African Development Community (SADC) Art. 100 et seqq.

61 See *supra*.

mentioned above. Hence, the rules on conditionality entailed in the SADC-Agreement are much weaker than in the agreement with Ukraine, but the agreement is also far more symmetrical than the one with Ukraine, and in effect, in line with the general idea that equal powers should conclude an equal treaty.

2. Intermediate Results

The new SADC-Agreement is the next step in opening up the markets between the SADC-countries and the European Union. It is, from the point of view of its scope and content, more of a classic trade agreement in line with other Economic Partnership Agreements of the European Union. Its asymmetry is against the Union, which is granting more benefits to SADC members than vice versa, except South Africa, which falls under a special arrangement. The provisions on conditionality are also more in accordance with the general rules of treaty obligations applicable in Public International Law.

V. The Agreement Establishing the African Continental Free Trade Area (ACFTA)

With the signing of the ACFTA on 21 March 2018, another layer of free trade norms of continental-wide scope and application was introduced. Currently, ACFTA has forty-nine signatures and seven ratifications and it will enter into force thirty days after the deposit of the 22nd instrument of ratification. This also applies to its Protocols on Trade in Goods and Trade in Services; on Rules and Procedures on the Settlement of Disputes; and on Investment, Intellectual Property Rights, and Competition Policy.[62]

The adoption of ACFTA marks the culmination of negotiations, which commenced in June 2015[63], for the establishment of a continental free trade area with the aim of integrating Africa's markets in line with the objectives and principles of the 1991 Abuja Treaty Establishing the African Economic

62 Agreement Establishing the African Continental Free Trade Area (ACFTA) Art. 23 (1) and (2).

63 Decision on the launch of continental free trade area negotiations, AU/Dec. 569 (XXV), 1.

Community. The objectives and institutions provided for in the Abuja Treaty were largely subsumed by the 2000 Constitutive Act of the AU, which, in any event, takes precedence over any inconsistent and contrary provisions of the Abuja Treaty.[64]

1. Objectives and Principles

ACFTA's relationship with the regional economic communities (REC's), such as SADC[65], forms part of the agreement's objectives in that ACFTA aims at contributing to the movement of capital and natural persons and to facilitating investments by building on the initiatives and developments within states parties and the REC's.[66] Linked to this is the objective of resolving the challenges presented by overlapping memberships and to expedite the regional and continental integration processes.[67] Where the agreement deals with the principles that will govern ACFTA, the REC's Free Trade Areas are considered as 'building blocks' for the ACFTA[68] with the result that best practices in the REC's will govern actions taken under the agreement.[69] Other principles that are worth mentioning are flexibility and special and differential treatment; transparency and disclosure of information; preservation of the acquis; most-favoured-nation treatment; national treatment; reciprocity; substantial liberalisation; consensus in decision-making; and international conventions binding the AU.[70]

In none of its substantive provisions does the agreement contain formulations that approximate the market access and common values conditionalities mentioned in the other examples above. The closest one gets to a common values conditionality is a non-descript formulation in the preamble to the effect that the agreement recognises "the importance of international security, democracy, human rights, gender equality and the rule of law, for the development of international trade and economic cooperation".

64 Constitutive Act of the African Union Art. 33 (2).
65 See Agreement Establishing the African Continental Free Trade Area (ACFTA) Art. 1 (t).
66 ACFTA Art. 3 (c).
67 Ibid. Art. 3 (h).
68 Ibid. Art. 5 (b).
69 Ibid. Art. 5 (l).
70 Ibid. Art. 5.

2. Conflicting Obligations

Given the scope of ACFTA, namely its intention to "cover trade in goods, trade in services, investment, intellectual property rights and competition policy"[71] it is a trade agreement that aims at establishing a deep and comprehensive free trade regime for the African continent in cooperation with member states and the REC's. For this purpose phase II negotiations, to be undertaken in successive rounds, shall be pursued by member states in the areas of intellectual property rights, investment and competition policy.[72] Given these developments and other agreements AU member states have become party to, such as the EU-SADC EPA discussed above, it may be of particular importance to consider the issue of conflicting obligations member states may assume under different treaty regimes. Various provisions in ACFTA and the Protocols, which will form an integral part of the ACFTA when they enter into force, are of relevance here.

The starting point is the disclosure obligation for member states in the ACFTA. According to Article 16 (1) states parties must promptly publish or make publicly available any other commitments under an international agreement relating to any trade matter covered by the ACFTA. This disclosure obligation applies to any commitment under a different international trade agreement adopted after the entry into force of the ACFTA and to any actual or any proposed measure which in the view of a state party might materially affect the operation of the ACFTA, or otherwise substantially affect the interests of the other states parties to the ACFTA. In both these latter instances the other parties to the ACFTA must be notified of the circumstances via the Secretariat.[73]

Once the ACFTA has entered into force, states parties, when implementing the ACFTA, shall accord each other, on a reciprocal basis, preferences that are no less favourable than those given to third parties.[74] Prior to the entry into force of the ACFTA, states parties are entitled to negotiate preferences granted to third parties on a reciprocal basis. A state party interested in such preferences must afford other states parties the opportunity to negotiate, on a reciprocal basis, taking into account the levels of development of

71 Ibid. Art. 6.
72 Ibid. Art. 7.
73 Ibid. Art. 17 (1) and (2).
74 Ibid. Art. 18 (1).

states parties.[75] It is then determined in clear terms that the ACFTA "shall not nullify, modify or revoke rights and obligations under pre-existing trade agreements that States Parties have with Third Parties".[76]

However, in the case of a conflict or inconsistency between the ACFTA and a regional agreement, the ACFTA shall prevail to the extent of the specific inconsistency, except as otherwise provided.[77] Notwithstanding this provision, states parties to other regional economic communities, trading arrangements and customs unions, which have attained among themselves a higher level of regional integration than under the ACFTA, shall maintain that higher level of integration.[78]

Relevant in the last instance is the Protocol on Rules and Procedures on the Settlement of Disputes. This Protocol is the outcome of the establishment, in Article 20 of the ACFTA of a dispute settlement mechanism, and the envisaged establishment, by means of the Protocol, of a Dispute Settlement Body (DSB). In terms of the Protocol, a 'dispute' "means a disagreement between States Parties regarding the interpretation and/or application of the Agreement in relation to their rights and obligations".[79] In dealing with such disputes the Protocol claims that the dispute settlement mechanism will form a central element in providing security and predictability to the regional trading system and that the rights and obligations of states parties under the ACFTA will be preserved "in accordance with customary rules of interpretation of public international law".[80]

Although this formulation may be susceptible to diverse interpretations, in essence it ought to be understood as a reference to Article 31 of the 1969 Vienna Convention on the Law of Treaties. The first paragraph of this provision contains the well-known and universally accepted rule that a treaty must be interpreted in good faith[81], in accordance with the ordinary meaning of the terms of the treaty in their context, and in light of the object and

75 Ibid. Art. 18 (2).
76 Ibid. Art. 18 (3).
77 Ibid. Art. 19 (1).
78 Ibid. Art. 19 (2).
79 ACFTA Protocol Art. 1 (e).
80 Ibid. Art. 4 (1).
81 See also Vienna Convention on the law of treaties (VCLT) Art. 26.

purpose of the treaty. In the case of the *Territorial Dispute* between Chad and Libya, the ICJ has confirmed the customary law status of this rule.[82]

Among the other interpretation aids mentioned in Article 31 (3) reference is also made to "any relevant rules of international law applicable in the relations between states".[83] It has been argued that this rule of interpretation views the international legal order as one single system and has the potential to avoid fragmentation and to ensure systemic cohesion by arriving at a meaning that would reflect the shared elements in the rules of an integrated international legal order.[84] The rule therefore allows (a) for treaty terms to be interpreted in the light of the terms of another treaty, especially if they deal with a similar subject-matter; (b) for customary international law to provide guidance on the preferred interpretation; and (c) for non-binding international law instruments to be relevant as interpretation aids.[85]

In the final instance the rules on norm-conflicts should be alluded to. These are covered in Article 30 of the Vienna Convention in the context of successive treaties and overlapping membership. As such, Article 30 is informed by the *lex posterior* and *lex specialis* rules. The relevant parts read as follows:

> 2. When a treaty specifies that it is subject to, or that it is not to be considered as incompatible with, an earlier or later treaty, the provisions of that other treaty prevail.
>
> 3. When all the parties to the earlier treaty are parties also to the later treaty but the earlier treaty is not terminated or suspended in operation under Article 59, the earlier treaty applies only to the extent that its provisions are compatible with those of the later treaty.
>
> 4. When the parties to the later treaty do not include all the parties to the earlier one:
>
> (a) As between States parties to both treaties the same rule applies as in paragraph 3;
>
> (b) As between a State party to both treaties and a State party to only one of the treaties, the treaty to which both States are parties governs their mutual rights and obligations.

These rules may find application in the context of the application and interpretation of Articles 18 (3) and 19 (1) and (3) of the ACFTA referred to

82 International Court of Justice, I.C.J. Reports 1994, 03.02.1994, *Territorial Dispute (Libyan Arab Jamahiriya / Chad)*, 21 – 22, para. 41.

83 Vienna Convention on the law of treaties (VCLT) Art. 31(3)(c).

84 Oliver Dörr, in: Oliver Dörr and Kirsten Schmalenbach (eds), *Vienna Convention on the Law of Treaties Commentary* (2nd Edition, 2018), 604.

85 Ibid. 603 – 608.

above but may also be rendered superfluous if the said provisions of the ACFTA settle a norm-conflict issue.

VI. Conclusion

By comparing two different sets of European Union agreements this chapter clearly showed the differences between the new types of association agreements and the new trade agreements of the Union by using the examples of the treaties with Ukraine and the SADC-countries, respectively. It is also clear that the Association Agreement with Ukraine is not only rather far-reaching in scope and comprehensiveness, but also asymmetrical in respect of the obligations of Ukraine for the fulfilment and implementation of the agreement. The reason can be found in the close proximity of the Ukrainian market to the EU and its relative weakness. The advantage of a deep and comprehensive free trade area is the almost full integration of the Ukrainian market into the EU market, but Ukraine is not entitled to influence the applicable legal rules, a clear disadvantage which creates considerable political problems if the aims of the agreement are not achieved soon.

The SADC-Agreement is a more traditional trade agreement with a different, more development-orientated objective. Its aim is not to integrate the economies of the SADC-countries into the European internal market and the provisions of the agreement are, as a result, more traditional trade-agreement like in nature. However, some similarities do exist, namely the establishment of a free trade area and rules on conditionality, although both sets of rules are far more limited than the ones in the EU-Ukraine Association Agreement.

Due to the long ratification history of the two agreements it is difficult to assess whether both or any-one of the two approaches will be successful. First, it can be safely said that the approach in the Association Agreement with Ukraine seems to lead to further problems due to Ukraine's inability to change its internal legal order as quickly as required by the agreement. Secondly, the lack of active reference-clauses in some parts of the agreement is a legal and political burden, too, because the transposition of already outdated clauses for the integration into another legal system does not seem to make much sense. Thirdly, the European Union's development policy cannot be regarded as a clear success story, thus the approach taken by the SADC-Agreement in opening up the EU-agricultural market seems to be the proper step in the right direction but the opening of the EU-market should be obligatory. These issues should be addressed in the negotiation of further agreements by the Union.

The situation on the African continent is rather different. South Africa is a party to the SADC and will be part of an even bigger African free trade area once the ACFTA has entered into force. However, the ACFTA still faces legal challenges which are difficult to solve in the future.

Bibliography

Finn Arnesen, 'Homogeneity and Disparity', in: Stefan Lorenzmeier and Hans-Peter Folz (eds), *Recht und Realität. Festschrift für Christoph Vedder* (Nomos, Baden-Baden 2017), 257.

Finn Arnesen, Halvard Fredriksen, Hans Graver, Ola Mestad and Christoph Vedder (eds), *Agreement on the European Economic Area*, Commentary (Nomos, Baden-Baden 2018).

European Commission, *Trade for all – Towards a more responsible trade and investment policy* (European Union, Luxembourg 2015), http://trade.ec.europa.eu/doclib/docs/2015/october/tradoc_153846.pdf (27-08-2018).

European Commission, *EU-Japan economic partnership agreement* (2017), http://ec.europa.eu/trade/policy/in-focus/eu-japan-economic-partnership-agreement/ (27-08-2018).

European Commission, *EU-Ukraine Deep and Comprehensive Free Trade Area* (2013), https://trade.ec.europa.eu/doclib/docs/2013/april/tradoc_150981.pdf (27-08-2018).

European Commission, *Global Europe competing in the world* (2006), http://trade.ec.europa.eu/doclib/docs/2006/october/tradoc_130376.pdf (27-08-2018).

European Commission, *Country report South Africa* (2018),

http://ec.europa.eu/trade/policy/countries-and-regions/countries/south-africa/ (27-08-2018).

European Commission, *ACP – The Cotonou Agreement* (2018), https://ec.europa.eu/europeaid/regions/african-caribbean-and-pacific-acp-region/cotonou-agreement_en (27-08-2018).

European Commission, *Communication on a new Africa –Europe Alliance for Sustainable Investment and Jobs: Taking our partnership for investment and jobs to the next level* (2018), COM(2018) 643 final, https://ec.europa.eu/commission/sites/beta-political/files/soteu2018-africa-europe-jobs-alliance-communication-643_en.pdf (17-09-2018).

Oliver Dörr and Kirsten Schmalenbach (eds) *Vienna Convention on the Law of Treaties Commentary* (2nd Edition, Springer, Berlin 2018).

Piet Eeckhout, *EU External Relations Law* (2nd Edition, Oxford University Press, Oxford 2011).

Peter Van Elsuwege and Roman Petrov (eds), *Legislative Approximation and Application of EU Law in the Eastern Neighbourhood of the European Union* (Routledge, New York 2016).

Karel De Gucht, *Trade as a cornerstone for the EU Eastern Partnership*, Speech at the European Parliament (Brussels 23 January 2012), http://trade.ec.europa.eu/doclib/docs/2012/january/tradoc_148967.pdf (03-09-2018).

Joni Heliskoski, *Mixed Agreements as a Technique for Organizing the International Relations of the European Community and its Member States*, (Kluwer Law International, Dordrecht 2001).

Christophe Hillion and Panos Koutrakos, *Mixed Agreements revisited* (Hart Publishing, Oxford 2010).

Frank Hoffmeister, 'The Deep and Comprehensive Free Trade Areas of the European Union – Concept and Challenges', in: Marise Cremona and Tamara Takács (eds), *Trade liberalisation and standardisation – new directions in the low politics of EU foreign politics* (CLEER, The Hague 2013), http://www.asser.nl/media/1641/cleer_13-6_web.pdf (27-08-2018).

Pieter Kuijper, Jan Wouters, Frank Hoffmeister, Gert De Baere and Thomas Ramopoulos, *The Law of EU External Relations* (Oxford University Press, Oxford 2013).

Adam Lazowski, 'Enhanced Multilateralism and Enhanced Bilateralism: Integration without Membership in the European Union' 45 (2008) *Common Market Law Review (CMLRev)*, 1433.

Adam Lazowski, 'Box of Chocolates Integration: The European Economic Area and the Swiss Model Revisited', in: Steven Blockmans and Sacha Prechal (eds), *Reconciling the Deepening and the Widening of the European Union* (T.M.C. Asser Press, The Hague 2008), 87.

Guillaume Van der Loo, *The EU-Ukraine Association Agreement and Deep and Comprehensive Free Trade Area* (Brill Nijhoff, Leiden, Boston 2016).

Stefan Lorenzmeier, 'Territorialer Anwendungsbereich von Assoziierungsabkommen – Im Hinblick auf umstrittene Gebiete', in: Stefan Lorenzmeier and Hans-Peter Folz (eds), *Recht und Realität. Festschrift für Christoph Vedder* (Nomos, Baden-Baden 2017), 336.

Marc Maresceau, 'Les accords d'intégration dans les relations de proximité de l'Union Europeénne', in: Blaude Blumann (ed), *Les frontiers de l'Union Europeénne* (Bruylant, Brussels 2013), 151.

Marc Maresceau, *Bilateral Agreements concluded by the European Community*, Recueil des cours Vol. 309 (Martinus Nijhoff, The Hague 2006).

Roman Petrov, 'Constitutional Challenges for the Implementation of Association Agreements between the EU and Ukraine, Moldova and Georgia' *European Public Law (EPL)* 2015, 241.

Herman van Rompuy, *Remarks of the President of the European Council at the press conference of the European Summit in Vilnius* (2013), http://www.consilium.europa.eu/uedocs/cms_Data/docs/pressdata/en/ec/139764.pdf (27-08-2018).

African Union, *Decision on the launch of continental free trade area negotiations* (2015), AU/Dec. 569 (XXV), http://www.un.org/en/africa/osaa/pdf/au/free_trade_negotations_2015.pdf (06.12.2018).

European Union, *EU-Ukraine Association Agreement enters fully into force* (2017),

https://eeas.europa.eu/headquarters/headQuarters-homepage/31591/eu-ukraine-association-agreement-enters-fully-force_en (27-08-2018).

European Union, *EU Treaties Office Database* (2018), http://ec.europa.eu/world/agreements/default.home.do (27-08-2018).

Bart van Vooren and Ramses Wessels, *EU External Relations Law* (Cambridge University Press, Cambridge 2014).

Bart van Vooren, *EU External Relations Law and the European Neighborhood Policy* (Routledge, London, New York 2012).

Register of Cases

European Court of Justice, Case 12/86, 30.09.1987, *Demirel v Stadt Schwäbisch Gmünd*, ECLI:EU:C:1987:400.

European Court of Justice, Opinion 2/15, 16.05.2017, *Free Trade Agreement with Singapore*, ECLI:EU:C:2017:376.

International Court of Justice, I.C.J. Reports 1994, 03.02.1994, *Territorial Dispute (Libyan Arab Jamahiriya / Chad)*, 21–22.